RAF
BOMBER
COMMAND
1936-1968

Patrick Stephens Limited, an imprint of Haynes Publishing, has published authoritative, quality books for enthusiasts for more than a quarter of a century. During that time the company has established a reputation as one of the world's leading publishers of books on aviation, maritime, military, model-making, motor-cycling, motoring, motor racing, railway and railway modelling subjects. Readers or authors with suggestions for books they would like to see published are invited to write to: The Editorial Director, Patrick Stephens Limited, Sparkford, Nr Yeovil, Somerset, BA22 7JJ.

RAF
BOMBER
COMMAND
1936-1968

CHRIS ASHWORTH

Patrick Stephens Limited

© R. C. B. Ashworth 1995

First published in 1995

British Library Cataloguing-in-Publication Data:
A catalogue record for this book
is available from the British Library.

ISBN 1 85260 308 9

Library of Congress catalog card No. 94-73834

Patrick Stephens Limited is an imprint of
Haynes Publishing, Sparkford,
Nr Yeovil, Somerset, BA22 7JJ

Typeset by Haynes Publishing Ltd, Sparkford, nr
Yeovil, Somerset BA22 7JJ.

Printed in Great Britain.

Contents

Introduction

MANY BOOKS AND articles have been written about RAF Bomber Command. Some provide a good overall picture of wartime activities; some go into great detail about single raids or particular targets; others are largely biographical. As far as I am aware none cover the history of the Command from start to finish, a situation which this book seeks to redress.

The sudden end of the 1914-18 War prevented the strategic bomber from fulfilling its promise but Trenchard, the Royal Air Force's dynamic chief, was in no doubt as to its potential and ensured that the lion's share of the meagre funds allocated annually for the home-based RAF during the 1920s was spent on the bomber force. Progress was bedevilled by the notorious but politically convenient 'Ten-Year Rule' and interminable disarmament conferences, and despite Trenchard's efforts the RAF was patently ill-equipped to face the dangers posed by the rise of Adolf Hitler in Germany. There had to be a massive expansion and it was soon obvious that the current command structure would be unable to cope. Functional 'Commands' were the answer and in 1936 Bomber and Fighter Command were born.

Politics, and the extraordinary (in hindsight) conviction that day bombers could fight their way through to a target even against a determined enemy, resulted in a force ill-trained to fight a real war. In 1940 it also came as an unpleasant shock to many in high places to discover that night bombers were not invulnerable and, perhaps worse, that their crews could not find their targets. Day bombing had to be all but abandoned, and it was accepted that night attacks on 'pinpoint' (i.e. precision) targets were a waste of effort – certainly until much-improved 'aids' could be devised.

Naturally mistakes were made, and critics soon emerged but never seemed to spell out what they would have done instead of bombing to bring war to the enemy's heartland in the dark days of 1941-42; or for that matter during 1943-44 when, with the massive help of the USAAF daylight bombing offensive, the tide was turned. 'Area' bombing came in for particular criticism, and certainly it was a blunt instrument – but the only one available. Once the necessary navigational equipment was provided, area bombing had a significant effect, both on factory output and the populace who, though often portrayed as innocent victims, did produce the munitions and equipment that supported Germany's armed forces!

Since the Second World War, hostile attention has focused on the best-known of the Commander-in-Chiefs, 'Bomber' Harris, with particular reference to the bombing of Dresden. Harris was a gifted leader and an exceptionally strong personality. He was also very obstinate and it is certainly arguable that he continued the policy of bombing towns and cities for longer than was necessary. It can also be argued that Dresden had no strategic value; but it was one of the communications centres ahead of the Russian advance and the western Allies had agreed to attack such centres. Harris did not take the final decision to include Dresden and neither did Bomber Command act alone, for the USAAF was also involved. One wonders, therefore, why the Americans are not similarly castigated over Dresden, or why their area bombing of towns and cities in Japan in the latter months of the Pacific War are so rarely criticized. Subsequently politicians, notably Churchill, distanced themselves from such bombing, despite agreeing to it at the time – typical buck-passing which leaves a nasty taste. Understandably, Harris and the whole of Bomber Command felt let down during the post-war debate on the subject, the denial of a campaign medal being a particular bone of contention.

Post-war came the inevitable cutbacks, followed by the learning of new skills and tactics as jet bombers were introduced. The coming of the nuclear age brought in the V-bombers, Bomber Command reinforcing its position as the main offensive weapon possessed by the British armed forces during the early years of the 'Cold War'. Whether it need have been such an expensive weapon was a different matter, for while the 'belt & braces' attitude which put both the Vulcan and Victor into small-scale production and service may well have been justified by the quantum leap in design involved, was there any logical reason why Mk.2 versions of both were ordered?

The steadfastness of the crews in the face of setbacks and appalling losses from both the weather and the opposition during the Second World War was admirable. To enter the maelstrom existing over a well defended German city once must have been daunting, but to do it again and again needed courage of the highest order. Post-war the problems were different, but none the less real. Seemingly endless stand-bys and alerts took their toll and inevitably there were also dramas such as the Suez débâcle, the Cuban missile crisis – and the sudden grounding of the Valiant. All subsided or were overcome and Britain's oft-debated nuclear shield was proudly maintained – and eventually handed over intact to Strike Command.

No book of this nature could be written without reference to a wide selection of earlier publications and recourse to primary sources at the Air Historical Branch, MoD, and the Public Records Office at Kew. Photographs are a vital adjunct to the text and it would have been difficult to illustrate the book adequately without access to the photographs held by the Imperial War Museum (IWM) and the RAF Museum (RAFM). I also acknowledge the invaluable assistance of individuals who provided me with information and/or photographs. I am grateful to them all and in particular would mention John and Kay Bartholomew, Chaz Bowyer, Mike Garbett, Brian Goulding, Jim Oughton, Brian Pickering of Military Aircraft Photographs (MAP), John Rabbetts, John Rawlings, Bruce Robertson, Ray Sturtivant, Andy Thomas, Alan Todd and Brian Webb. The interpretation of events is, of course, entirely my responsibility.

R. C. B. Ashworth
Padstow, August 1994

CHAPTER 1

Small Beginnings 1914-1939

THE ROYAL FLYING Corps (RFC) was still settling into its reconnaissance role in support of the British Expeditionary Force (BEF) in France when the Royal Naval Air Service (RNAS), lively as ever, made the first successful raid on Germany. This was on 8 October 1914 when Flt Lt Marix flying a Sopwith Tabloid of the RNAS detachment at Antwerp dropped two 20-lb Hale bombs on an airship hangar at Düsseldorf. Inside was the brand new Z.IX which exploded spectacularly, sending debris high into the air.

Despite such early success the RFC was slow to endorse bombing, and when it did it was only concerned with operations in direct support of the Army. The RNAS remained more belligerent, forming a Bombing Wing at Detling at the end of 1915 as part of a proposed Anglo-French force specifically intended for attacks on Germany. Renamed No.3 Wing the unit moved to Manston, and in July 1916 to Luxeuil in the Nancy area of France. This was within reach of a large number of important German industrial and munition centres and on 30 July three Sopwith 1½ Strutters accompanied six French aircraft of No. 4 Group to bomb Mülheim. It was only a gesture, for the strength of the force remained insufficient for sustained operations until the autumn because of aircraft transfers to the RFC, but it was the first strategic bombing operation. The first properly constituted attack was on 12 October when 20 Sopwiths and six Breguet Vs of the RNAS joined 38 French machines in an attack on the Mauser works at Oberndorf, 109 miles from Luxeuil. Unfortunately it

Sopwith 1½ Strutters of No.3 Wing, RNAS, the first strategic force. (DND RE14471)

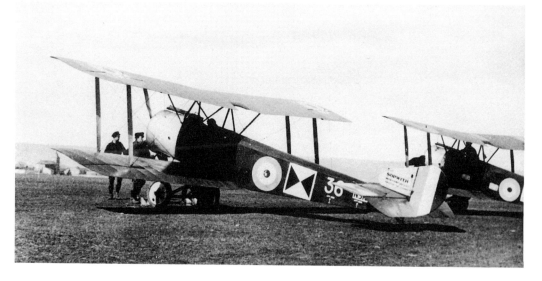

was not a success, only nine British and nine French bombers reaching the target, while the six Breguets of No.3 Wing bombed Donaueschingen by mistake. The many detractors were given plenty of ammunition and RFC leaders, including Maj Gen H.M. Trenchard, remained implacably opposed to the idea of strategic bombing. In May 1917 they got their way; the Admiralty was forced to disband No.3 Wing and the aircraft were dispersed, the two Handley Page 0/100s, the first truly strategic bomber on strength, going to join other 'Bloody Paralyzers' (as the type was nicknamed) with No.5 Wing at Coudekerque for attacks on airfields and coastal targets.

It was therefore somewhat ironic that at much the same time the RFC were starting to venture across the front-line trenches by day using newly delivered DH.4s, and at night operated a few FE.2Bs on bombing raids. Such activity was low-key however, and doubtless would have remained so had it not been for the public outcry resulting from German air raids on Britain during the summer of 1917. Lt Gen J.C. Smuts was instructed to investigate and suggest remedies. He produced a wide-ranging and radical report which recommended, amongst other things, the creation of a separate air service and the development of a strategic bombing force able to attack Germany in strength. With some reluctance both recommendations were accepted and Trenchard, in command of the RFC in the Field, was told to take action against those German homeland targets which could be reached from bases in France.

The result was the formation of the 41st Wing on 11 October 1917 specifically for attacks on the Saar and Ruhr using DH.4s (55 Sqn) for day bombing and FE.2Bs (100 Sqn) and Handley Page 0/100s (16 Naval Sqn) at night, all operating from Ochey, near Nancy, south of the Metz salient. The Wing started badly for

the force was too small, and the French, fearing reprisals, offered only minimal co-operation. On 28 December 1917 the Wing became the 8th Brigade, which was wrested from Army control in June 1918 when it became the 'Independent Force', some 142 raids, 57 over Germany, having been made since October 1917. The new organisation was often incorrectly referred to as the Independent Air Force, even by Trenchard, who after a brief period as first Chief of Air Staff, returned to France to take charge of strategic bombing and prepare for a sustained offensive against German munition factories. Already bolstered by two new DH.9 squadrons in May, the 41st Wing was joined by the 83rd Wing on 1 July, the latter taking over the 0/100- and 0/400-equipped squadrons; and when the Armistice was signed in November the 85th and 88th Wings were both working up prior to joining the Independent Force. The end of the war also saved Berlin from attack, secret plans having been made to move six Independent Force 0/400s to Prague to put them in range of the German capital, while in England the first of the new four-engined Handley Page V/1500s were being readied for attacks on the same target direct from the United Kingdom. The Independent Force had dropped 550 tons of bombs during its five months of operations, and had reached as far as Cologne, a round trip of 342 miles which took five hours. Poor weather and a slow build-up had prevented the Independent Force from demonstrating its full potential; indeed it is unlikely that anything significant could have been achieved before the spring of 1919. But despite the problems, Trenchard became convinced that strategic bombing was not only viable but essential – and there is no one more committed than a convert.

With the Armistice the DH.10 and Vickers Vimy twin-engined bombers, both about to enter service in

In majestic flight, the Handley Page 0/400, which followed the 0/100 into service with the Independent Force. (Central News Ltd)

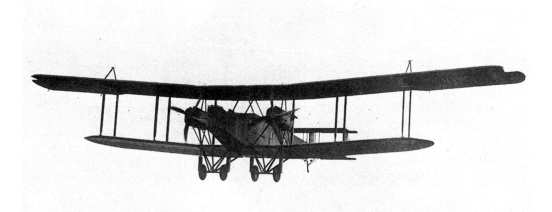

The Handley Page V/1500, designed specifically to bomb Berlin, probably at Bircham Newton.

France, were sent elsewhere and the Independent Force was disbanded, its squadrons coming under the direct command of GHQ Royal Air Force at Andre aux Bois on 14 November 1918. Sir Hugh Trenchard was again appointed Chief of Air Staff on 31 March 1919 and immediately started work on his proposals for the reorganization of the RAF. Determined to prevent a return to the pre-April 1918 organization and to maintain an offensive posture while still mindful of the 'Ten Year Rule' (contained in a Government policy statement issued on 15 August 1919 which in part read: 'It should be assumed, for forming revised estimates, that the British Empire will not be engaged in any great war during the next 10 years.'), Trenchard advocated a force largely based overseas on 'policing' duties but with a strong training organization at home, the latter providing a nucleus on which to build. In October 1919 the confusing Areas and Groups into which the RAF had been divided soon after the Armistice were rationalized, just two geographical Areas, Northern and Southern, remaining to cover the UK, while a third Area, Coastal, controlled all maritime air forces.

Trenchard's memorandum formed the basis of a White Paper which provided for an annual sum of £17m, judged sufficient for 40 squadrons if rigid economy was maintained. It was laid before Parliament on 11 December 1919 by Mr W. S. Churchill and subsequently a Bill was passed. But contraction continued, and on 1 April 1920 Northern and Southern Areas were amalgamated as 'Inland Area'. For a short period there were no operational aircraft in the 'Home Establishment' at all, and even

when a modest expansion was started the budget provided by the parsimonious Treasury was insufficient. By the summer of 1921 only three of the four UK-based squadrons, two bomber and one fighter, were up to strength. Both the former were single-engined day bomber squadrons (Nos.39 & 207) and it was not until March 1922 that twin-engined heavy bombers returned to home-based service when No.100 Squadron, recently transferred from Ireland, received four Vimys and an Avro 504K to form 'D' Flight.

Amid fears about French intentions the Government sanctioned a Metropolitan Air Force of 23 squadrons, 14 of them to be equipped with bombers. This was a considerable expansion, but the takeover bids by both the Admiralty and the War Office which had been beaten off in 1921 continued to be pressed strongly, and in March 1923 a Committee chaired by the Marquess of Salisbury was appointed to study the submissions. Again the bids were rejected; indeed the Committee recommended that the projected home defence force should be further increased to 52 squadrons (35 bomber and 17 fighter; a ratio of 2:1). Trenchard thought that the plan could be completed by 1928, but although approved in June 1923, severe financial restrictions and the Locarno Pact of December 1925, which settled the question of the Rhineland and guaranteed Germany's frontiers with France and Belgium, resulted in the Government delaying implementation. However, some progress had already been made, the Vimys of No. 7 Squadron (formed from 'D' Flight, No.100 Sqn) which had represented the RAF's entire home-based heavy bomber force for nearly a year, being joined by Nos.9, 58 and 99 Squadrons in April 1924 for 'night flying duties concerned with Home Defence'! At the same time Trenchard hatched another of his schemes, introducing Special Reserve and Auxiliary bomber units as an inexpensive way of bolstering the home establishment. Authorized on 9 October 1924, the first of the Special Reserve units, No.502 Squadron, was formed at Aldergrove, Northern Ireland, on 15 May 1925 with Vimys, manned by 'regulars' supplemented by a few reservists. The Auxiliary squadrons were quite different, being equipped with single-engined day bombers and staffed almost entirely by part-time volunteers, recruitment starting in time for the first Auxiliary unit, No.602 Squadron, to be formed on 12 September 1925.

Originally intended to consist of a Fighting Area and three geographical Bombing Areas, Air Defence Great Britain (ADGB) was formed on 1 January 1925 to take control of home-based operational aircraft. In practice it was divided into just two Areas, the Wessex Bombing Area and the Fighting Area, formed on 12 April 1926 within Inland Area, and not transferred to ADGB until 1 June. Wessex Bombing Area units were concentrated west of London and the Fighting Area in the south-east of England, squarely facing France. A separate Air Defence Group within ADGB administered the Special Reserve and Auxiliary Air Force units as they formed.

Air defence exercises, now so much a part of the aviation scene, were slow to become established. The first annual ADGB test was held from 25–29 July 1927 when four day and four night bomber squadrons took part in 'attacks' on London, largely for the benefit of defence staffs. Valuable lessons were said to have been learnt, though there was no obvious improvement in realism during the succeeding ten years.

Post-1918 bombers were now well established in service, but undemanding specifications and Air Staff planning which still envisaged France as the potential aggressor resulted in aircraft whose performance was little better than that obtainable from the wartime Vimy and DH.9A. Orders were small and spread thinly across the industry, aimed largely at keeping firms in business. No attempt was made to improve range and bomb load, with the result that the Handley Page Hinaidi night bomber entered service in October 1929 with a cruising speed of 75mph and a range of 850 miles – the earlier Vimy had averaged 80mph and 900 miles. Day bombers did a little better, largely due to the influence of the 'private venture' Fairey Fox which could travel 500 miles at 130mph, and the Hawker Hart which entered service in January 1930 with a cruising speed of 140mph. The Hart had a maximum level flight speed of 184mph and like the Fox could embarrass fighter pilots of the day by outrunning them; the result of the Trenchard doctrine which continued to put the maximum effort into offence and the minimum into defence. Despite this situation 'heavy' bombers continued to be lumbering monsters, it being perceived wisdom that there was no effective defence against night attack, so there was no need to press for improved performance.

Mainstay of the heavy bomber force during the 1920s was the Vickers Virginia. J7711 entered service as a Mk.VI in November 1925 and after much modification was still in service as a Mk. X in December 1935. (MAP)

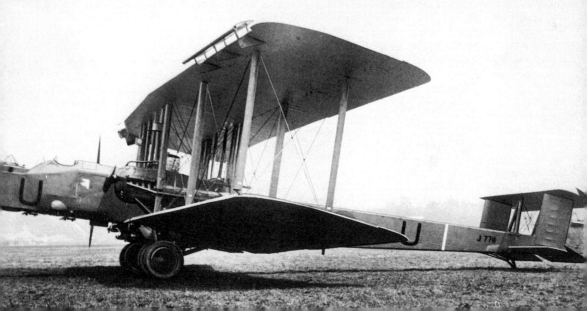

The light bomber which could out-perform contemporary fighters – the Fairey Fox. J7943 of No.12 Squadron was a Kestrel-powered Mk. 1A.

Since 1925 the world powers had been seeking agreement on disarmament. They had no success, so in 1932 the League of Nations sponsored a Disarmament Conference at Geneva to try and agree armament limitations. Amongst the worthy proposals put forward was a total ban on bombing, but more realistic was a suggested bomb load limit of three metric tons, (approximately 6,300 lb) on an aircraft's maximum tare weight (the basic empty weight plus fixed fittings). The Government, already struggling with the world-wide economic recession, seized the opportunity to freeze defence expenditure pending the results of the conference, and the planned expansion came to a complete standstill having reached 26 regular and eleven auxiliary/reserve units. Worse, the winner of the B.19/27 contest, the Handley Page Heyford biplane, was delayed, with the result that it was completely outdated when it finally entered service in November 1933.

The 'Ten Year Rule' had been officially abandoned in March 1932, and with the failure of the Geneva Conference in 1933 plus belated recognition that Germany and Italy were the potential enemies, re-armament began again in earnest – there was a lot of ground to be made up. Activity surged in the bomber field* and planning started in the first of a long series

*See Chapter 13

of 'Expansion' schemes. In preparation the Wessex Bombing Area was split on 1 October 1933, the Central Area controlling airfields and units in Oxfordshire and East Anglia, while Western Area administered those on or near Salisbury Plain in Wiltshire.

On 31 March 1934 there were 316 home-based bomber aircraft in 28 squadrons – still way below the figure of 35 squadrons agreed in 1923. The Air Estimates for the year allowed for the creation of two more squadrons; but with the seriousness of the situation recognized at last, and the Prime Minister, Mr Baldwin, declaring 'in air strength and in air power this country shall no longer be in a position inferior to any country within striking distance of our shores', such a modest increase in strength was clearly inadequate. Under Expansion Scheme A, approved by the Cabinet in July 1934, the bomber force was to increase to 41 squadrons by March 1939, enabling Baldwin to repeat his promise – this time with particular reference to parity with Germany. Not mentioned in public, however, was the situation concerning reserves – they would not be adequate in material or men until 1942!

A year later, after Hitler had formally revealed the existence of the Luftwaffe, it was belatedly recognized that none of the bombers in service, and few of those on order, were fit for operations over Germany, even

The twin-engined day bomber concept was kept alive by the agile Boulton Paul Overstrand, the first RAF aircraft with a powered turret. Illustrated is K4561/U of No.101 Squadron. (MAP)

The Handley Page Heyford was a large aircraft. K6872 joined No.166 Squadron in 1936 and is seen at Leconfield in 1939. (MAP)

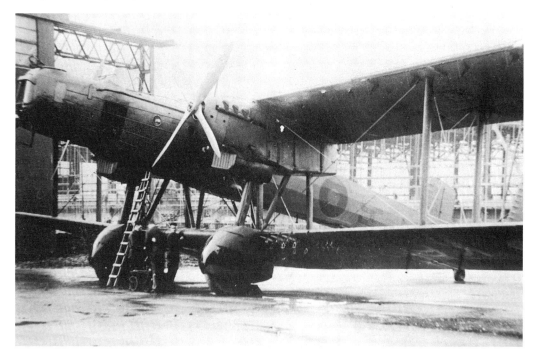

Hawker Hind K5558 of No.107 Squadron at Old Sarum in March 1937 soon after moving from Andover.

at night. Although Germany was unlikely to be ready for war in the immediate future, time was not on Britain's side and it was decided to order aircraft 'off the drawing board' as additional gap-fillers while new aircraft were designed, developed, and put into service.

In practice, Baldwin's 1934 claim of parity by 1939 was completely bogus, for no one could calculate accurately how quickly Germany could re-arm; and worse, 22 of the 41 RAF squadrons would be equipped with light bombers. Scheme C, approved in May 1935, sought to remedy this by calling for 68 'metropolitan' bomber squadrons by March 1937; but this was impracticable and Scheme F which replaced it in February 1936 proposed the same number of units, strengthened by reserves of aircraft, but not due for completion until 1938. Though more realistic, Scheme F still meant that everything would have to be put 'in the shop window' – the number of squadrons boosted to the detriment of the training organization.

Scheme F also restated the case for the bomber as the principal weapon for winning a war on the continent of Europe, rather than merely part of home defence, and it was decided to separate it from the fighter element by splitting ADGB into two functional Commands, each with a number of regional Groups. The plan was left in some disarray during the summer of 1935, when it was decided to reinforce RAF units in the Middle East following Italian threats against

Abyssinia (now Ethiopia). In June five ADGB light bomber squadrons were warned of overseas duty, their aircraft were crated in September, and personnel left the UK early in October. Despite such upsets the nucleus of No.2 (Bomber) Group formed-up on 20 March 1936, followed by No.6 (Auxiliary) Group (formed by renaming No.1 Air Defence Group) and Nos.1 and 3 (Bomber) Groups (from Central and Western Areas respectively) in May. ADGB closed down at 2359 hours on 13 July, Fighter and Bomber Commands being born at 0001 hours on the 14th.

The 20 regular squadrons forming Bomber Command were evenly split between Nos.1 and 3 Groups, the former with light day bombers (Harts/Hinds) and the latter equipped mostly with night bombers (Heyfords/Virginias) but with one twin-engined day bomber unit (Overstrands). The 12 auxiliary units of No.6 Group fielded a mixed bag of Hart, Hind, Wapiti and Wallace aircraft. However, this all-biplane force was soon to change out of all recognition as new aircraft entered service and additional squadrons were formed. Each reformed squadron was based on a nucleus from an established unit, and this admirably achieved the desired effect of increasing the apparent front-line strength. Unfortunately it also diluted experience levels and, coupled with the massive retraining task associated with new aircraft, resulted in a Command largely unfit for general operations.

This unhappy situation had little effect on the deliberations of the Chiefs of Staff in February 1937, it being agreed that Bomber Command would provide assistance to both the Royal Navy and the Army in the event of war, but primarily wage a strategic offensive against the Luftwaffe and German industry. This was little more than a restatement of earlier objectives, but for the first time it led to serious discussion of how Bomber Command could and should be used – and to the production of a series of war plans which became known as Western Air Plans.

Meanwhile the 'interim' Harrow, ordered into production in August 1935 and notable only for being the first RAF aircraft to have power-operated nose, dorsal and tail turrets, entered service in January 1937. Within five months the Whitley, Battle and Blenheim were appearing on squadrons and a delivery trickle turned into a flood as a sense of urgency spread through the aircraft industry, aided by the Government's obvious commitment to quantity production, as demonstrated by the Shadow factory scheme introduced in April 1936, and amplified by the construction of State-owned factories in 1938 for management by the aircraft industry. The new aircraft were monoplanes with complications such as electro-hydraulic or pneumatically operated systems for flaps and retractable undercarriages; and variable-pitch propellers. Crews were expected to transfer from their comparatively simple biplanes with minimal instruction, but it was a big jump – one which resulted in many accidents.

Schemes H and J (issued in October 1937) included proposals for 90 home-based bomber squadrons and critics argued, quite reasonably, that each of the larger aircraft due to enter production would be so much more effective than the light bombers currently in service that the number of squadrons could be reduced. Of course this took no account of the efforts being made to increase the size of the force to match the Luftwaffe which in September 1937 was thought to have a mobilizable bomber strength of over 500 – 250 of which were JU86s, He111s and Do17s – and the Italians who could muster 400, while Britain could manage just 96 bombers (36 Blenheims, 36 Wellesleys, 12 Battles and 12 Harrows). Sir Thomas Inskip, Minister of Co-ordination of Defence, contended that such an enlarged force could not be afforded, and in any case the RAF should be adopting a more defensive posture with more fighters at the expense of bombers. This was tantamount to heresy in most Air Ministry corridors and the Chief of Air Staff, Air Chief Marshal Sir Cyril Newall, fought hard to preserve the offensive doctrine. However, Inskip had the Government's ear, and his view was accepted by the Cabinet on 22

December 1937. Scheme J was thrown out and under the revised Scheme L the Air Ministry had to accept a slimmed-down expansion of the bomber force – 77 squadrons by March 1940. It was the end of the race for parity but at least it was fairly realistic, which is more than could be said for Schemes H and J.

No.4 (Bomber) Group had been formed on 1 April 1937 and No.5 (Bomber) Group on 1 July, both with a nucleus provided by No.3 Group. On 29 June No.4 Group took over Leconfield (97 & 166 Sqns); Driffield (75 & 215 Sqns); Dishforth (10 & 78 Sqns); Finningley (7 & 76 Sqns); and Linton-on-Ouse, to which Nos.51 and 58 Squadrons were transferred from Boscombe Down on 20 April 1938. Similarly Spitalgate (113 and 211 Sqns), Waddington (44, 50 & 110 Sqns) and Hemswell (61 & 144 Sqns) were transferred to No.5 Group in September 1937. Thus the geographical locations of the Groups, so much a feature of wartime operations, were starting to appear, though aircraft standardization still had some way to go.

Meanwhile, after much discussion 13 very wide-ranging Air Plans had been devised, based on the assumption that accurate day bombing, supplemented by some night bombing, would be possible. Priorities were agreed at an Air Ministry meeting on 1 October 1937 and these were passed to HQ Bomber Command on 13 December with orders to commence detailed planning. Time was to show these plans to be extremely far-sighted as objectives for a successful campaign against Germany, but the C-in-C, ACM Sir Edgar Ludlow-Hewitt, realized that they were beyond the current, or foreseeable, ability of Bomber Command to carry out. Shortly after taking over in October 1937 he had toured his Stations, and in a report a month later did not mince his words. While paying tribute to the efforts of all ranks coping with the problems produced by the rapid expansion, he went on to state that Bomber Command was 'entirely unprepared for war, unable to operate except in fair weather, and extremely vulnerable both in the air and on the ground'. He was equally hard-nosed over the priority Western Air Plans which covered attacks on the Luftwaffe (WA.1), communications (WA.4), and Ruhr industries (WA.5). WA.1 and WA.4 were dismissed by his Air Staff as inappropriate for a strategic bomber force on the grounds that aircraft could be widely dispersed and the German communication system was such that alternative routes could always be found; while knocking out the whole of the Ruhr with the bombers available in 1939 was considered impractical. Concentrating on power generation seemed to offer more, the 'experts' calculating that 3,000 sorties (each aircraft on an operation counting as one sortie) would be sufficient

A representative selection of Bomber Command aircraft at Harwell on 9 May 1938 when HM King George VI visited, accompanied by the Chief of Air Staff, ACM Sir Cyril Newall. In the background are a Battle of No.105 Squadron, Blenheim of No.90 Squadron, Harrow of No. 115 Squadron, a Whitley and a Wellesley. (W. Booth)

to knock out 19 Ruhr power stations and 26 coking plants, which they estimated would bring about a complete shut-down of industry in the Ruhr Valley.

Air Ministry staff favoured attacks on dams rather than power stations, and it was left to Ludlow-Hewitt to point out that all the targets in the Western Air Plans required precision navigation and bombing, neither of which could be attained without the proper equipment and training. He detailed his priorities as the provision of navigational aids of the radio beam type and good training facilities for all aircrew; in particular, the provision of more bombing and gunnery ranges. His views were met with much hostility by many in high places who could not, or would not, understand the problems faced by the crews, and who had a blind faith in the bomber.

The Handley Page Hampden entered service with No. 5 Group in September 1938 just days before tension over German intentions regarding Czechoslovakia resulted in the 'Munich Crisis'. The Government ordered mobilization on 10 September and the sorry state of Bomber Command was highlighted for those privy to the information. Fifteen of the regular squadrons could not be properly mobilized, 10 being equipped with the operationally useless Heyfords, Hinds and Hendons, and five more were rearming. Of the rest, just 10 were equipped with 'heavy' night bombers (Whitleys and Harrows), and some 50% of the mobilized crews were unfit for operations. Both Ludlow-Hewitt and the Air Ministry were forced to favour a 'softly softly' approach and were relieved when the restrictions which had been

Whitley II K7244 of No. 7 Squadron in 1939 carrying its newly introduced code, LT-G. (RAFM P4403)

outlined by the Government in June were confirmed. In essence, if it came to war, only military targets involving no risk to civilians would be attacked unless, as feared, the Luftwaffe had already bombed towns in Britain, specifically London.

In the event, the crisis was resolved by the politicians giving in to Hitler. Neville Chamberlain, Britain's Prime Minister, returned from meeting the German dictator waving a piece of paper and declaring that he had 'secured peace for our time'. The readiness state was relaxed on 7 October and it is generally argued that this 'agreement' bought precious time for the Allies, though it is also contended that only the Czechs were ready for war in 1938, and that Hitler would have backed down if the Allies had been more resolute. So much for theory. What is certain is that Hitler became convinced that when it came to the crunch the Allies would not support the next victim either. War then became inevitable.

It was a demoralizing climb-down but the crisis served to test the Command structure of the RAF as a whole more effectively than any number of exercises. At Bomber Command the 'two-pronged' organization, with the Senior Air Staff Officer (SASO) and his team dealing with operational matters while the Air Officer in Charge of Administration (AOA) ran the 'domestic' side, worked well. Group HQs had, however, been deliberately restricted to operational matters, and the small administrative staff proved unable to cope with the strain of mobilization. It was here that the chain, stretching from the Cabinet, through the Air Council, Air Ministry, Commands, Groups to Stations, broke. The Groups were therefore reorganized on the same lines as Commands,

allowing more detail to be dealt with at the lower level; a change which was to prove a conspicuous success.

The 'Munich Crisis' also precipitated furious efforts to reduce deficiencies in the numbers of men, aircraft and what would now be called infrastructure (airfields, maintenance and stores units, etc). Sir Kingsley Wood MP, Secretary of State for Air, wrote on 25 October 1938: 'We must make every effort to escape from the position in which we found ourselves during the recent crisis when we had less than one week's reserves behind the squadrons. This would have resulted in a rapidly declining scale of effort...' The result was Scheme M, a supplement to Scheme L, which increased the number of fighters by 30% at the expense of bombers, but also confirmed that all Bomber Command squadrons would ultimately be equipped with 'heavy' aircraft.

The Vickers Wellington, which had taken so long to develop, entered service with No.3 Group in October 1938 and the stage was set for the replacement of the last of the biplanes with monoplanes, a process accelerated by the transfer of auxiliary squadrons to Fighter Command on 1 January 1939. No.6 (Auxiliary) Group became No. 6 (Bomber) Group, and slowly built up as an operational light bomber organization, leaning heavily upon No. 2 Group. Meanwhile, after years of pretence, the 'bullet' was finally bitten in February 1939 when a number of bomber squadrons were declared non-mobilizable and used for training purposes, mainly of Volunteer Reserve personnel, their 'operational'-type aircraft being supplemented by Ansons. On front-line bomber squadrons the training, which for many years had

Blenheim 1 L1132 of No.82 Squadron with light series bomb carriers under the fuselage, early 1939. (MAP)

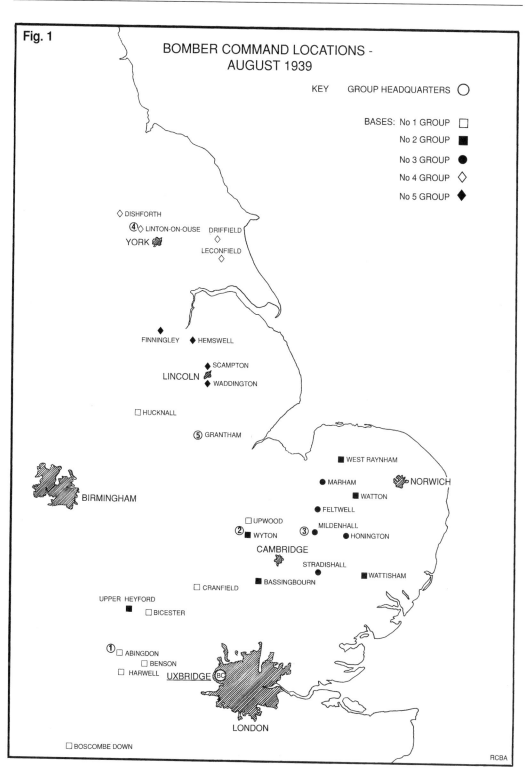

Fig. 1

BOMBER COMMAND LOCATIONS -
AUGUST 1939

KEY   GROUP HEADQUARTERS ◯

BASES: No 1 GROUP ☐
No 2 GROUP ■
No 3 GROUP ●
No 4 GROUP ◇
No 5 GROUP ◆

◇ DISHFORTH
④◇ LINTON-ON-OUSE   DRIFFIELD
YORK   ◇
LECONFIELD
◇

◆ FINNINGLEY   ◆ HEMSWELL

◆ SCAMPTON
LINCOLN
◆ WADDINGTON

☐ HUCKNALL

⑤ GRANTHAM

■ WEST RAYNHAM

● MARHAM   NORWICH
■ WATTON
● FELTWELL

BIRMINGHAM

☐ UPWOOD   MILDENHALL
②■ WYTON   ③●
●HONINGTON
CAMBRIDGE
STRADISHALL
●
☐ CRANFIELD   ■ BASSINGBOURN   ■ WATTISHAM

UPPER HEYFORD
■ ☐ BICESTER

①☐ ABINGDON
☐ BENSON
☐ HARWELL   UXBRIDGE ⦿BC

LONDON

☐ BOSCOMBE DOWN

RCBA

Battle K9423 of No.63 Squadron photographed from a Lysander, June 1939. (G/Capt W.S.G. Maydwell)

consisted of simple cross-country flights, camera obscura 'bombing' (worked by projecting an image of the aircraft onto a screen in a hut on the airfield, thus allowing the accuracy of a dummy attack to be assessed), the annual defence exercise and a three-week armament practice camp, was intensified. Operational exercises were increased in number and scope to include practice bombing on ranges and more realistic gunnery, fighter co-operation and night flying. At last Ludlow-Hewitt's efforts were bearing fruit, though he was still unable to get anywhere with the provision of navigation aids and the formation of a bomber development unit, nor in raising the status of air gunners – all subjects aired in his reports.

Operational plans also came under close scrutiny following the 'Munich Crisis', and though the 'softly

softly' approach was officially confirmed, resulting in very restricted WA.1/WA.4 objectives being considered, those covering co-operation with the Royal Navy (WA.2, WA.7 and WA.12) and for independent air attack on German industry (WA.5) were brought up to date in case the situation changed suddenly. The latter plan even involved the despatch of light bombers to France to put them in range of targets in Germany, though details of the deployment, called the Advanced Air Striking Force (AASF), had not been formally agreed with the French, and earlier studies had shown such aircraft as the Fairey Battle to be useless strategically.

In February 1939 the Cabinet accepted that detailed plans had to be agreed not only with the French, but with other European countries, additional

The Wellington 1, last of the new breed of bombers to enter service before the outbreak of war – and the most effective. No. 149 Squadron over Paris on Bastille Day 14 July 1939. (RAFM 5871-5)

Hampden L4076/QX-D of No. 50 Squadron, Waddington 1939. (via No. 50 Squadron records)

urgency being provided by the complete dismemberment of Czechoslovakia by Germany the following month. As tension mounted Kingsley Wood was able to state that Scheme F would shortly be completed (it was the only one to be completed, for most 'rolled on' to the next Scheme); but the situation again stabilized and Bomber Command continued its re-equipment programme, the last of the general purpose Wellesleys being withdrawn in April, leaving a few Heyfords to linger on until September, and the Hendon until December. Anglo-French Staff Conversations (what a marvellously descriptive name) started in the spring of 1939 and continued into the summer, resulting in broad agreement and a guarantee of assistance to Poland, a country under pressure to cede Danzig to the Germans. Detailed joint planning was undertaken, communications between France and Britain improved and bomb dumps were positioned in

the Reims area in readiness for the AASF. Consideration of a joint strategic air offensive against Germany lagged badly, however, partially because Bomber Command was still bound by a 'wait and see' policy, but largely because such French bombers as were available were purely tactical aircraft.

Navigational exercises were held from 11-25 July, some 240 Bomber Command aircraft carrying out 'show of strength' flights over central and southern France – the first really long-distance overseas sorties by many of the participants. The results were not encouraging, Ludlow-Hewitt still being faced with the fact that over 40% of crews were unable, in his words, 'to find a target in a friendly city in broad daylight'. From 5-11 August the annual air defence exercise was held, a total of 1,300 aircraft and 53,000 men taking part, including many from Bomber Command. Three weeks later the United Kingdom was at war.

CHAPTER 2

Stalemate and Disaster 1939-1940

ON 23 AUGUST 1939 messages were exchanged between Chamberlain and Hitler, the Prime Minister warning that Britain was prepared to help Poland forcibly, and Hitler stating that he would not renounce Germany's claim to Danzig. Unless one was bluffing, war was inevitable. Royal Air Force personnel had already been recalled from ordinary leave and on the 24th Readiness State C was declared and mobilization commenced. Aircraft were put on 12-hour stand-by, 'special leave' personnel were required to return to duty within six hours of recall, and members of the Auxiliary Air Force and the Volunteer Reserve were instructed to go to mobilization centres. No. 1 Group became the AASF. On the 25th Hitler ordered an attack on Poland the following day, but hesitated on

learning that British guarantees had become a firm alliance, and that Italy was not ready to take part in a war. In the UK there was also uncertainty, but Readiness State D was promulgated on 26 August when aircraft were dispersed around airfield perimeters, all personnel recalled, and E-Class Reservists started arriving on units.

Bullying tactics having failed, Hitler engineered a pretext and at 0445 hours on 1 September started an all-out assault on Poland. In an effort to prevent indiscriminate bombing, rightly perceived as one of the worst horrors of war, the President of the United States, Franklin D. Roosevelt, appealed for restraint, asking that no attacks be made on undefended towns, or any target where civilians might be hit. Britain and

Three Battles of No.218 Squadron which went with the AASF to France, September 1939. K9324 survived the experience but K9325 and K9353 were lost after the German breakthrough. (IWM C2116)

France agreed at once (Germany subsequently followed suit on 18 September, when the Polish campaign was nearly over) and strict instructions were issued stating that in the event of war Bomber Command was not to attack any target on German soil – only ships at sea or moored in harbours were to be bombed (War Plan 7b). Flights could be made over Germany but only for reconnaissance and the dropping of propaganda leaflets. It was not a policy received enthusiastically by bomber crews but, as was seen in Chapter 1, it suited the C-in-C well, anxious to conserve his Force while it gained strength and experience.

The next day nine squadrons of Fairey Battles (No.88 Sqn followed on 11 September) flew to France as the advance echelon of the AASF, and on Sunday, 3 September Britain and France declared war on Germany. Most bomber aircraft were immediately 'scattered' around the country and remained dispersed for a week or so – returning to their bases when the anticipated Luftwaffe attack did not materialize.

Six squadrons of Blenheims from No.2 Group were expected to join the AASF in Phase II of the deployment but Gen Vuillemin, the French Air Force Commander, intervened and it was decided to retain them in Britain to cover a possible attack through Belgium. The two squadrons earmarked for the Air Component, Nos.18 and 57, did go, crossing the English Channel on 24 September to join the British Expeditionary Force (BEF). A further 14 squadrons had already been transferred to No.6 (Training) Group, when it formed on 5 September, and six more were declared 'non-mobilizable', leaving 23 operational bomber squadrons in the UK, of which just 17 were capable of making a contribution to a strategic air offensive. Of these, six were equipped with Wellingtons (3 Group), five with Whitleys (4 Group) and six with Hampdens (5 Group). Each squadron had an establishment of 16 aircraft and by the end of September average availability was 77 Wellingtons (80%), 61 Whitleys (76%), and 71 Hampdens (73%). Thus, apart from light bombers, Bomber Command could only field a daily force of just over 200 aircraft. But even more serious was the shortage of trained men, both on the ground and in the air.

Despite the restrictions imposed, Bomber Command planned an attack on the German Fleet as soon as war was declared, with the object of causing as much damage as possible before the ships sailed or defences became too strong. A reconnaissance Blenheim stood by from 1 September, and a striking force from the 2nd. At 1200 hrs on the 3rd, one hour after the declaration of war, Flg Off A. McPherson of No.139 Squadron set off on the first wartime sortie, and in clear weather the crew sighted several warships in the Schillig Roads off Wilhelmshaven. Unfortunately the W/T set was unserviceable and the crew, which included a naval observer, Commander Thompson, were unable to report until they landed at Wyton at 1650 hrs. Eighteen Hampdens and nine Wellingtons were despatched, but worsening weather and the approach of darkness defeated their attempts to find the ships. As they returned, 10 Whitleys of Nos.51 and 58 Squadrons were setting out on the first night operation of the war –

Blenheim IV L8756/XD-E of No.139 Squadron, a contemporary of the aircraft which made the first operational sortie by Bomber Command on 3 September 1939. (via Chaz Bowyer Collection)

leaflet-dropping over Northern Germany and the Ruhr.

The following morning McPherson went reconnoitring again, bad weather forcing him to fly low, but warships were seen and photographed at Brunsbüttel, Wilhelmshaven and the Schillig Roads. This time the airborne recce report was corrupted, and again action had to await the aircraft's return. Fifteen Blenheims of Nos.107, 110 and 139 Squadrons and 14 Wellingtons of Nos.9 and 149 Squadrons were despatched, the Blenheims carrying out a low-level attack on the pocket-battleship *Admiral Scheer* and the training cruiser *Emden*, both in Wilhelmshaven harbour. None of their bombs exploded, three bouncing off the *Admiral Scheer*, while the *Emden* suffered minor damage and seven casualties when a No.110 Squadron aircraft crashed on the ship. Four other Blenheims were also shot down by 'flak' and at Brunsbüttel (Kiel Canal) two Wellingtons of No.9 Squadron were lost, probably victims of Bf109s. Only four of the Wellingtons found 'suitable' targets and one of them mistakenly dropped two bombs on the Danish town of Esberg, over 100 miles north of Brunsbüttel! Almost totally unproductive, these attacks resulted in the loss of seven aircraft and their crews (23.3% of the sorties despatched). Such losses could not be sustained for long.

Somewhat optimistically the Commander of the AASF, Air Vice Marshal P.H.C. Playfair, declared his

Battle-equipped squadrons operational on 6 September, and four days later three aircraft of No.150 Squadron patrolled the Franco-German border for the first time. Activities were confined to reconnaissance, the ban on bombing land targets applying to the AASF just as much as UK-based units. Such flights continued without incident until 20 September when three Battles on No.88 Squadron's first operational mission were attacked by Bf109s. Two Battles were lost, but the leader's gunner shot down one of the fighters – the first German aircraft shot down during the second World War by an Allied airman. Ten days later, five No.150 Squadron Battles were intercepted by 15 Bf109s; four Battles were shot down and a fifth so badly damaged that it crash-landed. If proof of the helplessness of unescorted Battles was needed this 100% loss provided it, and high-level daylight flights over German territory were stopped immediately. In addition a roster system was introduced, two squadrons providing the aircraft for each 24-hour period, enabling the other units to rest or train, though the poor weather which started in October gave little opportunity for the latter.

Most reconnaissance flights over the Heligoland Bight resulted in reports of warships, but it took four hours to mount an attack following the sighting, and by then the vessels were back in their heavily defended ports and could not be touched because of risk to civilians. Sweeps of the Bight by nine or more

In France conditions were far from ideal. Battle K9180/MQ-X of No. 226 Squadron is 'bombed up in the field'.

The Hampden – a mainstay of early daylight operations, though P1170 of No.61 Squadron did not last long, being written off on 14 October 1939. (RAFM P16258)

aircraft were tried, the first on 26 September being uneventful. Not so three days later when 12 Hampdens of No.144 Squadron were despatched in two separate formations. One aircraft returned early but the other crews swept the area, the three led by Sqn Ldr W.H.J. Lindsay attacking two destroyers without success. The other formation, led by the CO, Wg Cdr J.C. Cunningham, was intercepted by Bf109s and all five were shot down, the Germans losing two fighters in the process. It was a devastating blow for No.144 Squadron but the daily 'on call' system whereby 24 Bomber Command crews stood by for operations under Coastal Command control continued. They were little used, only 61 Hampden and Wellington sorties being flown between 8 October and 30 November because of the restrictions. The situation caused considerable friction between the two Commands and even the War Cabinet became restless, deciding that a more aggressive policy was warranted following the Germans' mounting success with U-Boats and mines. The Air Ministry was therefore authorized to carry out attacks on German warships anywhere, providing that such attacks were 'not likely to result in losses to our own air forces disproportionate to those inflicted on the enemy' – a classic piece of buck-passing!

The chance came on 3 December when the weather cleared and 24 Wellingtons from Nos.38, 115 and 149 Squadrons set out for Heligoland. Two cruisers were sighted and bombed from medium altitude without discernible result, though a 'hang-up'

The 'fighter-type' cockpit of the Hampden was unique amongst the twin-engined bombers. (via Chaz Bowyer Collection)

which dropped off over Heligoland Island caused a stir – it was the first bomb to explode on German soil during the Second World War. The Wellingtons were intercepted by Bf109s and Bf110s but suffered no losses, one of the attackers being shot down by a rear gunner; a result hailed as confirmation of the long-held theory that an efficient day bomber, flown in a formation providing good all-round defensive fire, could successfully penetrate a well-defended target and fight its way out again!

Attacking fighters were again ineffective on 14 December, but five out of 12 Wellingtons of No.99 Squadron were lost over the Schillig Roads to increasingly dangerous 'flak'. Four days later another armed recce was made of the Schillig Roads and Wilhelmshaven areas, this time by 22 Wellingtons of Nos.9, 37 and 149 Squadrons. In the meantime the Germans had re-thought their tactics and radar-directed Bf109s and Bf110s deliberately approached in the Wellington's blind spot – on the beam and from above – with devastating results. The formation was broken up and the bombers picked off one by one. Twelve Wellingtons were shot down in flames, for the loss of three German aircraft. Despite this evidence of vulnerability, No.3 Group's hierarchy insisted that poor positioning was responsible for the losses, and more immediate concern was centred on the Wellington's lack of self-sealing fuel tanks and consequent tendency to catch fire.

Meanwhile No.2 Group and Air Component Blenheim crews had started flying photographic reconnaissance sorties over Germany, though success was limited by problems with the cameras. The main task was checking activity behind the fortified Siegfried Line to establish whether an attack on France was imminent following the end of the Polish campaign. Nothing significant was spotted but such operations continued until late November when deteriorating weather brought the flights to a halt. Replacement of Battles commenced in December when Nos.15 and 40 Squadrons of No.71 Wing returned to Britain for re-equipment with Blenheim IVs, and were replaced by Nos.114 and 139 Squadrons already operating this versatile light bomber.

Operations by both the AASF and Air Component during the bitter winter of 1939-40 were almost non-existent – which was just as well, for the command and control structure, requiring Bomber Command HQ authority to launch AASF sorties, couldn't have coped with any pressure. This unsatisfactory state of affairs was finally rectified on 15 January when a new umbrella organization, British Air Force France (BAFF) commanded by Air Marshal A.S. Barratt, absorbed all RAF units in the country, and Bomber Command lost operational control of the AASF.

Almost unopposed leaflet 'raids' by the Whitleys of No.4 Group had continued, No.10 Squadron being the first to scatter paper over Berlin, on 1/2 October. They were joined by Hampdens and Wellingtons in January 1940, while a month earlier Whitleys started night-time harassment of German mine-laying He115 seaplanes based on Borkum, Norderney and Sylt. These armed 'Security Patrols' were taken over by Hampdens from February and like all the North Sea operations by Bomber Command, the crews found them a pretty thankless task. There were very few successes, day or night, outstanding being an opportunist low-level attack on a U-Boat off Borkum by Sqn Ldr M.V. Delap of No.82 Squadron on 11 March which resulted in the sinking of U-31, a Type VIIA. Delap's Blenheim suffered blast damage but survived the feat – and a feat it certainly was, as Coastal Command was discovering the hard way. By May 1940 Bomber Command had flown 861 sorties during which they dropped 61 tons of bombs, shot down 10 fighters, sank a minesweeper and U-Boat U-31 – but had lost 41 of their number.

The first *Nickel* delivery to Poland was made in March 1940, when airfields in France were often used as advanced bases for refuelling and diversions on longer-range sorties. Usually little more than endurance tests in aircraft inadequately heated and

Air Marshal Sir Arthur Barratt, AoC AASF in France, 1939. (via Chaz Bowyer Collection)

badly affected by icing, these flights were occasionally quite exciting, as on 15/16 March when Flt Lt Tomlin and his No.77 Squadron crew ran short of fuel while returning from Warsaw. They landed in a field, confident they were in France, but their first meeting with a local convinced them otherwise, and with German troops approaching they dashed back to their Whitley, started up and took off amidst a fusillade of rifle fire. Crossing the Franco-German frontier at low-level and with nearly empty tanks, they again landed safely in a field – the Whitley was that sort of aeroplane! On the same day the Luftwaffe accidentally dropped bombs on the Orkney Islands during an attack on Scapa Flow, killing a crofter and injuring six other civilians. A retaliatory raid was immediately planned, 30 Whitleys and 20 Hampdens being sent to attack the seaplane base at Hornum, Sylt, on the night of 19/20 March. It was the heaviest attack to date and the first on a German land target. Forty-one crews claimed to have bombed the target successfully, but in fact most bombs fell into the sea and there was little damage – a portent of things to come.

Supposedly valuable as part of the 'psychological warfare' battle, *Nickelling* was little more than a cover during March, when the primary objective was surveying potential land targets to check if they were identifiable in moonlight, and in April leaflet-dropping officially became a secondary task after 366

sorties and the loss of 10 aircraft. It had not been a success, the effect on the German population being minimal as crews were quick to realise, calling their sorties 'bumph raids'. However the missions did provide 'operational' experience at a time when offensive activity was severely restricted by the rules of engagement, and to this extent they were valuable.

It was at this point, on 2 April 1940, that Ludlow-Hewitt was replaced as C-in-C Bomber Command by Air Marshal C.F.A. Portal. Sir Edgar had been at the helm since September 1937, an arduous period, but it was unusual to replace a commander when it was pretty obvious that a major enemy offensive was about to be mounted – unless he was considered unsatisfactory. Ludlow-Hewitt had 'trodden on toes' with his outspoken reports on the state of preparedness of Bomber Command. He was regarded as too pessimistic and there were strong rumours that the outbreak of war prevented him being relieved of his post earlier. Now he was unfairly blamed for the poor performance of Bomber Command during the early months of the war and so had to go, though he was undoubtedly one of the ablest senior officers of the time.

Within a week of Portal taking command the German offensive in the West had started and stalemate was at an end. It was an obvious time to attack but the direction was undoubtedly influenced

Flt Lt Tomlin and his No.77 Squadron crew with Whitley V N1387/C, safe at Villeneuve, France, after first landing in Germany by mistake. (IWM C1011)

by Allied diplomatic activities in Scandinavia, which had been focused on stopping Swedish high-grade iron ore being exported to Germany since the war began. Anxiety in London and Paris about the whole of Scandinavia had increased when the Russians attacked Finland at the end of November 1939, and the Norwegian and Swedish Governments were requested to allow Allied units to transit across their territory to Finland – the idea being that not only could the Finns be helped, but ore exports from northern Norwegian ports could be stopped. Not surprisingly, both countries refused point blank; but Hitler judged that it would not end there, despite the Finnish cease-fire on 13 March 1940. He was right for on 28 March, after much indecision, the Allies decided to mine Norwegian waters and to send a force to northern Norway if the Germans reacted by invading the country. The mining force set sail with orders to start laying on 8 April, but unfortunately the Germans had already reacted, transports sailing for Norway on the 4th followed by major fleet units on the 6th. A sighting by a Hudson crew early on the 7th resulted in 18 Blenheims of Nos.82 and 107 Squadrons led by Wg Cdr Basil Embry attempting to bomb the ships, but without success. They were followed by 24 Wellingtons from Nos.9 and 115 Squadrons, but they failed to make contact in worsening weather conditions, which made it impossible to determine accurately the movements of the various German naval units at sea or work out their intentions. The consensus of opinion was that they were engaged on exercises, and surprise was complete when they arrived off Norwegian ports late on 8 April. The following day Denmark capitulated, and with the

Baltic secure the Germans started consolidating their positions all the way up the Norwegian coast, landing by air as well as sea.

As soon as the seriousness of the situation was appreciated, Bomber Command was ordered to do what it could to slow down the German advance in southern Norway, while a hastily assembled Anglo-French force prepared to land in the north. Incredibly the restrictions against bombing land targets in Germany remained in force and the Baltic ports were not attacked; but Norway was different, and during the afternoon of 9 April 24 Wellingtons from Nos.9 and 115 Squadrons set course for Bergen, followed an hour later by 12 Hampdens of No.50 Squadron. Their targets were the light cruisers *Köln* and *Königsberg*, but as usual SAP bombs failed to do any damage, the only small consolation being the shooting down of a Do18 flying boat on the way home. The first deliberate raid on Norwegian soil followed two days later when six Wellingtons of No.115 Squadron were led to Stavanger/Sola airfield by two Coastal Command Blenheims which strafed the airfield before the Wellingtons bombed, ineffectively. Night attacks by Whitleys and Hampdens on shipping in the Skagerrak and Kattegat were equally unsuccessful, one north-bound vessel being claimed but not confirmed.

Early on 12 April a reconnaissance Hudson sighted the battlecruisers *Scharnhorst* and *Gneisenau* south-bound off Lister and Bomber Command immediately ordered an attack. Twenty-four Hampdens from Nos.44, 50, 61 and 144 Squadrons were launched, followed by 44 Wellingtons from Nos.9, 37, 38, 75, 115 and 149 Squadrons. Unable to

Loading 1,000-lb and 500-lb bombs on a Wellington during the early war years. (via B. Robertson)

Hampden VN-G of No.50 Squadron at Waddington, late 1939. (N.D. Welch via MAP)

find the briefed targets, some Hampden crews went to Kristiansand to attack two reported naval vessels. They lost six aircraft – half their number – to 'flak' and Bf109s. Five of the Luftwaffe fighters were shot down by the bombers' gunners; a remarkable effort but no real compensation. Meanwhile the Wellingtons, searching close to the Norwegian coast, were attacked by twin-engined fighters. A Ju88 was shot down in the mêlée, but five Wellingtons were lost and another seven damaged, this disastrous affair resulting in the immediate cessation of large formation attacks by Wellingtons and Hampdens in daylight. At last it was accepted that their defensive firepower was inadequate against fighter opposition, and it was decreed that henceforth such tasks would be the unhappy prerogative of Blenheims. Meanwhile Hampdens, the only current Bomber Command aircraft capable of accommodating a 1,500-lb mine, started *Gardening* (the code-name for mine-laying,

the mines being known as *Vegetables* and the areas to be mined being identified by the names of flowers, vegetables and, as operations extended, shrubs and fish). Naturally the Baltic shipping lanes between Germany and Norway had priority, the first such operation of the war involving 15 Hampdens during the night of 13/14 April. One aircraft was lost, and during the following night two more went missing from a force of 28 sent to the same area. Mine-laying was no sinecure!

Now solely responsible for day attacks, No.2 Group detached Nos.107 and 110 Squadrons to Lossiemouth and tried to minimize losses by ordering crews to return without bombing if cloud cover was not available. Stavanger airfield was the main target by day and night, Wellingtons and Whitleys also carrying out night attacks on other Norwegian landing grounds, in a forlorn attempt to take the pressure off Allied troops who started landing on the 14th. They

Wellington 1As of No.75 Squadron 'setting out on a raid' in June 1940. (IWM CH463)

The standard night bomber was the Whitley, N1421 belonging to No.102 Squadron at Driffield, April 1940. (IWM C921)

Flying in characteristic nose-down attitude, two Whitley Vs of No.77 Squadron, N1373/J and N1347/E, April 1940. (Flight (Postcard Series))

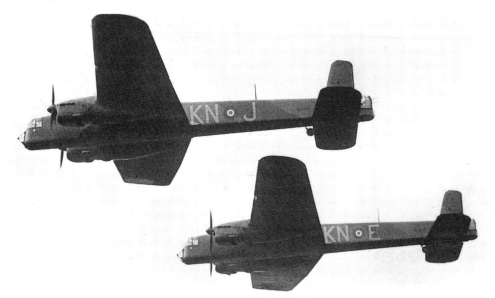

never got properly established in central Norway and started to withdraw on 28 April, a 50-strong force of Wellingtons, Whitleys and Hampdens bombing Sola, Fornebu and Aalborg airfields on the night of the 30th to bolster the support being given by Blenheims during the day. Some of the 'heavies' came under attack from Bf110s of 1./ZG1 – the first confirmed interceptions by German night fighters.

After final attacks on Stavanger and Rye airfields on 2 May, the Blenheims were also withdrawn from Norwegian operations, a German offensive in France being considered imminent! Seven Blenheims had been lost while at Lossiemouth, including one flown by Sqn Ldr K.C. Doran of 110 Squadron shot down near Stavanger on 30 April. Doran had led the first RAF bombing raid of the war, on Wilhelmshaven on 4 September 1939. With the evacuation of the Anglo-French forces from the central area all but complete by 4 May, Whitleys at Kinloss for night operations over Norway returned to their No.4 Group bases, and Hampden crews of No.5 Group extended their *Gardening* activities to the North Sea. Operations continued in northern Norway until 10 June, but Bomber Command took no further part in the latter stages. It was the end of an expensive fiasco, but nothing compared with what was awaiting the Allies during the next few weeks.

At dawn on 10 May the Luftwaffe attacked over 70 airfields in France, Holland and Belgium, glider-borne forces landing in the latter country to secure a bridgehead. The AASF was placed on 30-minute readiness for attacks on advancing troops – not the strategic targets for which they were officially in France, such operations having been tacitly abandoned in October 1939. Though understandable, the tactical use of the aircraft was directly contrary to BAFF operational instructions which stated 'It is not clear that a bomber force used against an advancing army well supported by all forms of anti aircraft defence and a large force of fighter aircraft, will be economically effective' – just the situation they faced. The AASF could have reached all parts of the front but its activities were concentrated on the southern sector, leaving the north-west almost exclusively to Bomber Command, who allocated seven No.2 Group Blenheim squadrons for day operations and two Whitley squadrons of No.4 Group for night attacks. Barratt could only request this help and there were grave misgivings at Bomber Command Headquarters about committing forces to the land battle. Indeed two

days before the German attack, Portal, writing about No.2 Group's planned involvement, expressed the view that 'the proposed employment of these units is fundamentally unsound...'. He was not alone in thinking that bombing based on target information necessarily some hours old would be unlikely to affect the outcome sufficiently to justify the crippling losses expected – but there was little choice, for Bomber Command could not stand idly by while the Wehrmacht swept forward.

It was also against Air Ministry policy to involve Whitleys in the land battle, not because it was thought that tactical targets could not be successfully attacked (there was still considerable faith in the ability of crews to find pinpoint locations even at night) but because the Air Staff wanted to use their 16 'heavy' squadrons for strategic operations against German industrial capacity, in particular oil resources. For months it had been argued, sometimes heatedly, that a German invasion of the Low Countries should be the signal for an all-out assault on the Ruhr, an area little

Right: *Propaganda leaflets being loaded aboard a No.102 Squadron aircraft at Driffield, April 1940... (IWM C912)*

Below: *...and despatched down the flare chute – a thankless task. (IWM)*

bigger than Greater London but containing 60% of German heavy industry. It was considered that not only would there be long-term damage to German industry, but that anti-aircraft gun and searchlight defences would have to be increased, diverting men and equipment from the battle front, and that there would be incidental damage to communications thus slowing down the Wehrmacht in the Low Countries. Not surprisingly the French did not agree for they had virtually no strategic bombers available and were naturally more concerned with stemming any advance into their territory by ground forces. However they could present no convincing argument against the British carrying out such raids, except one, rarely expressed – fear of Luftwaffe retaliation on French cities. It was a fear not lightly put aside for their air defences were pitiful – even worse than those in Britain!

Late in April the French had finally agreed that '...in the event of German aggression against Holland, or against Belgium, or against both countries, the British Air Force should be authorized, without further consultation, to attack marshalling yards and oil refineries in the Ruhr.' This seemed clear enough but it was not the end of the matter for the French or the British Army. The latter, having previously favoured the Ruhr plan, now took up the French stance. The War Cabinet, still led by Neville Chamberlain, also prevaricated, desperately anxious to confine bombing to purely military targets, at least until the Germans broke the so-called agreement. On 8 May Cabinet authority was finally given for 'harassing operations' against German rail marshalling yards if either of the Low Countries was attacked – with the aim of extinguishing the lights and thus reducing efficiency! The naïvety shown by such instructions would be laughable if the situation hadn't been so serious – and made worse by Bomber Command being expressly forbidden to attack their first choice of target, the power-generating resources of the Ruhr, without explicit War Cabinet permission.

In response to early reports of German troop movements on 10 May, two Blenheims of No.40 Squadron were despatched on pre-planned reconnaissance sorties. They were soon in trouble, one being shot down over the Dutch coast and the other, badly damaged by a Ju88, crash-landing back at Wyton. The crew's report convinced the Ops staff at No.2 Group that the situation was serious, and instead of following plans to attack troop columns, it was decided to tackle German forces already occupying Dutch airfields. Waalhaven was attacked by nine Blenheims from No.15 Squadron, hits being claimed on hangars and aircraft, and a little later No.40 Squadron sent twelve aircraft to Ypenburg, cratering

the airfield and damaging a hangar, but losing three crews in the process. Another 12 Blenheims from No.110 Squadron, accompanied by six fighter Blenheims of No.600 Squadron, bombed and strafed Ju52s on a beach north of The Hague. Night attacks followed, Waalhaven being visited by 36 Wellingtons, while nine Whitleys from Nos.77 and 102 Squadrons attempted to bomb bridges over the Rhine and troop transports near Goch.

No.2 Group came under the tactical control of Barratt's HQ in France on 11 May, but poor communications initially caused confusion in Operations Rooms and frustration for crews. When it became clear that the Wehrmacht were pouring over undamaged bridges in the Maastricht area, Nos.21 and 110 Squadrons, on stand-by since daybreak, were sent off mid-afternoon to bomb both bridges and troop columns. Tired and jaded after their long wait, the crews of No. 21 Squadron's 12 aircraft lost any element of surprise when their leader orbited over the target before attacking, and accurate ground fire damaged 11 of the Blenheims, further degrading the bombing. Surprisingly, all returned home but No.110 Squadron, making a direct attack, were not so lucky, losing two aircraft to 'flak'. That same night saw the first raid on a German town – the excuse, if one was needed, being that Munchen-Gladbach was a communications centre. Thirty-six aircraft took off: Whitleys of Nos.51, 58, 77 and 102 Squadrons and Hampdens of Nos.44, 49, 50, 61 and 144 Squadrons. Five of the Hampdens returned early, a large number for that period of the war, and only 15 crews claimed to have attacked the target. Two Hampdens and a Whitley were lost.

The situation around Maastricht on the Dutch/Belgium border was desperate by the early hours of 12 May. The River Maas which formed a natural barrier had been breached, and a number of key bridges across the Albert Canal which should have been blown up were already in German hands. Their leading armoured columns were across and fanning out to the west and it was obvious that they would soon be in contact with a tired BEF just completing a forced march to take up positions on the River Dyle, east of Brussels. Something had to be done and it was a day of high drama for the gallant crews of the AASF Battles. No.2 Group was also busy, Blenheims attacking bridges at Maastricht, Hasselt and Tongres. Aircraft of No.107 Squadron were first away, followed by Nos.15 and 82 Squadrons. All suffered badly from intense ground fire and waiting Bf109s, losing 14 of their number. Things were a little easier in the evening when nine Blenheims of No.82 Squadron cratered a road alongside the Albert Canal without loss and No.21

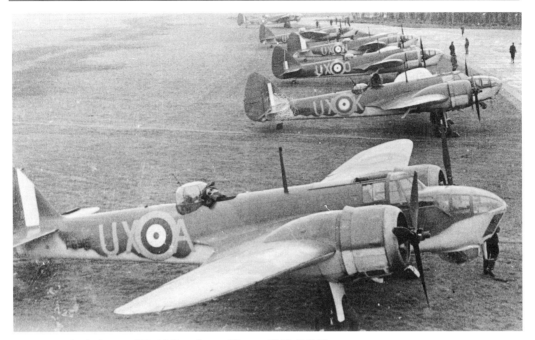

'Long-range' Blenheims of No.82 Squadron at Watton, 1940. (MAP)

Squadron carried out a similar attack on Tongres, losing one aircraft to 'flak'.

Poor weather and lack of serviceable aircraft prevented operations on the 13th, but with the Germans swarming over pontoon bridges thrown across the River Meuse at Sedan on the 14th, desperate efforts were made to contain them. No.82 Squadron tried blocking the road east of Breda but heavy 'flak' prevented accurate bombing, while attacks on the bridges themselves lost the AASF a staggering 35 of the 71 aircraft despatched. Later in the day, No.2 Group sent 28 fighter-escorted Blenheims drawn from Nos.21, 107 and 110 Squadrons to the same area, but in the face of overwhelming fighter strength and numerous 'flak wagons' they were lucky not to lose more than eight, one of which crash-landed at base.

During the afternoon, Rotterdam was heavily attacked by Ju87 dive bombers, before a surrender deadline had expired. It was the last straw and the following day the British War Cabinet, chaired by the new Prime Minister, Mr Winston S. Churchill, reacted strongly. Bomber Command was given clearance to carry out offensive operations across the Rhine and into the German heartland – the gloves were off at last!

The strategic offensive started immediately, 99 of

the 111 Wellingtons, Hampdens and Whitleys despatched during the night of 15/16 May going to 16 targets in the Ruhr Valley, the remainder hitting communications targets in Belgium. It was the first occasion when more than 100 aircraft were 'launched' in one night, and not one was shot down, the single loss being due to navigational error. A maximum of nine aircraft were allocated to each target, the crews being thoroughly briefed, even down to particular

The most powerful turret of the day, the Nash and Thompson tail turret of the Whitley V.

buildings in some instances, but were then left to their own devices as far as route and tactics were concerned – a situation which continued for months. After the horrendous losses over France the much lower casualties suffered on this and subsequent early night attacks, plus the successes claimed in good faith by the crews, were met with relief and a certain amount of complacency within Bomber Command and the Air Ministry – unfortunately later shown to be misplaced.

In France the AASF moved backwards as their bases were threatened, and with the BEF also forced to pull back under pressure, No.2 Group had to fill the gap. Twelve Blenheims of No.82 Squadron took off at dawn on 17 May to attack Panzer columns at Gemloux and when the promised fighter escort failed to turn up, pressed on alone, running into a heavy 'flak' barrage as they approached the target. The survivors then ran the gauntlet of Bf109s, and only one badly damaged Blenheim regained base. This disaster, unprecedented in No. 2 Group, prompted urgent debate, for it was obvious that the Blenheim force would be decimated if such losses continued. On the squadron the situation was seen in even starker terms, but the CO, Wg Cdr the Earl of Bandon, was determined to rebuild his unit and just three days later was able to declare No.82 again ready for operations – an extraordinary demonstration of one man's will-power and persuasiveness.

Night operations, already tried by the AASF Battle squadrons, were an obvious way to reduce casualties, but with untrained crews they were all but worthless, while operating by day only when fighter escort was available was too restricting. Crews had to fly,

escorted or not, and regardless of losses, as on 18 May when three of six No.15 Squadron aircraft attacking military transports and AFVs near Le Lateau were shot down. Occasionally things went differently of course, as on the 20th when 47 Blenheims with a fighter 'umbrella' suffered no casualties during an attack on Panzers threatening to encircle the BEF; a tribute to the escort, though 'flak wagons' were also less in evidence than usual.

Conditions in France were becoming chaotic, communications with some AASF squadrons being completely lost. Ever longer delays in getting vital target information to No.2 Group units resulted in more confusion, as did refugees caught up in the rapid German advance. Despite everything the Blenheim crews managed to keep up the pressure on German troop columns, assisted by the AASF whenever possible, and by aircraft of Nos.3, 4 and 5 Groups, switched on 19/20 May from attacks on oil installations to communications in northern France and Germany.

Operation *Dynamo*, the evacuation of the BEF, commenced on 27 May and largely completed by 4 June, saw 338,226 men, of whom 112,000 were French, being taken off the beaches. The surviving AASF and Air Component Blenheims had been flown back to Britain by this time, the remnants of No.114 Squadron being the last to depart, on 31 May. The fast-diminishing number of Battles remained, however, and for the next fortnight flew in support of the French and elements of the 51st Highland Division. No.2 Group continued attacking troop positions and communications targets from British bases, losses of

Bomber Command's transport squadron, No.271, flew a variety of aircraft from Doncaster, the most successful being the Handley Page Harrow. (No.245 Squadron records)

Many Battles and Blenheims ended their short careers in France as German booty – like L9241 of No.110 Squadron which crash-landed near Orchies, 14 May 1940. (via M.W. Payne)

Blenheims being relatively light – except on 6 June when 12 aircraft of No.40 Squadron were sent to attack armour in the Abbeville area with 250-lb bombs. Five Blenheims were shot down during the low-level attack, a blow somewhat mollified by the subsequent return of five crew members and information that all but three of the rest were PoWs.

On 10 June Mussolini, sensing German overall victory, declared war on France and Britain, a move not unexpected. Plans had been laid, No.71 Wing HQ, AASF, moving to the Marseilles area on 3 June to prepare two airfields for Operation *Haddock*, a planned attack by Wellingtons on targets in Northern Italy as soon as possible after any declaration. The plan caused alarm in the area, reminiscent of the reaction of the French in the north during May when the Luftwaffe attacked. A detachment from No.99 Squadron arrived at Salon during the afternoon of 11 June, to be met by a flurry of orders from increasingly senior Frenchmen stating that under no circumstances were the aircraft to take off. Meanwhile Group Captain R.M. Field, Officer Commanding No.71 Wing, was receiving conflicting instructions from Franco-British headquarters. He decided to act, and at midnight the Wellingtons began to move towards the runway, but they were blocked by French lorries! While this charade was in progress 36 Whitleys of Nos.10, 51, 58, 77 and 102 Squadrons, after refuelling in the Channel Islands, were on their way to bomb Turin and Genoa. Unfortunately only 13 arrived, bad weather defeating the rest, one of which crashed in France. Further north 59 Hampdens, Wellingtons and Whitleys bombed targets in Germany and France with slightly more success, though Wellington crews involved in dropping incendiaries in the Black Forest (the first of a series of attempts to start woodland fires in response to one of the more hare-brained pre-war Western Air Plans) wasted their time. Four nights

later, the lorry incident finally sorted out, eight Wellingtons of Nos.99 and 149 Squadrons took off from Salon for Genoa. Only one attacked, violent thunderstorms forcing the rest to return with their bombs. A further attempt was made by 22 aircraft the following night, 16/17 June, with more success, 14 claiming to have bombed their targets, but the next day the French sued for peace and Operation *Haddock* was at an end.

Meanwhile the AASF had been forced back onto four overcrowded airfields in the Nantes area. The situation was plainly hopeless so on 15 June Barratt ordered the evacuation of the remaining Battles. No.2 Group continued supportive sorties over northern France, bringing the Battle of France to an inglorious end on 18 June when six Blenheims attacked AFVs near Cherbourg. Attacks then switched to airfields in Holland, Belgium, Germany – and France.

Painfully, Bomber Command had learned that unescorted bombers were no match for German fighters by day, though at night the weather was seen as the principal enemy – a view that was subsequently to undergo some modification! Operational losses directly attributable to the campaign in France totalled 670, of which Bomber Command lost 97 Blenheims, 17 Hampdens, 26 Wellingtons and 26 Whitleys. The rest were AASF and Air Component aircraft, to which could be added over 200 from Fighter and Coastal Commands. Personnel casualties, dead, missing, wounded or captured were also horrendous, if possible made worse by being nearly all highly trained regulars, the natural leaders and instructors for the mass of volunteers flooding through the training organization. It had been a disaster, and Britain's outlook on her own was grim. Yet, overall, there was a curious sense of relief that the shadow boxing was over – and a new determination swept not only Bomber Command but the whole nation.

CHAPTER 3

Regroup and Reorganize 1940-1941

IN A SERIES OF brilliantly planned and executed operations the Germans had overrun Norway, Denmark, Belgium and much of France, gaining control of the coastline from North Cape to the Spanish border in less than two months. Only Britain stood in the way of Hitler's dream of total domination of western Europe and her situation looked hopeless. He paused, expecting that Churchill's new government would sue for peace. Instead, Britain remained defiant and on 16 July 1940 Hitler ordered the preparation of *Unternehmung Seelöwe* (Operation *Sea Lion*) – the invasion of Britain across the narrow waters of the English Channel.

First he had to gain air superiority in the skies over south-east England, and raids on airfields in the area were mounted with the aim of destroying the opposing fighter forces. It was the start of the Battle of Britain, three months of fierce fighting which ended with the

Luftwaffe forced to give up daylight raids and change to nocturnal operations against British towns and cities. It was Fighter Command's victory and the British fighter pilot's finest hour. Bomber Command played a supporting role, albeit an important one.

Half of Bomber Command's front-line strength at the end of April 1940 had been lost during the Battle of France, but operations continued into July without a break. The Blenheim squadrons, which had taken most of the casualties, were switched to daylight operations over Germany when cloud cover was available, and when it was not they attacked airfields in the occupied countries.

Meanwhile the 'heavies' of Nos.3, 4 and 5 Groups attempted to fulfil the latest in a long series of Air Staff Directives. Issued on 4 June it reflected the views of the Economic Intelligence Department of the Ministry of Economic Warfare in stating that if German oil

Blenheims and a Percival Q6 at Wyton during August 1940. R3741/VE-A, a No. 110 Squadron Blenheim appears to have a rear-firing gun in the engine nacelle. (IWM CH776).

stocks could be reduced by a minimum of 300,000 tons in the next three months the country would be in crisis, and so attacks on oil installations were the strategic priority. It was recognized that such installations were extremely difficult to identify at night so Bomber Command was also tasked with 'bringing about continuous interruption and dislocation of German war industry, particularly in areas within range where the aircraft industry is concentrated' – in other words the Ruhr Valley plus Hamburg, Bremen and Frankfurt. The Directive made clear, however, that night bombing was not to degenerate into indiscriminate attacks.

On 20 June Portal received another Air Staff Directive, stating that 'In the present situation [the anticipated Luftwaffe assault on Britain] it has been decided that the primary offensive of the Air Striking Force (i.e. Bomber Command) must be directed towards those objectives which will have the most immediate effect on reducing the scale of air attack on the country', and specifying six aircraft assembly plants. It is hard to see how such attacks would have an 'immediate' effect on the ability of the Luftwaffe to bomb Britain, but in the event Portal hardly had time to assimilate the order before it was overtaken by instructions to attack communications, continue sea mining (a nightly operation by No.5 Group Hampdens, usually six in number) and prepare to set alight crops and forests using a special incendiary device expected to be available shortly. The device sounded useful, but of more immediate interest was the first operational use of a 2,000-lb semi-armour piercing (SAP) bomb on 1/2 July by a certain Flg Off Guy Gibson during a raid on Kiel by 12 Hampdens.

With worries about an invasion mounting, Portal was informed on 4 July that priorities had changed again, to the bombing of ports and shipping, plus a three-fold increase in sea mining. Nine days later yet another Directive reached Portal; he was to concentrate on the aircraft industry, oil and communications. Five aircraft depots, at Diepholz, Eschele, Göttingen, Paderborn and Rotenburg and five assembly plants at Bremen, Gotha, Kassel, Wenzendorf and Wismar, were specified.

The effect of this flood of contradictory orders on Bomber Command operations staff can be imagined and Portal was very concerned, not only by the work load but because he felt it unrealistic to expect more than a very small proportion of his crews to find the latest priority targets. Most of them were at the limit of their aircrafts' range and in isolated positions which meant that 'near misses' would cause no damage or disruption. Such attacks would also have a minimal effect on German morale, and like some other senior officers he considered the lowering of morale a very important secondary effect of the bombing campaign. On 16 July he complained that he was being asked to do the impossible, but the only response was a restatement of Bomber Command's objectives as laid down by the Air Staff at the Air Ministry.

Attacks on barges massing in Low Countries' ports in readiness for *Sea Lion* commenced on 3 July when part of a force of 33 Blenheims bombed concentrations near Rotterdam. That night 27 Hampdens and Whitleys attacked communications, airfields, and more barges, a varied fare which, with mine-laying, continued for the rest of the month. The Luftwaffe reacted to the increasing number of night attacks by forming Nachtjagdgeschwaders (NJG: night fighter squadrons), the first becoming operational in July using Bf110s co-operating with searchlight batteries to stalk their prey. It is probable that their first success was on 8/9 July when a Whitley of No.10 Squadron was lost off Heligoland, and in an attempt to prove that two could play at the game Sqn Ldr Webster of No.15 Squadron loitered at low-level near an airfield at Caen during the night of 17/18 July, hoping to catch an aircraft landing or taking off. He was out of luck, but this was probably the first 'intruder' sortie of the war.

Another new idea was tried out on 20/21 July when nine Hampdens made a low-level attack on the battleship *Tirpitz* and pocket-battleship *Admiral Scheer* in Wilhelmshaven harbour. They used 'M' bombs, modified 1,500-lb sea mines with delayed-action fuzing, for this courageous attack made within the most strongly defended area in Germany. Four Hampdens were lost but no damage was done to either ship.

Meanwhile No.1 Group had been reformed on 18 June to control the remnants of the AASF Battle squadrons and was declared operational on 12 July. Four days later six aircraft from Nos.103 and 150 Squadrons were despatched to bomb oil tanks at Rotterdam but were unable to locate the target, and a raid on Schiphol airfield on the 22nd was the first meaningful operation by Battles under direct Bomber Command control. No.1 Group strength was soon diluted, however, the Battles of Nos.12 and 142 Squadrons being put at the disposal of Coastal Command, nominally for operations against E-Boats, on 7 August. A week later Nos.103 and 150 Squadrons were withdrawn for anti-invasion training, but the balance was redressed as Polish personnel, who had escaped from both Poland and France, converted onto Battles. They formed Nos.300 and 301 Squadrons during July and Nos.304 and 305 Squadrons in August, and were soon operational as part of No.1 Group.

For Wellingtons and Whitleys of Nos.3 and 4 Groups, journeys to the Ruhr Valley were becoming the 'norm', 43 crews being briefed for attacks on seven towns in the area during the night of 1/2 August. Some aircraft also carried leaflets, a practice which continued for the rest of the war, supplemented by Operational Training Unit (OTU) crews making *Nickelling* flights over enemy-occupied territory as part of their training – the first such sorties having been made over France on 18/19 July.

The *Razzle* incendiary device was probably first used on 11/12 August when the targets were again in the Ruhr Valley, the contents of tins of pellets being dropped down a special chute over adjacent forest areas. There was no obvious result and *Razzle* was never a success – the only enemy reaction being advice to the populace not to put the pellets in their pockets!

Hampdens still went on bombing raids as well as flying nightly mine laying sorties, and No.5 Group was making a name for itself on specialist tasks, such as attacks on the Dortmund-Ems canal. The canal had already been attacked on 10 occasions prior to the night of 12/13 August when 11 Hampden crews, six from No.49 Squadron and five from No.83 Squadron, were briefed for another attempt at breaching it. Two of the crews failed to locate the target and bombed Texel Island instead, four carried out 'diversionary' activities, but five found and attacked the old aqueduct carrying the canal over the River Ems north of Münster. By the time the last aircraft, flown by Flt Lt R.A.B. Learoyd of No.49 Squadron, commenced its run along the canal two Hampdens had been shot down by guns lining the bank, and the other two had limped away badly damaged. It was a daunting prospect but, almost blinded by searchlights and with the aircraft taking repeated hits, Learoyd continued down to 150 feet to press home the attack – and destroyed the aqueduct. Returning to Scampton he calmly circled overhead until dawn before landing his badly damaged aircraft. For his cool courage in making a determined attack knowing full well that the gunners were alert and had ranging and elevation all worked out, he was awarded Bomber Command's first Victoria Cross.

The following day No.2 Group was very active, six Blenheims carrying out a North Sea sweep, two reconnoitring the aqueduct attack, and 29 taking part in airfield raids. The latter proved disastrous, 12 of the 16 which made attacks being lost, eleven of them from No.82 Squadron which was virtually wiped out for the second time within three months.

On 23/24 August a large *Gardening* operation was mounted when 40 Hampdens laid mines in the coastal convoy routes. The following night they were joined by 28 Wellingtons, while 68 Whitleys and Wellingtons attacked German land targets, 25 Blenheims roamed over France, and 10 Whitleys visited Milan. The total daily weight of bombs was gradually increasing, though the weight aimed at individual targets was still small – too small to be effective.

On 24/25 August the Luftwaffe bombed central London unintentionally (the crews were briefed for night attacks on Rochester and Thameshaven), and against Air Staff advice the War Cabinet immediately authorized a retaliatory attack on Berlin. Some 80 aircraft from Nos.3, 4 and 5 Groups were despatched on 25/26 August to attack specific targets in the Berlin area. This was a much larger force than usually sent to one location but, as was standard practice, the crews made their way independently. Heavy cloud obscured Berlin and only 29 crews claimed to have identified their targets. In fact nearly all bombs exploded in open country to the south of the city. Strong headwinds during the return flight then caused difficulties, three of the six Hampdens lost that night 'ditching' when they ran out of fuel. The attack proved little more than a gesture, for even if crews found their targets at such extreme range the aircraft available in 1940 could not carry a worthwhile load to Berlin and return safely.

On 3 September 1940, the first anniversary of the outbreak of war, Prime Minister Churchill wrote one of his famous minutes to the War Cabinet, stating in part: '...the Navy can lose us the war but only the Air Force can win it. Therefore our supreme effort must be to gain overwhelming mastery in the air. The fighters are our salvation but bombers alone can provide the means of victory...' Angry over the disruption caused by German bombing around the country, Churchill followed this 'policy statement' with a memo suggesting that the RAF should spread its bombs as widely as possible over the cities of Germany – perhaps the first hint of an area bombing policy? Music to the ears of some advocates, but the Air Staff continued defending selective attack, supremely confident of Bomber Command's ability to hit individual targets. So sure were they that on 5

September Air Chief Marshal Sir Richard Peirse, Vice Chief of Air Staff, wrote to Prime Minister Churchill: 'There is little doubt that the reason for the effectiveness of our night bombing is that it is planned and relentless until the particular target is knocked out or dislocated whereas German night bombing is sporadic and mainly harassing.' This rosy view had no foundation in fact, but it was allowed to colour all the Air Staff Directives for months to come, being maintained even after the start of the London Blitz on 7 September; an event forewarned in a speech by Hitler on 4 September in which he announced reprisals for RAF attacks on Berlin.

On 11 September Portal, as a counter to Hitler's threats, proposed the selection of 20 German towns and due warning be given that every time a British town was attacked indiscriminately, one of them would be similarly raided by 150-160 aircraft carrying 130 tons of bombs. This seemed out of character, but Sir Charles was becoming increasingly doubtful about the ability of crews to find and hit pinpoint targets, and he thought it time to hurt the German people, and give a boost to the British. His suggestion was turned down, the Air Staff re-affirming on 21 September that their aim was 'Germany's economic disruption', though there was one rather surprising addition to the Directive. Berlin, said to contain no strategic targets, could now be attacked with the object of 'causing as much disturbance and dislocation to both industry and the population as possible'. Perhaps a little pressure had been applied!

Portal would certainly have had ammunition for his proposals if more photographic evidence of bombing results been available. The Photographic Reconnaissance Unit (PRU) was tasked with obtaining 'before and after' photographs but was swamped with

Its a tight squeeze in the locker room as a Wellington crew prepares for a flight. (IWM CH2205)

priority demands from the Admiralty, so No.2 Group Blenheim crews were given the job of reconnoitring 'heavy' bomber targets. Not surprisingly, they were largely unsuccessful, and though a few bombers were now carrying night attack cameras there was an art to analyzing 'time of release' photographs, and such expertise was not generally available.

Most Bomber Command operations reflected the priorities in the Directives, though on 2/3 September 30 Wellington crews made another attempt to start fires using *Razzle* and *Decker* incendiary leaves (known as *Razzling*) in the Black Forest without success, and 39 Hampdens attacked the U-Boat base at Lorient, the first such operation. The Battles of No.1 Group resumed bomber operations against invasion barges on 7 September, the Polish squadrons operating for the first time on the 14th when Boulogne was attacked. The heavier bombers continued to target oil depots and rail marshalling yards, but from the middle of the month most operations concentrated on barges. Among the 15 No.83 Squadron crews detailed for Antwerp on the 15/16th was one captained by Plt Off C.A. Connor. Over the target Connor's Hampden was repeatedly hit, and just after the call 'Bombs Gone' the aircraft was struck in the bomb bay, shrapnel piercing the fuel tanks and turning the rear fuselage into a blazing inferno. Sgt J. Hannah, occupying the upper gun cupola, could have baled out with other crew members but instead fought the fire with extinguishers, a log book, and his bare hands – and put it out. Crawling forward he reported to Connor and though badly burned, assisted with the navigation during the return to Scampton. On 1 October Connor was awarded the DFC and Hannah the VC, the latter not universally acclaimed by bomber crews at the time. Some felt that he had little choice because his parachute was already smouldering and probably unusable – an understandable reaction from men who had seen comrades perform acts of great valour and receive no recognition, but unfair, for whatsoever the truth about his chances of baling out, Hannah undoubtedly demonstrated extraordinary courage in the face of an appalling situation, saved the aircraft and probably the pilot.

Of the vessels assembled for Operation *Sea Lion*, German records reveal that 21 troop transports, 214 barges and five tugs had been sunk or badly damaged by September 21. This, together with the failure of the Luftwaffe to subdue the RAF in the Battle of Britain, had already resulted in the postponement of the invasion, but barges in Channel ports continued to be the main target until 30 September when Bomber Command was officially informed that the danger of imminent invasion had passed and that the strategic bomber 'offensive' could be resumed. In practice the latter had not ceased completely, 129 Hampdens,

Wellingtons and Whitleys having been sent to Berlin on 23/24 September, but generally aircraft had been thinly spread over the ports and German rail network. Poor weather over Berlin largely nullified the raid, but better conditions on 30 September/1 October resulted in 17 crews claiming to have identified and attacked the Reichsluftfahrt Ministerum on the Leipzigstrasse. Whether they had actually done so was a moot point for while there was no reason to doubt their sincerity, without photographs their claims couldn't be checked.

The C-in-C was in the throes of trying to get his own PRU established when he relinquished the post on 4 October 1940. Like his predecessor, Portal had differences with his Air Ministry masters, but he stepped firmly up the ladder to become Chief of Air Staff. He was succeeded by Air Chief Marshal Sir Richard Peirse, author of many of the Directives – a case of the biter bit!

On 9 October 1940 No.419 (Special Duties) Flight was transferred to Bomber Command and reluctantly added to No.3 Group's Battle Order, its Whitleys operationally controlled by the Air Ministry (Directorate of Plans) for secret 'special' duties with the Special Operations Executive*. In Bomber Command's view it was as much out of place as No.271 Squadron, which had joined No.3 Group six months earlier equipped mainly with Harrow and Bombay transports responsible for moving units of all Commands around the UK.

The last operation by the single-engined Battle was on 15/16 October, after some 237 sorties under direct Bomber Command control. All eight No.1 Group squadrons were then re-equipped with Wellingtons, an aircraft steadily increasing in numbers and gaining in reputation.

The Germans had also started 'intruding' with long-range fighters, and it was only a matter of time before they had some success. It came on 20/21 October after a British attack on the Skoda works at Pilsen, Czechoslovakia. The victims, the tired crew of a No.58 Squadron Whitley, were nearly home when they were shot down by a marauding Bf110 flown by Hauptmann Karl Hulshoff of I/NJG2 – an activity which became an increasing problem for both sides.

Three weeks after taking over Bomber Command, Peirse received his first Air Staff Directive. German oil production and stocks remained priority targets, but some recognition of the difficulty of attacking them was indicated by the instruction that only the best crews should be used for such raids. It also included a long list of other important targets, to which Peirse objected, wishing to concentrate on oil. He also pointed out that although theoretically Bomber Command's aircraft

*See Chapter 8

strength had doubled since the outbreak of war, less than half were of any real use against German targets. (When Peirse took command 100 Wellingtons, 70 Hampdens and 60 Whitleys were available for the strategic offensive.) The response was a clarification of sorts, stating that 'he was to concentrate on oil and attack other targets if the opportunity arose'!

The difficulty of finding specific targets was being increasingly recognized, but the suggestion that complete towns were being mis-identified was largely ignored until raids started involving more than one Group. Then reports began to conflict, the catalyst for action being an attack on Essen on 7/8 November when, at the same time as Wellington crews of No.3 Group reported leaving the target in flames, No.5 Group Hampdens were said to be overhead a completely untouched Essen. The Air Ministry finally accepted that Bomber Command needed its own reconnaissance organization so that the situation could be properly checked and No.3 PRU formed under No.3 Group control on 16 November, the first operational sortie being flown over Cologne on the 29th. As before-and-after flights became routine, target files were opened on all major cities and industrial sites in Germany, but the results were not encouraging; even 'specials' like Operation *Abigail Rachel* mounted on 16/17 December with the express authorization of the War Cabinet following Luftwaffe attacks on Coventry and Southampton being seen to be unsuccessful. The plan called for 200 aircraft, but was cut to 134 because of poor landing forecasts. Eight experienced Wellington crews were briefed to provide an aiming point for the remainder of the force by starting fires in the centre of the city using incendiaries, and on a clear moonlit night 102 crews claimed to have bombed the 'markers' and left Mannheim in flames. Unfortunately the photo mosaic obtained five days later showed scattered bombing

causing considerable damage but mainly in residential areas. Some of it was in Ludwigshafen on the other side of the Rhine. It was a terrible disappointment but both Peirse and Bottomley, AoC No.5 Group, managed to find excuses, still unable to accept that such a powerful force could not accurately bomb such a large target.

The 1,350-mile round trip to Milan or Turin, with its double crossing of the Alps, was always a challenge but small-scale operations continued against these targets in northern Italy. Nearer to home, No.1 Group started Wellington operations on 20/21 December with a raid on Ostend, and 1941 started well with an accurate attack on Bremen where the Focke-Wulf factory in Hemelingen suburb was hit. These were successes but too often Bomber Command was despatching aircraft in such small 'packets' that the effect on the German 'war machine' was negligible.

Though reduced in numbers following the transfer of four squadrons (Nos.15, 40, 57 and 218) to No.3 Group in November 1940 for re-equipment with Wellingtons, No.2 Group Blenheims gained a new task at the end of the year. Designed to help Fighter Command bring the Luftwaffe into combat over Belgium and France, the plan involved sending a small number of Blenheims to an inland target as 'bait', any Luftwaffe interceptors being attacked by a strong fighter force lurking in the area – a mission known as a *Circus*. On the first *Circus*, despatched on 10 January 1941, six Blenheims of No.114 Squadron escorted by 72 fighters, bombed a German ammunition dump in the Foret de Guines, south of Calais. The operation was uneventful, and so was the second *Circus*, flown by No.139 Squadron on 2 February; but three days later Bf109s did attack and though no Blenheims were shot down in the ensuing mêlée, nine RAF fighters were lost – a poor exchange

Blenheim IV V5458/RT-O of No.114 Squadron at West Raynham – painted black for night operations. (via Chaz Bowyer Collection)

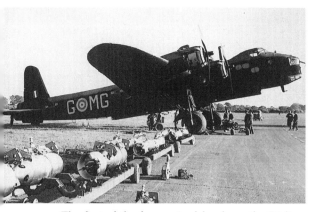

The first of the four-engined bombers, the Stirling, became operational in February 1941. W7444/MG-G of No. 7 Squadron is seen being loaded with 1,000-lb bombs. (RAFM P4033)

for one Bf109, shot down by Flt Lt B.F 'Paddy' Finucane.

Poor weather during December 1940-January 1941 restricted strategic operations but gave new crews time to settle down on 'freshman' targets. With German night fighter forces still weak, Peirse anticipated that he would be able to step up attacks as the weather improved without incurring crippling losses, and confidently forecast further improvement as new, more powerful aircraft entered service. He therefore received the Air Staff Directive of 15 January, which called for attacks on oil targets to the virtual exclusion of all else, with equanimity for he had already decided to make one full-scale raid on an

industrial city each month using the new moon, spending the remaining moonlit nights on oil-related sites. He was also happy to provide eight Whitleys for Operation *Colossus*, an audacious paratroop attack on an aqueduct over the River Tragino in southern Italy. After intensive training the crews, from Nos.51 and 78 Squadrons, took off from Malta on 10 February 1941, but the drop was only partially successful and the troops were only able to damage the structure.

Hanover was chosen for the next major raid, 222 aircraft, including 34 Blenheims, being despatched on 10/11 February, and most crews claimed to have bombed their primary targets. Proof of increasing strength was provided by an attack that same night on oil storage tanks at Rotterdam by 43 aircraft, including three four-engined Stirlings of No.7 Squadron – the first operational sorties by the aircraft after a six-month work-up with the unit. As February progressed oil targets at Bremen, Nordsten, Hamburg, and Sterkrade (on the Kiel Canal) were unsuccessfully attacked before the weather and new orders intervened. The latter required the bomber force to concentrate on harassment of German capital ships, the first 'warship' operation being on 24/25 February when 57 aircraft visited Brest. Amongst the bombers were six Manchesters of No.207 Squadron, a unit reformed on 1 November 1940 in No.5 Group to bring this new twin-engined aircraft into operational service. On 10/11 March Le Havre was attacked by a curiously small force, eight Blenheims and six Halifaxes, No.35 Squadron making the latter aircraft's operational debut. There were no losses due to enemy action but sadly a Halifax was shot down by mistake by an RAF

A salvo of bombs goes down over France during one of the first daylight raids made by Stirlings, 1941. (British Official/PNA)

A typical 'damage assessment' photograph by No.3 PRU of Bremen on 15 March 1941. Highlighted are: 1) Sheds over rail sidings being repaired; 2) Small craters on west side of Gropelinger heerste; 3) Destroyed buildings near craters. (British Official)

fighter pilot over Surrey during the return flight. All three aircraft types developed in response to the important specifications issued in 1936 were now operational, and the long-promised re-equipment of Bomber Command was really underway.

Already involved in the maritime war by virtue of its attacks on ports used by major German Fleet units, Bomber Command now became further embroiled. The war at sea was going very badly and there was a real risk of Britain's lifeline to the Americas being cut by a combination of U-Boats, long-range bombers and surface raiders. The Prime Minister issued another of his famously abrupt orders, repeated in the Air Staff Directive of 9 March 1941 to Bomber Command as follows: 'We must take the offensive against the U-Boat and the Focke-Wulf [Fw200 Condor long-range reconnaissance bomber] wherever we can and whenever we can. The U-Boat at sea must be hunted, the U-Boat in the building yard or in dock must be bombed. The Focke-Wulf, and other bombers employed against our shipping, must be attacked, in the air and in their nests'. Bomber Command's part in this onslaught was clear, involving attacks on U-Boat

production and facilities, the Focke-Wulf factory at Hamburg and bases at Stavanger in Norway and Merignac in France – plus a part in a sea blockade.

No.2 Group was given the latter task. Nos.107 and 114 Squadrons were already operating under Coastal Command orders from Thornaby and Leuchars, now Nos.21, 82 and 139 Squadrons joined in the anti-shipping war along the French, Belgian, Dutch and Danish coasts. They remained under No.2 Group control and were joined by the rest of the Group as units reverted from night bombing to the ultra low-level daylight operations required for the blockade – which was extended south to Bordeaux and northwards up the Norwegian coast.

Peirse was not happy about this diversion from his main strategic aims and was only slightly mollified by being allowed to continue expending some of his effort on oil-related targets. Portal on the other hand made no attempt to oppose the order, probably relieved that the Prime Minister had saved him from awkward decisions. He was now convinced that until much improved navigational and bombing aids were introduced, the only effective attacks were those on coastal targets, or on cities where 'secondary' damage resulted from bombing errors. Indeed, the March Directive went on to state: 'Priority selection should be given to those [targets] in Germany which lie in congested areas where the greatest morale effect is likely to result'. In a short follow-up Directive signed by the Deputy Chief of Air Staff (DCAS), Mannheim and Stuttgart, both of which contained U-Boat manufacturing facilities, are mentioned as 'suitable as area objectives and their attack should have high morale value'. The DCAS was AVM A.T. Harris, undoubtedly in full agreement with the sentiments expressed, but not the final arbitrator in such matters.

On 12/13 March Hamburg was the target for 88 aircraft including small numbers of Manchesters and Halifaxes, the first time they had bombed Germany. Twenty high-explosive (HE) and many incendiary bombs fell on the Blohm und Voss U-Boat yard, four other shipyards were hit and a large warehouse burnt out. Another 86 aircraft went to Bremen and reconnaissance photographs showed that the Focke-Wulf factory had been hit by 12 bombs. The pressure was now unrelenting, 139 aircraft being sent to Hamburg on 13/14 March when once again the Blohm und Voss yard was hit. The next night an oil plant at Gelsenkirchen was put out of action and on the 18/19 March there was more damage in the Deutsche Werke U-Boat yard and in Kiel city centre. Just as encouraging were aircraft losses, which were light throughout March, both over Germany and on anti-shipping sweeps, but worrying was the very slow initial production rate and teething troubles of the new 'heavies'. The Halifax had to be withdrawn for a month due to hydraulic faults, followed immediately by the grounding of the Manchester by the first of seemingly endless problems with its Vulture engines. More than ever the Wellington was proving the mainstay of the force, in service with Nos.1 and 3 Groups and joining No.4 Group.

In an effort to make the anti-shipping sweeps by No.2 Group Blenheims more productive, it was decided to include attacks on land targets of 'opportunity'. The first occurred on 31 March, when gun positions and troops parading in Holland were bombed. It turned out to be a good day, six aircraft from No.82 Squadron led by Wg Cdr S.C. Elworthy hitting two tankers off Le Havre, while No.21 Squadron crews damaged one of two destroyers sighted off the Frisian Islands. That night 28 Wellingtons went to Bremen and others to Rotterdam and Emden, the first 4,000-lb high-capacity (HC) blast bomb being dropped by a specially modified aircraft of No.149 Squadron on the latter target. One of the most effective British bombs of the war, it was known as the *Blockbuster* or *Cookie*.

The return of the *Scharnhorst* and *Gneisenau* to Brest heralded a sustained attack on the port by Bomber Command starting on the night of 30/31 March and continuing for a fortnight, day and night. Little damage was done to the two battlecruisers, but the bombing did force the captain of the *Gneisenau* to move his ship out into the harbour where it was attacked by a Beaufort torpedo bomber of No.22 Squadron, Coastal Command and put out of action for six months. Further afield, Berlin was attacked twice during April, by 80 aircraft on 9/10 March and 118 on 17/18 March, when one Stirling took part. Three Stirlings had been despatched on the 9/10 March raid but failed to reach the target.

Anti-shipping operations by Blenheims were producing results, though at increasing cost as the Germans introduced specialized 'flak' ships. Worse was to follow when it was decided to try and close the Strait of Dover to enemy shipping, using Blenheims by day and Royal Navy motor torpedo boats (MTBs) by night. A Flight from No.101 Squadron moved to Manston on 24 April for the operation which, known as *Channel Stop*, started four days later when three heavily escorted Blenheims attacked trawlers off Calais. One of the ships was sunk and escorting Spitfires drove off a Bf109, but a Blenheim was lost to 'flak'. The following day two 1,500-ton ships were intercepted off Nieuport and again Bf109s were driven off; then, with the Blenheim complement doubled, a 2,000-ton ship was claimed sunk off Ostend on 2 May. The next day a small convoy off Boulogne was the target but 'flak' claimed two Blenheims, and on 6 May another was badly damaged during a pitched battle between escorting Spitfires and Bf109s. It was time to call a halt and *Channel Stop* was temporarily suspended, though the main anti-shipping operations continued unabated.

An attempt to block the Kiel Canal by 23 Blenheim crews during the night of 8/9 May was unsuccessful, but an audacious daylight raid on the Friedrichskoog naval barracks and ships in the canal by No.105 Squadron on 2 June resulted in two ships being claimed 'damaged' and the blocking of the canal for at least 10 days. The Germans were caught napping and all nine Blenheims returned safely, though of the other 35 No.2 Group aircraft on anti-shipping work that day two were lost. Increasing losses were sapping No.2 Group's operational strength, but attacks by 'heavies' on sea ports were having some success, especially when the destructive power of the 4,000-lb *Cookie*, was used in built-up areas.

Attempts to sink, or at least badly damage, the two battlecruisers in Brest harbour continued throughout May and into June when the heavy cruiser *Prinz*

Above: *Wellington 1C of No.149 Squadron with a 2,000-lb armour-piercing bomb at Mildenhall, 1941. (via B. Robertson)*

Right: *Emden 31 March 1941 – an early night photograph recording the first use of a 4,000-lb Blockbuster. (British Official)*

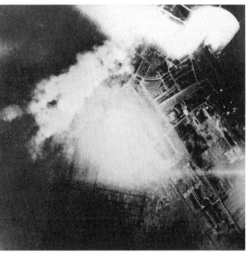

Eugen joined them, but none of the hits claimed could be confirmed. Ships, even big ones, remained very difficult targets. Somewhat easier were rail marshalling yards, though the weather was a key factor, as on 12/13 June when poor visibility meant that less than half the 314 crews despatched claimed to have bombed the primary targets at Soest and Schwerte. The 80 Whitleys sent to the latter target were accompanied by three Wellingtons of No.405 Squadron, RCAF (formed on 23 April 1941 in No.4 Group), making the first operational flights by a Canadian bomber unit. Better results were reported at Hamm and Osnabrück, and that same night 11 Halifaxes and seven Stirlings attacked a chemical works at Huls, reporting fires in the target area – this being by far the largest number of four-engined bombers operating to date.

Operation *Channel Stop* had restarted on 26 May when No.110 Squadron arrived for its two-week stint on this dangerous work, but Coastal Command aircraft were also operating in the area and the ad hoc control arrangements soon led to friction between Peirse and Joubert (C-in-C Coastal Command). On 27 June it was finally agreed that anti-shipping *Roadsteads* between Cherbourg and Texel were the responsibility of Bomber Command, and that *Channel Stop* would be increased to two-squadron strength, No.59 Squadron being loaned to Bomber Command to assist in the task. To suppress the dangerous 'flak' ships escorting German convoys, Fighter Command agreed to provide Hurricanes to attack them while the Blenheims ran in at mast height on the supply vessels, and Spitfires to deal with enemy fighters. But it was still no picnic!

At Cherbourg on 10 July 1941 a direct hit was made on the west quay of Darse Translantic, flames rising 250 feet (1), close to a tanker (2). The photograph was taken from a No.21 Squadron Blenheim. (British Official via B. Robertson)

By June one out of 10 bomber aircraft carried night cameras. They were treated with suspicion by the crews who naturally objected to a 'spy in the sky', and also did not like having to maintain steady flight with bomb doors open for what seemed an eternity after the call 'Bombs Gone'. At Bomber Command cameras were considered vital, and so was No.3 PRU, but despite fighting 'tooth and nail' Peirse could not prevent the unit being merged with No.1 PRU to cut down duplication of effort. No.3 PRU disbanded on 16 June 1941, the amalgamated unit remaining under the operational control of Coastal Command, though tasked by the Air Ministry.

By late June Stirlings, Halifaxes and Manchesters were all operating at 'double figure' strength, but despite increased bomb loads attacks on inland towns were still largely ineffective. On 27/28 June the crews even found Bremen difficult to find, many attacking Hamburg, 50 miles away, due to a combination of bad weather, icing and, for the first time, 'intense night fighter attacks'. Eleven Whitleys and three Wellingtons were lost, the heaviest casualties in a

Aircrew of No. 408 Squadron examine a dinghy of the type installed in their Hampdens. The CO, Wg Cdr N. W. Timmerman, DFC, is on the left of the group. (Public Archives of Canada PL 4545).

single night thus far. German night fighters, still not equipped with airborne radar, relied on a tight control system involving *Himmelbett* (four-poster bed) 'boxes' or 'zones' within which ground controllers using *Freya* and *Wurzburg* radars, linked searchlights and a fighter could vector the latter to within 400 yards of a bomber. The first three night fighter 'zones' had been formed in October 1940 and during 1941 the number of 'boxes' increased, strung out in a line covering the Ruhr, and later the whole of Germany's western border – known to the British as the *Kammhuber Line*, after the commander of the organization. With night attacks proving so disappointing, there was renewed discussion about daylight operations over Germany now that new heavy bombers with improved defensive armament were available. *Circus* operations were still being flown, but most of Germany was too far for fighter escort and it was decided to try sending Halifaxes on their own. Six aircraft of No.35 Squadron set out for Kiel on 30 June and despite heavy 'flak' they bombed successfully, but one Halifax was lost and another badly damaged when the formation was attacked by Bf110s. It was quickly agreed that such attacks were still not viable unless escorted, so only short-range targets could be contemplated.

Meanwhile the Germans had attacked Russia on 22 June 1941, and it was decided that with the Luftwaffe engaged in the east, No.2 Group could be used to support our new allies by deep penetration daylight attacks on communications in Germany itself – codenamed Operation *Manicure*. Eighteen Blenheims sent to Bremen on 28 June had to turn back and 'cloud cover' raiders on the 30th were equally unsuccessful. But No.2 Group was determined to get through and on 4 July 15 crews of Nos.105 and 107 Squadrons were briefed for another attempt under the leadership of Wg Cdr H.I. Edwards. Three crews turned back soon after take-off but the rest pressed on in close formation and at very low-level. As they made their approach to Bremen in good visibility they met intense flak and, as briefed, opened out for individual attacks. Edwards bombed the dock area then circled over the city at roof-top height, drawing fire for 10 long minutes. Four Blenheims were shot down and there is little doubt that losses would have been higher but for the leader's efforts. He was awarded the VC for 'displaying the highest possible standard of gallantry and determination'.

Just one week later, on 7/8 July, came another display of raw courage. That night 114 Wellingtons went to Cologne, while 54 Whitleys and 18 Wellingtons of No.4 Group were sent to Osnabrück and 49 No.3 Group Wellingtons were despatched to Münster. Amongst the latter was a No.75 Squadron aircraft captained by Sqn Ldr R.P. Widdowson and carrying 22-year-old Sgt J.A. Ward as second pilot. Suddenly the Wellington was raked by cannon fire from a Bf110 night fighter. The rear gunner promptly shot it down, but the damage had been done, a fuel-fed fire torching over the wing behind the starboard engine. Ward insisted on climbing out through the

Blenheim IV V6014/J of No.105 Squadron at Luqa during the summer of 1941, on attachment for Mediterranean operations. It did not return to No.2 Group, joining No.203 Squadron in the Western Desert and being posted 'missing' on 27 April 1942. (IWM CM1357)

The Operations Room of a bomber station 'somewhere in England', 1941. (British Official)

astro hatch, and roped to another crew member crawled across the wing to the engine using hand and foot holes kicked in the fabric covering. Despite the freezing slipstream and his bulky parachute he forced a canvas cockpit cover into the flaming hole and dampened down the fire before the cover was blown away. Almost completely exhausted he managed to crawl back to the comparative safety of the fuselage as the fire died down and burnt itself out. Widdowson force-landed the aircraft at Newmarket, and when the Squadron Commander's recommendation for a VC

for Ward was approved and gazetted on 5 August, the whole of Feltwell went mad – it was a very popular award indeed.

Variations on the *Circus* theme were now being tried. One, code-named *Circus Blot* was a small force intended to draw attention away from the main attack. Another scheme involved aircraft operating in waves, but the Luftwaffe generally chose to ignore such activities and they were soon abandoned, leaving standard *Circus* operations to continue despite heavy losses. At the end of July training for a special mission

The Knapsack and Quadrath power stations near Cologne were attacked by 54 Blenheims during a daring daylight raid on 12 August 1941 – seen from the turret of a No.18 Squadron aircraft as bombs burst on Knapsack. (British Official)

commenced. Intended to further encourage the Luftwaffe to withdraw fighters from the Russian front, it was an attack on the enormous power station at Knapsack and the somewhat smaller one at Quadrath, both near Cologne and deep in enemy territory. Nos.21 and 82 Squadrons were to attack Quadrath, while Knapsack was the target for Nos.18, 107, 114 and 139 Squadrons; a total of 54 Blenheims, escorted as far as possible by Whirlwinds and Spitfires. Four Fortresses and a number of No.5 Group Hampdens were to carry out diversionary tactics. The force set out during the morning of 12 August, each Blenheim carrying two 500-lb bombs. Both targets were successfully attacked though the 'flak' was fierce and 10 aircraft, 18.5% of the force, were lost. It remained No.2 Group's deepest penetration for some time.

The Directive received on 9 July released Bomber Command from its four-month offensive against maritime targets – a decision met with universal relief, though the Admiralty still retained the right to ask for 'occasional' raids on naval bases in France. Moonlit nights attacks were now concentrated on the Ruhr rail network and on Germany's inland waterways, replaced by 'morale' attacks on Rhine cities during moonless nights. If the weather was unsuitable in the Ruhr area the more distant major industrial towns of Bremen, Frankfurt, Hamburg, Hanover, Mannheim and Stuttgart could be targets. No time was lost in implementing the new Directive, Aachen being heavily bombed in a general area attack on 9/10 July by 82 Hampden, Whitley and Wellington medium

bombers, resulting in extensive property damage. The same night 57 Wellington crews were briefed for a raid on Osnabrück and many reported 'bursts in the target area'. Actually the raid was a complete failure, missing the town completely, a mistake by one crew attracting many others to the wrong area while more confusion was caused by false 'target' fires lit by the Germans in open country.

Four-engined Boeing B-17C Fortress high-altitude day bombers were now operational with No.2 Group. No.90 Squadron had reformed to operate them and after several months of frustrating servicing and operating problems, the unit was deemed ready in July, three being sent to Wilhelmshaven to attack the U-Boat dock. Two bombed the primary target and one the Frisian Islands.

The German capital ships could never be neglected for long and a day raid on the *Scharnhorst, Gneisenau* and *Prinz Eugen* sheltering in Brest by 150 medium and heavy bombers, escorted by five Spitfire squadrons, was planned for 24 July. Unfortunately the *Scharnhorst* was moved to La Pallice, some 200 miles to the south, and in case the ship was being prepared for another Atlantic foray the attack plan had to be changed at the last moment. The heavy bombers were withdrawn from the Brest operation, six Stirlings of Nos.7 and 15 Squadrons attacking the *Scharnhorst* on the evening of the 23rd, followed by 15 Halifaxes of No.35 and 76 Squadrons on the 24th! They met fierce opposition, one Stirling and five Halifaxes being shot down, but five direct hits were claimed. It was

The second unit equipped with Halifax bombers was No.76 Squadron, L9530 being the mount of Plt Off C. Cheshire, brother of the bomber 'ace'. On 12/13 August 1941 this aircraft was shot down over Germany and Cheshire became a PoW. (MAP)

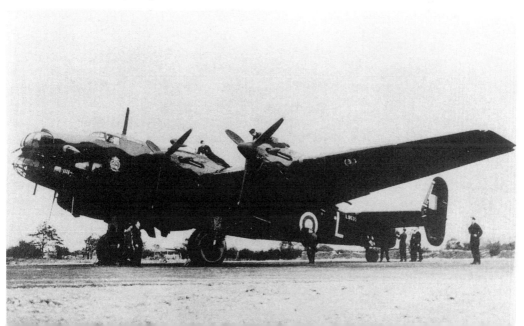

Operating in comparatively small numbers were Merlin-powered Wellington IIs, an example being Z8345/EP-S of No.104 Squadron at Driffield. (MAP)

Another example was W5458/LN-Z of No.99 Squadron which operated a few Mk.IIs alongside Pegasus-powered Mk.Is from late 1941 to early 1942. (Sqn Ldr J.W. Gee)

subsequently discovered that three of the armour-piercing (AP) bombs had gone through the ship without exploding, the other two causing slight damage. The ship started taking in water and was forced to return to Brest for repairs. The Brest raid went ahead, the mixed Fortress, Hampdens and Wellington force facing heavy 'flak' and fighter attack resulting in the loss of 10 Wellingtons and two Hampdens. Claims were made of hits on the *Gneisenau* but could not be substantiated, and the case for daylight attacks suffered another setback!

These mixed fortunes increased the opposition to the Air Ministry's call for a 4,000-heavy bomber force, despite assurances that it would bring Germany to its knees. Such a force would be extremely expensive and absorb a large part of the war effort, and there were many officials and politicians unconvinced that Bomber Command could make good its claims. They had good reason, for there was precious little to show for the effort and sacrifice already made in the bombing campaign. In addition, Bomber Command's contention that they had no chance of success against German capital ships and had uselessly thrown 750 tons of HE into Brest harbour hardly helped their submission. The argument raged on indecisively, but more serious was the Butt Report which brought into question whether the Command had a strategic future at all?

The Butt Report was commissioned by Lord Cherwell, the Prime Minister's advisor. He arranged for some 650 target photographs taken by bomber crews on 48 nights between 2 June and 25 July 1941 and their interpretation reports to be examined by a member of the War Cabinet secretariat, Mr Butt. His report, issued on 18 August, concluded that of those crews recorded as attacking their target only one-third got within five miles, the remainder of the bomb loads being dropped on the wrong target, in open country, or on excellent decoys provided by the Germans! This overall average was however distorted by the conditions and the target, only one in four crews reaching German targets, and over the well-defended and haze-covered Ruhr just one in 10 managed to place their bombs within five miles of the aiming point. The figures were not claimed to be infallible, for not all the photographs could be accurately plotted and some of the reports were inadequately completed, but the author was confident that the report presented a true overall picture.

Naturally the report caused a furore at Command and Group level. Peirse and his SASO, AVM Saundby, refuted it on the grounds that the known damage could not have been achieved if the report was accurate, and that the period chosen was not typical. They were unable to produce any concrete evidence, however, and the Air Ministry had to fall back on the argument that

there was currently no other way to carry the war to the heart of the enemy, and that if attacks were sustained German morale would break.

Meanwhile the real war continued, and far from increasing the size of the bomber force the problem was to prevent it dwindling in strength, despite rising production. Losses, equipping of Operational Conversion Units (OCUs) and diversion of aircraft and crews to other Commands (Nos.37, 38, 40 and 104 Squadrons to the Middle East and detachments to Coastal Command) combined to keep the overall strength down, and throughout 1941 the availability of four-engined bombers never exceeded 50! It was going to be a long haul even if the priority position enjoyed by Bomber Command was sustained.

No.455 Squadron, RAAF, flew the Australians' first operational sortie on 29/30 August, the crew joining 142 others briefed for an attack on Frankfurt. The same day Peirse received another Directive, adding 21 selected small towns on main railway routes to his bombing list. On 11 September the ball bearing town of Schweinfurt was added – another panacea target, like oil, beloved of the Ministry of Economic Warfare but extremely difficult to hit. During September attacks on German cities continued at a steady rate, 197 aircraft including 10 Stirlings, six Halifaxes and four Manchesters, going to Berlin on 7/8. German reports admitted that residential areas were hit, but with nothing like the weight of bombs claimed by crews. Hamburg was attacked on 15/16 September and reports indicated severe damage, but this was an easily identifiable target, and it was very different on 12/13 October when a strong force was sent to Nuremberg. The city received only a few bombs while small towns up to 95 miles away were heavily attacked, crews apparently deceived by their similar positions on the banks of wide rivers.

The considered response of the Air Ministry to the Butt Report was conveyed to the Prime Minister by the CAS, Sir Charles Portal, on 2 October. Somewhat ambivalently, Churchill replied five days later, supporting continued expansion of the force 'as circumstances permitted', but counselling against extravagant claims for its results, and casting doubt on the assertion that German morale would break if the force suggested was applied. Portal replied on 13 October: 'I am now completely reassured that you accept the primary importance of our bomber operations and of building the bomber force on the largest possible scale.' This rather rosy interpretation was not challenged and, mollified and reassured, the Air Staff turned its attention to the issues facing Bomber Command if it was to retain the backing of the Prime Minister. The Butt Report had opened everyone's eyes, some very reluctantly, to the question

The Avro Manchester entered service with No.207 Squadron in November 1940, initially with an ugly central fin and two small endplate fins/rudders. L7380/W was attacked en route Berlin on 8 September 1941 and force-landed in Holland. (RAFM P4023)

of navigation. Obviously it needed to be improved dramatically if night operations were to become effective and this could only be achieved by improved aids and, in the opinion of increasing numbers of middle rank officers, target-finding equipment. Fortunately the first of a series of radar navigation aids, *Gee*, was well advanced,* but it could be some time before production deliveries were sufficient.

Further operations by No.90 Squadron revealed the unsuitability of the Fortress I aircraft. An attack mounted from Kinloss on the *Admiral Scheer* in Oslo harbour on 6 September was a complete failure, and a repeat on the 8th was a disaster when two aircraft were lost and another badly damaged. Continued serviceability problems, but primarily the weather, aborted further attempts to operate and on 27 October four Fortresses were sent to the Middle East and the remainder transferred to Coastal Command the following month.

Other No.2 Group squadrons were sent to the Middle East during 1941. A trial detachment to Malta by Blenheims of No.21 Squadron in April demonstrated that it was a hazardous business getting there, and operations against Axis supply ships crossing to North Africa were no easier, but the detachment commander, Sqn Ldr L.V.E. Atkinson, deemed it feasible despite the poor conditions at Luqa

*See Chapter 13

Manchester 1A, L7515/EM-S of No. 207 Squadron; its appearance considerably enhanced by the cleaner tail unit, being shown off by Flt Lt Herring DSO, DFM in November 1941. (Hawker Siddeley/BAe)

Air Commodore H.P. Lloyd, who had been SASO at No. 2 Group, was sent out to command the forces on Malta and after a short visit by No.139 Squadron, the first full-scale detachment, from No.82 Squadron, arrived early in June. The plan was for each squadron to complete a five-week detachment then ferry the aircraft to Egypt, some of the crews staying with them, others returning to No.2 Group. No.82 Squadron attacked every southbound convoy bar one during June 1941 and despite strong air and surface escorts, damage to Axis shipping steadily mounted, helped by an audacious raid on a convoy sheltering in Palermo harbour which resulted in three large vessels being put out of action for no loss. No.110 Squadron arrived in July, followed by Nos.105, 107, 18 and 21 Squadrons respectively, most of which stayed longer than originally intended and overlapped to increase the force available and allow land targets to be attacked. Increasing flak took its toll, but the Blenheims, together with Wellingtons and Swordfishes operating at night, forced the Axis to stop operating convoys west of Malta altogether, with disastrous effect on Rommel's supply situation.

Generalfeldmarschall Kesselring was given the job of restoring the supplies and neutralizing Malta and started 'round the clock' bombing of the island's airfields in October. Losses from operations and the bombing were horrendous, and despite the 'highjacking' of crews and aircraft being ferried through to Egypt, the sortie rate started to fall in January 1942 under relentless Luftwaffe pressure (whose sortie rate rose from 60-70 per week in November 1941 to over 500 per week in early January 1942) and heavy rain which turned all the landing grounds into quagmires and forced severe overcrowding at Luqa. Two large convoys got through to Tripoli and Rommel's position was transformed, enabling him to launch a surprise attack on 21 January. The situation in the Western Desert rapidly deteriorated and this, combined with the rapidly declining stocks of fuel, food and ammunition on Malta, forced the move of the Blenheims to Egypt and the cessation of the detachments.

Meanwhile Fighter Command had taken over the *Channel Stop* commitment in October 1941 and with the weather worsening *Circus* operations were halted in November, as were *Roadsteads*, the results no longer justifying the losses. Since March 1941 No.2 Group had lost 139 aircraft on low-level shipping attacks which the Admiralty assessed were responsible for 101 ships (328,000 tons) sunk or badly damaged (post-war examination of German records reduced the figures to 29 ships (29,836 tons) sunk and 21 ships (43,715 tons) badly damaged), but the Blenheim loss rate was escalating rapidly. It was obvious that daylight

operation of the Blenheim in the European theatre was no longer practical, but with deliveries of its intended replacement, the Douglas Boston, only slowly gaining pace it had to remain in service. The answer was to use the aircraft to assist No. 11 Group night intruder operations and during November intensive night flying training was given to the crews of those squadrons expected to retain Blenheims during the winter. A briefed attack on Soesterburg airfield in Holland by No.82 Squadron on 27/28 December was followed by the first real night 'intruding' by No.2 Group the next night. Though weather often interfered, some successes were recorded by Nos.82, 110 and 114 Squadrons.

Probably frustrated by a lengthy period of poor weather and equally poor bombing by the strategic force, Peirse ordered a maximum effort on 7/8 November with Berlin the main target and Mannheim an alternative. Despite a weather forecast indicating storms, hail and severe icing affecting the Berlin route, Peirse refused to change the plan, though he did allow AVM Slessor, AOC No.5 Group, to withdraw his aircraft and send them to Cologne instead. Only 73 crews out of the 169 despatched claimed to have reached Berlin and none of the targets were successfully attacked. Thirty-seven aircraft were lost, 9.4% of the 392 which took off – more than double the number lost on any previous night's operations. Many were thought to have crashed in the North Sea iced up or with fuel tanks empty, but others succumbed to German defences which were becoming formidable, many 'flak' and searchlight batteries being radar-controlled.

The Air Staff, already concerned that the bomber offensive was straying from the Directive, were appalled by the apparent lack of judgement displayed by the decision to proceed with the Berlin raid. The resultant loss rate was bad, but just as worrying in their view was the likely impact on the crews. There was already evidence that some were questioning the point of pressing on to the target in the face of bad weather and strong enemy defences; such decisions and losses could only increase this tendency. Others were worried too, it being a measure of the general unease that Sir Richard Peirse was summoned to Chequers the next day to meet the Prime Minister and discuss his problems. The War Cabinet then considered the situation at length and decided to reduce operations drastically during the coming winter so that Bomber Command could gain strength (more than half the 84 Halifaxes built by the end of 1941 had been lost on operations or through accidents) and give time for a new policy to be formulated. The order was passed down through the Air Ministry to Bomber Command on 13 November, and though unpalatable it was undoubtedly the right decision.

Some pretty large operations were still mounted,

such as the despatch of 181 aircraft to Hamburg on 30 November/1 December, but the rate was much reduced, the next 'big' night being on 7/8 December when Aachen was the target for 130 aircraft. Other operations included an abortive dusk attack on Brest during which the first operational *Trinity/Oboe* trials were carried out by Stirlings of Nos.7 and 15 Squadrons* on 7/8 December. The third Halifax squadron, No.10, rejoined the ranks in December, its first operation with the new aircraft being on the 18th when, as the result of yet another Directive placing 'the highest priority for operations on the destruction of capital ships', another daylight attack was tried on Brest. Code-named *Veracity I*, the raid involved a mixed force of 18 Stirlings, 11 Manchesters and 18 Halifaxes with fighter escort. Despite careful planning it went badly wrong, the only success being a lucky hit on the lock gates which trapped the *Scharnhorst* for a whole month. Another attempt on 30 December was just as disastrous. Poor weather prevented Nos.3 and 5 Groups taking part and it was just 16 Halifaxes escorted by Spitfires which carried out *Veracity II*. 'Flak' and fighters put up a strong defence and the ships were obscured by a smoke screen, producing an inconclusive result for the loss of three Halifaxes and damage to most of the rest. The Air Staff decided that the 'heavies' would be reserved for night operations for the foreseeable future (in practice until May 1944 except for one or two 'special' raids); indeed they went further, confining operations to nights when the forecast provided a good chance of success – that was the theory anyway!

A diversion from the major tasks of the Command was provided by the first combined operation of the war, launched on 27 December, when Commandos landed on the Norwegian island of Vaagso to destroy installations and capture troops or *Quislings*. Bomber Command provided 19 Blenheims from Nos.110 and 114 Squadrons for support operations by attacking the fighter airfield at Herdla some 80 miles south and shipping off Oberstad, while 10 Hampdens of No.50 Squadron laid a phosphorus bomb smoke screen and bombed gun positions on the approaches to Vaagso. As a test of inter-service co-operation it was a great success, though limited in scope, but Bomber Command lost five Blenheims and two Hampdens, and had several more aircraft damaged.

On 8 January 1942 Air Marshal Sir Richard Peirse relinquished his command, removed by the Air Ministry. It had become accepted that the results achieved had not warranted the losses sustained during July to November – equivalent to the loss of the entire front-line strength (414 night and 212 day bombers). Peirse had found it particularly difficult to accept clear evidence that the Command's night-time navigation and bomb aiming was of a generally poor standard, but he was not alone in this and it is arguable whether anyone else could have done better given the resources available. However, the loss of confidence in him following the night of 7/8 November, and the resultant acrimonious discussions, meant that Peirse had to go – to become Commander-in-Chief of Air Forces in India.

Bomber Command itself was also in trouble, Hitler's invasion of Russia, anxiety over the Atlantic U-Boat war, and Japan's aggression in the Far East all combining to make people in high places question again whether the resources being poured into the bombing campaign would not be better employed elsewhere. Some of the pressure was relieved by the Arcadia Conference in Washington, DC, from 22 December 1941-7 January 1942, when Churchill and Roosevelt formally agreed that Germany should be beaten before the Allies turned their full strength on Japan and also supported the continuance of the bomber offensive against Germany, strengthened as soon as possible by American participation. However, the realization at last that precision bombing of specified targets would remain impracticable for some time gave the critics much ammunition, and despite support at the highest political level Bomber Command as constituted remained on a knife-edge!

*See Chapter 13

Brest under daylight attack by Halifaxes, 18 December 1941. The Scharnhorst *and* Gneisenau *are top left, partially obscured by a smoke screen, while the* Prinz Eugen *is top right. (British Official/PNA).*

CHAPTER 4

The Tide Turns – 1942

WITH THE REMOVAL of ACM Peirse on 8 January 1942 AVM J.E.A. Baldwin, the Air Officer Commanding No.3 Group since 29 August 1939, took temporary charge of Bomber Command. Baldwin was not expected to introduce changes while 'holding the fort' and in general he did not, attacks on Brest continuing to be interspersed with quite large raids on German towns and cities such as Bremen, Hamburg, Mannheim, Münster and Wilhelmshaven. There was one exception, made in response to German naval moves following the Commando raid on Vaagso in December 1941.* The raid had convinced Hitler that the British were planning an invasion of Norway, and he had the *Tirpitz* moved up to Aasfjord 18 miles east-

*See Chapter 3

north-east of Trondheim as a countermeasure. In turn Churchill and the British Admiralty saw the ship as a threat to Atlantic and Russian convoys and an attack by Bomber Command, oddly named Operation *Oiled*, was laid on for the night of 29/30 January. Seven Stirlings of No.15 Squadron joined nine Halifaxes from Nos.10 and 76 Squadrons at Lossiemouth in northern Scotland for the operation, but bad weather prevented any of the crews sighting the ship, and after waiting a week with no forecast improvement the bombers returned to their bases.

On 2 February the Admiralty issued a warning signal stating that the *Scharnhorst* and *Gneisenau* were expected to break out from Brest in the near future. Bomber Command operations virtually ceased, for in accordance with an agreed contingency plan

Hampden Is of No.408 Squadron, P1166/EQ-K in the lead. (MAP)

code-named *Fuller*, 250 aircraft, practically the whole bomber force, were placed on two hours' stand-by. This was tantamount to 'immediate readiness' and despite a Coastal Command appreciation indicating that the breakout was likely between 10-15 February, Baldwin was forced after a week to reduce the state of readiness, but kept 100 aircraft on a four-hour stand-by. It was No.5 Group's turn on stand-by on the 12th when soon after 1100 hrs the dramatic news that the ships were practically through the English Channel reached Bomber Command. The first bombers got airborne at 1330 hrs and after frantic efforts others followed in three waves, a total of 242 aircraft (92 Wellingtons, 64 Hampdens, 37 Blenheims, 15 Manchesters, 13 Halifaxes, 11 Stirlings and 10 Bostons, the latter still officially non-operational) from all the operational Groups. The weather was appalling, few crews found the ships and no damage was done by the bombs which were dropped. None of the other forces involved did any better, and Bomber Command came out quite well at the subsequent inquiry, credited with damaging both capital ships when they hit mines laid by No.5 Group Hampdens near the Frisian Islands. British pride was badly dented but the move of the ships to German ports did have benefits for Bomber Command. It meant the end of the raids on Brest which had cost the Command 127 aircraft and diverted much effort from the attack on Germany.

Two days later the famous, or infamous, 'area bombing' Directive arrived on Baldwin's desk. It stated: 'It has been decided that the primary objective of your operations should be focused on the morale of the enemy civil population and in particular of industrial workers.' This was clear and unequivocal and had indeed been the Air Ministry's, and in particular Portal's, unspoken policy for months, convinced for some inexplicable reason that German morale was suspect. In the past morale had been considered a by-product, now it was the primary objective!

Bomber Command was instructed to strike at the industrial heartland of Germany for the next six months with 'full force', and was also cleared to attack factories in occupied territory known to be working for the Germans. The Directive included a list of suitable targets but there was no immediate assault. Instead a small force of six Halifaxes, four Manchesters and four Stirlings was sent to bomb airfields in Norway on 21/22 February as a diversion for a Fleet Air Arm (FAA) strike by Albacores off HMS *Victorious* on the *Prinz Eugen*, sheltering near Trondheim after being damaged by a submarine. Poor weather caused the FAA attack to be cancelled and one Manchester was lost. Six other Manchesters

carried out mine laying off Wilhelmshaven – probably the first use of the aircraft in this role.

Air Chief Marshal Sir Arthur Harris was appointed C-in-C on 22 February 1942, eight days after receipt of the new Directive. He inherited a force numerically no stronger (469 night and 78 day bombers) than a year earlier, with Wellingtons still predominant. However, the percentage of 'heavies' was gradually increasing and there was a new four-engined bomber on strength – the Lancaster.

All successful commanders need luck and Harris was lucky to arrive at the same time as the Lancaster. Indeed he was doubly lucky for the navigation aid, *Gee*, was in full production and being installed in front-line aircraft. It proved easy to use and provided reliable fixing of position up to 400 miles from the transmitting station. Thus it could put crews overhead the nearer German cities, provide much improved wind-finding, and reduce the problem of getting home, especially welcome after a long tiring flight in difficult weather.

Harris was not just lucky though, he soon proved to be a tough and resourceful leader ready to introduce radical changes. He increased the use of incendiaries and concentrated the effort, not only by putting virtually the whole available force on one target, but also by reducing the time between the first and last bombs. He did not immediately increase the number of operations and most early attacks under Harris's stewardship continued to be on maritime targets. Kiel and Wilhelmshaven were regularly raided, the accommodation ship *Monte Sormiento* being burnt out on 25/26 February, and the *Gneisenau* so badly damaged the following night that she was not repaired. On 27/28 February, almost a year after Operation *Colossus*, No.51 Squadron Whitleys were again dropping parachutists on an audacious combined operation, *Biting*, which captured a *Würzburg* radar site at Bruneval, France, and took away equipment for examination.

During the night of 3/4 March, four Lancasters of No.44 Squadron laid mines off the north-west German coast – the traditional way of entering operational service – but of more immediate interest was an Air Ministry-inspired attack on the Renault works in the Billancourt district of Paris where lorries were made for the Wehrmacht. A technique, code-named *Shaker*, had been devised for such attacks, the plan requiring 20 *Gee*-equipped Wellingtons to drop flares so that 50 'target markers' could identify the target and rain incendiaries down to start a concentrated fire into which the 'followers' would aim their bombs. If the target was cloud-covered, both 'finders' and 'markers' would drop blind on *Gee* – a technique known as *Sampson*. Although the *Gee* ground stations were not

A 4,000-lb Cookie being loaded aboard a Wellington III. (Author's collection)

yet ready it was decided to try out the marking system. The factory was surrounded by workers' apartment blocks and to reduce French casualties the attack was to be at low-level and concentrated so that 'creep back' was kept to a minimum – the first time a genuine 'saturation' raid had been attempted. A strong force, 235 aircraft, was despatched and 460 tons of bombs dropped in under two hours, by far the highest concentration so far. It was very successful, some 40%

of the factory being destroyed, and losses were confined to one Wellington, extraordinary considering it was a low-level night attack for which the force was not trained. Unfortunately, despite the general accuracy of the bombing, 367 French civilians were killed and another 340 badly injured.

The first 'real' Boston operation (an uneventful anti-shipping patrol on 16 February was officially the first 'op') took place on 8 March when 12 aircraft

Claimed as Bomber Command's first major success. French workers clear debris from the Renault works after the attack on 3/4 March 1942. (Author's collection)

from Nos.88 and 226 Squadrons followed up the Renault night raid with a day attack on the Ford works at Poissy, south-west of Paris. Eight of the Bostons bombed successfully while another 12 flew diversion *Circus* operations to Abbeville and Comines, typical No.2 Group tactics.

During the evening of the 8th, 210 'heavies' took off for an attack on Essen – yet another first in that 74 of the leading aircraft were using *Gee* and the full *Shaker* technique was employed. It did not work well, the flares being so widely spread that the Krupps works escaped damage yet again and the Germans could not decide which town was the target. Follow-up raids during the next two nights were equally unsuccessful and only noteworthy for the inclusion of two Lancasters of No.44 Squadron on 10/11 March – the first to attack a land target.

More was being asked of *Gee* than it could guarantee to provide, but three days later came the first successful attack using the equipment, several important works in Cologne being put out of action for a month. More successful still was the raid on the ancient Hanseatic port of Lübeck on 28/29 March. Although the target was outside the range of *Gee* it was used by the leaders to check the wind, and with a full moon and light defences the bombers were able to attack accurately at a comparatively low level. A high

proportion of the bombs dropped were incendiary and it was fire that destroyed large areas of the old town; a successful test of theories propounded during the autumn of 1941, the many wooden buildings making it an ideal target for such an attack. It caused controversy because the Red Cross were using Lübeck for shipment of their supplies and they subsequently obtained an undertaking that the town would not be bombed again.

To protect the Russia-bound convoy PQ13 another attempt was made on the *Tirpitz* on 30/31 March, this time by an all-Halifax force of 34 aircraft from Nos.10, 35 and 76 Squadrons, operating from the Scottish airfields of Kinloss, Lossiemouth and Tain. The weather was clear but a smoke screen obscured the ship and yet another maximum range mission failed. Six aircraft did not return, probably running out of fuel. A series of unsuccessful raids on German cities followed and Harris was not a happy man, the gloom at Bomber Command headquarters only relieved by the dropping of the first 8,000-lb HC bomb, on Essen from a Halifax of No.76 Squadron during the night of 10/11 April.

To make matters worse he was under pressure to relinquish some of his best aircraft to bolster Coastal Command's efforts in the anti-submarine war. He was able to demonstrate how much he was already helping

Engines let the Manchester down but the airframe could take it, as demonstrated by R5830/L of No.83 Squadron, peppered with 'flak' during the 29 March raid on Lübeck. (via Chaz Bowyer Collection)

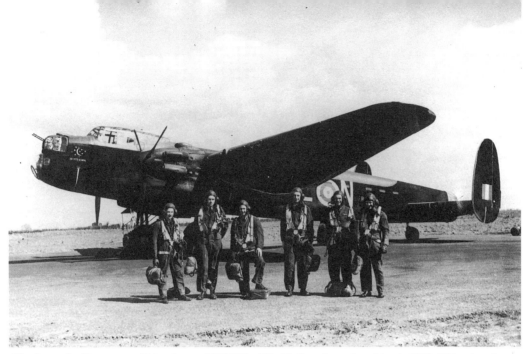

The happy-looking crew of Manchester R5833/N of No.83 Squadron circa March 1942. This aircraft was transferred to No.50 Squadron the following month. (The late Sqn Ldr J. Busby)

by mining (Stirlings had joined the mining force on 23/24 March 1942 and by the end of the year were laying them from the Baltic to the Bay of Biscay, having been allocated five of the seven 'areas') and attacks on towns containing U-Boat construction plants, and received a sympathetic hearing from Churchill. The Prime Minister was rapidly regaining confidence in the abilities of Bomber Command under its new and impressive leader – a man not unlike Churchill himself in many respects. Despite this

welcome support, Harris felt he had to do something dramatic to show his commitment to the anti U-Boat 'war' and demonstrate his Command's capabilities. He therefore decided on a long-range low-level penetration of Germany, a round trip flight of 1,250 miles, to attack the M.A.N diesel engine works at Augsburg, southern Bavaria, using Lancasters of Nos.44 and 97 Squadrons. Given a week's low-flying practice, seven crews from each squadron were very carefully briefed on 17 April 1942 for the operation,

Preparing to 'bomb up' Stirling W7451/MG-D of No.7 Squadron during the winter of 1941/42. (Public Archives of Canada/DND)

The Lancaster entered service early in 1942. L7578/B is seen indulging in some low flying in preparation for the Augsburg raid on 17 April 1942. (Hawker Siddeley/BAe A9/1/192)

which was to be supported by diversionary raids by Bostons of Nos.88 and 107 Squadrons escorted by Spitfires, while other Fighter Command units carried out a large-scale *Rodeo* over the Pas de Calais. Taking off at 1500 hours the twelve Lancaster crews (the other two were spares) formed up in two groups, the first led by Sqn Ldr J.D. Nettleton of No.44 Squadron, the second by Sqn Ldr J.S. Sherwood, No.97 Squadron. Over the Channel they descended to very low level and stayed low over France. At first all went well, but the *Circus* operation had been brought forward for reasons unknown, and intercepting Bf109s and Fw190s of II/JG2 returning to base sighted the Lancasters passing Evreux. For 15 minutes they harried the force and four aircraft of No.44 Squadron went down. Sherwood's formation got through unscathed and followed Nettleton as he carried on towards Munich before suddenly turning north for Augsburg. Nettleton released his four 1,000-lb delayed-action bombs on the target followed by Flg Off A.J. Garwell – who was shot down immediately afterwards. Sherwood ran in as the leader left and all his formation bombed the factory, though the Lancaster flown by WO T. J. Mycock was already engulfed in flames. Sherwood, Mycock and Flt Lt E.A. Deverill went down in the target area and only five of the 12 aircraft returned. The attack was hailed as a brilliant feat of arms, but it is exploding bombs on

target that matter, and of the 17 which landed on the engine works five failed to detonate. The raid had little effect on U-Boat engine production and such losses could not be sustained, Harris privately accepting that the raid had been a failure – though that did not stop him trying again. Nettleton was awarded the VC for his unflinching determination, valour and leadership.

Despite the evidence, some commanders were not convinced that *Gee*, an excellent navigational aid, was practically useless for bomb aiming, so a strong force of *Gee*-equipped Wellingtons and Stirlings was sent to Cologne on 22/23 April, the crews under orders to use the equipment for blind bombing. The results were pretty conclusive, reports indicating that of the 69 aircraft despatched only 15 bombed the city, other bombs exploding up to 10 miles away! Harris turned to the easily identifiable Baltic port of Rostock and in four 'Lübeck-type' attacks the damage was such that for the first time the Germans called them *Terrangrift* (Terror raids).

High- and medium-altitude attacks on the *Tirpitz* had proved unrewarding so it was decided to go in at low-level using a new weapon, the 1,000-lb Special Mine. The operation involved both Halifax (Nos. 10, 35 and 76) and Lancaster (Nos.44 and 97) Squadrons flying from the usual Scottish airfields of Tain, Kinloss and Lossiemouth. Thirty-one Halifaxes and 12 Lancasters set off on 27 April, the plan being for the Lancasters and No.76 Squadron's Halifaxes to drop HC and MC bombs from 6,000 feet to distract the defences, while Halifaxes of Nos.10 and 35 Squadrons, each carrying four or five mines and flying at 200 feet, attempted to lay them alongside the ship. The *Tirpitz* was found, but as the aircraft made their run she was obscured by a smoke screen and no damage was done. Four Halifaxes and a Lancaster were lost, one of the former flown by Wg Cdr D.C.T. Bennett, CO No.10 Squadron, who baled out and evaded capture. Another, flown by Plt Off D. McIntyre, crash-landed on a frozen lake and in 1982 was salvaged and partially restored, and is currently in the RAF Museum at Hendon. A reduced force, 23 Halifaxes and 11 Lancasters tried again the next night, and hits were claimed but not confirmed. Another two Halifaxes were missing and some of the mines were found on the hillside above the *Tirpitz*, leading to reports that it had been intended to roll them down onto the ship. The spherical mine was not used again.

April 27/28 was also the last night the Whitley operated as a front-line bomber (although OTU aircraft took part in the 'Thousand Bomber' raids and other major operations until September 1942 and continued leaflet-dropping until July 1944), No.4 Group being completely equipped with Halifax aircraft at last. Some of the Whitleys were transferred to Coastal Command, Nos.51 and 77 Squadrons temporarily and No.58 Squadron permanently, together with Hampdens of No.144 Squadron and Wellingtons of Nos.304 (Polish) and 311 (Czech) Squadrons, all the result of Admiralty demands made

The Hercules-powered Wellington III was in widespread service in 1942. Illustrated is X3763/KW-E of No.425 Squadron, RCAF. (MAP)

in February for the 'immediate transfer of 6½ Wellington squadrons to Coastal Command'.

Though he minimized the 'damage' by releasing his least effective aircraft, this forced transfer of squadrons infuriated Harris, already complaining bitterly about the continuing diversion of aircraft and newly trained crews to other Commands. His strongly worded comments bore some fruit, Portal informing him on 13 May that both Coastal and Army Co-operation Commands would no longer draw on Bomber Command for trained crews, but any hope that calls on Bomber Command's strength were over evaporated when Sir Philip Joubert, C-in-C Coastal Command, requested Lancasters to fill the gap produced by the unexpectedly slow delivery of

Halifax II W7676/TL-P of No.35 Squadron, May 1942. The aircraft failed to return from Nuremburg on 29 August 1942. (MAP)

Liberators. Harris was very angry and pointedly remarked upon Coastal's lack of success against the U-Boat at sea compared with Bomber Command's record against Germany's submarine production facilities, and contribution to sea mining operations, the latter far outstripping those of Coastal Command. In fact the effectiveness of Coastal's anti-submarine force was improving and U-Boats were being forced further out into the Atlantic which was why long-range aircraft were required. Britain's lifeline from the Americas was threatened, but this was not Harris's immediate problem, and he was too single-minded to see that unless losses were reduced the fuel for his aircraft would not be forthcoming in the future. Naturally the Air Ministry had a broader view and had to balance priorities, but in the end they did not divert Lancasters to Coastal Command, ordering Harris to lend squadrons to meet particular maritime threats instead. This was very much a second best solution for the detached crews were not trained in the very demanding anti-submarine role – but it was all Harris would swallow.

It was Stuttgart's turn for a series of medium-strength raids at the beginning of May, but this was a difficult target and all three attacks were unsuccessful, as was a raid on Mannheim on 19/20 May. For the rest of the month operations were largely confined to mine-laying while Harris husbanded his bomber force, knowing that the future of Bomber Command still remained in some doubt. Influential scientists and politicians were again casting doubt about the viability of the bombing offensive and Harris was determined to show that he could repeat the successes of Lübeck

and Rostock on a major city and grab the headlines in the process. His plan was certainly attention-getting, for it involved the despatch of 1,000 bombers to attack a single target. With a regular force of some 400 aircraft in his operational Groups the plan appeared impossible, but there were a considerable number of additional aircraft in the Conversion Flights attached to squadrons, and in Nos.91 and 92 Groups. He intended to use all these, crewed by instructors and advanced trainees.

Both Portal and Prime Minister Churchill were impressed by the idea and agreed to the basic plan, but when realistic serviceability figures were used Harris still had a shortfall and he invited the C-in-Cs of Coastal and Flying Training Command (FTC) to help. They agreed willingly, Air Chief Marshal Sir Philip Joubert immediately offering 250 bombers, many from squadrons recently transferred from Bomber Command, while Air Marshal Sir William Welsh earmarked 50 twin-engined ex-bomber trainers. To concentrate this unprecedented force over the target new tactics were formulated. The aircraft were to fly in a carefully regulated 'stream' taking a common route to and from the target and flying at a set speed. Each aircraft was to be allocated a height and time to enter the 'stream' to minimize the risk of collision (as recommended by Bomber Command's Operational Research Section, which had been tasked with determining the probability of collisions if 1,000 bombers concentrated their attack within one hour. The answer was one!). It was also hoped that such tight control would mean the majority of night fighter 'boxes' could be avoided, and that the controllers in

A dramatic sight – Halifax II W1170/U of No.10 Squadron about to set out from Leeming on a bombing operation, mid-1942. (via B. Robertson)

those that had to be penetrated would be swamped, thus reducing the overall number of interceptions. The plan aimed to get the whole force over the target within 90 minutes, which, it was hoped, would also overwhelm the anti-aircraft defences and fire/rescue services.

The detailed planning for Operation *Millennium* was complete when the Admiralty dropped their 'bombshell'. They refused to let Coastal Command take part, even though the choice of target was the port of Hamburg! Despite this bitter blow Harris was determined to have his 1,000 bombers and ordered his staff to find the aircraft and crews. By a supreme effort 1,047 bombers were ready on 26 May, all from within Bomber Command except four Wellingtons, the only aircraft FTC could produce that were adequately equipped for night operations! The weather held up *Millennium* and after three days the ancient cathedral city of Cologne had to be substituted as the target because the continuing delay was badly affecting training schedules. The aircraft despatched to Cologne were 602 Wellingtons, 131 Halifaxes, 88 Stirlings, 79 Hampdens, 73 Lancasters, 46 Manchesters and 28 Whitleys, while diversionary operations aimed at German night fighter airfields involved 34 Blenheims of No.2 Group, 15 Blenheims of Army Co-operation Command and seven Havocs from Fighter Command.

Gee-equipped Wellingtons and Stirlings of Nos.1 and 3 Groups started the attack and 90 minutes later the fastest aircraft, Halifaxes, Manchesters and Lancasters of Nos.4 and 5 Groups, were over the target – followed by a few stragglers. The total time over the target was longer and the attack less concentrated than planned, but from the C-in-C's viewpoint it was a great improvement on earlier raids. The crews were less enthusiastic, never really coming to terms with the undoubted collision risk, though losses from all causes were under 4% which was considered 'satisfactory'. Among them was a Manchester of No.50 Squadron captained by Flg Off L.T. Manser which was hit by 'flak' immediately after dropping its load of over 1,000 4-lb incendiaries. The controls were damaged and the port engine burst into flames. With the propeller feathered the fire finally went out at 2,000 feet but, barely controllable, the aircraft continued to lose height and Manser ordered the crew to bale out. The co-pilot, Sgt L. Baveystock, tried to clip Manser's parachute pack onto his harness but was waved away as the pilot struggled to keep the aircraft flying. Baveystock leapt out of the front hatch, his parachute having no time to deploy fully before he hit water in a Belgian dyke, the aircraft crashing only yards away and bursting into flames. Following interrogation of crew members who escaped with the help of the 'Underground', Manser was posthumously

awarded the VC for his gallant efforts to give his crew a chance with no thought for his own survival.

Even before the mighty *Millennium* force had returned, Mosquito IVs of No.105 Squadron were being prepared for the aircraft's first Bomber Command operation – to Cologne to harass the defences and photograph the city. The first off, flown by Sqn Ldr A.R. Oakeshott, found Cologne obscured by smoke rising to 14,000 feet; of the second nothing more was heard. Further attempts at reconnaissance later in the day were similarly frustrated by smoke and it was not until the evening of 1 June that photographs were obtained and the widespread damage could be seen. The Mosquito was still officially secret at this time and its part in the operation remained unpublicized for some months, a situation which suited Bomber Command very well for its 'top brass' were still finding it hard to accept the idea of an unarmed bomber and were unsure how to employ it.

Harris had planned to carry out a second 'Thousand Bomber' raid during the full moon period before dispersing his force and Essen was attacked on 1/2 June, though the number of aircraft despatched unavoidably dropped to 956. No.2 Group again provided Blenheims for 'intruder' operations on German airfields supported by Army Co-operation and Fighter Commands. The overall plan was similar to the attack on Cologne but more flares were dropped by the 'lead' Wellingtons of No.3 Group. Unfortunately, hazy conditions made such marking difficult and the Essen attack was not a success, though losses were again light: 3.2% of the aircraft despatched.

Eleven days later the first Lancaster detachment to Coastal Command started, six No.44 Squadron aircraft, their air crew and groundcrew arriving at Nutts Corner, Northern Ireland. The next day they started patrols which continued until 6 July, flying 61 hours and attacking U-Boats on two occasions without obvious result. One Lancaster was lost.

Emden and Essen were the main targets during June but on 25/26th came another 'Thousand Bomber' raid, this time on Bremen. The actual number despatched was 1,067, of which 102 Hudsons and Wellingtons were provided by Coastal Command (after Churchill had insisted that the Admiralty release them) and Army Co-operation Command sent five Blenheims. Some aircraft were given specific targets, these including the Focke-Wulf works (No.5 Group) and the Deschimag shipyard (Coastal Command). Unfortunately the city was cloud-covered, and though extensive fires were started the bombing was scattered and the damage was little more than that achieved by 170 aircraft earlier in the month, and much less than resulted from three smaller follow-up raids. 'Intruder'

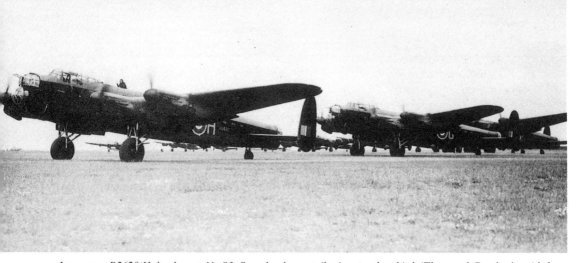

Lancaster R5620/H leads out No.83 Squadron's contribution to the third 'Thousand Bomber' raid from Scampton on 25 June 1942. Piloted by Plt Off J.R. Farrow, it was the only Lancaster lost during this attack on Bremen. (No 83 Squadron records)

operations were again flown, Bostons and Mosquitoes joining Blenheims in this task and losses for the night were considerable, totalling 55 aircraft (4.9% of the total force), mostly due to night fighters. The unsuccessful Manchester was withdrawn from operations following this raid.

Despite the comparative failure of the Essen and Bremen raids these massive attacks did show what could be done with a large force, and in doing so probably saved Bomber Command. They also proved the 'concentration' tactic and the increased control on routes to and from the target which remained features of all later operations.

The method used to choose a target and order the attack remained much the same throughout the war, though once Harris was in charge there was, in general, firmer control by the C-in-C. Almost invariably the daily planning conference commenced at 0900 hours in the Operations Room at High Wycombe, attended by most senior air staff officers and, from August 1942, a representative from the USAAF's 8th Air Force. After a short review of any operations carried out the previous night, the weather 'brief' was given and a decision made on whether to lay on an attack. Following an affirmative decision, the C-in-C was briefed on American plans and the priority list before announcing the target. He then briefly discussed the number of aircraft required, the routeing and any tactical ploys with his deputy before departing. Detailed planning then followed and the information signalled to participating Groups, which in turn decided on the units involved and informed the Stations. Squadron Commanders chose the crews and checked on aircraft preparation. The crews, who generally slept late, had a leisurely breakfast and if flying on operations air-tested their aircraft, then attempted to rest before assembling for briefing. With charts prepared, rations collected, signals bags signed for, they kitted up and after collecting their parachutes assembled to await transport to the aircraft dispersals. On return they attended debriefing by the intelligence officer, had a meal and staggered off to bed, often as dawn was breaking – a topsy-turvy existence.

No.2 Group's second Mosquito squadron, No.139, made its first raid as part of the back up for *Millennium II*, the Bremen operation, when a single crew, in a No.105 Squadron aircraft, joined in a low-level attack on Stade airfield, Wilhelmshaven. On 2 July, a more ambitious Mosquito operation was sanctioned, a low-level attack on U-Boat construction yards at Flensburg by six aircraft led by Wg Cdr A.R. Oakeshott. It was a disaster, intercepting fighters shooting down the leader, and another Mosquito, flown by Gp Capt J.C. MacDonald, crashed in Germany following 'flak' damage. Such operations were immediately suspended while their future was considered, No.105 Squadron finding itself on daily stand-by for weather checks prior to 'main force' operations.

Another experimental daylight attack by Lancasters was mounted on 11 July when 44 aircraft from Nos.83, 97, 106 and 207 Squadrons of No. 5 Group were sent to Danzig, where it was reported that U-Boat sections were being constructed on a production line basis. The plan involved low-level formation over the North Sea before climbing independently into the cloud forecast for the Baltic leg, to arrive over the target at dusk so that the journey back was in darkness – a round trip of 1,500 miles. Most crews had difficulty identifying the shipyards and had to bomb the town. Two Lancasters were shot down and the intended target survived unscathed. Further cloud cover daylight attacks were made during the following week, small numbers of Stirlings going to Lübeck, Lancasters to Essen, and Wellingtons to Emden and Essen, all intended to disrupt work over a large area. Other innovations included Bostons hunting in pairs at low-level for 'targets of opportunity', and Mosquitoes of No.105 Squadron operating singly using the aircraft's high-flying abilities to escape interception.

Meanwhile Halifaxes from Nos. 10 and 76 Squadrons (subsequently forming No. 462 Squadron) were sent to the Middle East early in July ostensibly as an anti-shipping force and a second Lancaster detachment, nine aircraft of No. 61 Squadron, went to St Eval on the 14th to take advantage of Admiral Doenitz's new orders to U-Boat commanders to remain submerged except when recharging batteries while transiting the Bay of Biscay. This greatly increased the chance of day sightings, and three days later Flt Lt P.R. Casement's 61 Squadron crew spotted a large oil patch and then a conning tower. The aircraft's complete load, 10 Mk.VIII depth charges and two 250-lb AS bombs were dropped in three runs across the U-751 (Type VIIc) which slowly sank stern first. The detachment returned to Syerston briefly for attacks on Hamburg and Saarbrucken at the end of the month, but were back in Cornwall to resume patrols on 3 August alongside 16 Whitleys of No.10 OTU, Bomber Command. The Whitleys, flown by staff and students during the last three weeks of each course, were used exclusively for Bay of Biscay patrols and were to remain at St Eval for almost a year.

On 19 August a 12,000-ton tanker, the SS *Corunna*, a blockade runner, was sighted and it was decided to use the bombing skills of the Lancaster crews to sink it. No.61 Squadron were joined briefly by No.50 Squadron but neither unit had any success, losing four aircraft in the attempt. Both units left for home on 22 August, the groundcrew in five Harrows of No.271 Squadron.

Bomber Command attacks during early July were concentrated on Duisberg (four times) and Hamburg (twice). More specialized was Operation *Pandemonium*, an attack made on the 16th by 21 Stirlings on the U-Boat assembly works 4½ miles NE of Lübeck, using a cloud-covered approach and dusk attack. Unfortunately only eight crews were able to bomb, and another dusk raid, by 99 Halifaxes, Stirlings and Lancasters on the Vulcan U-Boat yard at Vegesack, was even less successful. More standard in every way was a heavy attack on Düsseldorf by 630 aircraft, over 100 of them Lancasters, on the last night of the month. Damage was assessed as heavy, borne out by German records examined post-war.

The morale of the crews had been bolstered by the arrival of the dynamic Harris and the first 'Thousand Bomber' raids despite continued heavy losses, but the

Lancaster I R5554/Q of No.44 Squadron in August 1942 when it had completed 10 operations. Lost on 20 September during the long haul to Munich. (A.H. Collinson)

generally disappointing results since the end of May and the continued technical problems experienced by Stirlings and Halifaxes were having their effect. No.4 Group was particularly affected and in August the whole of the Halifax force had to be stood down from operations for nearly a month while tailplanes were modified. Harris blamed the manufacturers, in his opinion abysmally slow introducing essential modifications. His comments on Handley Page in particular were vitriolic, and his temper was not improved by a campaign orchestrated by Gp Capt S.O. Bufton, Director of Bomber Operations at the Air Ministry, for a Target Marking Force (a form of target marking using a timed run from a known position had been tried as early as June 1940) which had been gaining ground since the end of 1941.

There was no disagreement about the need for 'raid leaders' but Harris was firmly against any elite organizations within the Command, preferring experienced crews to remain with ordinary squadrons. In this he had the support of his Group Commanders, and ultimately Portal had to choose between the opposing views, and came down on the side of his own staff. On 11 August 1942 Harris was ordered to establish the marker force, which he insisted on calling the Pathfinder Force, to work directly under the planners at Bomber Command HQ, though administered by No.3 Group. Gp Capt B. Embry was suggested as commander of the new force, but in the event the Australian, Wg Cdr D.C.T. Bennett was given the job and turned out to be an inspired choice.

Each of the 'heavy' Groups were required to 'donate' one squadron to the Pathfinders. Bufton wanted the units to be manned by selected crews from all the squadrons in the Group but Harris refused to instruct his Group Commanders to 'head hunt' and the units, No.7 Squadron (No.3 Group) with Stirlings; No.35 Squadron (No.4 Group) with Halifaxes; No.83 Squadron (No.5 Group) with Lancasters and No.156 Squadron (No.1 Group) with Wellingtons were basically transferred *en masse*. In addition, No.109 Squadron joined No.83 at Wyton to operate independently in 'association' with the Pathfinder Force until formally absorbed later in the year. Bennett did not get the pick of the crews; nor did he necessarily get the best replacements, and the task was not made any easier by having four types of aircraft.

Harris had warned Bennett that the Pathfinders had to be operational immediately on arrival at their new East Anglian bases, but the weather intervened and there was a 24-hour delay before the first Pathfinder-led attack on 18/19 August. It was not a success, the intended target, Flensburg, being untouched while a large part of Denmark to the north received a scattering of bombs. The errors were doubtless compounded by jamming of *Gee* which had occurred for the first time on 9/10 August during an attack on the same target, but an anti-jamming device was rapidly produced and fitted to aircraft. It was not perfect but did allow the signals to be read through the 'clutter'.

On 19 August 62 Bostons of No.2 Group (Nos.88, 107 and 226 Squadrons) carried out smoke-laying in support of the Dieppe landings, losing three aircraft in the process. This was Bomber Command's only part in the operation, for though Mosquitoes were making daily sorties it was in small numbers because deliveries of the de Havilland aircraft were very slow,

it being December 1942 before No.139 Squadron had its own Mosquitoes. Other aircraft were entering service with No.2 Group, Venturas (a bomber version of the Lockheed 18 airliner) with No.487 Squadron, RNZAF and Mitchells with Nos.98 and 180 Squadrons, enabling the weary Blenheims to be withdrawn at last, their final sorties being flown against Dutch and German airfields on 17/18 August.

On 27/28 August Kassel was the main target and the Pathfinders had their first success, illuminating the city with flares. Casualties were high, over 10% of the force being lost, mostly to night fighters. Amongst the Lancasters sent to Kassel were nine from No. 106 Squadron, some of which carried on across Germany to Gdynia, Poland, 950 miles from their base. Their target was the almost completed aircraft carrier, *Graf Zeppelin*, and for the attack a new weapon, the 5,600-lb Capital Ship bomb was deployed. Led by Wg Cdr G.P. Gibson the crews had trained hard for this mission for several weeks. It was risky, for with the bombs loaded the aircraft were 7,000-lb overweight, but the small force reached Gdynia where the visibility was so poor that the ship could not be identified and the weapons had to be dropped in the general harbour area. They did little or no damage – a great disappointment. The next night Nuremburg and Saarbrücken were the targets, those Main Force aircraft going to Nuremburg having the advantage of Pathfinders carrying, for the first time, target indicators called *Red Blob Fire*, which burned brightly for some time. The bombing was reasonably concentrated – much better than at Saarbrücken – but losses were high, 14.5% of the force, Wellingtons

Boston IIIs of No.88 Squadron at Attlebridge. On 31 October 1942 W8297/RH-A was destroyed when a bomb exploded during arming. (Gp Capt J.E. Pelly Fry via A.S. Thomas)

No.2 Group also received Venturas, AE660 joining No.21 Squadron on 5 June 1942, transferring to No.487 Squadron in October. (RAF Museum P3457)

being particularly hard-hit.

On 3 September the Air Ministry issued a new Directive stating yet again that the Axis oil situation was critical and emphasizing it as a priority target. Harris ignored it, convinced that until the promised bombing aids were available his crews were unable, except by pure chance, to hit such difficult targets as the specifically mentioned hydrogenation plant at Pölitz.

On 4/5 September the Pathfinders tried a new technique, providing 'illuminators' with white flares to light up the area; 'visual markers' who, having identified the aiming point, dropped coloured flares; and 'backers-up' releasing incendiary loads on the 'marker' flares. It was a success, the centre of Bremen being badly damaged, and it was a technique used for the remainder of the war.

A heavy raid on Düsseldorf followed on 10/11 September and included a considerable number of aircraft from Nos.91, 92 and 93 (Training) Groups. It was another success for the Pathfinders, who were using a proper marker for the first time, an awesome device nicknamed the 'Pink Pansy' which weighed 2,800 lb. Bremen suffered another heavy attack on the 13/14th and the following night Hampdens operated with a front-line bomber squadron for the last time, leaving the Wellington as the only pre-war bomber remaining fully operational.

Gradually, very gradually, the strength of Mosquito raids was increasing, though not with any great success so far. Six Mk.IVs of No.105 Squadron were despatched to Berlin on 19 September, but only three got there, and an attack on the Gestapo HQ in

Olso on the 25th, timed to coincide with a rally of Norwegian Nazi sympathizers, did little to improve the aircraft's image. As the aircraft approached Oslo at low-level they were intercepted by Fw190s and one Mosquito went down, unsettling the other three crews. Five buildings around the HQ were hit and fierce fires broke out, but the Victoria Terrasse itself survived – a great disappointment after all the effort involved in getting the bombs there.

These daylight attacks, resulting in the Mosquito being publicly revealed, were followed by another 'Bomber' Harris 'special' using Lancasters. The Schneider works at Le Creusot, the French equivalent of Krupps, in the eastern region of Saone-et-Loire, had long been on the list of priority targets. Harris decided to attack by day, at low-level, using all nine No.5 Group Lancaster squadrons, obstensibly a repeat of the Augsburg disaster! In fact lessons had been learnt, and it was hoped that intense security, disciplined low flying and a carefully planned route would reduce casualties to acceptable levels. Low-flying practice started on 1 October, the numbers building up until the whole Group was flying together in loose formation. Within the squadrons there was much debate over possible targets, accentuated by several false alarms when aircraft were bombed-up in readiness. The delays were caused by the weather but on 17 October it was declared right and Operation *Robinson* was 'on'. Ninety-four Lancasters took part, 88 briefed to attack the factory area while six went for the nearby Montchanin transformer station which provided power for the site.

The aircraft, led by Wg Cdr L.C. Slee, CO 49

Squadron (the other units were Nos.9, 44, 50, 57, 61, 97, 106 and 207 Squadrons), flew out into the Bay of Biscay at 1,000 feet, then turned, descended to keep below radar cover, and crossed the French coast at 100 feet near Ile d'Yeu, 48 miles south of St Nazaire. The only German fighters thought to be in the area were at Vannes near Lorient, and it was hoped that a planned American raid would occupy them. The raid did not take place but the Lancasters remained unchallenged as they raced across France at tree-top height. Excellent navigation brought the force to Nevers at the confluence of the Rivers Allier and Loire, where the aircraft turned to starboard for the target and climbed to bombing height. Arriving at dusk, the target was easily identifiable and the attack was over in seven minutes – and considered accurate. Unfortunately recce photographs showed that most of the bombs had dropped short and hit workers' houses, the very thing that Harris had feared would result from a night attack. Only light 'flak' was encountered and no aircraft were lost from the Le Creusot attack, but one of those bombing the transformer site hit a building and crashed. Another aircraft had suffered engine failure and the crew had to turn back while still over the Bay of Biscay. Intercepted by three Ar196 floatplanes, the Lancaster's gunners promptly shot down two of them!

During the autumn, Halifaxes which had undergone drag reduction modifications started to appear in numbers, and losses dropped markedly. Lancasters, however, were plagued with pump problems which caused fuel starvation above 12,000 feet, but they still took part in a series of attacks on Genoa and Milan to coincide with Montgomery's El Alamein offensive in North Africa, one of them a risky daylight attack on Milan by 88 Lancasters of No.5 Group on 24 October. They flew at low-level over France before climbing to cross the Alps and the element of surprise worked, losses being confined to four aircraft, one of which crash-landed on return.

Operation *Torch* resulted in the whole of No.405 Squadron and half of No.158, 20 Halifax IIs, being sent to Beaulieu on 24 October for anti-submarine operations over the Bay of Biscay in support of supply convoys. In Harris's eyes this was another unnecessary diversion but several submarine sightings were made, some resulting in attacks, and on 27 November U-263 was damaged by a No.405 Squadron crew. No.158 Squadron's detachment ended in December 1942 but No.405 remained with No.19 Group, Coastal Command, until 1 March 1943 when the unit returned to Topcliffe.

Ventura operations commenced on 3 November 1942 when three crews attempted, unsuccessfully, to bomb a factory at Hengelo, Holland; but the fortunes of Mosquito crews were improving, six No.105 Squadron Mosquitoes making out a low-level attack on a 5,000-ton blockade runner in the River Gironde on 7 November, while Boston crews hit a large German merchantman at Le Havre and put it out of action for months.

The attacks on northern Italy continued until mid-December, *Boozer** being used for the first time on 13/14 November during a raid on Genoa, while one of

*See Chapter 9

the heaviest raids, on 28/29 November, witnessed the

Halifax II srs 1 W7710/Q of No.405 Squadron, RCAF, named the Ruhr Valley Express. (Public Archives of Canada/DND)

first use of the 8,000-lb bomb on an Italian target. Stirlings of No.3 Group also struggled over the Alps, one flown by F/Sgt R.H. Middleton of No.149 Squadron, having considerable trouble. As Turin was sighted he started a rapid descent and almost immediately the aircraft was hit by 'flak', one shell badly injuring Middleton. He lost consciousness but regained it in time to make a run over the target. The bombs released, he set off back over the Alps, refusing to leave the controls to the inexperienced co-pilot. With fuel almost gone as they reached the English coast Middleton gave the order to abandon the aircraft, five of the crew parachuting to safety, while the pilot and two members of his crew went into the sea with the aircraft. Middleton was awarded the VC for unsurpassed determination to give his comrades the best possible chance of survival.

Attacks on targets in German-occupied countries always posed risks to the civilian population, especially so when towns were involved. Sometimes hard decisions had to be made, but past experience showed that night raids should be the last resort. Thus when it was decided that the Philips radio and valve works in the Dutch town of Eindhoven had to be attacked, the planners opted for a daytime raid. Initially another Lancaster 'spectacular' was mooted – but quickly rejected: it would be suicidal in the middle of a German fighter belt. More attractive was a Mosquito mission, but the factories were large and dispersed and insufficient aircraft were available, so it was agreed that the whole of No.2 Group would be required, despite the problems involved in operating four types of aircraft of very different performance on

The famous low-level daylight raid on the Philips works at Eindhoven by No.2 Group, 6 December 1942. A Boston is seen overflying with its bomb doors open. (British Official)

a raid which, to maintain surprise, had to be concentrated in time and space. At a late stage the brand-new Mitchells had to be withdrawn because the crews were not ready for operations, and it was a mixed force of Bostons, Venturas and Mosquitoes that was finally scheduled for the two-pronged low-level operation, code-named *Oyster*.

Led by Wg Cdr J.E. Pelly-Fry of No.88 Squadron the force consisted of 47 Venturas (Nos.21, 464 and 487 Squadrons), 36 Bostons (Nos.88, 107, and 226) and 10 Mosquitoes (Nos.105 and 139 Squadrons), of which 24 Bostons and 17 Venturas were to attack the Emmasingel valve factory while the rest went for the

Boston III AL754/D of No.107 Squadron took part in the raid on the Philips factory, crash-landing at Great Massingham on return. (MAP)

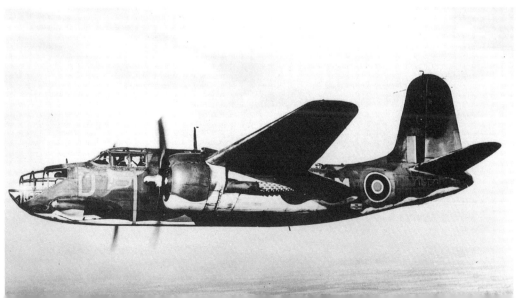

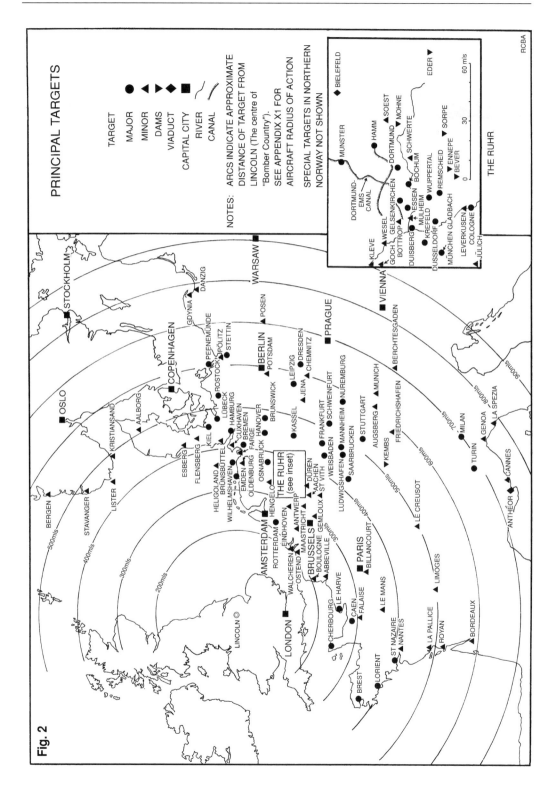

Fig. 2

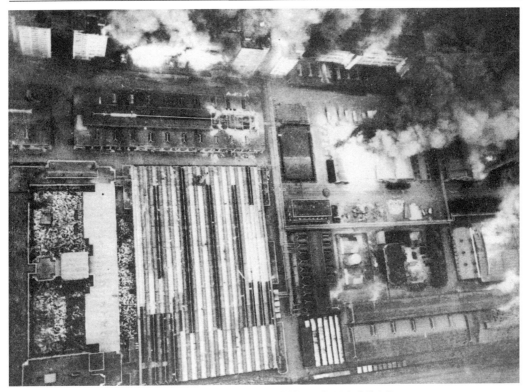

Half an hour after the attack on the Philips works, fires still blaze. (British Official)

Stryp Group works. Taking off at carefully timed intervals during the late morning of 6 December, the Bostons and Venturas flew the same route from their landfall at Colinsplatt, while the Mosquitoes flew a 'dog-leg' before joining the rest near Oostmalle for the run-in to the target. A strong diversionary force of B-17s, escorted by Spitfires, bombed Lille while Mustangs of No.268 Squadron went on *Rhubarbs* over the Continent to further confuse the defences. Both factories were severely damaged and there were few 'loose' bombs; but losses were high, nine Venturas, four Bostons and a Mosquito being brought down, mostly by fighters. Three more aircraft crash-landed in England, a total loss of 19%, which was certainly unsustainable, and the Eindhoven raid remained a 'one-off', the most famous and successful No.2 Group operation while part of Bomber Command.

With *Gee* in widespread service and fully accepted by the crews, other help was on its way. Since August No.109 Squadron had been carrying out trials on *Oboe*, an incredibly accurate aid which could be used for blind bombing. *Oboe* crews were given a geographical point 10 minutes' flying time (the 'switching on' point) from the target, an Estimated Time of Arrival (ETA) and a two-letter code. A

listening watch was commenced and on hearing their code they switched on the *Oboe* equipment. Their actual position in relation to the 'Bailey Beam' (an imaginary beam from the 'switching on' point to the target) was indicated by continuous 'dots' or 'dashes', a steady tone denoting 'on beam'. The aircraft had to be flown at a set speed and height, the distance to the target being indicated by single-letter transmissions, the release point by the cessation of the steady beam signal. The equipment had range limitations, but more importantly was restricted in the number of aircraft each pair of stations could handle per hour. It was therefore reserved almost exclusively for target marking, and pinpoint targets such as the power station at Lutterade, Holland, attacked by six *Oboe*-equipped Mosquito IVs on 20/21st December. It was chosen as a 'virgin' target so that the accuracy of the attack could be calibrated, but unfortunately the area was found to be smothered in bomb craters from earlier 'loose' bombs. Equipment malfunction prevented three crews from using *Oboe*, but the others bombed the target, reportedly none too accurately. As usual it was taking time for the equipment to settle down and for crews to gain experience, but results were better on 23/24 and 24/25 December, the Krupps works being hit on both nights, while a trial marking

Mosquito IVs DZ353/E and DZ367/J of No.105 Squadron, the first unit equipped with the bomber version. (RAFM 5948-1)

operation (the first *Wanganui*) over Düsseldorf, by two Mosquitoes for eight Lancasters of the Pathfinder Force on 31 December, resulted in some damage in the city. So that Main Force crews knew which type of marking was being employed, code-names derived from the birthplaces of Pathfinder personnel were used. *Newhaven* was ground marking by visual means, *Paramatta* was ground marking by H2S and *Wanganui* was sky marking. *Musical Parramatta* and *Musical Wanganui* indicated use of *Oboe.*

It was the end of an eventful year – a year of innovation during which, despite many distractions

and disappointments, real progress was made in upgrading Bomber Command's aircraft and the ability of ordinary crews to find and bomb targets. Losses, increasing steadily as German ground-controlled fighter interception systems improved were giving cause for concern, but the strenuous efforts made to perfect countermeasures were starting to bear fruit, as *Mandrel* and *Tinsel** became operational. They did not defeat the night fighters but they heralded much better equipment to come.

*See Chapter 9

CHAPTER 5

Battles – Ruhr and Hamburg 1943

JANUARY 1943, four months into the fourth year of war, and suddenly everything seemed to be going right for Bomber Command. The promised navigation and bombing aids were appearing in squadron aircraft and the use of H2S, originally vetoed until April, was brought forward to the beginning of the year. A squabble over the number of H2S-equipped aircraft required was soon resolved, Harris directing that it was to be fitted to all four-engined bombers except Lancaster IIs which had bulged bomb doors, ventral gun turrets and were earmarked for *G-H*. The Halifax was getting over its technical troubles at last and all three types of four-engined bombers were rolling off production lines in numbers which allowed the reliable but obsolete Wellington to be gradually withdrawn from the operational scene.

Even the number of Groups was increasing, No.6 Group, RCAF starting full scale operations on New Year's Day when Canadian squadrons, formed in No.4 Group during the summer and autumn of 1942, were officially transferred to the new organization. A few days later the Pathfinder Force was upgraded as No.8 Group. 'Bomber' Harris, as the Press called him, had tested his theories, refined them and, apart from No.2 Group which featured little in the C-in-C's plans, had firm ideas as to how he intended to employ his force.

As so often in the past a setback to the C-in-C's plans was not long in coming, and almost inevitably it was caused by the war at sea. An upsurge in U-Boat activity in the mid-Atlantic, where the Germans were successfully using pack tactics, resulted in calls for action to reduce the number of submarines available to the enemy, and the War Cabinet approved a renewed bombing campaign against French bases. On 14 January Harris was ordered to concentrate his night attacks on Lorient, St Nazaire, Brest and La Pallice,

with the object of destroying submarines and their maintenance facilities. The first attack was made that night on Lorient and in the course of nine heavy raids during January/February the town was completely destroyed. Harris then turned on St Nazaire, using *Oboe*-directed ground marking (*Musical Parramatta*) for the first time on 28 February. Only one *Oboe* station was in use but accurate marking was achieved, the town being devastated after four attacks. But it soon became obvious that only the French were suffering, the massive U-Boat pens built after the 1941 attacks being impenetrable using weapons currently available, while German personnel either stayed in shelters at night or were dispersed into the countryside.

Meanwhile British and American leaders had met at Casablanca during January and thrashed out their war policy differences. Before the conference was over the *Pointblank* Directive was issued by the Combined Chiefs of Staff, it stating that both Bomber Command and the United States' 8th Air Force were to participate in 'the progressive destruction and dislocation of the German military, industrial and economic system, and the undermining of the morale of the German people to a point where their capacity for armed resistance is fatally weakened'. A list of target systems was attached, the intention being that the Americans would make precision attacks by day and Bomber Command area attacks by night. There was nothing particularly new about this, but it reinforced the political backing for the planned bomber offensive, and when received officially by Harris on 4 February it undoubtedly further increased the 'feel good' factor permeating the HQ at High Wycombe.

Concentration on the U-Boat pens did not preclude other targets completely, Berlin being raided on 16/17 and 17/18 January by Pathfinder-led Lancasters and Halifaxes. These were the first major operations involving only four-engined aircraft, and the first using production target indicators (pre-production TIs had been in use since November 1942), but neither attack was particularly successful for none of the new aids could be used, and No.8 Group was unable to accurately mark the centre of the city due to haze.

No.2 Group Mitchells started operations on 22 January when 12 aircraft of Nos.98 and 180 Squadrons attacked oil targets near Ghent. It was not an auspicious start, three Mitchells being lost, and it also proved a false one, the Mitchells being immediately withdrawn from operations while armament and fuel problems were sorted out.

Oboe Mosquitoes used 250-lb ground markers in place of parachute flares for the first time during a raid on Düsseldorf on 27/28 January. Pathfinder Lancaster 'backers-up' reinforced them accurately and bombing was well concentrated on the southern side of the city, causing considerable damage. Very different Mosquito missions followed two days later when the Nazi leaders Goering and Goebbels were due to address large rallies in Berlin and their speeches broadcast. After calculations showed that Mosquitoes could fly an indirect 1,145-mile route to the German capital, much of it at low-level, and still carry a full bomb load it was decided that the RAF would take part. Three No.105 Squadron aircraft, led by Sqn Ldr R.W. Reynolds, flew at low-level until 30 miles south of Bremen, then climbed to 25,000 feet and at precisely 1100 hours, when Goering was scheduled to start his speech, they laid a trail of bombs across Berlin. The Mosquitoes had been tracked and in mounting confusion German radio announced a postponement just as the bomb explosions started. The aircraft returned safely just as three No. 139 Squadron aircraft were despatched, their crews briefed to interrupt Goebbels. This time the defences were ready and one Mosquito was shot down, but the missions remained a propaganda success and

No.139 Squadron was completely equipped with Mosquitoes early in 1943, DZ515/XD-M being delivered in March. (Author's collection).

gave a much needed boost to No.2 Group.

That same night came another 'first' when H2S-fitted Pathfinder Stirlings and Halifaxes of No.7 and 35 Squadrons led the way to Hamburg. The city was an ideal target for the new equipment, coastlines and rivers being the most easily identifiable features on the display, but set failure and poor definition were problems with early Mk.1 H2S and the crews suffered both in full measure during this raid – which was not a success. Three nights later, on 2/3 February a No.7 Squadron Stirling was shot down by a night fighter and the Germans salvaged the set and learnt its secrets. It was inevitable that this would happen but unlucky that it occurred so quickly for it gave them an early opportunity to develop a jammer and a homer, the latter code-named *Naxos*.

On 4/5 February 156 out of the 188 aircraft despatched successfully bombed Turin, causing widespread damage. They were accompanied over the Alps by four Pathfinder Lancasters which carried on to the port of La Spezia to test a 4,000-lb bomb fitted with a new proximity fuze. It was designed to detonate a few hundred feet above the ground and thus increase blast damage, but its effectiveness proved hard to judge.

It was hoped that H2S would not only aid navigation when outside *Gee* cover, but also be useful for blind bombing as serviceability improved and crews gained confidence in it. An early opportunity to demonstrate its potential came on 11/12 February when the Pathfinders found complete cloud cover over Wilhelmshaven and had to 'skymark' using flares released on H2S target information. Everything worked perfectly, resulting in accurate marking and effective Main Force bombing, helped by a direct hit on the naval ammunition depot at Mariensiel which exploded causing widespread devastation. But it was a 'false dawn', similar attacks later in the month being failures. A panacea marking aid had still to be discovered! However, despite this setback, Main Force crews were instructed to bomb the TIs rather than try and identify the target themselves, a sure indication that the Pathfinders had graduated from a target-finding to a target-marking organization!

Meanwhile No.2 Group was in turmoil. All three Boston squadrons were stood down on 15 February, most of their crews being sent to North Africa, where Blenheim Vs had suddenly been replaced by Bostons, and then, at the end of the month the Venturas of Nos.21, 464 and 487 Squadrons and Mitchells of No.98 Squadron were involved in the large-scale Exercise *Spartan*. For over a fortnight the Mosquitoes of Nos.105 and 139 Squadrons were No.2 Group's only operational aircraft.

Another heavy attack was made on Berlin at the

beginning of March and the city maintained its reputation for being a difficult target, Pathfinders' H2S failing to 'print' any detail of built-up areas. By chance the Telefunken works was hit and the H2S set 'captured' on 2/3 February was destroyed. But fate plays many tricks, the Germans recovering a practically intact set from a No.35 Squadron Halifax which crashed in Holland the same night, and their examination of the equipment suffered little delay!

On 3 March an outstanding raid by nine Mosquitoes of No.139 Squadron led by Wg Cdr P. Shand was made on the important molybdenum mine at Knaben, Norway, To confuse the defenders the crews attacked in two waves, the first low-level, the second in a shallow dive. The ploy was successful in that the mine was badly damaged, but one aircraft was shot down by Fw190s, maintaining the high average loss rate of 7.5%. It was a rate worrying for advocates of the unarmed aircraft, though it was more a function of the small numbers of aircraft employed and the difficult targets involved than poor tactics – and the crews were now getting results.

Harris had carefully husbanded his forces through the winter while engaged on maritime 'diversions', content to let the Command gain experience with the new equipment while experimenting with target-marking. But by March 1943 he was ready to start the sustained attack on Germany that *Pointblank* required, and which he was convinced would break the fighting resolve of that country. Aircraft deliveries had built up, allowing squadron establishments to be increased to 27, and by delaying the 'declaration' of aircraft until mid-day availability was increased because a better serviceability estimate could be given.

Berlin was tempting but the Ruhr was the obvious choice because blind marking could be provided by *Oboe* and raids could be made under the cover of darkness. However, it would have been fatal to allow the Germans to concentrate 'flak' and fighter defence forces in the Ruhr by ignoring the rest of the Continent, and 40% of operations continued to be on targets scattered across Europe, including Berlin. In practice they did reinforce Ruhr defences but it could have been much worse!

With the size of the Groups expanding steadily AOC's found it increasingly difficult to exercise operational control over their stations, and in March 1943 the 'Operational Base' system was formulated. A Base consisted of a parent station, commanded by an Air Commodore, and one or two sub-stations. One, sometimes two, squadrons were housed on each airfield, full administrative and technical backing being the responsibility of the Base. A few of these Base HQ stations were pre-war brick-built permanent stations but most were standard wartime heavy

This Ventura II of No.464 Squadron was a survivor; 20 'ops' was good going on No.2 Group daylight raids over the Continent. (Fox Photos 294711).

bomber airfields similar to their satellites. Three runways, the main one approximately 6,000 feet in length and the other two 4,800 feet, were laid out in a triangular pattern, a 50-foot-wide perimeter track encircling the airfield. Dispersals were scattered about, aircraft only going into hangars for major servicing. Communal sites were spread haphazardly around the surrounding countryside up to a mile away from the main camp, and were in general both uncomfortable and inconvenient. In contrast Messes, though just large huts, were usually pleasant and friendly places – just as well for many camps were very isolated. On 16 September Bomber Command directed that the Bases should be numbered, the first digit indicating the Group, the second identifying the base; e.g. Linton-on-Ouse became No.62 Base.

Other changes affected personnel more directly. At the beginning of the war a tour was 200 'operational' hours but following studies it was limited to 30 completed sorties, and because of the effects of battle stress, 40 became the age limit for operational aircrew. A tour-expired crew was split up and 'rested' at a training unit or on 'desk jobs' for at least six months, after which aircrew could be ordered back for a second tour embracing 20 operations. Survivors of two tours were not required to fly again on operations though some did, just as some volunteered to stay on 'ops' after the first 30 rather than face instructional duties. The first six operations, while gaining the experience that no amount of training could provide, remained the most dangerous but the survival rate of the first complete tour did improve. In 1942 only three crews in 10 survived, from 1943 onwards it was some 50% – not good, but better – a combination of improved aircraft, aids and training!

The Battle of the Ruhr, as Harris so aptly called it, opened early in March, though he was required to expend effort on the U-Boat pens for a further month. Some 600 aircraft were now available, four-fifths of them four-engined bombers, and the numbers continued to increase as the battle progressed. A significant addition to No. 8 Group was No.1409 Flight, formed on 31 March by the transfer of eight Mosquitoes from No.521 Squadron, Coastal Command, to carry out *Pampa* weather flights exclusively for Bomber Command. The addition of the aircraft was balanced out by the transfer of No.271 Squadron to Transport Command on 25 March 1943.

These pre-raid meteorological sorties, pioneered by No.105 Squadron, resulted in much improved forecasts and together with the steadily improving marking by *Oboe* Mosquitoes, lifted the morale of Main Force crews, who at last could see real results – results which made the heavy casualties sustained more bearable.

The Battle of the Ruhr officially opened on 5/6 March when 442 aircraft were despatched to Essen. The marking was good, a number of TIs falling into the Krupps complex, and the results excellent, target photographs indicating that 153 crews had dropped their bombs within three miles of the aiming point. It was Essen which took the most attacks with Duisberg a close second, while Bochum, Cologne, Dortmund, Düsseldorf, Geilenkircken, Krefeld, Mülheim and Wuppertal were all heavily attacked during the 24 major raids despatched in the four months covering the Ruhr offensive. During the same period another 15 major attacks were made on towns as far apart as Aachen in the west, Stettin in the north-east, Pilsen in Czechoslovakia and Turin in Italy. In all, 18,506 sorties were despatched from which 827 aircraft failed to return; a casualty rate of 5% (not including crashes in the UK). Almost without exception the *Oboe*-marked Ruhr attacks were successful and really affected German industrial output for the first time, while raids outside *Oboe* cover were generally failures. There were spectacular slices of luck of course, the destruction of a secret stores complex in woods south-west of Berlin on 27/28 March being a case in point. The bombing concentration on the area was so good that the Germans concluded it was the target – and were impressed!

No.2 Group Venturas re-joined Mosquitoes on operations on 15 March when 11 aircraft of No.21

Squadron bombed La Pleine airfield in Brittany while operating with a No.10 Group *Circus*, but Mitchells were still non-operational and the Boston squadrons were working up with new aircraft and crews. Venturas were despatched in large numbers on occasion, 60 on 4 April when an airfield, a shipyard and railway installations were attacked, but they were unwieldy aircraft, unpleasant to fly and not fast enough for the type of operation forced upon No.2 Group – in short, they were heartily disliked by their crews.

A particularly heavy attack was made on Kiel on 4/5 April when 577 aircraft were despatched, but it was not very successful, increasingly sophisticated decoy fires and 'markers' being blamed for the dispersed bombing. A medium-weight attack on La Spezia in northern Italy on the 13/14th caused heavy damage in the dock area, but it was particularly noteworthy because for the first time the crews of three damaged Lancasters flew on to recently captured airfields in North Africa, rather than face the hazardous return crossing of the Alps.

On the same night No.2 Group tried a new tactic, six Mosquitoes of No.105 Squadron carrying out high-level 'nuisance' raids on Bremen, Hamburg and Wilhelmshaven. These were the first non-*Oboe* Mosquito night operations, soon to be strengthened by No.139 Squadron.

Large-scale minelaying was carried out, 160 aircraft being sent out on 27/28 April when 458 mines were laid off Biscay and Brittany ports and around the Frisian Islands. The next night 207 aircraft were despatched, 593 mines being laid off Heligoland, in the entrance to Hamburg docks and the difficult waters of the Little and Great Belts around the Danish island of Funen. Twenty-two aircraft were missing from the operation – nearly 11% of the force and the heaviest losses while minelaying during the war.

In the midst of all this activity came *Chastise*, the famous Ruhr operation using a weapon specially developed by Dr B.N. Wallis and codenamed *Upkeep*. The story of the Dams raid has been recounted in great detail many times and here a brief factual record will suffice. The idea of attacking the dams, which provided hydro-electric power and water for much of the Ruhr, was not new. It had been under consideration by the Air Ministry since 1938 and in June 1940 the C-in-C Bomber Command had written: 'I am given to understand that almost all the industrial activity of the Ruhr depends upon the water contained in and supplied by the Möhne Dam, and that if it was destroyed, not only would most of the industry in the

Lancaster III ED817 during the Upkeep *trials. Though coded AJ-C of No.617 Squadron, it remained a reserve aircraft. (via J.D. Oughton).*

Ruhr be brought to a standstill, but very great havoc would be wrought throughout the length of the water course!' Rightly or wrongly this view was widely supported, the problem was the lack of a suitable weapon. Barnes Wallis, a brilliant scientist interested in weapons, evolved a rotating mine which in theory would work, and after trials using a Wellington proved the concept early in 1943 the Air Ministry's scepticism evaporated. Portal advocated that full-scale trials should be carried out, but Harris, bombarded with wild schemes of all sorts, was firmly against the project. In mid-March he was bluntly told that the Dams operation was 'on' and that 20 Lancasters were being modified to carry the 9,250-lb weapon, and to provide a means of rotating it at a pre-determined speed.

Detailed planning started immediately, for if the dams on the rivers Möhne, Sorpe and Eder were to be full when attacked time was extremely short. AVM the Hon Sir Ralph A. Cochrane, AOC No.5 Group, was ordered by Harris to form a special squadron, provisionally known as 'X', and personally selected Wg Cdr G. Gibson as CO. Gibson was told he could choose his crews from volunteers, none of whom knew what they were letting themselves in for. Established at Scampton on 21 March 'X' Squadron became No.617 Squadron six days later and the crews underwent six weeks of intensive training on standard Lancasters. The weapon had to be dropped at exactly 60 feet above the water, 400-450 yards from the dam wall at a ground speed of 220 mph – an accuracy not required of crews before or since. The special aircraft with cut-away bomb doors and electro-hydraulic weapon rotation gear started arriving late in April, together with inert training weapons. Filled *Upkeeps* arrived during the night of 13/14 May, and with top-level approval for *Chastise* granted it was obvious that the operation was imminent. With the weather forecast favourable the decision was taken to go on the night of 16/17 May, the targets (most crews expected it to be the *Tirpitz*) being revealed at the briefing for the first time. The plan was for nine aircraft to go to the Möhne Dam, five to the Sorpe and five more, taking off two hours later, were to act as an airborne reserve filling in as instructed by the AOC No.5 Group. The aircraft left the English coast at low-level and stayed low throughout the operation. One struck the sea and returned without its weapon, five were either shot down or crashed *en route*, and another was so badly damaged by 'flak' that the crew had to turn back. The Möhne Dam was breached by the fifth aircraft to attack, flown by the deputy leader, Flt Lt H.M. Young, but it did not collapse until after Flt Lt D.J.H. Maltby's attack. Gibson and Young then accompanied the three crews still with weapons to the Eder Dam some 40

miles away. It proved difficult to find and equally difficult to attack but both Flt Lt D.J. Shannon and Plt Off L.G. Knight hit it and it was spectacularly breached. The Sorpe Dam was also attacked by two crews but it withstood the onslaught, while a crew from the reserves ordered to the Ennepe Dam (also referred to as the Schelme, the name of the river on which it stands) may have dropped their *Upkeep* on the Bever, some five miles to the south-west. Three Lancasters were shot down after they had attacked, bringing the total to eight out of the 19 despatched. Grievous losses, but not surprising in view of the extremely hazardous nature of the operation, the crews having misty conditions to contend with as well as the defences.

Although not as disastrous for the Germans as had been anticipated, the devastation caused was considerable, and there is no doubt that *Chastise* was a success from that viewpoint alone. It was also a great feat of airmanship which had a considerable uplifting effect on the British population as a whole, the squadron becoming famous as the 'Dambusters'. Without doubt the successful breaching of the Möhne Dam in the face of intense 'flak' was at least in part due to Gibson flying alongside the attacking aircraft and drawing the fire. He was awarded the VC for leadership, determination and valour of the highest order. Another 34 decorations were awarded to survivors.

The navigational skill demonstrated by the 'Dambusters' was exceptional, reliant as they were on a mixture of 'dead reckoning' and map reading. Many Main Force crews, even with the assistance of *Gee*-fixing over 300 miles from the English coast, strayed off track and became easy prey for gun concentrations and night fighters. Losses were often much higher on the homeward journey, sometimes double, due to

Lancaster III ED932/G of No.617 Squadron, the famous 'Dambusters', carrying the Upkeep *weapon, May 1943. This was Gibson's aircraft on the raid. (RAF Museum P11916).*

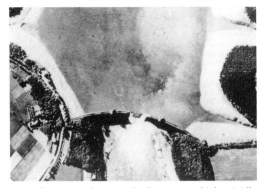

A well-known photograph, but one which vividly shows the result of the attack on the Möhne Dam during the night of 16/17 May 1943. (British Official).

lapses of concentration and a tendency to leave the briefed track early and make straight for base. The dangers of such actions were pointed out, but often fell on young and very deaf ears with disastrous results.

Boston crews of No.107 Squadron resumed operations on 1 May with an unsuccessful attempt to disrupt railway communications at Caen. They failed again the next day when attacking the Ismuiden steelworks, though Ventura crews who accompanied them were luckier. However, raised spirits were soon dashed by the events of 3 May when 12 Venturas of No.487 Squadron, escorted by three Spitfire squadrons, were sent to the Amsterdam power station as a diversion for an attack on the Royal Dutch Steel Works by six Bostons. The Boston crews missed the steel works, badly damaging an adjoining power station, and lost one aircraft, but a mistimed No.11

Group *Rodeo* sweep alerted enemy defences and the 11 Venturas (one had turned back) ran into a 'swarm of hornets' – experienced fighter pilots attending a conference at Schipol. The escorting Spitfires were overwhelmed, and the Venturas were picked off one by one. Nine were shot down before reaching the target, and another badly damaged. Only the leader, Sqn Ldr L.H. Trent, was left and he just had time to see his bombs overshoot the power station before coming under intense fire from both 'flak' and fighters. Reduced to a wreck the Ventura entered an uncontrollable spin before exploding, hurling Trent and his navigator, Flt Lt V. Phillips, into space. Both became PoWs and the full story only became clear after they were repatriated. On 1 March 1946 Trent was awarded the VC for determined leadership and devotion to duty.

Early in the spring of 1943, Air Chief Marshal Sir Arthur Tedder, AOC-in-C Mediterranean, asked for a six-week loan of three Wellington squadrons for night attacks on enemy airfields and communications prior to the invasion of Sicily. As usual Harris was against such a plan but was overruled by Portal, and with the whole-hearted agreement of Air Marshal Harold Edwards, AOC-in-C RCAF Overseas, 60 Wellingtons of Nos.420, 424 and 425 Squadrons departed for the Middle East on 16 May. Tedder managed to hang on to them until the Salerno landings, the Wing flying its last operation on 5 October 1943. The squadrons then returned to No.6 Group and re-equipped with Halifaxes.

Mitchells were finally deemed ready for operations early in May and, after recalls on the 7th and 11th, attacked railway communications at Boulogne on the

Mosquito IV DK300 flew with No.109 Squadron, a No.8 Group Pathfinder unit, during 1943. (RAFM P19850).

13th, losing one aircraft. Ten days later the Venturas of a rebuilt No.487 Squadron resumed operations with an attack on a power station/coking plant at Zeebrugge, bombs falling on adjoining railway yards, but it was the Mosquitoes which were demonstrating their worth at last, though losses from 'flak' were still high. Nos.105 and 139 Squadrons were regularly sending small numbers of high-flying Mosquitoes over Germany, nine going to Berlin on 16/17 May, but more spectacular was a low-level 'special' to Jena on 27 May for an attack on the Zeiss optical instruments factory. Fourteen Mosquitoes from the two units were despatched, 11 reaching the target 48 miles south-west of Leipzig and 500 miles from the coast, just as darkness fell. The bombing was accurate but two aircraft had collided *en route*, another was shot down and two more crash-landed on return – a total loss of five aircraft and crews (35%).

The Ruhr offensive continued, one of the most successful attacks being on a new target, Wuppertal, on 29/30 May when over 700 aircraft were despatched. Marking was very accurate and so was the Main Force bombing, resulting in over 80% of the old town being completely destroyed, largely by fire.

On 31 May, as a last flourish, 30 Venturas, 12 Mitchells and 12 Bostons were sent to attack targets in Holland and France. The next day No.2 Group, apart from the Mosquitoes of Nos.105 and 139 Squadrons, left Bomber Command. No.105 Squadron became the second No.8 Group *Oboe* unit alongside No.109, while No.139, much to the aircrews' annoyance, were 'retrained' for high-level 'nuisance' attacks, even though they had flown such operations mixed in with low-level work while in No.2 Group.

A Joint Planning Team had been formed to co-ordinate the efforts of the 8th Air Force and Bomber Command, and following the Washington Conference of May 1943 a revised *Pointblank* Directive was issued on 10 June. The objectives were not changed but priority was given to destroying the German fighter defence force – in service and in the factories. Harris did not believe, rightly, that his bombers could take on German fighters and remained sceptical about attacks on specific factories. He managed to successfully argue that there were legitimate factory targets in practically every German town and city, and that his operations should continue unabated and unchanged – but in doing so he brought controversy into the open.

Experimental raids continued at intervals, a secondary attack made on the night of 11/12 June being a case in point. The main target was Düsseldorf, but No.8 Group also sent 72 aircraft to Münster on an H2S radar and marker trial. It was very successful, the marking and bombing being both accurate and concentrated, lasting less than 10 minutes and overwhelming the civil defence organization. On 19/20 June the Schneider armament works and Breuil steelworks at Le Creusot were the main targets. Pathfinders dropped flares and Main Force crews were briefed to make two runs, dropping sticks of bombs each time. Unfortunately, crews were getting so used to bombing on TIs that many found it difficult to visually identify the target. The same problem even afflicted No.8 Group during a secondary attack on Montchanin power station the same night. H2S-equipped Pathfinders dropped flares for 26 Lancasters of the Group, but most crews mis-identified the target

Lancaster III DV156/VN-C of No.50 Squadron, almost certainly in North Africa in between the so-called 'shuttle' raids on Friedrichshafen (20/21 June) and La Spezia (23/34 June). (D. Grant).

and no bombs hit the transformer complex. H2S was still not the hoped for target finder!

The next night a special raid was mounted on the Zeppelin works (manufacturing *Würzburg* radar equipment) at Friedrichshafen on the shores of Lake Constance. The operation developed further the idea of a 'controller' pioneered by Gibson during the Dams raid, and was split into two distinct phases, the first involving Main Force crews aiming at Pathfinder target indicators, while the second used a technique being developed by No.5 Group, a timed run from a feature easily recognizable on the H2S indicator – in this case a prominent lakeside point. Despite problems caused by incorrect winds both methods produced reasonably accurate bombing, and German attempts to arrange an 'ambush' on the long return flight over France were thwarted by all 60 Lancasters flying on to North Africa. Three nights later the aircraft completed the first 'shuttle' raid, attacking La Spezia *en route* to Britain. No losses occurred on either operation.

Cologne received three heavy raids between 28/29 June and 8/9 July and despite indifferent weather and trouble with Oboe unserviceability, considerable damage was caused to industrial premises, over 5,000 people were killed and 350,000 made homeless. The Luftwaffe tried a new tactic on 3/4 July, using the light of flares, fires and searchlights to visually intercept the bombers for *Wilde Sau* (*Wild Boar*) single-seat fighters of JG300, and of the 30 bombers lost that night 12 went down over Cologne. Previously, night fighters operating on the so-called *Kammhuber Line* defence system had rarely been seen over the target, and crews were unused to such attacks – it was a disturbing innovation.

After some hesitation it was decided to retain No.617 Squadron and use it for independent No.5 Group precision attacks, despite Harris's well-known dislike of elite units. The squadron's first operation since the Dams raid was an attempt to disrupt troop and equipment reinforcements to the battle front in Sicily by attacking two railway transformer stations in northern Italy on 15/16 July. Twelve Lancasters took part but the attack made on these difficult targets was a failure. No.5 Group tried again the next night, selecting two more stations, one of which was hit. In both cases the Lancasters carried on to North Africa, and 33 of them bombed Leghorn docks on the way home on 24/25 July.

Long before the Battle of the Ruhr was over (with an air attack on Aachen on 13/14 July 1943), Harris was considering his next move and on 27 May ordered his Group Commanders to start preparing for Operation *Gomorrah*, an assault on Hamburg, Germany's second-largest city. Already the subject of 98 not very successful raids, it was heavily industrialized, but the British plan was to attack the port and factory complexes indirectly by paralyzing the city. For the first time the USAAF's 8th Air Force was invited to join in a Bomber Command offensive with follow-up daylight attacks, but after 252 sorties the Americans withdrew because dense smoke prevented visual sighting of their briefed targets, and they would not officially countenance area bombing.

The 'Battle of Hamburg' opened on 24/25 July

Well-known as the Ruhr Express, KB700, the first Canadian-built Lancaster, joined No.405 Squadron, RCAF, at Gransden Lodge in late 1943 for Pathfinder duties, but was soon transferred to No.419 Squadron. (DND PL26189).

AVM D.C.T. Bennett, AOC No.8 Group and Gp Capt J.E. Fauquier, OC No. 405 Squadron, in front of the Ruhr Express. (via Chaz Bowyer Collection).

force, undoubtedly due to the use of *Window* for the first time. *Window* was a strip of aluminium foil of precise length, which when dropped in large numbers produced hundreds of false returns, swamping ground-controlled interception radars. It had been ready for use since April 1942, but at the instigation of the AOC-in-C Fighter Command, Air Chief Marshal Sir Sholto Douglas, had not been used because of the feared effect on Allied defences if copied. Against this, Bomber Command had lost 2,200 aircraft during the embargo and it is reasonable to suggest that at least some would have been saved had *Window* been employed.

Harris had intended to return to Hamburg the next night, but fearing that the city would still be obscured by smoke and taking maximum advantage of the disruption caused by *Window*, he sent Bomber Command to Essen instead. Marked for the first time by *Oboe* Mk.II-equipped Mosquitoes of No.105 Squadron, the area of the city containing the Krupps armament factories was badly damaged. The pressure was kept up on Hamburg by six Mosquitoes of No.139 Squadron during the nights of 25/26 and 26/27 July before the second major attack was mounted, one of No.83 Squadron's Lancasters carrying Bgdr Gen F.L. Anderson, Commander of the American 8th Bomber Command, who was keen to gain first-hand knowledge of night operations. Almost exactly the same number of aircraft bombed the target as on the

with the despatch of 790 aircraft. Well outside *Oboe* range, the marking relied on a mixture of H2S and visual identification of the distinctive river and dockyards layout. It was largely successful and considerable damage was done even though a significant 'creep-back' developed. The attack was over in 50 minutes and losses were light, 1.5% of the

One of the last units to use Stirlings on Main Force bomber operations was No.149 Squadron at Lakenheath, among them EF411/K. (RAFM P14534)

first attack, but the Stirlings carried more incendiaries because a change in routeing increased the distance and loads had to be adjusted. This was not the main reason for the horrific events of the night, however, a long dry spell combining with particularly good marking and concentrated Main Force bombing providing the catalyst for a 'firestorm'. It started with a large number of individual fires amongst the densely-packed tenements on the eastern side of the city centre. Roads were blocked by the rubble of destroyed buildings and the emergency services could not reach the fires which joined up and started drawing in air. The resulting 'wind' increased to gale force and spread the fires still further. They raged out of control for three hours, only subsiding when all combustible material had been consumed. Some 40,000 were killed, many through lack of oxygen, and two-thirds of the population, some 1,200,000, abandoned the city.

No.139 Squadron visited Hamburg yet again on 28/29 July and the following night came the third major attack. The marking, entirely by H2S, was less accurate on this occasion, but the subsequent bombing, assisted by the use of *Zephyrs* (a target wind obtained by averaging out winds found by selected crews and broadcast to the Main Force), was very effective and considerable damage resulted in the outer suburbs. Two nights later came a devastating *Oboe*-marked attack on the Ruhr town of Remscheid which resulted in an estimated 80% of the buildings being destroyed or damaged, and for a short while Bomber Command's offensive appeared unstoppable. On 2/3 August Harris returned to Hamburg. A force of 740 aircraft was despatched but heavy thunderstorms over Germany caused chaos. Many crews turned back and very few reached the target. It was a complete failure, made worse by the loss of 30 aircraft (4.1%) against the 57 (2.4%) during the first three Hamburg raids of the series when 2,353 sorties had been flown and approximately 7,100 tons of bombs were dropped

Halifax B.V LK640/SE-Q of No.431 Squadron, RCAF, under maintenance at Tholthorpe in August 1943. (DND PL26140).

on the city. The effect of the Hamburg attacks on the Germans was considerable, for it appeared that *Window* would defeat both radar-predicted bombs and night fighters as well as the control system, and it was the general opinion that the destruction of another six large towns would cripple the country's ability to sustain the war. The confidence of the German leaders was badly shaken, but they recovered remarkably quickly, increasing the use of *Wilde Sau* and re-organizing the defences to minimize the problems caused by the metallic strips. In any case, it was beyond the capability of Bomber Command to repeat the Hamburg scale of damage, much of it due to an unusual combination of circumstances, and the apparent opportunity to shorten the war soon passed.

Early in August the Air Ministry ordered Harris to lay on a series of attacks on Italian cities in an attempt to speed up surrender – for Italy was war-weary. Lancasters of Nos.1, 5 and 8 Groups attacked Genoa, Milan and Turin on 7/8 August and it was these cities that also took the brunt of five follow-up raids, the one on Milan on 12/13 August being particularly heavy. On the same night Turin was attacked by a smaller force and two Stirlings were lost. Another, already badly damaged by 'flak' as it approached the city, was fired on by a trigger-happy rear gunner. The navigator was killed instantly and the pilot, F/Sgt A.L. Aaron of No.218 Squadron, badly injured. Made as comfortable as possible between the wing spars, he insisted of being kept informed of the situation while F/Sgt Larden, the bomb aimer/co-pilot flew the aircraft south. Aaron lapsed into unconsciousness but four hours later, as the effects of morphine wore off, he crawled forward and took control for a landing at Bone, North Africa. With a shattered jaw and only one usable arm, he could only communicate by head movements and had difficulty in positioning the aircraft for an approach. After several 'overshoots' and with fuel running low, Larden had to forcibly take over and succeeded in making a rough but safe belly landing. Aaron was rushed to hospital only to die nine hours later, his chances of survival undoubtedly much reduced by trying to help his crew despite great pain and shock from his appalling injuries. He was posthumously awarded the VC, while Larden received a well-deserved CGM.

On 16/17 August Lancasters made another attack on Turin, the last by Bomber Command on an Italian city. The next night Harris mounted Operation *Hydra*, an operation long in the planning, which broke several of his own rules, for it was a full-scale assault at long-range on a precision target in moonlight! Rumours of fearsome weapons had been rife for years and more recently the German people had been promised that revenge in the form of the long-range bombardment of

No.426 Squadron, RCAF, was the first Canadian unit to be equipped with Lancasters, including DS713/OW-J, a comparatively rare Hercules-powered Mk.II with enlarged bomb doors. (E.C.G. Jones)

Britain would soon be theirs. Following good intelligence work and luck there was now positive proof of the existence of such weapons and their connection with the experimental station at Peenemünde, an isolated spot on the Baltic coast, close to what had been the Polish border. The threat was very real and Bomber Command was ordered to destroy the test facilities and kill the scientists on the site. A conference held on 7 July determined the outline plan and agreed that the whole site had to be destroyed during one attack – it would be too well defended afterwards for any subsequent raid to be successful. The site was long and thin, and the plan envisaged three aiming points: the living quarters, the rocket factory and the experimental station itself. No.8 Group was to carry out most of the marking with, for the first time on a full-scale operation, a 'Master Bomber', Gp Capt J.H. Searby, controlling the Main Force. No.5 Group squadrons, attacking last, were expected to be hampered by smoke screens, so they were allowed to employ their timed run technique, using Ruden Island to the north of the target.

Some 600 Lancasters, Halifaxes and Stirlings of Nos.1, 3, 4, 5, 6 and 8 Groups took off on the raid, taking the route usually used by Berlin-bound aircraft, and eight Mosquitoes did visit the city on a successful attempt to draw night fighters away from Peenemünde. Some marking mistakes were made and it appeared that No.5 Group's timed runs had much to recommend if an easily identifiable starting point was available. Forty aircraft were lost, mainly from Nos.5 and 6 Groups, still in the area when night fighters arrived in force, some of them Bf110s fitted with *Schrage Musik* upward-firing cannon. The raid was a success, much of the experimental station being destroyed and some 180 Germans killed, several of them senior scientists. Unfortunately the foreign workers' camp was also hit and between 500-600 were killed.

A series of heavy raids employing between 600-700 aircraft followed, those marked using *Oboe* proving generally successful while others, despite the increasing fitment of H2S in Main Force aircraft, were usually disappointing. Berlin remained one of the most difficult targets, the extremely heavy defences usually resulting in 'creep-back'; 30 miles along the approach route on 1 September! Most towns were chosen because they housed aircraft or equipment factories, but other targets were also visited, such as the gun positions at Boulogne on 8/9 September. This attack, code-named *Starkey*, was notable for the inclusion of five B-17s of the 422nd Bomb Squadron, USAAF, part of a very mixed force of 260 aircraft. Despite the use of *Oboe* the target was poorly marked, resulting in equally poor bombing.

On 14/15 September eight Lancasters of No.617 Squadron armed with the new 12,000-lb HC bomb* took off to attack the Dortmund-Ems canal but were recalled. They went again the next night and though visibility was poor, two crews managed to bomb the canal near Ladbergen – but did not breach it. Four Lancasters were shot down and another crashed, but despite these heavy losses the squadron was attacking the Antheor railway viaduct on the Marseilles-Genoa line near Cannes the following night, accompanied by Lancasters of No.619 Squadron. The crews attacked from 300 feet but failed to hit the viaduct, only damaging the line. Understandably this succession of failures was taken as proof that low-level operations by heavy bombers at night were not cost-effective. They were abandoned and No.617 Squadron was retrained as a high-level bombing unit, but still employed on specialist weapon attacks.

It had been noted that the experimental Münster operation of 11 June had attracted more night fighters than the diversions by No.139 Squadron Mosquitoes, and it was decided to try 'spoof' raids. The first was on 22/23 September when 21 Lancasters and eight

*See Chapter 11

The V-Weapon research station at Peenemünde was attacked by a strong force of Lancasters, Halifaxes and Stirlings on 17/18 August 1943. It was not a completely successful raid, but some sites like this one were badly damaged. (British Official)

Mosquitoes of No.8 Group went to Oldenburg, and it appeared to be successful, losses on the main Hanover attack being a comparatively low 3.7%, while there were no losses at all on the 'spoof'. Such tactics could not be used routinely, however, especially on distant targets, because the longer the flight the more obvious it became which was the Main Force and the destination. Such a target was Munich, attacked on 2/3 October by some 290 Lancasters accompanied by two B-17s of the 422nd BS (both dropping 10 500-lb GP bombs). The raid was only partially successful because it used No.5 Group's timed run techniques and unfortunately crews could not identify the briefed start point, the Wurmsee Lake. The 422nd BS took part in its third and last Bomber Command operation on 4/5 October when Frankfurt was the target, and one of the three B-17s was lost. Good marking resulted in good bombing, the city being extensively damaged. The same night Ludwigshafen was attacked by Lancasters as a diversion, and the first operational trial of *G-H* blind bombing equipment (basically *Oboe* in reverse) was carried out by a Mosquito over Aachen – unsuccessfully.

Because No.101 Squadron's Lancasters were low on the H2S installation list, they were chosen to carry *Jostle* which was capable of automatically jamming German R/T frequencies. But the equipment was delayed and *Airborne Cigar* (ABC), which required an operator capable of understanding German* was fitted instead. By 6 October over half the squadron's aircraft had the equipment installed and it was first used operationally on 7/8 October when Stuttgart was attacked. (One source suggests that the first operational use was on 22 September during a raid on Hanover, but it is thought that this, and a follow-up on the 23rd when the single *ABC*-equipped aircraft despatched was lost, were actually familiarization flights.) At least eight *ABC* Lancasters, spaced at 10-mile intervals in the stream, were required to cover a raid and the equipment's effectiveness was not really put to the test that night, the German fighter controller being confused by a Mosquito diversionary raid on Munich so that fighters only reached the Stuttgart area as the last of the all-Lancaster force was leaving. *ABC* accompanied all subsequent major attacks, however, and is generally agreed to have proved its worth.

The attack on Hanover the following night was also successful, the city receiving its heaviest pounding of the war despite the fighter controller correctly assessing it as the major target, and not Bremen which received the attentions of a large diversionary force. The Hanover raid was also noteworthy for being the last in which Main Force Wellingtons (26 from Nos.300 (Polish) and 432 (RCAF) Squadrons) took part.

Production difficulties delayed the widespread introduction of H2S but by early October 70 Stirlings, 155 Halifaxes and 225 Lancasters had been equipped. Attrition had already accounted for 149 of them – a sobering indication of the losses being suffered. It was to be a long time before the majority of aircraft had H2S and the associated *Fishpond* warning device fitted.

In addition to *Oboe* marking, small numbers of Mosquito bombers continued to operate nightly, sometimes on diversionary attacks for the Main Force, more often singly on 'nuisance' raids. Their

*See Chapter 9

numbers gradually increased, as many as 28 going to Berlin, Branweiler, Cologne and Emden on 20/21 October when an all-Lancaster Main Force went to Leipzig. Such diversionary tactics often worked well, but so did decoy TIs; an increasing problem as they became more sophisticated. Almost invariably some Main Force crews attacked them, and if fires developed more joined in.

The most devastating attack since the Hamburg firestorm was made on 22/23 October – the target Kassel. All three Henschel factories in the town were badly damaged, a major set back for the V-1 'flying bomb' programme. At 43, aircraft losses were severe (7.6%) but not unduly high for a target so far into Germany, the Luftwaffe controller correctly determining the attack on Frankfurt as a diversion.

On 3/4 November Lancaster IIs from No.115 Squadron, the first No.3 Group unit with these Hercules-powered aircraft, joined others from No.6 Group in the first large-scale operational testing of the *G-H* blind bombing aid. They attempted to bomb a precision target, the Mannesmann steel works, while a general area raid on Düsseldorf was in progress. For various reasons, including equipment failure, only 15 of the 38 Lancaster IIs reached the works, but the attack could be described as successful for several fabrication sheds were burnt out. During the general Düsseldorf raid the Lancaster of No.61 Squadron flown by Flt Lt W. Reid was attacked by a Bf110 night fighter over the Dutch coast and the cockpit windscreen exploded in a shower of perspex. Reid's face was cut to shreds by slivers of steel and perspex fragments, but ascertaining that the rest of the crew were uninjured he continued the sortie. Shortly

A Lancaster can be seen against the fierce incendiary fires burning around the plainly identifiable city centre of Hanover in this night attack photograph taken during 8/9 October 1943. (British Official)

afterwards the aircraft was raked by cannon fire from a Fw190. The navigator was killed, the wireless operator fatally wounded, and Reid was again injured. Judging it more dangerous to turn back in the face of the bomber stream than continue, Reid calmly navigated by the stars until he identified the target and the bombs were dropped. Heavy flak over the Dutch coast outbound was little more than a nuisance for the desperately tired crew, much worse was the sudden failure of all four engines. The Flight Engineer quickly rectified the situation and they continued on their way, Reid lapsing into semi-consciousness and allowing the Flight Engineer to fly the aircraft. Reviving slightly as they crossed the coast and seeing a cone of searchlights indicating an airfield, Reid made an approach with the bomb aimer behind him ready to grab the controls if he fainted. The damaged undercarriage collapsed as the aircraft touched down –

A late-series Halifax II srs 1A with low-drag nose, four-gun dorsal turret and enlarged 'square' fins. HR926/TL-L of No.35 Squadron went missing from a raid on Kassel 23 October 1943. (RAFM P12018)

at Shipham, a USAAF base. It was the AOC himself, AVM the Hon R.A. Cochrane, who extracted the details from Reid in hospital and recommended the survivors for awards. He was also able to tell Reid that he was to receive the VC for, amongst other things, his 'tenacity and devotion to duty beyond praise'.

On 11/12 November came another attack on the Cannes marshalling yards which went badly wrong, most of the bombs dropped by Main Force Halifax crews hitting residential areas despite good marking, while 10 No.617 Squadron Lancasters using the new Stabilizing Automatic Bomb Sight (SABS) for an attack on the nearby Antheor Viaduct with 12,000-lb bombs missed completely. Six days later came a comparatively successful, though light, raid on Ludwigshafen, but Harris was more concerned with the next phase of his battle, convinced that Bomber Command was now ready to take on Berlin in spite of worsening weather and a re-organized German night fighter force.

* * * * *

The period covered by this chapter was one of consolidation as new equipment and techniques, particularly in the marking field, were introduced. *Oboe* had proved an outstanding success, but even with the third set of ground stations in operation only 18 aircraft per hour could use the system, and the Mk.1 version was becoming susceptible to jamming. H2S proved a mixed blessing, for the Germans were now able to track bomber streams using the equipment's transmissions. They also triggered

Identification Friend or Foe (IFF) which crews continued to use over Continental Europe despite firm instructions to the contrary. Out of *Oboe* range, bombing was still erratic. No.5 Group's timed run system could not be used universally, and *G-H*, though promising, was suffering teething troubles. On a less gloomy note, the Mk.XIV bomb-sight, now in general Main Force use was a great advance, and for specialist work SABS promised to be even better.

Harris could point with satisfaction to a strengthening of Bomber Command in both quantity and quality, and to some spectacular successes amongst the failures. Worryingly, German defences continued to improve despite the countermeasures being brought into service* and the Stirling gave much cause for concern. It had a significantly greater loss rate than the other four-engined bombers because its operational ceiling was some 8,000 feet lower, and orders were issued requiring Halifax and Lancaster crews to stay at 'Stirling' heights when operating with them. Unfortunately, when night fighters were active most of the bomber crews immediately climbed; a natural reaction, but short-sighted for it destroyed the protective cover of the 'stream'. Harris was entitled to feel vindicated over his attitude concerning taking on the German fighter force, for until long-range fighter escorts became available American losses had been horrendous, their claims exaggerated, and the results of their 'precision' bombing less than encouraging.

*See Chapter 9

'Nose art' was widespread in Bomber Command, as depicted on this Halifax II Srs 1A of No. 429 Squadron, RCAF, at Leeming on 22 November 1943. (DND PL261644)

CHAPTER 6

Berlin and *Overlord* 1943-1944

ON 3 NOVEMBER 1943 Harris wrote to the Prime Minister: 'We can wreck Berlin from end to end if the USAAF will come in on it. It may cost us 400-500 aircraft. It will cost Germany the war.' This was the sort of talk Churchill could not resist and despite American refusal to take part the RAF was authorized to launch another 'Battle of Berlin.'

The new offensive started on 18/19 November when 440 Lancasters and four Mosquitoes were despatched to a cloud-shrouded Berlin. The city was hit but not heavily, and losses were light at 2%, probably because the night fighters were busy with a large diversionary raid on Mannheim/Ludwigshafen

which lost 23 aircraft (5.8%). Here bombing was scattered due to cloud cover, but considerable damage was caused, especially to the Daimler-Benz factory, an indication of the progress made in both weight of attack and navigational accuracy – a year earlier the twin towns would probably have escaped altogether! Other improvements included Fog Investigation Dispersal Operation (FIDO), the installation at Graveley enabling four Halifaxes of No.35 Squadron returning from a failed attack on Leverkusen the following night to land safely despite thick fog – though it was a fearsome business, crews describing it as 'landing in Hades'.

An 8,000-lb Blockbuster *is positioned for loading in a Lancaster's bomb bay, December 1943. (IWM CH10941)*

Berlin was visited again on 22/23 November when 764 aircraft, including the first Canadian-built Lancaster Mk.X, were despatched. As usual the target was obscured by cloud but marking and bombing was correctly assessed as accurate, for this was the most effective raid on the city throughout the entire war. A swathe of destruction right across the central districts resulted, and the bad weather kept most German fighters on the ground so losses were fairly light for this target – 26 aircraft (3.4%). Five of them were Stirlings, 10% of the 50 despatched, and with losses consistently above 6% over the last four months the decision was taken to withdraw them from operations over Germany, though Stirling squadrons continued to bomb less well defended targets in France and to assist Wellington crews in the unglamorous but extremely important mining task. Plans were made to re-equip No.3 Group with Lancasters as quickly as possible, and two squadrons, Nos.196 and 620, were transferred to No.38 Group (via No.93 Group) for transport duties.

On the 23/24th Berlin was again the target, this time for 365 Lancasters, 10 Halifaxes and eight Mosquitoes. The latter dropped 'spoof' flares to divert the strong fighter defences, and broadcasts were made on fighter controller frequencies – all of which caused some confusion but did not prevent 20 Lancasters

being shot down. Despite the usual cloud cover, the use of sky markers and fires still burning from the previous night resulted in accurate bombing and much further damage.

Helped by the many crews who, regardless of instructions to the contrary, switched on their H2S on leaving the English coast, German controllers could now track the bomber stream from its start. In order to make their task more difficult indirect routeing was usually employed for the more distant targets, but for some reason this ploy was abandoned for the next batch of Berlin raids. The result was heavy losses, only marginally offset by the success of the gambit employed on 3/4 December when the 'heavies' flew directly towards Berlin, then suddenly turned for the real target of Leipzig leaving nine Mosquitoes to continue on to the 'Big City' taking most of the night fighter force with them. Such ploys could not be used too often and Harris soon turned his attention back to Berlin, an attack on 16/17 December being notable in that losses due to bad weather on return (29 Lancasters) were greater than the number (25) lost due to 'flak' damage or night fighters despite infiltration of the bomber stream over Holland, and at intervals all the way to the target.

That same night two precision attacks were made on small sites near Abbeville in northern France, one

No.199 Squadron continued as a Window *dropper into 1944. The Duke of Gloucester inspected the unit shortly before its transfer to No.100 Group in May of that year. (D. Lockett)*

of them by 26 Stirlings of No.3 Group, the other by nine Lancasters of No.617 Squadron. Both appeared unlikely targets for 'heavies' but were the first of many, part of concerted operations by the USAAF, the 2nd Tactical Air Force (TAF) and RAF Bomber Command against a new menace – the V-1 'flying bomb'. Armed with the knowledge that the missiles were being prepared for an assault on London, weeks of intense activity by photo-reconnaissance units, interpreters and intelligence agencies had finally identified the sites and worked out their purpose – now Operation *Crossbow* was launched to destroy them. The *Oboe* marking by Mosquitoes was good, but not good enough for such small targets, and it could be said that the 12,000-lb bombs dropped by the Lancasters were too accurate, none being further than 100 yards from the markers but causing no damage to the launching sites.

Crossbow operations continued but Bomber Command had little success and Wg Cdr G.L. Cheshire, recently appointed CO No.617 Squadron, became very unhappy with the marking by No.8 Group on these and other pinpoint targets. He started his own experiments and put them to the test on 4/5 January 1944 when 80 aircraft, mainly Stirlings but including eleven No.617 Squadron Lancasters, were sent to attack two *Crossbow* sites in the Pas de Calais

and another near Cherbourg. With Flt Lt Martin as his deputy, Cheshire dropped hooded flares at 12,000 feet and then dived to low-level and accurately marked the site allocated to the Lancasters. The 617 Squadron crews, using stabilized sights, dropped their 12,000-lb HC bombs squarely on the target which was virtually destroyed. It looked as if the answer had been found and further proof of the accuracy of the method was provided a month later, on 8/9 February, when 12 Lancasters from the squadron went to Limoges in the Haute-Vienne region of France 210 miles south of Paris, to attack the Gnome-Rhone aircraft engine works. To minimize risks to French civilians Cheshire flew low over the factory to warn workers, then dropped a cascade incendiary which was backed up by Martin using 'red spot' fire markers. After checking the marker accuracy Cheshire called in the rest of the crews who bombed from 10,000 ft with incredible precision, nine hitting the target. Production virtually ceased, and low-level marking continued to be a tactic employed by No.5 Group, though resisted by the Pathfinders of No.8 Group, and never used for large-scale Main Force operations. Pride and prejudice ran deep!

Main Force attacks continued at a steady rate, raids on Berlin being interspersed with other long-range targets to take advantage of the long winter nights,

The weather was often as much the enemy as the Germans. The Australians of Nos.463 and 467 Squadrons at Waddington must have found the winter of 1943/44 particularly hard to take. (RAF Waddington records)

No.8 Group expanded its light night bomber force steadily. A 4,000-lb Cookie *is shown being loaded into the 'bulged door' bay of black-painted Mosquito B.IV DZ637 of No.692 Squadron at Graveley during the spring of 1944. (Keystone Press)*

though the more uncertain weather could ruin an attack or face crews with difficult landing conditions, sometimes both. Losses due to night fighters also increased during the winter of 1943/44. *Window* had effectively destroyed the German 'box' system but paradoxically it liberated night fighter crews, because the controller could only direct them to the 'stream' and then leave it to their initiative. *Wilde Sau* fighters remained a potent force, especially over Berlin, but increasingly it was the *Zahme Sau (Tame Boar)* twin-engined, two-seat night fighters flying in the bomber 'stream' that did the real damage. Their new SN-2 AI

The morning briefing in No.8 Group Operations Room, Wyton 1944. From the left: J.Jukes, Ops research; Wg Cdr M.J. Thomas, Group Met Off; AVM Bennett, Gp Capt C.D.C. Boyce, SASO; Sqn Ldr W. Rathbone, Group Armament Off; and Duty Ops Off (back to camera).

Early 1944 and the excellent Hercules-powered Halifax B.III was appearing on squadrons. NA570/MP-P of No.76 Squadron is seen at Holme-on-Spalding Moor. (Gp Capt J.E. Pelly Fry via AST)

radar was unaffected by bomber countermeasures, and now that the Stirling had been withdrawn it was the Merlin-powered Halifax IIs and Vs which bore the brunt of casualties. These averaged 9.8% early in 1944 despite the diversionary raids and the efforts of No.100 Group*.

Meanwhile the Mosquito force continued to gain in strength and potency. No.692 Squadron, formed in No.8 Group on 1 January 1944, were equipped with specially modified Mosquito IVs capable of carrying a 4,000-lb bomb (first proposed in April 1943 but delayed by instability problems), the first operational drops being made on Düsseldorf during the night of 23/24 February. Together with Nos.139 and 627 Squadrons, the latter having been formed in November 1943, the new unit constituted the nucleus of the Light Night Striking Force (LNSF), a title coined by Bennett which stuck despite being disliked by Harris. No.139 Squadron was designated the marker squadron for the LNSF and No.8 Group turned to H2S for longer-range sorties, using it operationally for the first time in a Mosquito on 27 January 1944. Five days later H2S marking was used by a small force attacking Berlin, during which No.692 Squadron made its debut over the city.

Another attempt was made on the Antheor viaduct by No.617 Squadron on 12/13 February. The low-level marking technique was used, but did not work because of the difficult terrain and 'flak' damage to both Cheshire's and Martin's Lancasters. Two nights later, after resting his force for a fortnight, Harris sent 891 aircraft to Berlin, the largest number during the whole war. Despite the seemingly inevitable cloud cover and loss of 43 aircraft (4.8%) it was rated a

successful attack, considerable damage being caused.

Such losses were having an effect on bomber crews, the number of 'early returns' and bombs dropping short of the target to lighten the load, steadily increasing as the winter progressed. Indeed the situation was getting so serious that after an attack on Leipzig on 19/20 February, when harrying of the 'stream' all the way from the Dutch coast and heavy 'flak' in the target area resulted in 78 aircraft (9.5%) being lost, Harris felt he had to act. Thirty-four of the lost aircraft were Halifaxes, most of them Mk.IIs (a loss rate of 14.9%), and with the much improved Hercules-powered Mk.IIIs now reaching the squadrons in numbers, he decided he could not expect crews to fly the Merlin-powered variants over Germany any longer. They joined Stirlings on operations against more poorly defended targets and mine-laying which meant a temporary reduction in Main Force strength, most new production of both Lancasters and Halifaxes being absorbed as replacements, but it allowed withdrawal of Wellingtons from mine-laying on 3/4 March. Prominent amongst the mine-layers were Halifax II/Vs of No.6 Group, Nos.419 and 428 Squadrons pioneering the use of mines capable of being dropped from heights up to 15,000 feet – a great boon. The scheme was tested over Kiel Bay on 24 February when the two squadrons marked for aircraft of Nos.3, 4 and 6 Groups so successfully that they were ordered to continue the work for the next three months. Included was the largest *Gardening* operation of the war, carried out by 74 aircraft on 22/23 March with Kiel Bay again the target.

During February a genuine attempt was made to co-ordinate the American and British bomber offensives and day/night raids on the same town or

*See Chapter 9

city did have some success. On 24 February 266 B-17 Fortresses of the 1st Bomb Division, 8th Air Force, were despatched by the USAAF deep into Germany to attack ball-bearing factories at Schweinfurt, one of the panacea targets which if destroyed was expected to drastically curtail fighter deliveries to the Luftwaffe. Bomber Command followed during the night with a new tactic, the force being split into two roughly equal parts separated by two hours. The intention was to pose problems for the night fighters, and it appeared to work for the second wave suffered few losses due to them. The tactic was tried again the next night coupled with the now commonplace diversionary raid, the target being Augsburg, and again losses were well below the average for a 'deep penetration' raid. The Pathfinders were very accurate and the centre of the town was completely destroyed. Controversy followed because of art treasure losses, the damage to the facilities of the M.A.N. engineering works being conveniently ignored by the critics, as was the loss of life – both apparently of less importance to them than paintings.

Other innovations were the use of *Oboe* Mosquitoes to lead medium bomber units of the 2nd TAF attacking 'flying bomb' sites, and for 'heavy' bomber assaults on targets in France. The Directive of 4 March specifically listed such targets in order to 'obtain experience of the effects of night attacks on airfields, communication centres and ammunition dumps before Operation *Overlord*', the invasion of Europe, and all six named marshalling yards had been attacked by the end of the month with considerable success.

Despite all sorts of diversionary tactics, including the shovelling out of vast quantities of *Window* by mine-laying aircraft, and large-scale flights over the North Sea by training units to divert attention, the average loss rate on German targets remained stubbornly at 5.5%. This was an unsupportable figure if the Main Force strength and its efficiency were to be maintained, the problem being highlighted when Bomber Command suffered a loss rate of 8.9% (72 aircraft) during an attack on Berlin on 24/25 March – the 'night of the strong winds'. Though not forecast, these were so strong that the wind-finding equipment available to crews was unusable. The force became scattered and many aircraft strayed over heavily defended areas on the way home, some 50 falling to radar-predicted 'flak'. For various reasons, not least the losses, this turned out to be the last Main Force attack on Berlin of the war, though the LNSF continued visiting regularly.

Berlin had defeated Bomber Command for the second time. The distance of the city from bases in the UK made it difficult to concentrate attacks and meant that the 'Battle of Berlin' had to be fought in the winter, with all that entailed for the crews. Even the new H2S Mk.III did not 'map' the area well and Berlin's size and layout made target identification difficult, a problem accentuated by persistent cloud which also made ground markers largely useless. When blast damage was caused it tended to produce fire breaks which reduced the effectiveness of later attacks, and frankly, Harris underestimated the capacity of such a large, dispersed city to absorb punishment. During the first four of the 16 attacks, which ended on 24/25 March 1944, 7,000 tons of ordnance was dropped with little overall effect – the same tonnage had devastated Hamburg!

Another disaster was the attack on Nuremburg made on 30/31 March 1944. The forecast suggested that the brilliant half moon would be obscured by high

A Lancaster II of No.426 Squadron, Linton-on-Ouse, being refuelled and oiled in March 1944. (Public Archives of Canada/DND)

cloud cover over the target, but the crew of a No.1409 Flight *Pampa* Mosquito reported that it was not present. Despite this the raid went ahead, the crews' problems compounded by hopelessly wrong forecast winds, and an astute German controller who ignored all diversionary tactics, and positioned his fighters well. A fierce battle developed and continued for an hour, *Zahme Sau* tactics by the night fighter crews causing most of the 95 bomber casualties (11.9%). The bomber crews were badly shaken and the attack itself was a shambles. Most of the marking was poor and a long 'creep-back' developed, while some 15% of the crews attacked Schweinfurt, some 50 miles north-west of Nuremburg, one captained by Plt Off C.J. Barton of No.578 Squadron probably among them. His Halifax III had been attacked and badly damaged by a Ju88 night fighter as it turned onto the final leg of the journey to the target. With leaking fuel tanks, the starboard inner engine on fire, and the intercom knocked out, the navigator, bomb aimer and wireless operator baled out, having misunderstood the emergency light signals being used to communicate between gunners and pilot. After the propeller of the No.3 engine flew off and the fire subsided Barton decided to continue the sortie, though he had little idea of his location after the violent evasive action he had taken. Reaching a city under attack, he dropped the bombs and turned for home, but having crossed the Belgian coast it appears that Barton became disorientated and flew parallel to the English east coast. At dawn he turned inland and as the aircraft reached the coast the engines failed – they had run out of fuel. Ordering the crew to crash positions Barton fought unsuccessfully to control the engineless bomber, demolishing a house before crashing into a railway cutting.

The gunners and flight engineer survived comparatively uninjured in the rear fuselage, but Barton was badly hurt and died on reaching hospital. He was posthumously awarded the VC for 'unsurpassed courage and devotion to duty'.

It did appear that the Luftwaffe night fighters were getting the upper hand, and it was perhaps fortunate that the disastrous Nuremburg raid signalled a scaling down of Main Force operations against Germany as attacks on less well defended French targets assumed greater importance in the run-up to *Overlord*. Such attacks, mainly against communications targets, had been steadily increasing, and though Harris was openly sceptical of Bomber Command's ability to hit small targets, he reluctantly accepted that he had to share the burden alongside the American 8th Air Force and Allied Tactical Air Forces. In fact the results of night precision attacks on French targets were generally excellent, owing much to the comparatively short

Briefings were now highly organized affairs. At Snaith, No.51 Squadron crews gather before the ill-fated Nuremburg *raid of 30/31 March 1944. The squadron lost six of the 17 Halifax IIIs despatched. Gp Capt N.H. Fresson, Station Commander, sits in the front row with the squadron 'leaders'. (IWM CH12598)*

distances involved, the use of the 'Master Bomber' technique and to low-level marking, experiments using Mosquitoes of No.627 Squadron having shown that dives from 3,000 feet with release of markers as low as 100 feet were feasible, and very accurate. On 5/6 April No.617 Squadron's CO, Wg Cdr Cheshire, who had already demonstrated the value of low-level marking, tried using a Mosquito instead of the unwieldy Lancaster for an attack on an aircraft factory at Toulouse. With his markers backed-up extremely accurately, the Main Force crews of No.5 Group were able to concentrate their bombing on this difficult target. The factory was badly damaged, but some bombs did fall outside the target area and hit surrounding housing, killing 22 of the French inhabitants, a tragic but almost inevitable result of such attacks, which worried the crews, Command staffs and Churchill.

One of the standard Lancaster loads: a 4,000-lb MC bomb and 12 incendiary canisters. (via P.H.T. Green)

Harris immediately sanctioned No.5 Group to operate as an independent force using its own marking techniques and more Mosquitoes were delivered to No.617 Squadron. No.627 was transferred from No.8 Group with Nos.83 and 97 Squadrons, the two Lancaster units, which as far as No.5 Group was concerned had only been on loan to the Pathfinders. The low-level identification and initial marking method was not infallible of course, but in the right circumstances it was much more accurate than release on *Oboe* signals which No.8 Group used for most French and Belgium targets, as well as any German ones in range. 'Creep-back' was the main problem, usually caused by the original markers being obscured by smoke. To overcome this the No.5 Group marker force started to deliberately place their illuminants 300 yards upwind of the target and broadcast a false wind such that crews aiming at the unobscured markers would land their bombs on the target. Alternatively, the markers were sometimes placed further away and a timed run employed.

The use of *Gee* for bombing was still prohibited but crews were required to practice the technique in case it became necessary for bad weather operations over northern France. When operating alone No.3 Group frequently used *G-H*, but when the whole Command operated together it was No.8 Group which almost invariably led and marked the target, and they stuck to *Oboe* or H2S.

LNSF operations were gaining in strength and effectiveness, the Mosquito XVI providing a significant advance in performance and versatility. In addition, more H2S-fitted aircraft were entering service and improving the marking of distant targets such as Berlin, and on 13/14 April Mosquito XVIs of 692 Squadron went to the 'Big City' carrying a 4,000-lb *Cookie* and two 50-gallon drop tanks each, the first time this combination had been used. In contrast, a series of Pathfinder-led Mosquito VI attacks were made on V-weapon sites and railyards later in April, but results varied wildly and such operations ceased on 26 May.

On 14 April the strategic bombing forces in Europe were placed under the direction of Gen Eisenhower, Supreme Commander Allied Expeditionary Force, for operations in support of *Overlord*, though Bomber Command was not immediately diverted on to tactical targets. Between the 14th and 28th there were five medium to heavy raids on Germany; Cologne, Düsseldorf, Munich and Friedrichshafen all suffering severe damage. In his despatches Harris described the raid on Friedrichshafen as one of the outstanding raids of the war, all six important factories in the town being devastated. An attack on Schweinfurt was a failure

however, the low-level marking by No.627 Squadron being inaccurate, a problem compounded by the late arrival of Lancaster back-up markers and the Main Force from Nos.1 and 5 Groups. Worse, the delay allowed night fighters time to reach the town while the raid progressed and 21 Lancasters, 9.3% of the force, were lost. One of them was a No.106 Squadron aircraft flown by Flg Off F. Mufflin. Just as he turned away from the target the aircraft was attacked by a Fw190 which raked the fuselage and set fire to the starboard inner engine. Sgt N.C. Jackson, the flight engineer, operated the engine fire extinguishers with partial success and then, with a portable extinguisher stuffed in his battle dress blouse, he donned his parachute, pulled the ripcord and with the canopy held by two of his companions, climbed out onto the wing. Somehow he found foot and hand holds and played the extinguisher onto the fire which was dying down just as another burst of gun fire hit the aircraft – and Jackson. He lost his grip and slid off the wing and past the tail before being jerked to a halt by the rigging lines frantically being paid out by Flg Off Higgins (navigator) and F/Sgt Toft (bomb aimer). Suddenly he was free and landed safely, but badly injured. He managed to crawl to a cottage where he was taken prisoner and paraded through the local town before being taken to hospital. When the surviving crew returned from PoW camp and reported the full story he was awarded the VC. Nothing less would have sufficed as recognition of such bravery.

The main weight of Bomber Command was now being directed towards France where several marshalling yards were completely destroyed, and a raid on a large munitions dump at Maintenon by Lancasters of No.1 Group on 30 April/1 May led by the Group Marking Flight from Binbrook, resulted in a spectacular firework display. Problems arose, sometimes of the most unexpected kind, as on 3/4 May when accurate marking of a large military camp at Mailly-le-Camp by No. 617 Squadron Mosquitoes could not be followed up immediately because the orders of the Main Force Controller were blotted out by an American Forces Radio broadcast. When the Deputy Controller took over using HF some 1,500 tons of bombs rained down on the camp and it was virtually destroyed, but the delay resulted in heavy casualties, 42 Lancasters, 11.6% of the force being shot down.

Airfields and coastal batteries also came under attack during May, the raids spread both east and west of the intended invasion areas to prevent compromising the plan. Attacks on communications were steadily widened too, Mosquitoes IV/XVIs of No.692 Squadron, No.8 Group, closing the Kiel Canal for a week in May by low-level mining, such

French marshalling yards were prime targets during the run-up to D-Day. Aulnoye was only slightly damaged by two attacks... (British Official)

...but completely destroyed after 223 aircraft of Nos.4, 6 and 8 Groups attacked on 27/28 April. (British Official)

operations a relief for the crews, always worried about killing or injuring civilians when operating over France or the Low Countries. On occasion the Master Bomber would even suspend the bombing, as on 27/28 May when he decided half way through an attack on a railway junction at Nantes that the job was done and ordered the remaining aircraft to take their bombs home, rather than risk more casualties on the ground.

On 5/6 June, the night before the *Overlord* landings, Bomber Command flew over 1,200 sorties – a new record. Over 1,000 aircraft visited 10 coastal

Servicing Halifax B.III QO-E of No.432 Squadron at East Moor, 26 May 1944. (RCAF/DND)

gun batteries, dropping more than 5,000 tons on the cloud-covered sites using *Oboe* marking. At the same time, 16 Lancasters of No.617 Squadron were simulating a large convoy crossing the Channel to the Cap d'Antifer area, 15 miles north of Le Havre, by dropping vast quantities of *Window* while using *Gee* to perform meticulously flown 'racetrack' orbits which advanced at seven knots. The crews had practised for Operation *Taxable* for weeks, as had No.218 Squadron which carried out Operation *Glimmer*, using six *G-H* Stirlings to 'paint' a spoof naval force making for the Boulogne area of the Pas de Calais on the screens of German radars purposely left undamaged in the run up to D-Day. Meanwhile, 36 Halifaxes and Stirlings of Nos.90, 138

(SD), 149 and 161 (SD) Squadrons dropped dummy parachutists and devices simulating the noise of airborne landings at Yvetot, Maltot and Marigny as part of Operation *Titanic*, and No.101 Squadron Lancasters prepared to disrupt German night fighter controllers' R/T, using their *ABC* jamming equipment alongside the more sophisticated jammers of No.100 Group*.

Immediately after the landings attention switched to communications around the battlefield, including four rail centres near Paris at Achires, Juvisy, Palaiseau-Massy and Versailles-Matelet which were all badly damaged. On 8/9 June No.617 Squadron dropped the first 12,000-lb *Tallboy* deep penetration bomb on a railway tunnel near Saumur, with the object of preventing a Panzer division reinforcing German front-line troops. One bomb scored a direct hit and brought masses of rock down by the 'earthquake' effect of the weapon, the tunnel being blocked for months.

Gen Eisenhower asked Harris to join the USAAF on a renewed campaign against oil-related targets as soon as possible after D-Day, and Bomber Command started on 12/13 June with a heavy attack on the Nordstern synthetic oil plant at Gelsenkirchen. Using *Oboe* marking, the raid by 280 Lancasters was exceptionally accurate and all production ceased for several weeks, but generally such targets were difficult and Harris remained unenthusiastic. Communications were not forgotten, railways in France being attacked the same night by over 600 aircraft with varying

*See Chapter 9

ABC-equipped Lancaster B.1 LL757/W of No.101 Squadron at Ludford Magna, May 1944. The equipment's two long dorsal aerials are prominent while the one under the nose is just visible in this photograph taken from inside a hut. (E.H. Manners)

success and the loss of 17 Halifaxes and six Lancasters. Amongst the latter was a No.6 Group aircraft from No.419 Squadron, set on fire by a Ju88 night fighter. Realizing that the situation was hopeless the pilot ordered the crew to bale out and Plt Off A.C. Mynarski from Winnipeg, Canada, left his mid-upper turret and made for the escape hatch. Glancing rearwards he saw that the tail gunner was trapped, so he scrambled through the flaming rear fuselage and desperately tried to free the turret with his bare hands. Covered in hydraulic oil he was soon on fire, but continued to attack the turret until it was obvious he could do nothing to move it. He dived through the hatch, his parachute ablaze, and died soon after hitting the ground. Amazingly the tail gunner survived the Lancaster crash and after repatriation the full story was told and Mynarski was posthumously awarded the VC.

The threat to cross-Channel convoys posed by a strong force of E-Boats at Le Havre was taken very seriously, and to deal with them Bomber Command mounted the first daylight Main Force raid since the departure of No.2 Group in May 1943. Regarded by Harris as a risky experiment, the attack was made during the evening of 14 June in two waves, both escorted by No.11 Group Spitfires. The force included 22 Lancasters of No.617 Squadron armed with *Tallboys* for an assault on the reinforced E-Boat pens and several direct hits were scored, one bomb penetrating the roof. The rest of the force bombed the port area accurately and the threat was removed, but unfortunately there were French casualties in other parts of the town. The next day a similar raid was

made against German light naval forces in Boulogne and again the port area was devastated. Such results were encouraging and so were the light losses, one Lancaster being shot down on the 14th and a Halifax on the 15th. Lancasters, Halifaxes and Mosquitoes of Nos.4, 5 and 8 Groups also attacked crossroads at Aunay-sub-Odon and Evrecy, near Caen, at short notice following reports of German armour approaching from the south-west. The targets were accurately bombed and virtually obliterated – a striking demonstration of the abilities of a force which could, at last, be considered mighty.

On 13 June the long-awaited V-1 offensive against Britain opened and evoked a rapid response. Bomber Command started on 16/17th with a heavy attack on four launching sites in the Pas de Calais area, supplementing 8th Air Force daylight operations. A series of attacks were then mounted against 'flying bomb' storage areas, but were largely rendered ineffective by bad weather which persisted until 23/24 June. Attacks on German oil-related targets were similarly disrupted and also resulted in heavy losses, a disastrous raid on Wesseling by 133 Lancasters on the 21st/22nd producing a casualty rate of 27.8%, mainly due to the activities of well-controlled night fighters.

On 25 June daylight raids were made on three V-1 sites, the one at Siracourt being attacked by No.617 Squadron. Wg Cdr Cheshire used a Mustang, delivered that day, for initial marking, backed up by two Mosquitoes. Seventeen Lancasters then bombed, scoring three direct hits with *Tallboys*. Much the same force was used against a bomb store in a cave at St Leu d'Esserent on 4 July, with similar results. Two days

Merlin-powered Lancasters with bulged bomb doors were comparatively rare, though No.75 Squadron were so equipped for some time. (R.D. Mayhill)

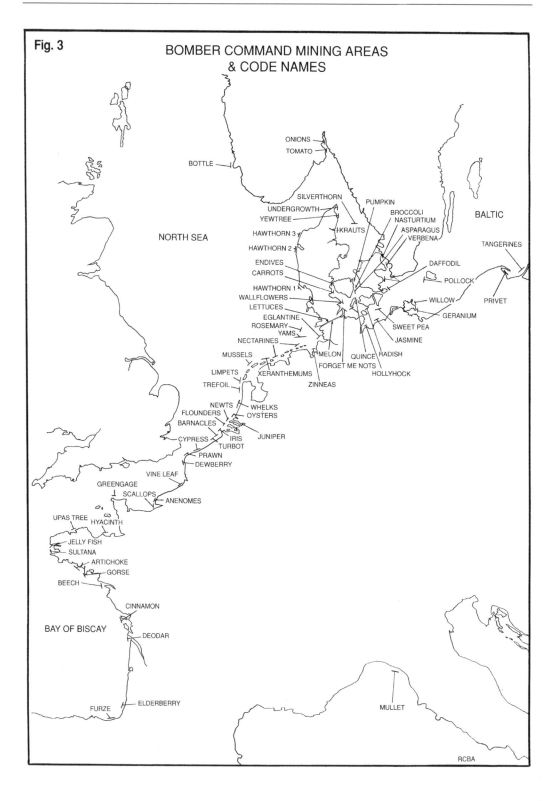

Fig. 3

BOMBER COMMAND MINING AREAS
& CODE NAMES

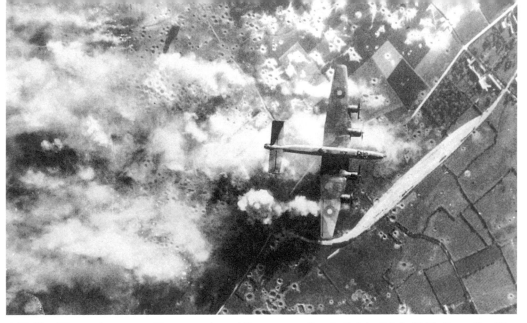

A Halifax III over the target, a V-weapon site at Mimoyecques, Pas de Calais, 6 July 1944. (Australian War Museum)

later Cheshire, who had flown 100 operations, was posted on the direct orders of the AOC No.5 Group. He later received the VC for sustained courage throughout four operational tours.

With the Canadian 1st and British 2nd Armies attempting to capture Caen, but held up by well dug-in German forces, it was decided to try the effect of tactical heavy bombing. On 30 June a road junction at Villers-Bolage, south-west of Caen, was accurately bombed by Lancaster and Halifax crews, and this success encouraged their further use in the battle area, 450 Bomber Command aircraft attacking fortified villages on the northern outskirts of Caen during the

evening of 7 July. Controlled by a Master Bomber the raid was accurate and mind-numbing, but unfortunately the bomb-line had been moved back because of worries about the safety of Allied troops, and though gun emplacements were largely destroyed the forward German defences survived. It did however enable the northern half of Caen to be captured after two days of vicious fighting, and Gen Montgomery got agreement for another attack prior to the launching of Operation *Goodwood*, the attempted breakout from the bridgehead. On the 18th over 1,900 aircraft of Bomber Command, the USAAF and the Allied Expeditionary Air Force (AEAF) dropped 7,700 tons

Mosquito B.XXV KB416/AZ-P of 'B' Flight, No.627 Squadron (part of No.8 Group's Pathfinder Force), during July 1944. (D. Garton via P.H.T. Green)

of bombs on Colombelles, the eastern suburb of Caen. The ground advance initially went well, but became bogged down in bad weather and the congestion caused by the total devastation of the area. The breakout failed but Montgomery was able to claim that his efforts had held the Panzers at Caen and relieved pressure elsewhere.

Despite the problems caused at Caen, and the heavy casualties suffered by French civilians, such bombing was continued, a USAAF raid being made on the 25th, followed on the 30th by Bomber Command and the AEAF dropping over 2,300 tons of bombs on the Villers Borage-Caumont area. The attack was not a success due to cloud cover and had to be repeated on 7/8 August when over 1,000 Bomber Command aircraft were sent to attack German positions south of Caumont immediately before an assault by Canadian troops. The final Main Force battle area operation came a week later on 14 August when 800 aircraft bombed German positions holding up Operation *Tractable*, the advance of the 3rd Canadian Division on Falaise. It was an accurate attack, controlled as usual by a Master Bomber, but at some stage yellow identification flares were lit by leading Canadian troops – the same colour as the TIs being used by the marker force. Despite warnings by the Master Bomber the inevitable happened, some 70 crews bombing the Canadian positions, killing 13 and injuring 53 – a tragic but understandable mistake in the heat and confusion of battle.

Raids on oil production plants and V-1 sites had continued throughout the Normandy campaign, No.8 Group trying a new method of concentrating bombing

Diane Cupid, a Halifax III of No.420 Squadron, RCAF in July 1944, with a 'scare' gun in the nose cupola. Second and third from left are Sgts W. Halborton (bomb aimer) and G. Burton (flight engineer). (G. Burton via AST)

on a small target on 11 July using a 'flying bomb' site at Gapennes. An *Oboe*-fitted Lancaster of No.582 Squadron with Wg Cdr T.F. Grant, CO No.109 Squadron on board, led a 26-strong formation briefed to release their bombs when they saw the leader do so. The 'carpet' effect was apparently successful and gave hope that it was possible to bomb small targets effectively from above cloud when the surrounding area was unpopulated, but a *G-H* blind bombing trial on the 27th produced poor results, and Harris continued to have his doubts about the ability of the Main Force to hit pinpoint targets except by luck, even in daylight. He was supported by the statistics, only one in four attacks appearing to do any damage.

Lancaster I W4783/AR-G of No.460 Squadron, RAAF, at Binbrook was withdrawn and flown to Australia in October 1944 after completing 90 operations. G-George *now rests in the War Museum, Canberra. (British Official)*

CHAPTER 7

Victory over Germany 1944-1945

FOR TWO MONTHS, while the Main Force was busily engaged in tactical operations over France, the LNSF carried the war to Germany single-handed, and Harris was very relieved when he was able to resume the strategic offensive on 23/24 July with an attack on Kiel. It was a model raid, the force of 612 Lancasters and Halifaxes suddenly emerging from a *Mandrel* screen and in a concentrated attack badly damaged the port area and U-Boat yards, the city being paralyzed for three days. Three heavy raids on Stuttgart

followed, the city being virtually destroyed, but the momentum was lost when Bomber Command had to return to attacks on oil, communications, and 'flying bomb' storage areas, daylight onslaughts on the latter in the Bois de Cassan, Foret de Nieppe and at Trossy St Maxim being particularly heavy on 3/4 August 1944.

During the Trossy St Maxim raid the No.635 Squadron Lancaster flown by Sqn Ldr I.W. Bazalgette was set on fire as he approached the target. Both

Air Chief Marshal Sir Arthur Harris, AoC-in-C Bomber Command, February 1942 to September 1945. (IWM CH5493)

Lancaster I HK551/A4-E of 'C' Flight, No 115 Squadron, is sent on its way from Witchford by well-wishers. An ex-75 Squadron aircraft, it had 'bulged' bomb doors and lacked H2S. (R.S.G. MacKay via A .S. Thomas)

starboard engines were put out of action but he carried on with his marking mission, controlling the aircraft with increasing difficulty. As he cleared the area four of the crew were able to bale out, but the mid upper gunner was unconscious and the bomb aimer badly wounded, so Bazalgette attempted a crash-landing near Sanantes in France. Tragically the aircraft exploded and all three were killed, the pilot subsequently being awarded a posthumous VC.

Only formed in No.8 Group during March 1944, No.635 Squadron was selected to carry out the operational trials of the Lancaster VI, a variant fitted with powerful Merlin 85 engines. Three went to Bremen on 10/11 August on a diversionary attack carrying new 10,000-lb bombs – the first operational use of the weapon. Experimentation was rife at this time, No.5 Group Lancasters trying 2,000-lb armour-piercing bombs on U-Boat pens on the 11th but they hardly chipped the concrete, and on 12/13 August a medium-sized force of Lancasters and Halifaxes went to Brunswick and bombed without Pathfinders or marking of any kind. The object was to determine whether a successful raid could be mounted using H2S alone. Apparently it could not, for the bombing was very scattered indeed, towns up to 20 miles away being attacked. Bennett would not have been human if he had not felt encouraged by the result, though the attack on the Opel plant at Rüsselheim the same night by 191 Lancasters and 96 Halifaxes led by Mosquito Pathfinders was not perfect. 'Flak' and fighters upset the bombing and the main site escaped, but fortunately the repeat operation on 25/26 August was much better. Damage was considerable and production interrupted for several weeks.

The H2S trials resulted in renewed sniping at the equipment, made worse by uncorroborated statements concerning the abilities of *Naxos*, the German homing

device, to use the equipment's transmissions. Rumour spread through Bomber Command and it proved very difficult to reassure crews, even when it became clear that *Naxos* could not detect 3-cm radar transmissions, and was not as effective against 10-cm H2S as had been suggested. However, recent tests on a captured night fighter had revealed that the Germans could home on *Monica* and with the dangers of indiscriminate use of airborne transmitters fully realized, Harris ordered the equipment's immediate removal from aircraft. Crews operating *ABC*, *Mandrel* and *Tinsel* were already under orders not to switch on until close to enemy territory, now all Main Force crews received similar instructions regarding H2S, and were forbidden to use IFF except when approaching the UK or in an emergency.

Airfield attacks had only played a small part in Bomber Command's activities since early in 1943, but on 15 August heavy bomber attacks were made on nine Dutch and Belgian airfields in preparation for a renewed offensive on Germany. Stettin and Kiel were attacked on the 16/17th and other cities, notably Bremen, Rüsselheim and Darmstadt soon followed. The LNSF sent 46 Mosquitoes to Cologne on 23/24 August and considerable damage was done by the *Cookies* carried by some aircraft. On the 27th *Oboe* aircraft of Nos.105 and 109 Squadrons, together with Lancasters of No.8 Group, marked the Rhein-Preussen synthetic oil refinery at Meerbreck, Homberg, for 216 Halifaxes of No.4 Group under escort by nine Spitfire squadrons – the first major daylight raid on Germany by Bomber Command since 12 August 1941.

Most of the V-1 sites had been overrun by ground forces by 28 August when the last bombing attacks were made, the combined offensive by 2nd TAF, USAAF and Bomber Command having failed to

Oboe Mosquito B.IX LR503/F *of No.105 Squadron after completing 203 operational sorties. The equipment was housed in the 'blacked-out' nose. F-Freddie completed 213 'ops' and was then sent on a tour of Canada at the end of the war. Tragically it crashed at Calgary 10 May 1945, killing the crew. (G. Plumb via AST)*

completely stop launches of the weapons, but certainly reduced the numbers. A new menace, the V-2 rocket immediately took its place, and Bomber Command started attacking suspected storage areas in northern France. Other diversions from strategic operations included pockets of resistance like Le Havre, bypassed by the Allied advance but capable of causing trouble. Four Stirlings of No.149 Squadron were amongst the 308 'heavies' taking part in an attack on the port on 8 September – the last such sorties by the aircraft.

Bomber Command was formally released from the control of the Supreme HQ Allied Expeditionary Force in mid-September, though still expected to respond to any call for direct battlefield assistance. Royal Navy support also remained a high priority and the old adversary, the *Tirpitz*, still lurked in northern Norway, currently at anchor in Kaafjord, an inlet of Altefjord north-east of Tromso. In theory the ship was out of range of Lancasters carrying a worthwhile bomb-load, and in practice it was a very difficult target, surrounded by mountains and protected by radar, guns and smoke screens. But despite all the problems it was decided to have another go at the ship and the Russians were approached, agreeing in August that Yagodnik airfield, located on an island in the River Dvina south of Archangel, could be used for such an attack. Thirty-eight Lancasters of Nos.9 and 617 Squadrons, a film Lancaster from No.463 Squadron and two Liberator transports set out on Operation *Paravane* on 11 September after refuelling at Lossiemouth.

Poor weather, poor maps and radio problems resulted in six aircraft crash-landing in Russia and one turning back *en route*, but the remainder finally gathered at Yagodnik. Twenty-one aircraft loaded with 12,000-lb *Tallboys* and six with 500-lb *Johnny Walker* (*JW*) anti-ship bombs were prepared for the mission, and following a favourable weather report the operation, led by Wg Cdr J.B. Tait, CO No.617 Squadron, was mounted on the 15th. As feared, the smoke screen started as the ship came into sight and it was largely obscured by the time the aircraft were

A 12,000-lb Tallboy *with Type 78 tail fitted leaves the Bardney bomb dump on a Type H trolley, 3 September 1944. (RAF Bardney G70)*

overhead. Seventeen *Tallboys* and some *JW* bombs were dropped but no claims were made, and it was a bitterly disappointed detachment which returned to Yagodnik. In fact one *Tallboy* had hit the *Tirpitz* on the fore-deck and though still afloat the ship was badly damaged. After patching up she was moved to Haakoy Island four miles west of Tromso, and some 100 miles closer to the British Isles.

Operations in support of *Market*, the airborne drop in Holland, followed on 16/17 and 17/18 September, and attacks were also made on German garrisons still holding out in Boulogne and Calais. Lancasters and Mosquitoes of Nos.1 and 5 Groups went to the twin towns of Munchen-Gladbach/Rheydt on 19/20 September, the Master Bomber being Wg Cdr Guy Gibson. He was officially the Base Operations Officer at Coningsby but managed to carry out a couple of operational flights in a P-38 Lightning, and on this occasion was flying a Mosquito XX of No.627 Squadron. He co-ordinated the raid without a hint of trouble, but the aircraft crashed near the Dutch coast

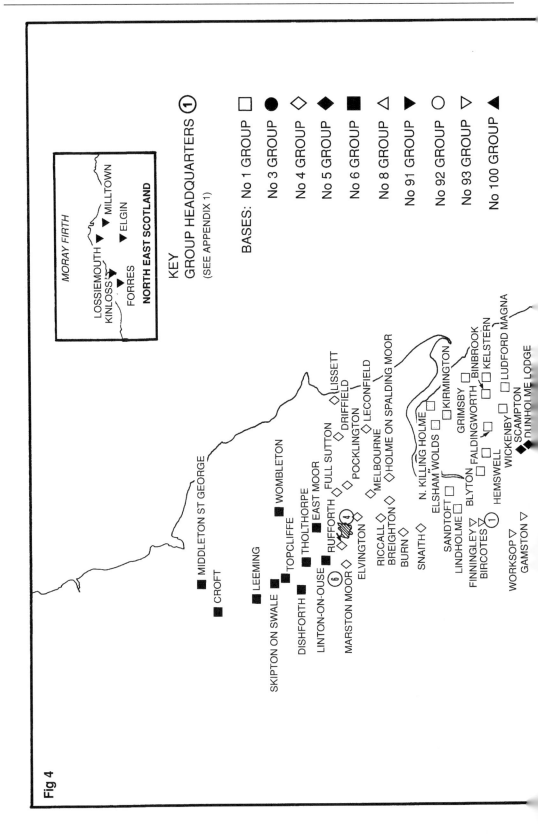

Fig 4

KEY

GROUP HEADQUARTERS ①
(SEE APPENDIX 1)

BASES: No 1 GROUP   □
        No 3 GROUP   ●
        No 4 GROUP   ◇
        No 5 GROUP   ◆
        No 6 GROUP   ■
        No 8 GROUP   ◁
        No 91 GROUP   ▶
        No 92 GROUP   ○
        No 93 GROUP   ▽
        No 100 GROUP ◀

MORAY FIRTH

LOSSIEMOUTH ▶
KINLOSS ▶   MILLTOWN ▶
FORRES ▶   ELGIN ▶

NORTH EAST SCOTLAND

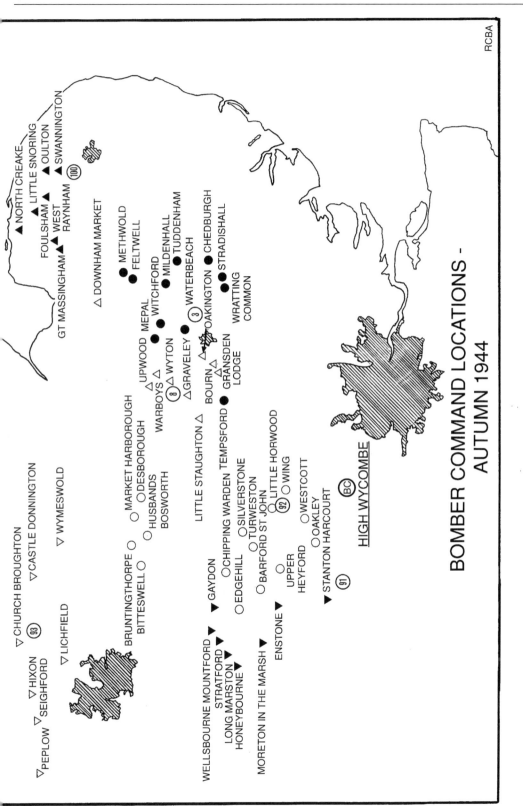

BOMBER COMMAND LOCATIONS - AUTUMN 1944

Above: *Lancasters of Nos.9 and 617 Squadrons flew to Russia on 11 September to mount an attack on their old adversary, the* Tirpitz. *Yagodnik was their destination but not all made it, among them PD211/M of No.9 Squadron which suffered a collapsed undercarriage on the rough wooden planking of Belomorsk airstrip. (W.R. Humphries)*

Below: *Photographed after 109 'ops',* Lancaster B.III EE139/B Phantom of the Ruhr *of No.550 Squadron went on to complete 121 operations, most of them from North Killingholme. (J. Foxon via AST)*

Bottom: *Close-up of* Phantom of the Ruhr's *nose, showing the patented Avro carrier in use. This was attached to the bomb while on the trolley and then winched into the bay, where it engaged latches in the roof. (J.Foxon via AST)*

on the way home, killing Gibson and his navigator, Sqn Ldr J.B. Warwick.

The Dortmund-Ems Canal, still a vital waterway, was the target for a strong No.5 Group force on 23/24 September which included 11 Lancasters of No.617 Squadron and five marker Mosquitoes from No.627 Squadron. The majority carried 1,000-lb bombs but No.617 Squadron took *Tallboys* and it was two of the latter that did most of the damage to the twin canal section near Ladbergen, north of Münster. A 10-mile stretch of the canal was drained, barges were stranded and it took six months to repair – a far cry from the gallant but unsuccessful attacks by Hampden crews in 1940. The canal was just as well defended though, and 14 Lancasters, 10% of the force were shot down. Less exciting, but just as important, was mine-laying. It continued apace, amongst the units heavily involved being the four RCAF squadrons, Nos.424, 427, 429 and 433, of No.63 Base, who methodically blocked the approach channels and ports of southern Norway so successfully that Oslo became virtually useless for German troop and equipment movements.

Behind the scenes a battle was raging over the future use of the rapidly expanding and evermore potent Bomber Command, 50% stronger than a year earlier. The Air Ministry, and very significantly, the Chief of Air Staff, Sir Charles Portal, were now convinced that the destruction of oil facilities was the most important task, certain that this would paralyze German forces and bring the war speedily to an end

without completely wrecking the country. Having seen what bombing could do to hamper the Wehrmacht in France the AEAF commanders, led by Sir Arthur Tedder, Eisenhower's deputy, favoured all-out attacks on communications, while a smaller group which included Sir Arthur Harris, distrusted all 'panacea' targets and wanted to continue bombing cities, still believing that Germany would collapse from within if pushed sufficiently. The Directive issued to Bomber Command and the USAAF 8th Air Force on 25 September made it clear who had won, for oil was the priority target for both bomber forces, and it was rather ironic that on the same day some 70 Halifaxes of No.4 Group (Nos.77, 102, 346 and 347 Squadrons) should start carrying jerricans of petrol to Belgium for Allied ground forces desperately short of fuel because Antwerp, though in Allied hands, could not be used with Germans controlling the approaches. Over the next week aircraft flew in some 430,000 gallons of fuel which alleviated the situation but did not cure it. Only the capture of Walcheren would do that and on 3 October eight waves, each of 30 Lancasters under the control of a Master Bomber, attacked the sea wall at Westkapelle. It was successfully breached and the sea rushed in, but it was not until 8 November, after bitter battles and several more bombing raids, that the garrison surrendered and clearance of the Scheldt Estuary and the approaches to Antwerp could begin.

With U-Boats forced out of Biscay ports the base

Halifax B.III MZ910/BM-Y of No.433 Squadron at Skipton-on-Swale after completion of 32 'ops'. (W. C. Pierce via AST)

at Bergen was expanded, and it was decided to attack it in daylight on 4 October using No.6 Group Halifaxes and No.8 Group Lancasters escorted by No. 100 Group Mosquitoes. Fourteen Halifax and six Lancaster crews were briefed to attack specific U-Boats while the rest of the 140 aircraft aimed at the pens. As usual little damage was done to the latter, but two small ships were sunk and three U-Boats and an auxiliary were damaged. Unfortunately the bombing spread to the town, a direct hit being made on a school, and of the 125 killed, 113 were Norwegian – a tragic end to what had appeared initially to be a reasonably successful 7½-hour operation.

American and French troops were now in the area of Mulhouse, eastern France, and it was feared that the Germans would release the water held behind the Kembs Dam on the Rhine, north-west of Basle, to disrupt the Allied advance. It was therefore decided to breach the dam so that the waters would subside before the next Allied forward thrust. Naturally No.617 Squadron was given the job and on 7 October 13 Lancasters were despatched, with long-range Mustangs of Nos.129, 306 and 315 Squadrons accompanying them as a 'flak' suppression force. Six of the Lancasters carried *Tallboys* with 30-minute fuzes and the crews were briefed to attack at low-level (500 feet) while German gunners positioned on the power station were hopefully occupied with the seven aircraft also carrying *Tallboys* but with 25-second fuzes for a high-level drop. The attack was successful, the sluice gates being hit, and when the delayed-action bombs exploded water poured through as the dam gave way.

Attacks on oil refineries and production plants were made whenever conditions were right, but despite the sophisticated aids now available they remained difficult targets, and Harris seized upon the next Directive with thinly disguised glee. Issued on 13 October, it consisted of two plans, *Hurricane I* and *Hurricane II*. *Hurricane I* was intended to demonstrate to the enemy the overwhelming superiority of the Allied Air Forces by applying within the shortest practical period, the maximum effort of Bomber Command and the 8th Air Force against targets in the densely populated Ruhr. The Americans were to attack specific targets while Bomber Command set about 'areas selected from undamaged parts of the major industrial cities'. *Hurricane II* concentrated on oil targets 'when weather permitted', Bomber Command being responsible for installations in the Ruhr and Rhineland. Within 24 hours nearly 1,000 Lancasters and Halifaxes, together with Mosquito markers, were over Duisburg, while 1,000 American bombers were despatched to Cologne. The following night Bomber Command returned to Duisburg with another 1,000 aircraft, and yet was able to mount a separate No.5 Group attack on Brunswick which destroyed the centre of the old town. Essen and Cologne were also the subject of concentrated attacks before *Hurricane I* came to an end having caused much damage and considerable suffering but with no noticeable effect on German resolve.

On 15 October No.9 Squadron had a go at the Sorpe Dam with *Tallboys* but without success for, as discovered in 1943, earthworks absorbed even direct hits much better than concrete or brick structures.

Halifax III LW179/DY-E of No.102 Squadron in 1944. It failed to return from Magdeberg 16 January 1945. (S.R. Cook via AST)

Three days later No.3 Group cut its newly independent teeth on Bonn using the *G-H* blind bombing equipment fitted to approximately one-third of its Lancasters. The raid was the first real success using *G-H*, measured by the damage caused, for the heart of the town was almost completely destroyed.

Operation *Ploughman*, which was intended to cause as much disruption as possible by spreading LNSF aircraft widely but thinly, was now largely abandoned. Instead effort was concentrated on one target, 48 Mosquitoes going to Wiesbaden on 19/20 October, and 60 making the long flight to Berlin on the 27/28th, many of them using the newly introduced Mk.XIV bomb-sight.

Continued concern over U-Boat operations from Bergen resulted in a strong No.5 Group attack on the pens on 28/29 October, but cloud cover prevented the raid developing properly and it was abandoned after

Above: ABC-*equipped Lancaster 'B' of No.101 Squadron, dropping Window over Duisberg, 14 October 1944. (Air Ministry CL1405)*

Below: *Halifax B.III MZ954/KW-M of No.425 Squadron at Tholthorpe, fitted with a .5-inch gun in place of the usual H2S scanner. (DND PL40557)*

the town was hit again. The next day Nos.9 and 617 Squadrons were back at Lossiemouth for another attempt on the *Tirpitz*. The removal of dorsal turrets, and extra fuel provided by the installation of additional tanks in the rear fuselage enabled the Lancasters to make a direct attack on the ship at its new moorings. Thirty-six aircraft set off, but just as they reached Tromso a change of wind moved cloud over the target and they had to blind bomb. Little or no damage was done to the ship and one aircraft crash-landed in Sweden. The charmed life of the *Tirpitz* seemed set to continue, especially as time was running out, for there would soon be no daylight at Tromso. Harris was determined to see the end of the ship, however, and after a cancellation due to weather on 5 November, the two squadrons were briefed for another attempt on the 12th. Thirty Lancasters plus the 463 Squadron 'camera ship' left Lossiemouth, led as usual by Wg Cdr Tait. They avoided the coastal radar by flying low, only climbing when screened by mountains, and this time the weather was clear and there was no smoke screen or fighters. The 'flak' was intense but inaccurate, and at least two *Tallboys* scored direct hits. The ship capsized and approximately 1,000 of the 1,900 crew were killed or injured – the *Tirpitz* had gone at last.

Early in November Portal, who had committed himself to supporting oil targets as the priority at the Quebec Chief of Staff Conference in mid-September, virtually accused Harris of disobeying orders by attacking cities rather than fuel supplies. It was indeed true that twice as many 'area' operations had been flown since the Directive of 25 September than against specific oil targets, but the situation was complicated by the *Hurricane* operation and the weather. Nevertheless it was noticeable that the

number of 'oil' operations doubled after Portal's letter, 20% of the total in November as opposed to 5% in October, and Harris's arguments in defence of his 'area' bombing policy were not altogether convincing. There was even talk of 'sacking' Harris, but his reputation was such that it was 'politically' impossible.

Harris was also called upon to continue attacks on communications and on 16 November supported Operation *Queen*, the US 1st and 9th Armies' thrust towards the Rhineland, by launching his heaviest tactical assault. Over 1,100 Bomber Command Lancasters, Halifaxes and Mosquitoes bombed Düren, Jülich and Heinsburg, small towns between Aachen and Cologne, to cut roads and railways behind German troops facing the Americans, while over 1,200 aircraft of the 8th AF bombed gun positions in the same area. In an attempt to prevent transfer of troops and equipment between east and west Germany attacks were made on rail centres, the marshalling yards at Aschaffenburg, east of Frankfurt, being the target on 21/22 November and those at Freiburg-im-Breigau, 30 miles north-east of Mulhouse were *Oboe*-marked on the 27/28th using mobile stations in France.

The continuing 8th Air Force attacks on oil targets, and to a lesser extent those by Bomber Command, were now having an effect, enabling the Allies to gain air superiority and RAF 'heavies' to operate regularly in daylight over Germany, sometimes escorted by fighters. No.8 Group's LNSF also took part, 30 Mosquitoes attacking tar and benzole plant at Meiderich, Duisburg, with Mustang cover on 29 November. It was intended as their first *Oboe*-led daylight raid, but the bombers failed to rendezvous with the markers and it was a shambles. The operation

Mosquito B.XVI MM183/P3-A of No.692 Squadron at Graveley on 20 November 1944 while operating as part of the LNSF. (IWM CH17858)

was repeated next day using 39 aircraft from four squadrons, Nos.128, 571, 608 and 692, and was much more successful, though the main target, the Gesselschaft Teerverwetung Works, had to be attacked again during December.

All 10 large synthetic oil plants in the Ruhr had been damaged by early December, some irretrievably, and it was assessed that German stocks were so low that they could not contemplate a ground offensive. The attack in the Ardennes on 16 December therefore came as a painful shock, but little could be done by bomber forces until the 19th because of appalling weather. Trier was then attacked by No.3 Group using *G-H* in an attempt to disrupt communications behind the forward enemy troops, and follow-up attacks were made on rail junctions and marshalling yards at Koblenz, Opladen and Gremberg (Cologne). Lack of expected cloud cover reduced the latter raid, made on 23 December, to a shambles and the intended *Oboe* marking was abandoned because of the risk involved in a long, straight run in clear weather. Unfortunately the crew of the lead marker Lancaster, a No.582 Squadron aircraft flown by Sqn Ldr R.A.M. Palmer of No.109 Squadron, did not receive the instruction, and though his aircraft was hit by 'flak' and set on fire Palmer continued on a steady run and bombed the target accurately. Immediately afterwards the blazing aircraft fell out of control and crashed, only the rear gunner managing to escape by parachute. It was Palmer's 110th operation and he was posthumously awarded the VC. Another six Lancasters and a Mosquito were lost, and all 22 surviving aircraft were

Right: *Plastered! – the Dortmund-Ems Canal in 1945. (British Official)*

Below: *A vic of No.90 Squadron, No.3 Group Lancasters* en route *for a G-H daylight attack. The leader is identified by special tail markings. (T.W.H. Saunders)*

Above: *Air Commodore 'Gus' Walker in his spartan office at Pocklington in 1944, during his time as No.42 Base Commander. No.42 Base also controlled Elvington and Melbourne. (IWM CH9326)*

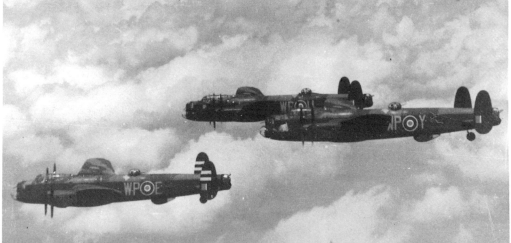

damaged to varying degrees; proof that the Germans were by no means defeated. Less disastrous were daylight raids on Christmas Eve, 338 aircraft (248 of them Halifaxes) attacking Lohausen (Düsseldorf) and Mulheim (Essen) airfields. Six aircraft were lost but the objective, the disruption of attempts to re-supply German forces in the Ardenne using transport aircraft, was probably achieved. The weather relented on Boxing Day and a major attack was made on St Vith in the middle of the Ardenne 'bulge' by a mixed force of Lancasters, Halifaxes and Mosquitoes.

On 31 December 1944, over two years after the first attempt, Mosquitoes again attacked the Gestapo HQ in Oslo. Twelve aircraft of No.627 Squadron set out in perfect weather and this time there was no fighter opposition. But there was 'flak'. All of the Mosquitoes suffered damage and again the main target escaped, largely because smoke obscured it after the first bombs exploded, and most of the second wave had to return to Peterhead with their loads intact. Unfortunately Norwegian casualties were high, 77 being killed and 58 injured, and yet again inner city pinpoint targets were shown to be fraught with difficulty.

On New Year's Day further efforts were made to disrupt supply routes with von Runstedt's troops in the Ardenne by blocking railway lines in the Eifel region, the crews of No.8 Group Mosquitoes (Nos.128, 571 and 692 Squadrons) attempting to place 4,000-lb Cookies in the mouths of railway tunnels from low-level – and four succeeded! The recently repaired Dortmund-Ems Canal was another communications target, and the 'heavies' started the New Year with an attack by over 100 No.5 Group Lancasters on the Ladbergen section. Yet again it was breached but two Lancasters were lost, one of them, a No.9 Squadron aircraft flown by Flg Off R.F.H. Denton being hit by deadly 88-mm 'flak' immediately after its load of 12 1,000-pounders was released. The rear fuselage became a raging inferno but the wireless operator, F/Sgt G. Thompson, disregarding his own safety dragged out the trapped mid-upper and rear gunners. Denton crash-landed the aircraft near Brussels, and Thompson was rushed to hospital only to die three weeks later from his terrible burns. He was posthumously awarded the VC for his courage and self-sacrifice.

Early on the morning of 5 January the French town of Royan was virtually destroyed by a strong force of Lancasters from Nos.1, 5 and 8 Groups. The town, at the mouth of the River Gironde, was still garrisioned by stubborn Germans preventing the desperately needed port of Bordeaux from being used – a thorn in the side of the Allies. Acting on intelligence which indicated that French citizens had been cleared from the town, SHAEF requested the attack to help the besieging French Resistance. Unfortunately some 2,000 civilians were still present in the town and at least a quarter of them were killed. Bomber Command was quickly exonerated, but arguments about who was to blame rumbled on for years.

Almost nightly visits to Berlin were now being made by the LNSF, the astonishing performance of the aircraft enabling Mosquitoes to take off early in the evening, bomb the German capital, return for refuelling and re-arming, repeat the sortie with a different crew, and be clear of Germany by dawn. Gp Capt J.E. Fauquier, the new CO No.617 Squadron also used a Mosquito to lead 32 Lancasters, 16 of them from No.9 Squadron, to Bergen on 12 January 1945 for an attack on the U-Boat pens. On this occasion the bombing was very accurate, three *Tallboys* penetrating the roof of the pens and causing severe damage, though not to the two U-Boats inside.

The German adventure in the Ardenne was over on 16 January, but resulted in another offensive on oil-related targets and communications, despite the Directive issued on 15 January which stressed the importance of attacking U-Boat facilities and the Luftwaffe, the latter enjoying something of a resurgence. As usual the results of attacks on fuel production plants were extremely varied, but the number of successful ones, like the Pölitz raid of 8/9 February which put out an important synthetic oil plant for good, was increasing. Gradually the noose was tightening, resulting in the virtual grounding of the Luftwaffe during the final months of the war in Europe.

In preparation for Operation *Veritable*, the advance into Germany from Holland by the British XXX Corps, the fortified towns of Goch and Kleve were bombed by over 750 Lancasters and Halifaxes from Nos. 1, 4, 6 and 8 Groups on 7/8 February. Kleve was reduced to rubble, the attack almost too successful for it proved impossible for army units to traverse the streets, the ground attack faltering when a thaw flooded routes around the town.

On 13/14 February Dresden was attacked by over 800 aircraft, nearly all Lancasters, in two distinct phases. The first was a No.5 Group affair only partially successful, but three hours later Nos.1, 3, 6 and 8 Group Lancasters using extremely accurate Pathfinder markers caused a firestorm which burnt out large areas of the city, and casualties were very high. The next day over 300 B-17 Flying Fortresses of the 8th AF bombed the city, and it was the target for another 200 American aircraft on the 15th when escorting P-51 Mustangs strafed traffic on surrounding roads. In the meantime 800 Halifaxes and Lancasters of Nos.1, 3, 4, 6 and 8 Groups had attacked

Chemnitz, another communications centre 40 miles to the south-west – but much less effectively.

There was nothing out of the ordinary about the RAF attacks on Dresden except the split into two parts and their devastating success, yet Bomber Command, and Harris in particular, have been villified for it ever since. In fact the raids on Dresden were part of a revised Operation *Thunderclap*, originally devised in July 1944 as an all-out attack on German civilian morale, but shelved, then resurrected in 1945 in revised form and intended to help end the war in Europe by knocking out communication centres ahead of the Russian advance, prevent reinforcement of the Eastern Front, convince the Germans that any organized resistance following a formal end to hostilities would be futile, and demonstrate to the Russians the awesome strength of the American/British strategic bomber force. It had been agreed at the highest level that the priority should be oil, communications, tank factories, jet fighter production and U-Boat construction, but under 'communications' stress was laid on movement in the evacuation areas behind the Eastern Front. The Chiefs of Staff were all attending the Malta and Yalta conferences while the detail was thrashed out, and it was Air Marshal Sir Norman Bottomley, Deputy Chief of Air Staff, who discussed the resurrected *Thunderclap* with Harris. As far as help for the Russians was concerned the plan only envisaged all-out attack on Berlin, but Harris suggested supplementary attacks on Chemnitz, Leipzig and

Dresden – all communications centres and long on his list of suitable targets. Portal was kept informed, and apart from Berlin, which he thought should be the subject of just one heavy attack, he agreed the overall plan. With the knowledge and tacit backing of Roosevelt, Stalin and Churchill he signalled back approval of the list which included Dresden, also granting permission to attack other centres where ensuing confusion could affect the situation on the Eastern Front. Thus Harris was not solely responsible for the choice of Dresden, and nor was Bomber Command the only force involved in the bombing of the city. His 'misfortune' was the success, in bombing terms, of the raid and others which followed, notably on 23/24 February when another communications centre, Pforzheim, 20 miles south-east of Karlsruhe, suffered a similar firestorm resulting in many deaths. During this raid, the Master Bomber, Captain E. Swales, SAAF, No.582 Squadron, continued broadcasting instructions despite two attacks by night fighters which holed fuel tanks and put out of action two engines and the rear turret. On the way home turbulent conditions made the Lancaster uncontrollable and Swales ordered his crew to abandon the aircraft, sacrificing his own chances to keep it as steady as possible while they did so. He was posthumously awarded the VC – Bomber Command's 18th and last. (Some were awarded later but for earlier actions.)

The raids continued unabated, though there were no *Thunderclap* attacks on Berlin, it being left to the

Halifax B.VI Rosie *of No.466 Squadron. (via Chaz Bowyer Collection)*

A Lancaster B.1 (Special) of No.617 Squadron releasing a 22,000-lb Grand Slam. (IWM CH15374)

LNSF which visited the city on 36 consecutive nights from 20/21 February to 24/25 March, causing misery if not overwhelming destruction. In all, 3,900 sorties were flown to the 'Big City' and more than 4,400 tons of bombs were dropped, including 1,479 *Cookies* – an extraordinary effort. Mannheim, Düsseldorf, Chemnitz, Duisburg and Dortmund were among Main Force targets, some raids involving more than 1,000 aircraft. By the end of March most of the Ruhr towns, even those the size of Cologne and Essen, were effectively paralyzed and could be ignored, but oil-related targets continued to be attacked and systematically eliminated, mainly by No.3 Group using *G-H* as a bombing aid.

On 3/4 March No.5 Group attacked, yet again, the Ladbergen viaduct, this time putting it out of action for the rest of the war, while the same night over 200

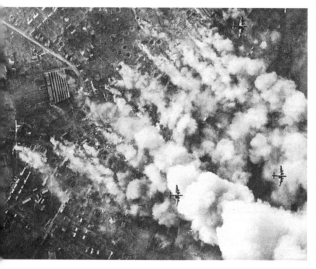

Halifaxes of No.4 Group, accompanied by No.8 Group markers went to Kamen, near Dortmund. The target was only lightly defended, the reason becoming clear when bombers started to be shot down near their bases. The Luftwaffe had laid on Operation *Gisella*, some 200 night fighters following the bombers home, shooting down 19 operational aircraft and three on training flights. It was a shock but really only the last desperate gesture by the German night fighters, for it could not be sustained or even repeated.

On 8/9 March a strong force from Nos.4, 6 and 8 Groups, mainly of Halifaxes, went to Hamburg where the new, and extremely potent Type XXI U-Boats were being assembled. The attack was not a success and neither was the repeat performance at the end of the month – both due to cloud cover.

Viaducts continued to be the preserve of No.5 Group's Nos.9 and 617 Squadrons, but poor weather prevented success on the Bielefeld and Arnsburg rail/river crossings east of the Ruhr until 14 March when the first 22,000-lb *Grand Slam* to be dropped operationally helped No.617 Squadron collapse the Bielefeld viaduct. The Arnsburg viaduct survived No.9 Squadron's attack with *Tallboys*, but on the 19th No.617 Squadron used six *Grand Slams* to destroy it and were equally successful at Nienburg on 22 March.

Two attacks were made on Wesel immediately prior to the crossing of the Rhine north and south of the town by Field Marshal Montgomery's 21st Army Group on 24 March – the start of Operation *Plunder*. Some 97% of the town was destroyed and it was captured with just 36 casualties on the 24th, prompting 'Monty' to signal Bomber Command HQ: 'My

The ultimate — Halifaxes attacking the Ruhr in daylight, early March 1945. (via J.D. Oughton)

grateful appreciation for the quite magnificent co-operation you have given us in the Battle of the Rhine. The bombing of Wesel was a masterpiece and a decisive factor in our entry into the town before midnight.' Bomber Command continued tactical work, concentrating on towns behind the German positions to prevent reinforcement, but reverted to oil targets at the end of the month. A depot at Farge was attacked by over 100 Lancasters of No.5 Group on 27 March while 20 aircraft of No.617 Squadron visited the nearby U-Boat shelters with *Grand Slams*. Two penetrated the 23-foot-thick concrete roof and completely destroyed the complex. An attack on shelters at Hamburg on 9 April produced similar results, while at Kiel the following night the pocket-battleship *Admiral Scheer* was capsized and the cruisers *Hipper* and *Emden* badly damaged.

Encounters with jet fighters had occurred spasmodically and largely ineffectively since November 1944, but on 31 March about 12 Me262's of III/JG7 suddenly appeared over Hamburg at the end of a Main Force daylight raid. Escorting Allied fighters had left for home and five Lancasters and three Halifaxes of No.6 Group, plus three Pathfinder Lancasters, were quickly shot down. Had the Luftwaffe been able to operate these jet-powered aircraft freely the carnage would have been appalling – proof if any was required that the emphasis which had been placed on aircraft and oil-related targets was the right one.

Bomber Command had shown conclusively that it could now destroy any medium-sized town in Germany in one or two attacks, because the concentration achieved by *Wanganui* marking was so good.

Paradoxically this power, so painfully acquired, engendered doubts, and Churchill in particular had become concerned about the problem of dealing with a completely devastated Germany after capitulation. He started to distance himself from the area bombing policy he had supported enthusiastically for so long, and on 1 April he sent another of his famous notes to the Chiefs of Staff asking for a review of the area bombing campaign. Though not in total agreement

Operation Manna. *Lancaster NX561/L of No.15 Squadron flown by Flg Off C. Hall free-dropping sacks of food to the starving Dutch, 1945.*   (*C.J. Zwanenburg*)

No.149 Squadron Lancasters at Juvincourt near Reims on Operation Exodus, *the ferrying home of British PoWs, 21 May 1945. (via J.D. Oughton)*

with the Prime Minister's comments, the Service chiefs concurred and on 16 April a new Directive confirmed oil, communications and shipyards as priorities, and specifically banned area bombing purely to destroy German industry – such attacks were only to be made if directly assisting armies on the ground or disrupting communications. Behind-the-scenes arguments over who should sign the document delayed formal issue until 5 May, but Portal had sent Harris an advance copy and the last major Main Force raid on a German town was made on 14/15 April. The target was Potsdam, virtually a suburb of Berlin, 500 Lancasters and 12 Mosquitoes of Nos. 1, 3 and 8 Groups taking part, some using *G-H* marking following the setting-up of ground stations on the Continent which put the town within range. A diversionary raid on Cuxhaven and the 62 Mosquitoes of the LNSF operating over Berlin doubtless helped reduce losses, but the fact that such a large force could fly to the Berlin area and back for the loss of one

aircraft was indicative of the parlous state of German defences, once so powerful. Bombing of the 'Big City' itself ended on 20/21 April, a Mosquito XVI of the LNSF flown by Flg Off A.E. Austin believed to be the last aircraft to attack.

The long campaign against the larger German surface ships continued, eighteen Lancasters of No.617 Squadron flying to Swinemunde, 25 miles south-east of Peenemünde, on 16 April to sink the pocket-battleship *Lutzow*. On the 25th the coastal batteries on Wangerooge, a Frisian island controlling the approaches to Bremen and Wilhelmshaven, were attacked by Nos.4, 6 and 8 Groups unsuccessfully, and tragically six of the seven aircraft lost were victims of collisions. The same day Nos.1, 5 and 8 Groups went to Berchtesgaden, 18 miles south of Salzburg in the Bavarian Alps, where Hitler had his Eagle's Nest chalet and an SS guard barracks. It was not a target specified in the latest Directive, or any other, but it was feared that fanatical Nazis were planning to make a last-ditch stand there. *Oboe* marking proved impossible because of the mountains and it was difficult to distinguish the buildings, but they were hit and badly damaged, No.101 Squadron making the last of its 2,477 *ABC* sorties during this raid. The following night 107 Lancasters and 12 Mosquitoes of No.5 Group attacked the oil refinery at Tonsberg (Vallo) successfully – the final 'heavies' raid.

The war in Europe was plainly approaching its end and the Tonsberg raid was intended as the last Bomber

The damage inflicted on German cities only became truly apparent from low-level. Koblenz at the end of the war – a scene repeated all over the country. (K.M. Robertson)

Command operation. But there were indications that ships were gathering at Kiel ready to transport troops across to Norway where it was rumoured that another group of Nazis intended to continue the struggle. An LNSF attack was laid on to discourage such a move, 126 Mosquitoes being despatched to Kiel on 2/3 May in two groups, one hour apart. Though cloud-covered the area was accurately marked by *Oboe* and H2S and the large number of troops in the town dispersed soon afterwards.

Meanwhile Operation *Manna*, together with USAAF Operation *Chowhound* in which B-17s dropped 3,700 tons of food in 5,343 sorties, had been mounted to save from starvation the population of the part of western Holland still in German hands. In anticipation No.115 Squadron had already carried out dropping trials, and after a truce was arranged food drops started on 29 April, no less than 33 squadrons from Nos.1, 3 and 8 Groups being involved. The 6,280-lb pannier loads were dropped on Drop Zones (DZs) marked by Pathfinder Mosquitoes at Leiden (Valkenburg airfield), The Hague (Racecourse and Ypenburg airfield), Rotterdam (Waalhaven airfield and the Kralingsche-Plas) and Gouda while flying at 300 feet. *Manna* continued until 8 May when the surrender allowed road transport into the area. Figures vary but approximately 3,150 sorties were flown and 6,685 tons of food delivered. With *Manna* established, Operation *Exodus*, the flying home of liberated PoWs by aircraft of No. 1, 5, 6 and 8 Groups, started on 4 May using Brussels and Juvincourt airfields. Stripped of everything except essentials and flown by a 'skeleton' crew, each Lancaster carried 24 passengers, some 72,500 PoWs being transported in 2,900 sorties during the next 23 days.

The war in Europe ended at 2301 hours on 8 May 1945 and immediately attention turned to the Far East and the defeat of Japan. In fact, planning had been going on with varying intensity ever since the Japanese struck at Pearl Harbor and Malaya in December 1941. It had subsequently been agreed that Germany be defeated first, followed by an Allied assault on Japan, and in 1943 tentative plans were made for a British bomber force to be sent to the Pacific. By mid-1944 the Allied Combined Chiefs of Staff had accepted that some 40 Lancaster squadrons would participate, operating from one of the islands the Americans were already using as 'stepping-stones', but stating that actual numbers, bases and dates would have to await developments. Ambitious plans were made to use air-to-air refuelling, but long-range operations against the *Tirpitz* indicated that it would not be necessary if the load was limited to 4,000 lb and overweight take-offs were accepted. It was, however, suggested that two squadrons should be practised in the art of air-to-air refuelling so that *Tallboys* could be carried for attacks on 'special' targets. The carriage of a large 'saddle' tank on top of the fuselage was also considered but rejected, and by the end of 1944 the planning staff under the Force Commander Designate were working on Project *Tiger* as a three-Group force each with 12 squadrons of 16 UE Lancasters/Lincolns fitted with 400-gallon overload tanks in the bomb bay, and six Mosquito fighter squadrons for escort duties. Conflicting priorities forced the Americans to make it plain that the British force would have to be concentrated in a small area and when the *Tiger Force* was officially formed on 24 February 1945 under the command of AVM Sir Hugh P. Lloyd, it had been slimmed down,

Operation Dodge. *Lancasters at Pomigliano await a weather clearance while ferrying troops home from Italy, late autumn 1945. Almost all remaining Lancaster units in Bomber Command were involved. (M. Drackett)*

A post-war photograph of a No. 15 Squadron Lancaster, ME844, still proudly displaying its operational 'scoreboard' but carrying stylized LS-W *codes. (No. 15 Squadron records via AST)*

consisting of Nos.5 and 6 Groups, Bomber Command, each with 10 Lancaster (20 unit equipment) and two Mosquito squadrons.

During June 1945 the composition of the *Tiger Force* was sorted out. To maintain a Commonwealth balance No.75 (New Zealand) Squadron joined No.5 Group which already had Australian squadrons, and near tour-expired personnel were posted out. The Canadian squadrons involved were sent home *en bloc* for leave and re-equipment with modified Lancasters, the intention being to restart operations at the beginning of 1946. Ground personnel and equipment was already on the way to the Pacific as part of *Shield Force* when the Americans dropped atomic bombs on Hiroshama and Nagasaki, and the Japanese uncon-ditional sur-render was accepted on 15 August. *Tiger Force* training ceased immediately, and *Shield Force* shipments were recalled, or re-routed to India, the organization being officially disbanded on 31 October 1945.

No.4 Group was transferred to Transport Command immediately the war in Europe ended, the other Groups carrying out battlefield and bomb damage sight-seeing 'tours' for the ground crews, and the disposal of unwanted bombs in The Wash and off Heligoland. No.6 Group, RCAF, transferred its last four squadrons, Nos.424, 427, 429 and 433, to No.1 Group on 30 August (Nos.424 and 433 Squadrons disbanded on 15 October 1945 and Nos.427 and 429 Squadrons on 1 June 1946), and the Rear HQ at Allerton Park was then disbanded. Starting in September, Lancasters released from the *Tiger Force* joined others from Nos.1 and 3 Groups on Operation *Dodge*, the repatriation of some 100,000 troops from Italy. The aircraft flew out of Bari or Pomigliano, in southern Italy, but the weather steadily worsened and the programme was brought to a halt at the end of November for a couple of weeks. As a result it was late December before *Dodge* was completed by which time Nos.5 and 8 Groups had been disbanded, plans for a peacetime Bomber Command envisaging a force consisting of two operational Groups (Nos.1 and 3) supported by a training organization (No.91 Group).

Lincoln B.II RF385 taken on charge by No. 57 Squadron for service trials, 23 August 1945. (MAP)

CHAPTER 8

SIS/SOE Operations 1940-1945

THE SECRET INTELLIGENCE Service (SIS) owed its existence to the First World War when unobtrusive intelligence-gathering became a professional and organized affair. Reluctantly the Service also became involved in subversion and sabotage, Section D being created for the purpose, and in June 1940 it was this department which arranged for a Walrus amphibian to pick up Bgdr Gen Charles de Gaulle's family from France should their evacuation by British destroyer fail. The crew lost their way and were killed in a crash-landing, but the clandestine use of aircraft to get people in and out of Continental Europe obviously had potential.

At much the same time the War Office was considering the possibilities of guerilla warfare, and on 15 June 1940 the Directorate of Combined Operations was established. The following month the Ministry of Economic Warfare became involved, and pressed for a single body to control all 'irregular warfare' including subversive activities. Churchill approved the plan and the Special Operations Executive (SOE) was formed and took over Section D and a miscellany of embryo organizations.

The SIS agent network on the Continent had been virtually destroyed by the summer of 1940 and new operatives had to be trained and deployed. Most went into Europe by traditional overland routes but it was planned to send some by air and No.419 Flight was formed by Fighter Command on 21 August 1940 to handle the operation. By the end of the month two agents had parachuted from a Whitley, one into France, the other into Holland, and two Lysanders, aircraft capable of landing and taking off in very short distances from rough terrain, were also on the unit's strength for retrieval purposes.

Early in September 1940 the Flight moved to Stapleford Tawney, a most unsuitable location for Whitleys, and the anomaly of a unit using 'heavy' bombers being administered by No.11 Group also caused concern even though control was exercised by the Air Ministry through the Assistant Chief of Air Staff (Intelligence). On 2 October Bomber Command were asked to provide space for the Flight at Bassingbourn but they were not enthusiastic about the suggested location, or indeed any involvement. Reluctantly No.3 Group offered Stradishall which was accepted with alacrity and within days the Flight had moved in, the transfer marred by failure to properly address the control issue. As a result, SIS/SOE/PWE (Political Warfare Executive) operations were to remain an enigma at Command, Group and Station level, and a thorn in their side.

The first Lysander pick-up was arranged for the night of 19/20 October, the aircraft being flown to Tangmere, an airfield which became very familiar to the pilots of the organization. Delayed by weather Flt Lt W.R. Farley finally set off a day late, found the three-light signal laid out near Fontainbleau by agent *Felix* (code-name for Philip Schneidau who had parachuted into France from a Whitley 10 days earlier) and landed safely. *Felix* was quickly aboard using the ladder fitted to the Flight's Lysanders and Farley took off only to find that he was prevented from climbing by restricted elevator movement. While sorting out the problem the compass (between the pilot's knees) was smashed by a rifle bullet and Farley had to steer by the stars. He was soon completely lost, and it was hours later that *Felix* sighted some cliffs through a break in the clouds. With fuel almost gone they glided down and crash-landed – near Oban in north-west Scotland!

Operations were gradually extended as the crews gained expertise, a Whitley fitted with extra fuel tanks taking three agents and supply containers to Poland on

15/16 February 1941 – a flight of 11 hours 20 minutes. Unfortunately the drop was made 60 miles within the German border, and though the parachutists managed to complete their journey they were unable to recover their supplies. Despite this rocky start commitments steadily increased and attempts were made to enlarge the organization – all thwarted by other priorities, the only changes made being the renumbering of the unit as No.1419 Flight early in March, and the use of Newmarket as a satellite.

A second Lysander pick-up was made on 11 April 1941, and a third a month later, successes overshadowed by the desperate situation in the supply of longer-range aircraft. Air Marshal A.T. Harris, Deputy Chief of Air Staff, offered two Harrows from No.271 Squadron, then substituted a Whitley which merely replaced a missing aircraft. Bomber Command's solution was to raise the Flight to full squadron status as a bomber unit annotated for 'Special Duties' (SD) – a ploy quickly quashed by the Air Ministry without offering any alternatives!

No.1419 Flight moved to Newmarket on 22 May but little operational flying was done, only two Whitley sorties being completed during the whole of June. However, one of them, carried out during the

night of the 13/14th, when two containers were parachuted onto a dropping zone (DZ) east of Limoges in central France, marked the start of SOE operations, a standard procedure for such drops having been evolved. Sites were identified by a white light flashing a letter in Morse code, the DZ being marked by three red lights orientated to indicate the wind direction.

Upgrading finally came on 25 August 1941 when the Flight became No. 138 (SD) Squadron with an establishment of six Whitleys and four Lysanders. The new unit carried out its first operational mission that night when a Whitley flown by Flg Off R. Hockey dropped an agent near Châteauroux. Shortly afterwards, on 4 September, the Lysander Flight delivered the first agent into France, picking up another at the same time. Also successful was the drop of two agents and their equipment 80 miles east of Prague on 3/4 October, resulting in radio contact being established with the Czech Resistance movement for the first time since the occupation. The round flight, during which a railway line was bombed to disguise the purpose, took 11 hours 25 minutes, probably the longest SOE operation by a Whitley.

The Whitley establishment was now nine aircraft,

V8287 was a Lysander III (Long Range), a Special Duties variant used by Nos.138 and 161 Squadrons. (Westland Helicopters Ltd)

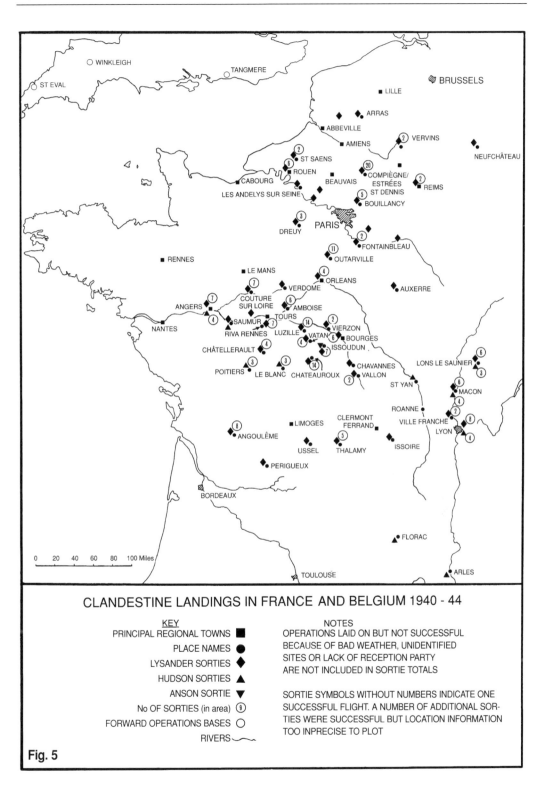

CLANDESTINE LANDINGS IN FRANCE AND BELGIUM 1940 - 44

KEY		NOTES
PRINCIPAL REGIONAL TOWNS	■	OPERATIONS LAID ON BUT NOT SUCCESSFUL BECAUSE OF BAD WEATHER, UNIDENTIFIED SITES OR LACK OF RECEPTION PARTY ARE NOT INCLUDED IN SORTIE TOTALS
PLACE NAMES	●	
LYSANDER SORTIES	◆	
HUDSON SORTIES	▲	
ANSON SORTIE	▼	SORTIE SYMBOLS WITHOUT NUMBERS INDICATE ONE SUCCESSFUL FLIGHT. A NUMBER OF ADDITIONAL SORTIES WERE SUCCESSFUL BUT LOCATION INFORMATION TOO INPRECISE TO PLOT
No OF SORTIES (in area)	⑨	
FORWARD OPERATIONS BASES	○	
RIVERS	⌒	

Fig. 5

but on 12 October the unit was notified that two Halifaxes had been allocated; tacit indication of the importance being attached to the work, for the Halifax was only just entering service with bomber squadrons. Fitted with an oblong trap door in the floor and static line strong points, the first Halifax arrived at Newmarket while the Polish crew were still undergoing conversion at Linton-on-Ouse. It was therefore flown to Linton and set off on its first sortie, Operation *Ruction* on 7 November, taking three agents and six containers to Poland. The drop near Poznan was successful but the hydraulic system failed, the flaps could not be retracted, and the undercarriage extended under its own weight. It was obvious that with the extra drag and against a headwind the British Isles could not be reached, so the crew set course for Sweden and crash-landed near Ystad on the southern tip of the country. They were later repatriated.

The Air Ministry may have regarded the unit highly, but its priority was low on No.3 Group's pecking order. They wanted Newmarket for a bomber squadron and suggested that No.138 Squadron should be moved to Graveley, an airfield still under construction. Rather surprisingly the plan was agreed, though for various reasons much delayed, and the SD organization thankfully remained at Newmarket for the winter.

Support for self-liberation armies, particularly those in Poland and Czechoslovakia, had been gaining ground during 1941, with plans to 'service' the armies by air drops being actively studied. *Barbarossa*, the German attack on Russia, and Stalin's subsequent call for active sabotage by Communist supporters in these countries complicated things, however, and aid plans were cut back severely. Priority moved to France where ambitious proposals for a 24,000-strong force equipped for a rising in concert with the invasion of Europe were being made. In the short-term, however, little changed and operations in support of Polish and Czech organizations continued until mid-February 1942 when appalling weather nearly resulted in the loss of a Halifax and its Polish crew. Flights were then suspended until the weather improved, an awkward situation for long trips over enemy-occupied territory had in any event to stop in May as the nights got shorter. Meanwhile, further north, difficulties with the Norwegian undercover 'army' delayed operations and it was not until 2/3 January 1942 that the first two agents were dropped into the country, it proving a slow business engendering trust.

The hair-raisingly difficult Lysander pick-ups continued intermittently, the eighth, flown by Sqn Ldr J. Nesbitt-Dufort on 28 January proving an epic. After successfully delivering one agent and picking up two others from a field near Issoudun, he was faced on the return journey with a massive bank of cloud on a very active cold front. In severe turbulence the Lysander became almost uncontrollable, and with the engine iced up and losing power he tried to make his

Accidents during clandestine operations were surprisingly few, but black Lysander T1508 of No.138 Squadron ended up on its nose near Châteauroux on 28 January 1942. The pilot, Sqn Ldr J. Nesbitt-Dufort, evaded capture and was airlifted out a few days later. (British Official)

Sir Archibald Sinclair, Secretary of State for Air, visited Tempsford on 4 April 1942 and talked to personnel, including Flg Off Badger in front of a No.161 Squadron Lysander. (via AST)

passengers understand instructions to bale out. Unsuccessful, he had to turn and fly back out of the storm and with fuel running low force-landed in a field, tipping up in a ditch. All three survived the crash and 'melted' into the countryside. Having evaded capture they were later flown out of France.

On 14 February 1942 No.138 Squadron was supplemented in its clandestine activities by No.161 (SD) Squadron, formed using the King's Flight as a nucleus and Wg Cdr E.H. Fielden as the CO. It was originally intended exclusively for SIS work, leaving No.138 on SOE operations, but this proved impracticable. Instead No.161 was made responsible for all pick-ups, some parachute drops and

As clandestine as any aircraft at Tempsford were the Wellingtons of the SIS Wireless Flight, No.161 Squadron, among them P2521/V in 1942. (M. Whinney/AST)

communications experiments using Lysanders and Whitleys, Wellingtons and a Hudson, while No.138 concentrated on long-range agent and supply drops by parachute with Whitley and Halifax aircraft.

No.161 Squadron carried out its first 'op' on 27/28 February when Flt Lt A.M. Murphy flew a Lysander from Tangmere to St Saens with *Anotok*, a female passenger, and brought out two agents. On 1 March the unit moved to Graveley and the same night Murphy flew a borrowed Anson via a circuitous route to Issoudun where Nesbitt-Dufort and three agents (two of whom he had gone to collect on 28 January) jumped aboard. While stationary the aircraft sank through the frost- hardened ground and was only freed by the occupants 'bouncing' it out by jumping up and down while full power was applied! After an agonizingly slow flight they arrived safely on English soil – a saga not repeated!

Although Graveley had potential, No.138 Squadron was sent to Tempsford in March 1942 when it vacated Newmarket, and was joined by No.161 early in April – the 'secret' squadrons had at last found a permanent home. It was a curious choice though, for activities were easily viewed from the main LNER railway line which formed the western boundary. This SD expansion coincided with the arrival of Air Chief Marshal Sir Arthur Harris as the new AOC-in-C Bomber Command, and it was fortunate that the re-organization had been agreed before he took command. He found it hard to accept SD units which were not even fully under his control, and he was also unhappy about the decision to give the organization its own airfield and the instruction that he was to give 'sympathetic consideration to any particular problems encountered by the Station Commander in the

provision of adequate facilities'. There was nothing he could do about it immediately, but the first clash, over the question of crew establishments, was not long coming and required the Deputy Chief of Air Staff, Air Chief Marshal Sir Wilfred Freeman, to sort things out despite the units having an agreed priority. It was obvious that the relationship would not be easy.

No.161 Squadron's Whitleys started operations on 1 April and for the next 3½ months concentrated on France, while Harris bombarded the Air Ministry with selected statistics aimed at illustrating how wasteful the two units were. He proposed that either they should leave Bomber Command and count as two of the squadrons he was being required to relinquish, or be fully absorbed. In the latter case he promised he would fulfil any 'reasonable' requirement by SIS/SOE from Command resources using standard bomber crews. This ignored the expertise involved in agent drops but fortunately Freeman, and even Portal who almost invariably took Harris's side, firmly rejected the arguments, the former writing a formal letter on 16 April which in effect instructed Harris to do as he was told with regard to the SD squadrons.

In fact the tempo of operations was gradually increasing, No.138 Squadron alone carrying out 45 missions during April 1942 while No. 161 Squadron was experimenting with their Wellington as a radio station, using French speakers to communicate with Breton fishermen supplying Naval Intelligence with information.

Harris was soon back with a new scheme, suggesting that No.161 Squadron be absorbed by an enlarged but 'more effective' No.138, and a new Wellington-equipped unit be formed which could be used for bomber operations when not required to

The first Halifax II with the 'Z' nose, W7776 became 'L' of No.138 Squadron. (Author's collection)

One of the two PRU Blue Havocs, AW399/X, which took over the SIS wireless task in October 1942. Note the extra underbelly aerials. (M. Whinney/AST)

supplement the specialist SD unit. He acknowledged that specialist navigation skills were necessary for the agent-dropping role; indeed, he wanted to use it for bombing attacks on pinpoint targets. The plan was considered at length, officially dropped, but actually taken up in a somewhat different form for on 31 May No.161 Squadron Whitleys started leaflet-dropping over France, Belgium and Holland, and on 2/3 June bombed marshalling yards at Tours. Such operations went some way towards Harris's demands and also provided useful navigation training for new crews,

but they remained the exception rather than the rule.

For some time the Poles had been campaigning for a separate Liberator-equipped Flight, to be used mainly on supply drops to the Home Polish Army. They canvassed the help of the Americans and discussions with the British were lengthy and sometimes acrimonious. Finally it was agreed that six No.138 Squadron Halifaxes would be fitted with special long-range tanks for Polish operations and flights to Poland resumed in September 1942 but became steadily more hazardous, losses reaching

Halifax II srs 1 L9613/V of No.138 Squadron far from home on an Egyptian airfield while on a cargo flight in 1942. (H. Levy)

nearly 50% as bad weather and an increasingly effective night fighter force took their toll.

In July 1942 two Havocs had been taken on No.161 Squadron charge and fitted with special equipment for recording messages from agents using short-wave radio. Intended as replacements for Wellingtons they were detached to St Eval in October for work with Breton fishermen. There they were joined by two Albemarles, which were under consideration for the job, but in practice were only used as escorts!

Both squadrons were now carrying out bombing whenever available, power stations, transformers and railway facilities being the targets until late October when locations of special interest to SOE became the priority. Much to Harris's chagrin the SOE were allowed to choose the sites which were then authorized by the Air Ministry, but it was the latter which ordered the use of Whitleys for carriage of urgent supplies to North Africa for Operation *Torch*. The SD units were also involved in the carriage of stores to Egypt, nine Halifaxes being attached to No.511 Squadron, Lyneham, early in November. The aircraft carried 5,500 lb of freight, flying via Malta to Cairo, returning a few days later via Malta and Gibraltar.

Operational Lysander flights were also increasing and on 18/19 November the first double pick-up was attempted, from a field near Châteauroux. Unfortunately the weather intervened and the agents had to wait until the 22/23 November. New establishments dated 20 November indicated that the obsolescent Whitley was to be completely replaced, No.138 Squadron being allotted 15 Halifaxes while No.161 was to have five Halifaxes and retain its Lysanders. The aircraft were supplied from Bomber Command resources and it was a measure of changing attitudes, and the improving supply situation, that they arrived promptly.

Bad weather during December dramatically demonstrated its effect on sorties, No.138 Squadron flying 19 of which 16 were unsuccessful, while No.161 only attempted two drops and six Lysander pick-ups of which only two succeeded. In January 1943 the Poles, led by Gen Sikorski, again asked the Americans to supply SOE Liberators, claiming that Halifaxes allotted to them by No.138 Squadron did not have the range to reach some of the DZs, or the speed necessary to operate on shorter summer nights. After more discussion reaching Vice Chief of Air Staff level, it was decided that three Liberators would be provided as soon as suitably modified for night flying (unlikely before June), and that the number of Polish crews on No.138 Squadron would be increased to six. The question of a separate Polish Flight was postponed until after the winter.

'B' Flight, No.161 Squadron, started Halifax SOE sorties on 14/15 January, but its first attempts to reach Czechoslovakia were unsuccessful. No.138's sorties to Poland and Norway were more profitable despite difficult weather which continued throughout the winter, but the Air Ministry's plan to 'misuse' six Halifax aircraft on Operation *Pullover*, the dropping of 20 soldiers at Alt Lake in northern Norway, met considerable opposition from the SOE. The troops were to destroy a viaduct on the railway line used to carry iron ore to Narvik, a task considered top priority and requiring the use of the 'Polish' long-range aircraft for the round trip from Kinloss, a distance of 2,150 miles. The Air Ministry insisted and the aircraft went to Kinloss on 13 February to await good weather. It never came and the operation was finally abandoned. More successful was the SOE Operation *Gunnerside* which involved the dropping of six Norwegians on 16 February from a Halifax flown from Kinloss by Sqn Ldr Gibson of No.138 Squadron. *Gunnerside* completed a series of operations which started with an ill-fated attempt to land troops in Norway in November 1942 by Horsa glider. The target was the Norsk heavy water plant located on a plateau halfway up the steep side of a deep valley near Rjukan, 70 miles west of Oslo in the Telemark region. Blind-dropped, the party made their way across the Hardanger Vidda glacier with their explosives and provisions, made a brilliant attack on the plant and escaped. About 350 kilogrammes of heavy water were lost and the plant put out of action for six months – a major setback to the German atomic bomb programme.

Meanwhile 'A' Flight, No.161 Squadron, was tasked with extending its pick-up operations deeper into France and the CO, Wg Cdr P.C. Pickard decided, after trials, that Hudsons could be used on specially selected fields. On 13/14 February he successfully landed five agents at St Yan near Charoules, 60 miles north-west of Lyon in central France, but the return passengers had not reached the rendezvous point and after five minutes on the ground Pickard left carrying a bag of agent's reports. A second Hudson flight went well, but on 24/25 February Pickard got bogged down in a field near Tournus, halfway between Dijon and Lyon. Feverish efforts by the reception party, agents and men from the nearby village were unsuccessful until a couple of horses were recruited. The aircraft finally got away over two hours after landing, crossing the French coast outbound with a hastily organized Typhoon escort just as dawn was breaking.

An SOE Directive issued in March 1943 laid down new priorities and instructions regarding the type of sabotage to be carried out. The official lack of enthusiasm for secret armies, now also applied to the French, was emphasized, clandestine operations being

HM King George VI and Queen Elizabeth at Tempsford on 9 November 1943. In the background are a Lysander and a Hudson of No.161 Squadron. (via H.G. Deblutt/AST)

much preferred. At the same time it was obvious that the demand on SD units was insatiable – up to twice what could be supplied. Efforts were made to increase the size of the airborne supply organization, 7½ squadrons being suggested, but understandably such expansion did not find favour with Harris, for he only had 40 operational bomber squadrons at his disposal and was desperately trying to enlarge the force.

Drops by Halifaxes of both squadrons were steadily increasing, 32 sorties being flown in April (plus 15 by Lysanders and two by Hudsons), but so were losses, now averaging six crews each month. The 'in-house' training system could not cope and it was decided by Bomber Command that all aircrew posted to SD units for 'heavy' operations would be put through the standard bomber course at No.1659 Heavy Conversion Unit and then be given an additional 10 hours' role-training at Tempsford. Ferrying was an added commitment during non-operational moonless periods, No.161 Squadron trying a shuttle operation combining an operational drop over France with freighting to North Africa, but it was not a success and the unit quickly reverted to separate sorties.

With the French Resistance organization the most active and important, supply drops over France were increased dramatically during the summer of 1943, resulting in more activity for the Lysanders and Hudsons of No.161 Squadron as agents came and

went in greater numbers. During August, a most successful month, 66 agents, 194 packages and 1,452 containers were dropped in 184 sorties, while 16 pick-ups were made. Havocs were also busy carrying out *Ascension* wireless flights for agents in France and the Low Countries.

Further Polish lobbying had resulted in the unit establishment of No.138 Squadron being increased to 18 Halifaxes and the formation of 'C' Flight from personnel of the disbanded No.301 (Polish) Squadron. But despite such additions aircraft shortages were biting deep, and the situation was not improved by the sudden departure of four Halifaxes to Tunis on detachment. However, help was at hand, for Stirlings were being withdrawn from the bomber force and No.3 Group agreed to allocate three aircraft and crews from No.214 Squadron for SD work on a trial basis. The first sortie was made on 18/19 September, the same night that the Polish Flight commenced Liberator operations having received three aircraft during August. The weather made it difficult to assess No.214 Squadron's results before the end of the moonlight period, but the Stirling detachment remained at Tempsford for training and was strengthened for the next operational period.

Hudsons took over the SIS *Ascension* wireless flights (using the *S-Phone* communication system) at the end of October 1943 and the Havocs were retired. Liberators started long-distance flights to Poland, one lasting 15 hours 5 minutes, while over northern Norway Halifaxes continued agent and equipment drops, operating from Kinloss on flights which often lasted well over 12 hours. Despite the less than enthusiastic reception of the Stirling, the Air Ministry decided that the aircraft would replace the Halifax on SOE work as soon as possible. This suited Harris, keen to find a use for the Stirling and to increase the numbers of bomber Halifaxes, but he insisted that the range of replacement aircraft had to match that of the Halifax (2,300 miles) or exceed it, 2,600 miles being preferable.

In November the Polish Flight was transferred to Tunis, moving to Brindisi a month later with three Liberators and three Halifaxes. They were immediately replaced by USAAF attachments to the Tempsford squadrons to gain experience in the work prior to the start of their own SD Liberator *Carpetbagger* operations over Europe.

Behind the scenes serious trouble was brewing, following the discovery by the SIS that the Dutch SOE network had been controlled by the Germans since 1942, new agents having been picked up as they arrived from May onwards – a disaster which was to take many months to rectify. Harris suspended all SOE flights on 1 December 1943 and although the order was soon partially rescinded, and SIS flights continued, it was a bitter blow for the SOE at a time when positive results were being achieved, especially in France. On 3 June 1943 the Michelin tyre works at Clermont-Ferrand had been badly damaged by sabotage and the following month SOE agents killed

12 Gestapo men. They also brought the canal system connecting the Ruhr with the Mediterranean to a standstill for four months, and disrupted rail communications almost daily. On 5 November the local Resistance, helped by agents, managed to place bombs in the Peugeot factory at Sochaux. Such activity gained a momentum of its own, but it needed the backing which could only be supplied by air.

Operations over France resumed after a week and on the 8th Wg Cdr Cheshire, newly arrived on No.617 Squadron, was asked to provide three aircraft and crews for a secret operation about which he was given no details. Reluctantly he despatched the Lancasters to Tempsford and the crews were briefed alongside men from the SD squadrons and No.214 Squadron for a special low-level supply drop in the Boulogne area. The target was located, but for No.617 it was a disastrous affair, two Lancasters being shot down. So important was the operation that it was repeated on 20/21 December when No.617 Squadron provided four aircraft, but none of the 'amateurs' identified the DZ, only serving to prove yet again the inadvisability of using untrained personnel for specialist operations.

Bad weather claimed five SD aircraft on 16 December, two of them from the close-knit Lysander Flight which lost two pilots and two agents, a considerable shock after 22 months during which only one operational fatality had occurred, and it was probably fortunate that the work load was so high. Commitments to Resistance groups required the dropping of 350 tons of supplies per month and resources were wildly overstretched, but yet again the

Stirling C.IV LK119 of No.138 Squadron in 1944, later transferred to No.161 Squadron and shot down 31 March 1945. (The late J.T. Breeze/AST)

answer was at least partially at hand, for the Stirlings, Halifaxes and Albemarles of No.38 Group, Transport Command, were available to supplement the efforts of the SD and bomber squadrons. Starting on 3/4 February they concentrated on supply operations to the French Resistance, leaving the Tempsford squadrons, supplemented by detachments from Nos.149, 199 and 214 Squadrons of Bomber Command, to carry out the more difficult sorties to other parts of Europe.

At the same time a message pick-up (MPU) system for the Lysander developed by ML Aviation was, after much official prevarication, approved for use, and Hudsons had a chute installed in the rear fuselage so that they could take over some of the agent drops from overworked Halifaxes. Stirling replacements were delayed by modifications which took longer than expected but standard bomber variants from Nos.75, 90 and 149 Squadrons were used for supply drops in March despite continuing poor weather. This caused problems in identification of DZs and accidents on return to base, but the French backlog was reduced.

During April the tempo increased further, No.138 Squadron on occasion fielding 16 Halifaxes, while No.38 Group provided up to 55 aircraft per night, supplemented by 18 Stirlings from No.3 Group. In retrospect the bomber and transport crews performed marvels, for even with the benefit of *Gee, Rebecca* and *S-Phone*, navigation was not always easy. If no recognition signals were displayed the standard procedure was to circle for a while and then go on to an alternative DZ, and these rarely had any navigational aids and crews had to rely on moonlight, often in short supply even in May. A big effort was planned for June, but Operation *Overlord*, the invasion of Europe, resulted in pre-planned special tasks being activated at short notice, all supply drops being suspended on receipt of the code-word *Titanic*. On the night of 5/6 June four Stirlings of No.149 Squadron were joined by seven Halifaxes from No.138 and four more from No.161 in dropping dummy parachutists, rifle-fire simulators and *Window*, in the Yvetot area of north-eastern France. The intention was to suggest an airborne landing, while on the Cherbourg Peninsula a single Halifax did drop two three-man SAS parties near Isigny – the first troops to land on *Overlord*!

The *Overlord* operations went well, but agent drops immediately after D-Day were not very successful, mainly because 'reception parties' were prevented from reaching the site, or were pinned down by German patrols. The long-awaited Stirlings joined No.138 Squadron in July 1944, No.161 continuing with Halifaxes, but increasingly used Hudsons for agent drops. Lysanders were still active on MPU and agent transfer sorties, one of the latter having tragic consequences on 7/8 July. Unable to locate the landing field a few miles south of Chenonceaux in the Indre et Loire region, the pilot aborted the mission but strayed off course and the Lysander was hit by 'flak', probably Allied, and forced to 'ditch' in the Channel. The aircraft turned over and the three passengers were

An interesting photograph of a No.161 Squadron Lysander showing the new 'JR' code introduced in April 1944 and the 'invasion stripes' painted on in June. (L. Newhouse/AST)

thrown out. Inflating his dinghy the pilot managed to get two passengers aboard, but the other drifted away and a second passenger died of exposure following rescue after 2½ hours in the water.

The Hudson Flight of No.161 Squadron also had its moments, a pick-up south-west of Châteauroux in central France during the moonless period nearly turning into a disaster on 27/28 July. The field, already marginal in size, had recently been ploughed by the Germans, but Wg Cdr A.H.C. Boxer landed safely and dropped off two agents and boxes of medical supplies. With four evaders embarked the take-off was more difficult and the Hudson literally staggered off the ground and just cleared the hedge!

The chaotic situation in France badly affected operations from Tempsford, the rapidly changing scene resulting in many last-minute cancellations, and with Tangmere too close to the fighting for comfort, Lysander pilots started using Winkleigh, Devon, as a forward base instead. During August, Stirlings became operational with No. 138 Squadron, but there was a further setback when 'B' Flight, No. 161 Squadron was temporarily made non-operational following urgent calls for Halifax reinforcements for Middle East SD units operating in support of the Polish Home Army after the Warsaw Uprising.

What turned out to be the last Lysander pick-up flights by No.161 Squadron were completed on 5/6 August and a month later, with much of France in Allied hands, the final Hudson sorties were made. Nine agents were successfully delivered into a field near the Swiss border and seven picked up, but at the other strip, north-west of Lyon, came tragedy. Inexplicably, some of the 'reception party' stood in the path of the aircraft, unseen until the pilot switched on his landing light just before touchdown. His desperate efforts to avoid them failed and two were killed, one of them the leader of the local Maquis – a sad end to an extraordinary venture.

Lysander and Hudson crews commenced special transport flights to France and Belgium during September 1944, and with virtual air superiority both No.3 Group SD squadrons started daylight supply drops to patriots in the area. Occasional agent drops were also made into Germany, and following withdrawal of the Mitchells of the 2nd TAF Special Signals Flight the Hudson crews of No.161 Squadron became solely responsible for maintaining the *Ascension* wireless flights – the last of the unit's truly clandestine activities – at the reduced rate of two sorties a day.

In November the Lysander establishment was savagely cut and No.161 was reorganised with Hudsons in 'A' and Stirlings in 'B' Flight. Both

Tempsford squadrons concentrated on Denmark and Norway where *Eureka* beacons were now in use to assist in identifying DZs, leaving No.38 Group units to cope with Holland. Losses were heavy in this area, German defences, especially over Denmark, taking a steady toll of aircraft on low-level supply drops, even small-arms fire proving effective.

Just four sorties were attempted in the appalling weather of January 1945, but they were amongst the most hazardous flown by Stirlings. Mounted from Kinloss the first sortie was aborted, and of the two despatched on 11 January only Sqn Ldr G. Watson's crew spotted the tiny lights laid out by a Resistance group 4,500 ft up in the mountains at Naushorn, west of Torslake. Fourteen food/supply containers were dropped, the crew receiving the ultimate reward for their 11 hour 44 minute flight in a signal from Norway which read: 'Thanks for the containers of food. Aircraft was 20 minutes early!'

In February the *Ascension* flights were suspended, but Hudson crews resumed agent drops, and from the middle of the month Stirlings operated over Norway in strength, the steadily improving weather enabling the backlog to be substantially reduced. It was not to last, however, for on 9 March Harris finally got his way, No.138 Squadron joining the main bomber force, having delivered 995 agents, 29,000 containers and 10,000 packages in 2,494 sorties, and lost 70 aircraft, while at Tempsford. At the same time No.161 Squadron was transferred to No.38 Group and out of Bomber Command – the SIS/SOE thorn had finally been removed!

The effectiveness of SIS/SOE air operations was often disputed, Harris being just the most voluble detractor. Indisputable was the remarkable bravery and skill demonstrated by the crews, for there can be few things more daunting than map-reading your way to a field somewhere in enemy territory by the light of the moon, landing on an unknown surface chosen by someone with only minimal knowledge of the requirements, facing an uncertain reception, and then getting airborne again, often overloaded, with unknown obstructions ahead. Agent drops by parachute were only slightly less hazardous for the lumbering Whitley, Halifax and Stirling. Sorties had to be flown at low-level and (except when *Eureka* was available) navigated at night, often deep into enemy-occupied territory by dead reckoning and map-reading alone, avoiding known flak defences, but always at the mercy of marauding night fighters and the weather. Postwar, Gen Eisenhower stated that the activities of the French Resistance, supplied by the British, had shortened the campaign in Europe by nine months. Impossible to verify, but an indication of the Supreme Commander's feelings on the subject!

CHAPTER 9

No. 100 Group Countermeasures & Bomber Support

No.100 (SPECIAL DUTIES) Group, Bomber Command was formed on 8 November 1943 using as a nucleus No.80 Wing, Fighter Command. No.80 Wing had been established in June 1940 to co-ordinate action against the German blind bombing *Knickebein* (*Crooked Leg*) system, identified by the Beam Approach Development Unit (BADU). On 30 January 1940 the BADU was re-designated the Wireless Intelligence Development Unit which in turn became No.109 Squadron in December and assisted No.80 Wing in virtually defeating *Knickebein* and the later

X-Gerat and *Y-Gerat* beam systems. Work was then concentrated on discovering how far Germany had progressed with radar, the *Freya* early warning radar being positively identified in February 1941 and the sites plotted. A second system, the *Würzberg*, was also identified by its transmissions and in November a site was finally discovered at Bruneval on the French coast. It became the subject of a daring commando raid on 27/28 February 1942.

On 19 January 1942 No.109 Squadron was divided into three Flights. The Headquarters & Wireless Development Flight moved to Tempsford, the Wireless Reconnaissance Flight to Upper Heyford, while the Wireless Investigation Flight (radio countermeasures (RCM)) remained at Boscombe Down, all under No.26 Group. However, the squadron was steadily becoming more involved in electronic bombing aids, and as a consequence shed the RCM/ELINT (electronic intelligence-gathering) task soon after the HQ moved to Stradishall in April 1942. 'A' Flight reformed as No.1473 Flight and remained at Upper Heyford to continue beam tracking and RCM equipment tests using five Wellingtons and three Ansons, while 'B' and 'C' Flights were transferred to Gransden Lodge with nine Wellingtons and became No.1474 Flight, leaving the squadron to concentrate on *Oboe* work*.

The Air Staff at Bomber Command was anxious about enemy radar developments but was resolutely against RCM, putting its faith in radio/radar 'silence'.

*See Chapter 13

Wg Cdr E.B. Addison commanded No.80 Wing and subsequently No.100 Group for the whole of its operational existence, and rose to the rank of Air Vice Marshal. (Author's collection)

Among No.100 Group's jamming 'targets' were German Würzburg *and* Freya *radars. This was the first positive identification of a* Würzburg - *at Bruneval in France, photographed from a PRU Spitfire on 5 December 1941. (British Official)*

It was left to Fighter Command, concerned about interceptions of *Circus* operations, to encourage the early development of countermeasures, but by mid-1942 it had become obvious that rising Bomber Command losses were directly attributable to radar-guided guns and aircraft. Additionally, the new navigation aids being developed would inevitably break radio silence and reluctantly Bomber Command's Air Staff started to take a real interest in the development of electronic aids designed to defeat the enemy's equipment or warn crews of its presence. Soon they were asking for it to be given top priority!

Meanwhile the first bomber support operation of significance had been carried out in May 1942 during the 'Thousand Bomber' raid on Cologne, attacks being made on night fighter airfields in the hope of suppressing their activities. During October Harris suggested to Air Chief Marshal Sir Sholto Douglas, C-in-C Fighter Command, that 'some Mosquito night fighters might profitably be mixed in with the bomber stream'. Sholto Douglas was keen on the idea, but use of Airborne Interception (AI) radar over enemy territory was banned and nothing could be done until there was a change in policy – in June 1943.

No.1473 Flight was working on the development of *Moonshine* equipment which picked up *Freya* early warning radar transmissions, amplified the pulses and re-transmitted them, a single aircraft producing a very large 'echo' which hopefully would decoy enemy fighters away from the bomber force. Fitted in Defiants, it was first used operationally in August 1942 and had some success. Less useful was the fitting of a 'J' (jamming) switch to bomber IFF sets which was supposed to jam *Würzburg* ground-controlled interception (GCI) radars but proved ineffective, as did a modification named *Shiver*. *Moonshine* was replaced by the higher-powered *Mandrel* which jammed early warning (EW) radars very successfully and was modified to cope with German refinements as they were developed. To interfere with night fighter control transmissions *Tinsel* was used. This required the operator to 'sweep' over a briefed waveband until he received foreign language R/T transmissions, then tune his aircraft transmitter to the same frequency and switch on a microphone situated in a noisy engine bay. The Luftwaffe quickly reacted by changing frequency but *Tinsel* was refined, *Special Tinsel* operators being instructed by W/T which frequencies to jam. Efforts were also made to learn more about German AI equipment, No.1473 Flight flying 'live bait' sorties over France, Belgium and Holland recording airborne intercept radar transmissions. The Germans were slow to bite, so on 3 December 1942 a Wellington from the unit accompanied bombers to Frankfurt – and produced the evidence the hard way, being attacked and badly damaged by a Ju88!

Meanwhile No.1474 Flight continued its work identifying enemy radar wavelengths and plotting coverage, forming the nucleus of No.192 Squadron on 4 January 1943 with 17 Wellingtons, three Mosquitoes and a couple of Ansons on strength. Some of the Wellingtons were replaced by Halifaxes in March and from June onwards signals were being routinely monitored from northern Norway to southern France.

Concern over the very efficient FuG 202/212 series of German airborne radars resulted in the introduction of *Ground Grocer* which became operational on 26/27 April 1943. It only proved a partial solution because its range was limited but fortunately *Window*, the oldest and simplest countermeasure of all, proved equally effective. First suggested in 1938 and introduced unsuccessfully in North Africa during 1941, *Window* was redeveloped in 1942 and finally cleared for use on 1 May 1943. The developed version consisted of thin strips of tin foil gummed to black backing paper packed in bundles of 2,000 and effective against both GCI and AI radars. Used over Europe for the first time on 24/25 July, *Window* blotted out the German radar 'picture' and caused total paralysis of the defences. Countermeasures were quickly produced but they were never completely effective, and *Window* remained one of the best, and certainly the cheapest, method for long after the war ended.

The Telecommunications Research Establishment (TRE) produced *Boozer*, a passive device which gave the aircrew an indication that German gun-laying and night fighter radars were active in the area via warning lights on the pilot's instrument panel. It went into service during the spring of 1943 and was followed in June by the Royal Aircraft Establishment (RAE)-developed *Monica*. This was an active radar with rear-facing scanner which generated a 'bleeping' sound on the intercom, increasing in rate as the range closed. Neither was totally successful because *Boozer* gave almost constant alarms while *Monica* responded to friend or foe, and there was always the fear that the Germans would use it to home onto the bombers.

Meanwhile Fighter Command started organized bomber support operations in June 1943 when Mosquito IIs of No.605 Squadron began *Flower* patrols – the first such 'intruder' sorties against Luftwaffe night fighter bases being made on the 11/12th. Beaufighters of No. 141 Squadron commenced operating within the bomber stream during the same month, using *Serrate*, a homer designed to give a bearing on German AI radars which was initially very successful.

With H2S now in general use a replacement for *Monica* was devised and developed by Dr Lovell at the TRE. Code-named *Fishpond* it used part of the H2S time base not employed for mapping to indicate on a separate scope any reflecting objects between the ground and the aircraft. Night fighters, or for that matter other bombers, could therefore be detected and a range and bearing obtained, fighters obvious by their more rapid movement across the screen. It entered service at the end of 1943.

In August Fighter Command started *Mahmoud* sorties with AI Mk.IV and *Monica*-fitted Mosquitoes of No.25 Squadron. The crews went to known German night fighter assembly points and offered themselves as 'bait', while non-AI Mosquitoes of No.605 Squadron started loose escort of the bomber stream and on 31 August 1943 even reached Berlin. Nos.264 and 410 Squadrons also took part in such operations during the autumn, while on the ground No.80 Wing was developing jammers and various 'spoofing' equipments such as *Ground Cigar*.

Jostle, a high-powered jammer intended to drown out German night fighter control frequencies, had been expected to enter service in July but was delayed, and in October 1943 *Airborne Cigar* (*ABC*) was introduced as a stop-gap. Developed by the TRE, *ABC* consisted of a receiver sweeping German night fighter control frequencies and three 50-watt transmitters providing frequency-modulated jamming signals. Initially carried by Lancasters of No.101 Squadron the equipment used three seven-foot aerials, two on top and one beneath the fuselage. An additional crew member was carried, trained to identify and jam German GCI controllers.

At much the same time *Corona* became operational. This equipment carried out a broadly similar function to *ABC* but used a No.80 Wing ground station for transmitting confusion, and was able to counter female controllers by training German-speaking WAAFs to imitate them. It was first used on 22/23 October 1943 during a raid on Kassel and though a failure on that occasion due to a lucky sighting of the Main Force by a German reconnaissance aircraft, it soon demonstrated its usefulness. In desperation the Germans turned to coded broadcasts on their Forces radio – dealt with by *Dartboard*, a high-powered transmitter – and then tried instructions in Morse code. The latter failed on two counts because most night fighter crews were insufficiently versed in the code, and *Drumstick* transmitters in England were quickly in use broadcasting meaningless Morse on German frequencies.

With diversionary raids, false target marking and deceptive routeing, the whole business was becoming both complicated and distracting, and Bomber Command's Operations staff suggested the formation

A Beaufighter IIF, representative of the aircraft equipping No.515 Squadron when it joined No.100 Group in December 1943. (MAP)

of a specialist organization to oversee both RCM and diversionary tactics. The proposal was accepted by the Air Ministry and No.100 Group was born. Even Harris was won over, for in a letter dated 7 December 1943 he wrote that, 'overriding priority should be given to the formation [of the Group] and equipment'. No.141 Squadron had already been transferred from Fighter Command four days earlier and by mid-December No.100 Group had seven airfields on which were Nos.141, 169, 239 and 515 Squadrons equipped mainly with Mosquito II and Beaufighter II aircraft for support operations, No. 192 Squadron and No.1473 Flight for RCM work, plus No.1692 Flight for *Serrate* training. Only No.1473 Flight and Nos.141 and 192 Squadrons could be considered operational though, and it was Wellingtons from the latter unit which had inaugurated the Group's activities on 30 November by flying RCM flights. The remaining units were either re-equipping or training for new 'support' roles, No.515 Squadron being in a particularly sorry state with equipment problems and unsuitable aircraft.

The first No.100 Group *Serrate* sorties were despatched on 16/17 December 1943 when No.141 Squadron sent two Mosquitoes and two Beaufighters to Berlin in support of a Lancaster/Mosquito raid on the city. Sqn Ldr F.F. Lambert and his navigator intercepted a Bf110 and claimed it 'damaged', and on 23/24 December Flt Lt Kelsey, the pilot of one of three Beaufighters patrolling the route to the same target, destroyed a Ju88 near Düren, south-west of Cologne.

No.192 Squadron were now flying Wellington,

Mosquito and Halifax aircraft, the latter especially well-equipped with two 'special operator' positions between the wing spars for the *Mandrel* gear, wire recorders and visual displays, the latter photographed by a 35mm camera. No.1473 Flight used its short-range Ansons to monitor enemy VHF transmissions, and Wellingtons/Mosquitoes for checks on the effectiveness of jammers such as *Ground Cigar*; work so similar to that of No.192 Squadron that it was absorbed in January 1944. The unit then concentrated on plotting enemy coastal radar coverage in preparation for Operation *Overlord*, the invasion of the Continent, a task which continued until June.

No.214 Squadron joined the Group with Stirlings in January and immediately started conversion to Fortress IIs as a jammer unit. Continuing delay in the delivery of *Airborne Grocer* and *Jostle* resulted in a number of the unit's aircraft being fitted with *ABC* equipment and the first operational sortie was despatched on 20/21 April. Operating alongside was the 803rd BS (P) of the 8th Air Force which flew B-17s fitted with *Mandrel* and *Carpet* from Sculthorpe and Oulton, under No.100 Group control in all but name.

The *Serrate* squadrons were now slowly getting into their stride as serviceability improved and retraining was completed. Between December 1943 and April 1944 only 220 patrols had been flown by the three squadrons, Nos.141, 169 and 239, but in May sortie rates increased markedly and the units were confident of much better results.

Above *Mosquito IIs supplemented the Beaufighters of No.515 Squadron in February 1944, both being replaced by Mosquito VIs in April 1944. (British Official)*

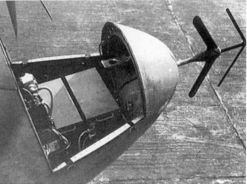

Left Serrate *equipment in the nose of an AI Mk.IV-equipped Mosquito II. The 'black boxes' replaced the .303-inch guns usually fitted in the night fighter variant. (British Official)*

So many trials were now underway that it was decided to form a dedicated unit to control them. Established at Foulsham in April 1944 as the Special Duty Radar Development Unit, it was given the more accurate title of Bomber Support Development Unit (BSDU) on 1 May and was soon designing and developing new equipment in addition to testing and devising tactics.

Also in May No.199 (SD) Squadron, previously a No.3 Group Stirling unit, joined No.100 Group for *Mandrel* work, its aircraft also fitted with *Shiver* (modified IFF Mk.II) and *Gee*. Up to eight *Mandrel* transmitters could be carried, additional alternators being fitted to cope with the electrical load, and the squadron was mainly responsible for the development of both 'permanent' and 'creeping' *Mandrel* screens. At last *Jostle* was declared operational and the first installations were made in No.214 Squadron Fortresses during the month, though the initial sortie using the equipment was not made until 4 July. *Monica III* tail warning radar was fitted at the same time but the *ABC* installation, specified in the RCM requirements for the aircraft, did not progress past a

trial fit because it was found easy to 'home' onto its transmissions.

The AI Mk.IV installed in the *Serrate* Mosquito IIs of Nos.141, 169 and 239 Squadrons was clearly inadequate, returns from the bomber stream often completely swamping the display when close escort was attempted. As a direct result of the disastrous raid on Nuremburg on 30/31 March 1944 when 95 aircraft were lost, Harris wrote a strongly worded letter to the Vice Chief of Air Staff on the subject of night fighters, suggesting that they could only be defeated by heavier bomber armament, which seemed impracticable in the short term, or greatly strengthening the No.100 Group fighter force and providing it with better radar. He proposed that an additional 10 squadrons, equipped with AI Mk.X Mosquitoes, should be transferred from Fighter Command, and that the ban on the use of the equipment over enemy-held territory should be lifted. A high-level conference at the Air Ministry on 20 April

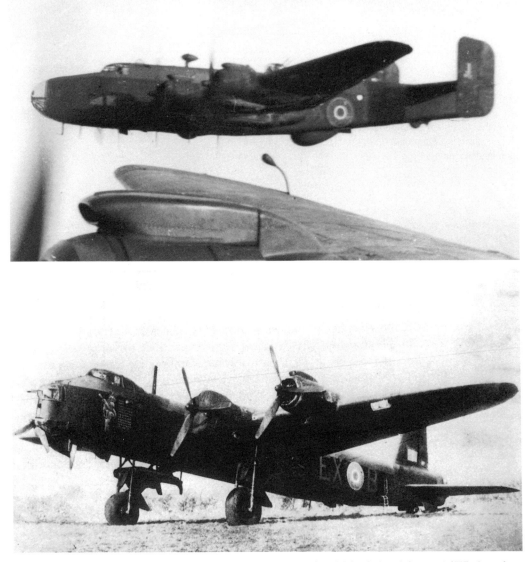

Top: *Halifax III PN375/EX-E of No.199 Squadron, another aircraft with* Mandrel *and the special* Window *chute aft of the radome. (RAF Museum P17222)*

Above: *Stirling III LJ514/EX-B of No.199 Squadron fitted with a* Window *chute and* Mandrel *aerials. (J.L. Smith/AST)*

agreed the use of centrimetric AI radar by No. 100 Group, but the allocation of squadrons was reduced to three, Nos.85 and 157 Squadrons with AI Mk.X transferring early in May, and No.23 Squadron arriving from the Mediterranean theatre at the beginning of June with Mosquito VIs. The latter were not fitted with radar but were used for 'intruding' alongside No.515 Squadron, with considerable success.

Nos.199 Squadron and the 803rd BS(P) were held at readiness so that the maximum effect of their *Mandrel* screen was felt during the initial stages of *Overlord*. Flying at 15,000 ft on the night of 5/6 June they set up their screen from Eastbourne to Portland

Bill, covering the advancing invasion fleet by flying pairs of aircraft on 'racetrack' orbits on 10 'stations' based on *Gee* chart lines. At much the same time, five Fortresses of No.214 Squadron joined 24 Lancasters of No.101 Squadron using *ABC* jammers and *Window* to simulate a bombing force approaching the Pas de Calais along the line of the River Somme – their aim being to distract attention from the transports and tug/glider combinations on their way to the DZs and LZs further west. Supporting the jammers were ground-based transmitters blotting out Luftwaffe night fighter frequencies. Altogether it was a devastating use of RCM power.

The Group's Mosquitoes were also active, 27 *Serrate* sorties being flown over France by Nos.141, 169 and 239 Squadrons, while the 'intruders' of Nos.85, 157, and 515 Squadrons flew 25 sorties, half over the beachhead and the rest over Dutch and Belgian airfields. Immediately after the invasion force had landed Main Force bomber squadrons started attacking German communications, supported by No 100 Group Mosquitoes, the latter claiming 32 enemy aircraft destroyed in June, even though Nos.85 and 157 Squadrons were temporarily transferred to ADGB towards the end of the month for anti-*Diver* (V-1) operations, the BSDU fitting the aircraft with *Monica* tail warners for this work.

Nos.85 and 157 Squadrons were partially replaced by No.23 Squadron, operational with the Group during the night of 5/6 July and subsequently, with No.515 Squadron, contributing 244 sorties on day and night *Rangers*. Meanwhile the *Serrate* squadrons had suffered a sudden drop in the number of contacts in June, and became almost totally ineffective at night – a very worrying development. The explanation came with the fortuitous arrival of a Ju88 night fighter at Woodbridge on 13 July 1944. It was equipped with SN-2 AI and a *Flensburg* homer, the AI working on a frequency unaffected by *Window* and undetectable by *Serrate*, while the homer could pick up *Monica* at an alarmingly long range. Modified *Serrate Mk.IV* and

Below: *Mosquito VI PZ181/YP-E of No.23 Squadron at Little Snoring during late summer 1944. (G. Stewart)*

Bottom: *Nos.85 and 157 Squadrons joined No.100 Group in early summer 1944 with Mosquito XIXs equipped with centrimetric AI. (British Official)*

Mosquito NF.XXX of No.85 Squadron at the start of another nocturnal mission. (via Chaz Bowyer Collection)

Perfectos were rapidly developed by the BSDU, the latter capable of providing homing, distance and positive identification by triggering German FuG 25A IFF.

The success of 'spoofing' on D-Day resulted in the formation of the Special *Window* Force (SWF) in July, which became operational on the 14/15th using *Mandrel* fitted aircraft of Nos.192 and 199 Squadrons. Its object was to divert attention away from Main Force raids by simulating the transmissions of such a force. It depended on accurate navigation and precise *Window* dropping to achieve success, plus a constant flow of new ploys as German controllers learnt to identify them. *ABC* was removed from No.214 Squadron Fortresses during the summer and they joined the SWF, to which the 803rd BS (P) (re-designated 36th BS on 14 August 1944) was also attached. Other aircraft operating with the 803rd/36th BS were *Droop Snoot* P-38 Lightnings and P-51 Mustangs which flew *Ferret* sorties under the control of No.192 Squadron, RAF. On 23 August No.223 Squadron, equipped with Liberators, joined No.100 Group for jamming work using *Jostle*, and the debut of the V-2 rocket resulted in the unit's aircraft being fitted for *Big Ben* operations, intended to jam the V-2 guidance mechanism in the understandable but mistaken belief that it used ground radio transmissions for this purpose.

On 29 August Nos.85 and 157 Squadrons returned to No.100 Group following the virtual defeat of the

V-1, and immediately resumed their low-level 'intruding' work. Trials by the BSDU on the American AN/APS-4 radar (known as AI Mk.XV in the RAF and *ASH* in the Fleet Air Arm) showed promise, and it was installed in Mosquito VIs of No.23 Squadron, while the *Serrate* squadrons, Nos.141, 169 and 239, were re-employed on day *Rangers* and as escorts to *Big Ben* sorties.

The *Mandrel* force was further strengthened during September when No. 171 Squadron was reformed from 'C' Flight, No.199 Squadron. The new unit flew its first operation on the 15th using Stirlings but was soon converting to Halifax IIIs. The SWF was very active at this time, and proved successful on 11/12 September when 13 No.100 Group 'heavies' accompanying 76 Halifaxes and Lancasters mine-laying in the Kattegat, 'spoofed' the Germans into thinking they were *en route* Berlin or Stettin and left the Main Force attack on Darmstadt, a town between Frankfurt and Mannheim, comparatively 'night fighter free'. The next night 31 RCM sorties were flown in the Karlsruhe area and the use of *Window* and *Mandrel* resulted in a strong night fighter response. In general, however, night fighter activity declined in the autumn of 1944, and as the Mosquito units all received aircraft fitted with either *ASH* or AI Mk.X radar their activities were merged. *Big Ben* sorties were also gradually reduced during November when the target for both V-1 and V-2 attacks changed to Antwerp, though No.192 Squadron continued its

Air and ground crew of Halifax III NA695/6Y-D of No.171 Squadron. (L.H.J. King/AST)

work, trying to discover whether radio beams were being used by He111s air-launching V-1s against Britain from over the North Sea.

It was found that AI Mk.X worked much better at high-level and so it was decided to feed Mosquitoes thus equipped into areas around the Main Force target, flying orbits known as the 'Clock Patrol' some 6-10 miles from the target itself. It was an immediate success, enabling the Mosquito crews to intercept incoming German night fighters. Other Mosquito units continued operations with the SWF and started 'nuisance' attacks dropping 500-lb bombs, while the SWF itself was further strengthened by the transfer of No.462 Squadron from No.4 Group, the unit introducing bombing by the 'heavies' of No.100 Group and also taking part in *Mandrel/Window*

Mosquito FB.VI RS566 of No.515 Squadron in 1944, equipped with ASH (AI Mk.XV) in a 'thimble' nose radome. (via R.W. Elliott)

Halifax III PN431/DT-A of No.192 Squadron over Norfolk. The Monica *aerial can be seen under the tail and the* Window *chute aft of the H2S radome. (RAFM 17224)*

'spoofing' while waiting for *ABC* equipment to be fitted to its Halifaxes.

During December the BSDU was transferred to Swanton Morley with its cosmopolitan collection of aircraft, which included Mosquitoes, Stirlings, Liberators, Beaufighters and even four Spitfire Vs, as well as the main workhorse, the Halifax. Tremendous effort was expended on a 'standard' jammer Halifax, an aircraft fitted with three *ABC* units, three *Carpet II* GCI jammers, three *Carpet IIIs*, an AN/APR4 search receiver, *Window* chute and TR1143A transmitter/ receiver. Unfortunately it was April 1945 before the 'fit' was finalised and the war in Europe was over before it entered service.

Nos.23 and 141 Squadrons both became operational with *ASH* radar during December 1944 and on 1 January 1945 No.141 Squadron claimed the equipment's first victim, a Ju88. Later in the month some of the *Serrate/Perfectos* Squadrons started to re-equip with Mosquito Mk.XIX and Mk.XXX night fighters, and Fighter Command provided additional support for Main Force bombers, Nos.151, 307, 406 and 456 Squadrons all joining the escort force as 1945 progressed.

The last Bomber Command Wellington sortie, an RCM flight over the North Sea, was flown by No.192 Squadron during the night of 7/8 January 1945, and the 36th BS was replaced by two new units on *Mandrel* patrols, the 857th and 858th BS(H), in

February. The 857th was soon disbanded but the 858th continued under No.100 Group control until April, by which time the amount of jamming, 'spoofing' and bomber support was overwhelming. New 'spoofing' included the dropping of TIs by No.100 Group Mosquitoes for a simulated Main Force from No.5 Group under the control of a Master Bomber transmitting on the usual frequencies. At last the Group had managed to standardize on the Halifax for *Mandrel* and *Window* work, but Nos. 214 and 223 Squadrons continued operations with Fortresses and Liberators respectively, because the ultra high-powered *Jostle* jamming transmitters could not be fitted in the Halifax.

No.141 Squadron started operations with its Mosquito Mk.XXXs on 4/5 April when the Group's sorties included a number of 'flak' suppression patrols in support of mining off Norway. On 17/18 April No.515 Squadron started 'Master Bomber' sorties, acting as a marker unit for other No.100 Group Mosquito units engaged on airfield attacks, and the following night seven No.141 Squadron Mk.XXXs dropped 1,400 gallons of napalm (an unpleasant jelly-like substance which ignites on contact with objects) on Neubiburg airfield. Code-named *Firebash*, other napalm attacks were made later in the month on Flensburg, Lübeck and Schleswig.

Both *Mandrel* and SWF operations were now being conducted ahead of the Main Force stream, the

SWF also carrying out full-scale raids on diversionary targets, such as on 13/14 April when an attack was made on Bioizenburg by 20 Halifaxes and eight Mosquitoes during the main raid on Kiel.

No.223 Squadron started conversion to the Fortress III during the month but they were not destined to see operational service, for the Germans were near to collapse and there were no offensive operations by Bomber Command from 26/27 April until 2/3 May. On this, the final night, No.100 Group despatched aircraft on a variety of tasks, 37 Mosquitoes joining forces with 16 from No.8 Group attacking airfields in the Kiel area, while 89 RCM aircraft supported the main assault on Kiel itself. The aircraft included Mosquitoes, Fortresses, Liberators and Halifaxes, the latter carrying five 500-lb bombs as well as their jamming equipment. Sadly one of No.169 Squadron's aircraft was lost during a napalm attack on Jagel, and two Halifaxes of No.199 Squadron crashed near Meimersdorf, probably following a collision. Fifteen airmen were killed in the two incidents, the last Bomber Command casualties of the war.

In June the *Window* Research Section, formed in February 1945 to develop a much-needed automatic *Window* dispenser was absorbed by the BSDU, and between 25 June and 5 July the unit was heavily engaged in Exercise *Post Mortem*. Simulated large-scale attacks on enemy territory were mounted to assess the efficiency of the German raid reporting system, and showed that Bomber Command's 'spoofing' and jamming techniques developed by No.100 Group were a great success. The final passage of the report said: 'On the whole, there appears no defence against the effective jamming of the *Mandrel* and *Window* forces.' Vindication indeed!

The BSDU was absorbed by the newly-formed Radio Warfare Establishment on 21 July and No.100 Group itself was rapidly run-down. It disbanded on 17 December 1945 having flown 16,746 operational sorties and lost 122 aircraft (0.7% of those despatched).

The results of *Post Mortem* and the rudimentary state of the radars available to the only likely opponent at the end of the Second World War, Soviet Russia, produced a hiatus in the further development of countermeasures. *Window* could easily confuse the EW radars available to the Russians and apart from a new tail warning radar, *Orange Putter*, developed for the Canberra in

Right: Jostle *IV VHF jamming equipment on its special transporter. (British Official)*

Below: *The size and power requirements of* Jostle *precluded carriage in the Halifax, so the Fortress III was used. The* Jostle *aerial is plainly visible on KJ101/BU-H of No.214 Squadron. (via J.D.R. Rawlings)*

No.223 Squadron also operated Fortress IIIs including KJ118/6G-H, seen at Lichfield post-war with codes painted out. (J. Rabbetts)

Another view of a Fortress III of No.223 Squadron showing its nose-mounted H2S radome. (J. Rabbetts)

The Fortress' replacement – Liberator VI 6G-M of No.223 Squadron at Oulton in 1945. (via J.D. Oughton)

1947, and *Red Garter* a similar device intended for V-Bombers but which failed to meet specifications, little was done until the early 1950s. By then the Russians, taking advantage of German know-how, had developed centrimetric radars. In response, No.199 Squadron was reformed on 16 July 1951 with Lincolns fitted with jamming gear, the unit transferring from No.90 Group to No.3 Group, Bomber Command, in April 1952 to continue its monitoring and training role. The first Canberra to join the unit arrived in July 1954 and on 1 October 1957 the Lincoln element became No.1321 Flight, the Canberras moving from Hemswell to Honington to join the Valiants of 'C' Flight, No.199 Squadron. The latter aircraft had very extensive jamming gear which included *ABC*, *Cornet 4*, *Window* dispensers, *Carpet III* and AN/APT-16A, a development of *Mandrel*. In December 1958 the Canberras were withdrawn and the Valiants transferred to Finningley,

the unit being renumbered No.18 Squadron on arrival.

It had been realized as early as 1955 that a single squadron could not cover a widely dispersed V-Force on operations. It was decided to equip V-Bombers with their own ECM equipment, though in practice the installation was confined to Victor and Vulcan Mk.2s and a number of Mk.1s, the latter fitted with additional alternators. The package included the *Red Shrimp* GCI radar jammer, *Green Palm*, a VHF jammer operating on Soviet fighter frequencies, and *Blue Saga*, a passive warning receiver. Also fitted was *Fishpool*, an upgrade of the wartime *Fishpond* using elements of the H2S Mk.9 radar to detect intercepting fighters, and a new tail warner, *Red Steer*, developed at TRE Malvern from AI Mk.13. It was this ECM package, together with *Window*, which remained effective long after the disbandment of Bomber Command in 1968, though new equipment was in prospect.

CHAPTER 10

From Bludgeon to Rapier 1946-1957

BOMBER COMMAND ENTERED the post-war era equipped almost entirely with Lancasters and Mosquitoes, the two most successful wartime bombers. The heavy bomber replacement, the Lincoln, suffered delays largely due to engine problems, but tentatively entered service at East Kirkby with the Trials Flight in August 1945, operating as part of No.57 Squadron. No.75 Squadron received a few Lincolns in September but was disbanded within a month, its aircraft passing to No.44 Squadron. Further deliveries were painfully slow and it was December 1946 before No.44 Squadron and the rest of No.1 Group were completely equipped, while No.3 Group had much longer to wait. The operational Mosquito force was quickly reduced to just three Mk.XVI bomber squadrons, No.109 with No.1 Group and Nos.105 and 139 in No. 3 Group, all operating as marker units. In further moves No.139 Squadron joined No.109 in No.1 Group, and in February 1946 No.105 Squadron disbanded.

Relieved of their *Tallboy* responsibilities Nos.9 and 617 Squadrons were re-equipped with Lancaster VIIs and in January 1946 went to India to replace Liberators of Nos.159 and 355 Squadrons

Waddington and snow seem synonymous. Lancaster III ME359 of No.50 Squadron stands outside the big Type C hangars in January 1946. (W.G. Rees)

relinquished under Lend-Lease agreements. In India the crews spent most of their time on photographic survey work, but were also placed on stand-by during an Indian Navy mutiny. They returned to the UK at the end of April and became involved in the experimental 'Binbrook Wing' project, Nos.9, 12, 101 and 617 Squadrons being effectively 'pooled'.

Disposal of surplus weapon stocks continued with Operation *Sinkum*, the 'ditching' of incendiaries in the Heligoland Bight and Cardigan Bay, and Operation *Mandarin*, which started in May and involved dropping 1,000-lb bombs on Heligoland; an action repeated at intervals to deter re-occupation until the island was officially returned to the Germans. Deep penetration bombing trials, code-named Project *Ruby,* were also carried out using B-17s and B-29s of the USAAF and Lancasters of Bomber Command on the nearly complete U-Boat pens at Farge, near Bremen. Among the bombs dropped were 22,000-lb *Grand Slams*, ex-617 Squadron Lancasters being used by No.15 Squadron for these tests which continued until the end of August.

Operation *Front Line*, a 'flag-waving' exercise in which up to 60 aircraft flew at low-level over Germany, became commonplace during 1946, and in June the first Operation *Sunbronze* detachment saw No.9 and 617 Squadron Lancasters at Pomigliano, though Luqa, Malta, was the more usual destination. However it was the first post-war goodwill tour by Bomber Command that attracted more attention, the crews of 16 Lancasters, nominally from No.35 Squadron, carrying out low-level formation flying practice in the Graveley area for several weeks prior to departure for the United States under the command of Gp Capt R.C.M. Collard. They arrived in the USA on 17 July 1946, visited seven airfields and took part in the Air Force Day celebrations before returning home

In warmer climes. Lancasters B.VII(FE)s NX746/B and NX782/T of No.617 Squadron 'show the flag' in India, early 1946. (RAFM P14751)

on 29 August. Other overseas flights followed, the first by a Lincoln in September when a No.100 Squadron aircraft accompanied Meteors of the High Speed Flight to Prague. The same unit provided three aircraft for a visit to Santiago, Chile, in October.

These high-profile events were good publicity but at squadron level demobilization was a having a drastic effect, it becoming difficult to provide crews or aircraft for normal daily training, while in the higher echelons a fierce debate was raging over the future of strategic bombing, a concept no longer universally accepted as desirable or even feasible. The advent of the 'atom' bomb and the turbojet had radically altered the situation and while the arguments continued the Air Ministry judiciously outlined specifications for unarmed, high-altitude jet-propelled bombers, light and heavy,* it being universally agreed that the Lincoln stood no chance of survival against the new breed of fighters on the drawing boards and that only a radical new generation of bombers could hope to survive once such fighters were operational!

In practice any decisions on strategic bombing were soon out of the Air Ministry's hands for as early as February 1946 it was clear that relations with the Soviet Union were not going to be harmonious, and a month later Churchill was talking of the 'Iron Curtain'. International tension, added to the sudden ending of Anglo-American co-operation in the nuclear field following the McMahon Act of 1956, caused alarm in Whitehall, and early in 1947 the political decision was taken to 'go it alone' and produce British atomic weapons and the aircraft to carry them. The circumstances in which such a force would be used were not spelt out but the Chief of Air Staff, Marshal

*See Chapter 13

of the Royal Air Force Lord Tedder, was determined that Bomber Command would not get involved in a nuclear war of attrition. He directed the planners to create 'a rapier rather than a bludgeon'.

Such plans were for the future. In the short term a 'bludgeon' was all that was available and to counter a Russian attack Air Staff Plan E of 1947 proposed a front-line strength of 41 piston-engined bomber squadrons, it being considered that such a force could still get through to Russian targets for the next few years. However, Britain's poor economic circumstances and assessments of Soviet capabilities suggesting that war was unlikely in the next five years mitigated against such a force, and inevitably it was slimmed down and in June 1948 the official strength was stabilized at 24 squadrons. The number of aircraft was 160 though manning levels reduced availability way below this figure. To those with long memories it all sounded distressingly like the 'Ten Year Rule' of 1919!

The flying that was done was a strange mixture. From January 1947 Lincolns of No.1 Group helped

During Project Ruby, No.15 Squadron used Lancaster B.1 (Special) aircraft, including PD131/V, to test-drop 22,000-lb bombs on the U-boat pens at Farge, Bremen. (Flight 17474)

Top: *Service trials of the Lincoln B.II were still under way in 1946. Among the aircraft used was RF388/KM-C of No. 44 Squadron. (J. Chatterton)*

Above: *After a slow start Lincolns steadily replaced No.1 Group Lancasters. RF472/B was on No.100 Squadron strength from April 1947 to February 1948. (Author's collection)*

out Coastal Command with meteorological flights, regular *Seaweed* sorties northwards to the fringe of the Arctic Circle, and *Pampas* which were flown and routed as required, usually out over the Atlantic for up to eight hours. Six specially-equipped Lincolns were used, these being passed from unit to unit with the 'Met' tasking. Bombs and ammunition continued to be dumped in Cardigan Bay under Operation *Wastage*, and four Lancasters of No.7 Squadron went to Singapore for Operation *Red Lion*, a trial two-month detachment 'showing the flag' and carrying out live bombing over Perak, Malaya. Operation *Hatbox*, a shipping target trial using 500-lb and 1,000-lb bombs, occupied Nos.15 and 44 Squadrons from May until October 1947, alongside the *Harken Project* which involved dropping special 1,000-pounders on the long-suffering Farge submarine pens.

In June 1947 AVM Stratfield, SASO Bomber Command, visited Egypt to prepare the way for Operation *Sunray* detachments, these being intended to provide crews with intensive practice bombing and gunnery on the ranges. No.207 Squadron arrived at Shallufa for the first *Sunray* on 19 July, and a steady stream of units followed, each staying for a month. During No.101 Squadron's detachment in October they were unexpectedly sent down to Khormaksar, Aden, to take part in attacks on Thumier, the 'capital' of the rebellious Quteibi tribe. The Lincolns dropped 60 tons of 500-pounders before returning home via a 10-day goodwill visit to Turkey – it would not be the only 'colonial policing' by Bomber Command.

Meanwhile 16 Lincolns, nominally from No.617 Squadron but including Nos.9 and 12 Squadron crews, left for the USA on 23 July for a five-week goodwill tour which also took in Air Force Day. The crews were welcomed in the usual American fashion, but in truth the aircraft were already considered an anachronism on both sides of the Atlantic and it was with relief that orders for prototypes of twin- and

Lancasters lasted longer with No.3 Group, one example being PA412, a B.1(FE) of No.115 Squadron, seen over London during the Battle of Britain Flypast on 15 September 1947. (via J.D. Oughton)

four-engined jet bombers, the latter with 'a novel wing shape', were announced in October.

A six-Lincoln *Sunray* detachment from No. 15, 90 and 138 Squadrons followed No.101 to Aden at the beginning of November for more tribal bombing, and during February/March 1948 No.57 Squadron spent two weeks attacking Bel Harith tribesmen in the Yemen. Other *Sunrays* included flights from Shallufa to Habbaniya, Khartoum and Nicosia, all aimed at increasing experience levels as the number of wartime personnel on operational squadrons gradually declined.

Heligoland was a favourite target for live bombing on Exercise *Bullseye* and in May 1948 was used by Nos.83 and 100 Squadrons to demonstrate the Lincoln's ability to Vice Commodore Armenanzas, AOC Lincoln Group, Argentine Air Force. Other exercises which became standard were *Ding Dong*, a navigational flight over Continental Europe, and target marking sorties which often included *Window* dropping to give air defence radar operators some experience of jamming. Nos.83 and 97 Squadrons operated as a 'Flare Force', their Lincolns carrying up to 12,000 lb of these dangerous pyrotechnics, dropping them as sky markers using H2S for positioning, or to enable Mosquitoes of Nos.109 and 139 Squadrons to visual mark from low-level.

Lincolns of No.97 Squadron left Hemswell on 28 April 1948 for Operation *Red Lion II*, remaining at Singapore for six weeks on anti-insurgent training.

The Mosquito marker force upgraded to the B.35 variant. TK635 of No. 139 Squadron is seen at Luqa, Malta, in 1949. (M. Olmsted)

They left just as the Malayan Communist Party (MCP) fomented the unrest which developed into full-scale guerilla operations – and the 'Malayan Emergency'.

In the UK inter-service exercises began in a small way during 1948. For *Dawn*, Bomber Command provided Lincolns and Lancasters for attacks on the Home Fleet on 13-14 May, while the Lancasters of the Stradishall Wing, Nos.35, 115, 149 and 207 Squadrons, took part in the similar *One Step* on 24 September. The first major post-war air defence exercise, *Dagger*, was also in September, Lincolns and Mosquitoes joining forces with USAF B-29s and Fighter Command Hornets in attacks on 'Northland' from 'Southland' via a circuitous route. Not surprisingly it was judged that the Lincolns were particularly easy targets to intercept, and their mass formation tactics were considered ill-judged.

In February 1949 the concept of 'linked' squadrons was authorized, the idea being to keep alive the 'number plate' of disbanded units earmarked for reformation during an expansion. Nine ex-Bomber Command units were so linked but it was never a very successful idea, the link hardly ever being acknowledged by the operational unit. The

deteriorating political situation following the blockade of Berlin by the Russians during 1948-49 accelerated the re-equipment of No.3 Group with Lincolns. The installation of improved H2S Mk.IVA in the aircraft was also made a priority, No.9 Squadron receiving the first operational Lincolns with this radar in June 1949. Exercises were stepped up following the formation of the North Atlantic Treaty Organization (NATO) in April, Bomber Command being involved in mock attacks on naval units, various UK air defence exercises such as *Foil*, *Verity* and *Tool*, and probes of Norwegian radar and control systems.

Direct flights to Shallufa for *Sunray* were now introduced using two 400-gallon tanks in the Lincoln's bomb-bay, and in October No.9 Squadron followed its Egyptian detachment with the last goodwill tour by Lincolns, a 12-day visit to Pakistan, during which live bombing demonstrations, including drops of 4,000-lb *Cookies* were made on Churna Island near Karachi.

In September 1949 the Americans announced that the Soviets had exploded an atomic weapon, adding to the general concern being felt about the speed at which the Russians were catching up. The unofficial 'five-year' rule was abandoned and re-armament plans accelerated, arrangements being made for the short-term loan of Boeing B-29s by the Americans under the Mutual Defence Assistance Program (MDAP). The concern expressed was understandable for at this time, early 1950, Bomber Command could field only 22 heavy bomber squadrons, 20 equipped with Lincolns, the other two, Nos.49 and 214, still having Lancasters. Hardly a credible force but at last

the meteorological flights which, following the Russian nuclear tests, had latterly included air sampling flights were relinquished just as re-equipment with Lincoln B.2/4As was completed. Soon afterwards came an increase in unit establishment from six to eight aircraft and a noticeable lift in the Command's morale as the basic bomber role was re-emphasized.

The last bomber Lancasters were replaced in March 1950 just as No.3 Group's Mildenhall Wing (Nos.35, 115, 149 and 207 Squadrons) was disbanded to provide crews for the B-29 Washingtons already being delivered. Meanwhile Benson and its three photographic reconnaissance units (PRUs), No.58 (Mosquito), No.540 (Mosquito/Spitfire) and No. 541 (Spitfire) Squadrons, were taken over from Coastal Command during January 1950, together with No.82 (Lancaster) Squadron on detachment in Africa, the Central Interpretation Unit and the OCU. The 'ownership' of the PRUs had been a bone of contention for over eight years – at last it was resolved in Bomber Command's favour.

Obsolescent they may have been, but for 'colonial' type skirmishes Lincolns were to prove very effective and as *Firedog*, the code-name for air support to the troops fighting Communist terrorists (CTs) in Malaya, broadened in scope Bomber Command became involved. Contingency plans were updated, Operation *Musgrave* was ordered, and No.57 Squadron arrived in Singapore on 20 March 1950. Two days later the unit made a 'maximum effort' attack on a 1,000 square yard area of jungle believed to contain CTs,

The stop-gap Washington B.1 - WF442/KO-J of No.115 Squadron in 1950. (J.D.R. Rawlings)

each Lincoln carrying 14 1,000-lb bombs and full ammunition trays. During a standard three-month detachment a crew could expect to complete 25-30 sorties, but some units stayed up to six months, operating alongside Lincolns of No.1 Squadron, RAAF.

On 25 June 1950 the North Koreans launched their unexpected attack on the South and Britain became involved in the conflict through its United Nations (UN) commitments, though direct RAF involvement was small. However, it was inconceivable that the Koreans would act without Russian consent, and it was feared that the latter would take advantage of the situation to attack in Western Europe. On 30 July the Government announced large-scale re-armament, and though there was no immediate effect on Bomber Command the planners had to burn the midnight oil and air defence exercises took on a new meaning. *Cupola* and *Emperor* were conducted during August and October 1950 respectively, Washingtons joining USAF B-50s in dummy attacks from high altitude, while Lincolns soldiered on at their usual 18,000 feet, their crews endeavouring to use *G-H* as a bombing aid for the first time since 1945.

Meanwhile the second Washington squadron, No.149, had reformed in August and on completing training moved to Coningsby in October 1950 to await aircraft, the Americans having temporarily suspended deliveries as a result of the Korean War.

Allied fears increased when the Chinese escalated the conflict in Korea by actively backing the North against UN forces. The United States tripled her military budget and on 29 January 1951 the British Prime Minister announced a further increase in military spending and the intention to order quantity production of four-engined jet bombers for Bomber Command.

The introduction of the twin-engined jet bomber, the Canberra, into Bomber Command was more immediate, though surprisingly it was not universally popular amongst senior officers, many of whom favoured heavier bombers to the exclusion of everything else – almost a repeat of the Mosquito story! Equally surprisingly, plans envisaged the Canberra's operation in a tightly bunched 'stream', much as the 'heavies' had been in 1943-45, and still very much the 'bludgeon'. The re-equipment plan envisaged 24 squadrons organized in six Wings, a total of 240 aircraft, though there were follow-up schemes for a force of 500 Canberras, including photo-reconnaissance variants, all in support of Supreme HQ Allied Powers Europe (SHAPE).

More evidence that things were stirring came the following month when two Lincolns joined No.58 Squadron at Benson to start production of a target information library for the new 'heavies', a task handed over to the Radar Reconnaissance Flight when it was born out of the squadron a year later. Meanwhile Bomber Command had been expressing doubts over the viability of the *Firedog/Musgrave* detachments, the Air Staff considering that the effort expended was not matched by the results at a time

The start of a new era: No.101 Squadron shows off the first Canberra B.2s to enter service, at Binbrook in 1951. (No.101 Squadron records)

SX926, a 'jamming' Lincoln of No.199 Squadron, 1954. (MAP)

when the Command was having difficulty in maintaining commitments to NATO whilst completing Washington training and preparing for the Canberra. With little concrete evidence of bombing effectiveness forthcoming from Far East Air Force (FEAF), the Air Ministry accepted Bomber Command's case and the detachment was withdrawn on 29 March 1951. The next month every available Lincoln was involved in Operation *Accent* which validated the new UK radar defences, the air defence exercise *Umbrella* following soon afterwards.

The first Canberra arrived at Binbrook on 24 May 1951 and re-equipment of No.101 Squadron commenced, though deliveries were at first painfully slow. The Washington re-arming programme had caught up, however, and Nos.15, 44 and 90 Squadrons were all 'operational' by the end of May, Nos.57 and 207 following in June. Finally No.35 Squadron, reformed in September from the Washington Conversion Unit (WCU) staff, completed the No.3 Group transformation just in time for Exercise *Pinnacle/Cirrus* which stretched Bomber Command to the limit.

No.101 Squadron was almost up to strength by the end of the year, and No.617 Squadron started Canberra conversion in January 1952. They were followed by Nos.9 and 12 Squadrons to complete the Wing at Binbrook, but not all the planned four-squadron Wings materialized, and the last one was sent to Germany because of a shortage of suitable accommodation in the UK.

At the end of 1951 there was considerable unrest in Egypt and in January 1952 rioting in Cairo culminated in the burning of Shepheards Hotel, long associated with colonialism. Reinforcement of units in the Canal Zone followed, No.148 Squadron being hurriedly despatched to Shallufa, the Lincolns making their presence felt by overflying towns in formation in addition to carrying out bombing training until mid-March when they returned to Upwood. In the UK *Bull's-eyes* were still being flown, many using Heligoland as a target until the island was returned to the German Government early in 1952, the last attacks being made by Washingtons of Nos.15, 44 and 149 Squadrons as part of Exercise *Bentover* on 21 February. At much the same time the very popular

Lone Ranger overseas flights were introduced on Lincoln squadrons – a way of gaining valuable experience while rewarding crews for good results.

Equipped with four Lincolns the Radar Reconnaissance Flight moved to Upwood in March, and despite the delivery of more modern aircraft Bomber Command's Lincoln strength was further increased the following month when No.199 Squadron arrived at Hemswell to join No. 1 Group and continue its radar jamming activities alongside the Flare Force (Nos.83 and 97 Squadrons).

In July the long expected military *coup d'état* took place in Egypt and King Farouk abdicated. The situation in the Canal Zone became very tense and in August it was decided to temporarily suspend Bomber Command detachments to Shallufa – a decision greeted with mixed feelings by the crews.

It was inevitable that the Canberra would become the next aerial ambassador for Britain and in October came the first goodwill tour, when four No.12 Squadron Canberras, one piloted by AVM D.A. Boyle, AOC No.1 Group, left Binbrook for South America on Operation *Round Trip*. They were away nearly seven weeks during which they covered 24,000 miles, visited 14 countries and displayed the aircraft to many thousands of people.

Less exciting but certainly just as important, were the exercises, both NATO and national, which came thick and fast during the second half of 1952. They included *Holdfast*, *Window Box*, *Mainbrace* (a maritime scenario) and most important for Bomber Command, *Ardent*, the first to involve the Canberra. A maximum effort by Washington, Canberra and Lincoln squadrons produced over 100 aircraft for 'raids' on Glasgow and London and the results were conclusive. Unless the weather was such that the fighters could not fly both the Lincoln and Washington stood little chance of survival, but the Canberra was difficult to intercept even when restricted to 30,000 feet, as during *Ardent*. It was a pity that the aircraft was not eligible for the annual Strategic Air Command (SAC) Bombing and Navigation Competition, for the Lincoln crews of Nos.83 and 97 Squadrons who accompanied Washingtons of No.15 Squadron to Davis-Monthan Air Force Base for the contest in 1952 were embarrassingly outclassed – a replacement was clearly overdue.

At the end of October the Lancasters of No.82 Squadron returned from East Africa on completion of a huge photographic survey task which had taken years, and in December 1952 No.540 Squadron started re-equipping with the badly delayed Canberra PR.3. A month later Lancasters and Mosquitoes took part in Operation *Floodlight*, surveying the East Coast

Among the PR units transferred from Coastal Command in 1950 was No. 82 Squadron using Lancaster PR.1s, among them SW302/G photographed at Khormaksar, Aden, in 1952. (R.B. Trevitt)

after the disastrous floods of January 1953. At the end of March the whole photographic reconnaissance organization moved to Wyton, and the three Canberra PR.3s on strength on 3 June were used to rush film of the Queen's Coronation across the Atlantic for Canadian and American cinemas and television. The operation was a success but the aircraft was still having teething troubles, resulting in Mosquitoes being retained until September.

Washingtons brought a new standard of comfort to Bomber Command but technically the aircraft was a nightmare. In particular the engines were very unreliable and spares backing was never satisfactory. The result was a poor standard of serviceability, and starting early in 1953 the aircraft was replaced as quickly as possible by Canberras. At the same time other squadrons were being reformed and equipped with Canberras, a general build-up of strength which enabled 48 of the aircraft (along with 36 Lincolns and 12 Washingtons) to represent Bomber Command in the flypast at Odiham on 15 July 1953 on the occasion of the Coronation Review. Six more were lined up as part of the equally impressive ground display.

It was to prove a hectic year. The remaining Lincoln units took on regular *Ranger* flights over Germany to maintain Allies' flying rights in the Berlin corridors, while continuing to take part in exercises like *Jungle King* in March, *Rat/Terrier* in May, *Coronet* in July and *Momentum* in August – plus the annual *Skyhigh* which exercised the whole Command, and monthly *King Pin* 'bomexs'.

The Waddington Wing (Nos.49, 61 and 100 Squadrons) moved to Wittering on 4 August so that the former airfield could be prepared for V-Bombers, and the following month *Firedog* detachments were resumed, eight Lincolns of No.83 Squadron going to Tengah for Operation *Bold* alongside the long-suffering No.1 Squadron, RAAF. During their four months in Singapore they carried out 211 sorties on 72 separate missions, including Operation *Bison* on 28 October when 15 million leaflets exhorting the CTs to surrender were dropped on 200 locations by the two Lincoln units.

Mariner, a large-scale sea/air exercise held during October 1953 had several objectives, amongst them fleet defence against land-based bombers which included Canberras. Their inclusion was not a success, which was not surprising considering the aircraft's lack of radar and generally poor navigational aids. A better opportunity to demonstrate the performance of the aircraft was provided by the New Zealand Air Race of October 1953 which captured the imagination of the Commonwealth peoples – certainly those from British stock. A special Flight was formed with Canberra PR.3s and a PR.7 and one of the former, flown by Flt Lts L.E. Burton and D.H. Gannon, was the first to reach Christchurch having covered the

Using pre-loaded carriers, Canberra B.2 WH914 of the Wittering Wing is loaded with 1,000-pounders. (via B. Robertson)

11,792 miles in an elapsed time of 23 hours 50 minutes, an average of 494 mph. Other Canberras finished 2nd and 3rd – a clean sweep of the speed section.

Meanwhile land-hungry Kikuyu tribesmen had been stirring up trouble in Kenya for some time by using Mau Mau witchcraft to coerce other tribes. Punitive action was called for and in April 1953 No.1340 Flight had started offensive operations using Harvards to bomb jungle hide-outs. They achieved results but in the autumn it was decided that known terrorist camps in the Aberdare and Mount Kenya hills should be hit harder. In November No.49 Squadron, in Egypt for a *Sunray*, was ordered to send three Lincolns south to Eastleigh for trial operations and the detachment was followed by others, the Lincolns usually bombing marked areas of jungle early in the morning, though occasionally night sorties were flown as well.

By the end of 1953 all three remaining PR units, Nos.58, 82 and 540 Squadrons (No.541 Sqn had moved to Germany in June 1951) were flying Canberra PR.3s, the Lancasters and Mosquitoes having left late in the year after completing a photo survey of western Germany. The PR aircraft had been joined at Wyton by No.1323 Flight for atmospheric radiation checks around the UK using Canberra B.2s fitted with 'sniffer' pods in place of wing-tip fuel tanks – this unit later moving to Australia for work on the nuclear weapons programme, taking part in Operations *Bagpipes*, *Dogster* and *Shiver*.

The Washington force, gradually reduced during 1953, was disposed of completely in March 1954, most of them returning to the USA. Their service had been brief but they had filled a gap at a very difficult time.

No.7 Squadron took over the *Firedog* detachment in January 1954, their first 'strike' being on an area north of Kuala Lumpur where CTs were thought to be hiding. They were partially relieved by No. 148 Squadron in April but took over again in July and both units assisted in Operation *Bagpipes* by flying radio isotopes part of the way from Australia to the UK. No.7 Squadron finally left the Far East in October when No.148 returned to Tengah, the latter soldiering on until the end of February 1955.

No.542 Squadron reformed with uprated Canberra PR.7s in May 1954, and as more Canberra squadrons became operational *Lone Ranger*s were extended, and other detachments increased, No.27 Squadron sending six aircraft on a Mediterranean tour. With the Lincoln squadrons overstretched by activities in Kenya and Malaya *Sunray*s were again discontinued, but the units managed to take part in major UK exercises, *Dividend* in July being followed in September by *Battle Royal*, a 2nd TAF exercise in which Bomber Command participated.

Evidence of healthy deliveries of Canberras as the re-armament programme accelerated was demonstrated by the increase in unit strength from eight to 10 aircraft during October. Less time was now being spent on demonstrations and goodwill flights as the aircraft's novelty wore off, and the squadrons concentrated on training, especially on *G-H* which

Lincolns carried out live bombing against dissidents of one sort or another in the Aden Protectorate, Kenya and Malaya, where No.148 Squadron are seen 'carpet bombing' Communist terrorist positions during the summer of 1954. (Author's collection)

No.138, the first V-Bomber squadron, received Valiant B.1s during 1955. (PRB 10305)

remained the primary high-altitude bombing aid following the failure of the intended radar to perform satisfactorily.

At the same time preparations were going ahead for the delivery of the first of the V-Bombers, the Valiant. Such preparation had been made more urgent by the testing of the first practical 'hydrogen' bomb at Bikini Atoll in March 1954 by the Americans, for it was obvious that the Russians would not be far behind and it was considered essential that Britain had a deterrent against the use of such weapons – the Defence White Paper of February 1955 confirming publicly that Britain was proceeding with development of such a bomb.

The first Valiant squadron, No.138, reformed on 1 January 1955 and aircraft deliveries commenced on 8 February, though it was May before the first crews completed their OCU training. Deliveries continued on schedule and the squadron moved to Wittering on 6 July with its full complement of eight aircraft, introducing to the RAF the American concept of 'crew chief', a senior non-commissioned officer (NCO) responsible for all technical aspects of a particular aircraft, and in charge of all who worked on it whether at base or elsewhere.

Canberras of No.101 Squadron took over the

In June 1954 the Binbrook Wing received upgraded Canberra B.6s, one of the early No.101 Squadron deliveries being WJ766. (via B. Robertson)

Canberra PR.7 WH800 of No.82 Squadron, Wyton PR Wing. (J.D.R. Rawlings)

Bomber Command commitment to *Firedog* from Lincolns in February 1955. Their initial task, checking the aircraft systems under tropical conditions was soon completed, and the four aircraft moved from Changi to Butterworth for operations in the north of the country. Code-named Operation *Mileage*, the detachments were continued successively by Nos.617, 12 and 9 Squadrons, all of which received the B.6 version of the aircraft during 1955. In practice the Canberra was not a great success as a replacement for the Lincoln, for its range was limited at the operating height, navigation was difficult, and the bomb load was insufficient to produce the concentration required for carpet bombing. More successful were Operation *Planter's Punch* detachments of Canberra PR.7s at Changi. These started in May 1955 and were continued intermittently by the Wyton Wing until October 1959, exclusively by No.58 Squadron from the end of 1956, Nos.82, 540 and 542 Squadrons having been disbanded during 1955-56.

Meanwhile the first jet bomber exercise in the Mediterranean area, *Blue Trident*, had been completed by Nos.21 and 27 Squadrons in February 1955 operating from Nicosia, Cyprus, and was followed by Exercise *Down Under* from Kasfareet in the Canal Zone during March. No.76 Squadron spent almost a month with its Canberra B.2s at Habbaniya and aircraft from the Wittering Wing were detached there again in May in connection with the Baghdad Pact signed by the UK, Iran, Iraq, Pakistan and Turkey on 4 April. Other overseas trips included No.21 Squadron's visit to Khormaksar in March and Operation *New World* in August when No.139 Squadron toured the Caribbean.

Anti-Mau Mau operations ceased in July 1955, by which time the terrorists were effectively beaten. Nos.100, 61, 214 and 49 Squadrons had taken part (in that order), two of the Lincolns on the final detachment being sent to Aden to join part of No.7 Squadron which had just arrived at Khormaksar for

more 'Colonial Policing'. Back at Upwood No.7 Squadron started to run-down in October and disbanded on 1 January 1956, the four aircraft of the Aden detachment equipping the newly-formed No.1426 Flight at Bahrain. At the same time the two Lincoln units at Hemswell, Nos.83 and 97 Squadrons, were renamed 'Antler' and 'Arrow' Squadrons respectively (the names taken from the unit badges) and became involved in radar training for the V-Force.

In September 1955 two Valiants of No.138 Squadron had made a proving flight to the Far East and went on to Australia and New Zealand for Operation *Too Right*, demonstrating the aircraft to the RAAF and RNZAF. Nearer home, air defence exercises *Beware* occupied the Command's Canberras and *Sunbeam* the Valiants, the latter part of a force of over 400 'attackers' attempting to overwhelm Fighter Command.

Rather surprisingly the second Valiant squadron, No.543, which reformed on 24 September 1955 was a PR unit. It replaced No.542 Squadron, which immediately reformed by renaming No.1323 Flight and, equipped with Canberra B.2/B.6 aircraft, continued plotting radiation fallout. No.543 Squadron arrived at Wyton in November to join the Strategic Reconnaissance Force, initially with four B(PR)Mk.1 aircraft but soon up to strength with seven, each carrying 10 cameras and equipped for radar reconnaissance.

No.76 Squadron moved from Wittering to Weston Zoyland in November 1955 and was joined by the reformed No.542 Squadron in December in preparation for more atomic test cloud-sampling and general radiation level measurement. Canberra tailplane trimming problems again came to a head late in 1955, but fortunately the modifications required to the B.6 were minor compared with those on B.2 aircraft and a 'crash' programme cleared No.9 Squadron for a tour of West Africa in January/February to coincide with Queen's visit to Nigeria and Nos. 76 and 542 Squadrons left for Pearce, Australia, in March for Operation *Mosaic*, the air support component of the atomic bomb tests on the Monte Bello Islands.

With continuing 'on time' deliveries and a steady production rate five more Valiant squadrons, Nos.7, 49, 148, 207 and 214, joined No. 3 Group in 1956, and it was two aircraft from No.214 Squadron which went to Idris in June 1956 for *Thunderhead*, the first overseas exercise involving the aircraft. Other such flights soon followed, including the first across the Atlantic when the CO No.207 Squadron, Wg Cdr L.H. Trent, VC, flew AVM S.O. Bufton, SASO Bomber Command, to the USA to observe the SAC Bombing Competition. Of these new units No.49 Squadron was

Canberra B.6s of No.12 Squadron at Hal Far, Malta, during the Suez Campaign, 1956. The aircraft carry 'Suez stripes' around the wings and fuselage and the unit's fox symbol on the fin. (Air Ministry CMP844)

'special', having reformed on 15 March from No. 1321 Flight, which had been engaged on trials of inert 'special weapons' since August 1954. The squadron had four Valiants, two of them, specially modified for atomic bomb testing, going to Edinburgh Field, south Australia, where they joined other units, including Nos.76 and 542 Squadrons, for Operation *Buffalo*. On 11 October 1956 the crew of one of the Valiants made the first 'live' drop of a British atomic device. It was a complete success.

No.9 Squadron replaced No.12 in Malaya in March 1956, coinciding with a lull in operations which enabled them to make a goodwill visit to the Phillipines. Indeed activity was so low that the crews of No.101 Squadron who relieved them in June became the last *Mileage* detachment, being recalled to Binbrook on 31 August as things hotted up in the eastern Mediterranean where President Nasser of Egypt had been flexing his muscles for some time. On 26 July he had nationalized the Suez Canal in breach of international agreements, resulting in the French and British Governments, neither prepared to see the waterway in the hands of such an unstable regime, conspiring with the Israelis to engineer a 'threat' to the Canal as an excuse for action. From August onwards Canberras of Nos.15, 21 and 44 Squadrons were engaged on Exercise *Accumulate*, ferrying bombs to Malta and in September RAF bomber units started deploying under Operation *Reinforced Alacrity*. Canberra B.6s of Nos.9, 12, 101, 109 and 139 Squadrons went to Hal Far and Luqa, followed in October by the shorter-range Canberra B.2s (Nos.10, 15, 18, 27, 44, and 61 Squadrons) to Nicosia, and Valiants (Nos.138, 148, 207 and 214 Squadrons) to

Luqa. In addition No.58 Squadron supplemented the resident No.13 Squadron with Canberra PR.7s at Akrotiri and the crews of Nos.35 and 115 Squadrons were used to reinforce the deployed units.

Israeli ground forces attacked Egyptian positions on 29 October, the Allied air offensive, Operation *Musketeer*, beginning at dusk on 31 October when over 200 Canberras and Valiants set off to bomb 12 Egyptian airfields. Target marking was by Nos.18, 109 and 139 Squadrons, the first bombs being dropped on Almaza by the crew of Canberra B.2 WH853 of No.10 Squadron. Although the targets were clearly visible the results of the high-level bombing were generally disappointing and most of the follow-up precision attacks were made by low-level strike aircraft. The RAF bomber force attacked Cairo West, Fayid, Kasfareet and Luxor airfields during the night of 1/2 November and during the following day Canberras bombed the Cairo radio station at low-level, escorted by French F-84 Thunderstreaks. That night the light and medium bomber force was in action again – against radar and other coastal installations at Alexandria followed by a final V-Force raid on Agami Island. On 4 November Hunters provided top cover for Canberras attacking a large Egyptian Army barracks and early on the 5th markers were dropped over Gamil airfield during a successful paratroop drop. Operations on the ground went well and the Commander was confident that the Suez Canal would be in Allied hands on the 6th or 7th. But politics intervened and a cease-fire was ordered for midnight on 6 November. Canberra sorties from Malta had totalled 72 and from Cyprus 206, while the Valiants flew 49. No Bomber Command aircraft was lost due

Canberra B.2 WD965 of No.44 Squadron in May 1957, still in its original colour scheme. (A. Pearcy/MAP)

to enemy action though it was reported that a Valiant was intercepted by an Egyptian Meteor night fighter. Over 1,400 1,000-pounders were dropped, but Bomber Command had not covered itself in glory. There were valid reasons, it being an 'out of area' operation for which the crews were not trained or equipped and in addition Valiant NBS was incomplete and the intended T4 bomb sights not always fitted.

British pride was badly dented by Operation *Musketeer* and its aftermath and the Government had to rebuild its image and that of the country. It was

decided that the best way was to emphasize the independence of the British nuclear deterrent and it was even suggested that instead of being restricted to 'retaliation', in some circumstances it might now be used much earlier in a conflict. Fortunately common sense prevailed when Macmillan succeeded Eden as Prime Minister in January 1957, and relations with the Americans, which had sunk to a very low ebb, improved rapidly.

With the end of *Musketeer* squadrons left their temporary and very crowded Mediterranean bases at a

No.76 Squadron carried out air sampling during the Monte Bello and Christmas Island nuclear tests. Canberra B.6 WH949 wears the unit's symbolic lion on the fin. (MAP)

steady rate, though No.61 Squadron stayed on into 1957 and was joined by Nos.15 and 44 Squadrons on Exercise *Gold Flake*, a precautionary move in the event of further trouble from Egypt or Nasser's sympathizers. Prior to the Suez affair, plans had been made to build up Canberra forces in the Middle and Far East by withdrawing units from Bomber Command as the V-Force expanded, and a Canberra Wing was formed at Akrotiri by re-equipping four ex-Venom squadrons already in-theatre. Five Bomber Command squadrons (Nos.10, 18, 101, 109 and 617) were disbanded almost immediately, followed by another six (Nos.15, 21, 27, 44, 57 and 115) by the end of 1957. The remaining Canberra units in Bomber Command were concentrated in No.1 Group and expanded in size, Nos.9 and 12 Squadrons at Binbrook increasing to 20 crews and 16 aircraft until the situation settled down. No. 12 Squadron returned to Malta in February 1957 for a six-week *Sunspot* detachment, followed by No.9 in April. Replacing the Shallufa detachments, *Sunspots* involved long navigation exercises and visual bombing on the local Maltese and Libyan ranges – a popular change from restrictive European conditions.

In April came Duncan Sandys' infamous Defence White Paper which announced the cancellation of the supersonic bomber project and stated that the *Blue Streak* ballistic missile would replace manned bombers when the V-Force was withdrawn. At the same time the Central Reconnaissance Establishment (CRE) was formed with operational control and policy exercised by the Air Ministry through Bomber Command, while administration was the responsibility of No.3 Group. The CRE controlled the UK reconnaissance force slimmed-down during 1956 to No.58 (Canberra) and No.543 (Valiant) Squadrons, the Joint Air Reconnaissance Intelligence Centre (JARIC) and Joint School of Photographic Interpretation. No.543 Squadron also had an air survey role, its first major overseas task, working from Khormaksar, being the survey of a large part of the Aden Protectorate.

Vigilant, the first air defence exercise built around a nuclear attack, was held in May, Valiants and Canberras (and the USAF) providing the really serious opposition for Fighter Command – and a far cry from Operation *Bulldog* in 1949 when Percival Prentice trainers acted as a low-level bombing force!

Canberras from Nos.76 and 100 Squadrons (plus two PR.7s of No.58 Squadron to fly radioactive samples to the UK for analysis) were in the Pacific area again for *Grapple* hydrogen bomb tests operating from Christmas Island. On 15 May 1957 the first thermo-nuclear device was dropped off Malden Island from Valiant XD818 of No.49 Squadron by a crew captained by Wg Cdr K.G. Hubbard.

Six days later the delta-shaped Vulcan B.1 entered service with No. 83 Squadron at Waddington. The crews used four aircraft on temporary loan from the OCU, the first of the unit's own aircraft arriving on 11 July. Re-equipment of No.1 Group had begun!

Valiant B(K).1 XD823 of No.49 Squadron, one of the specially modified aircraft used for the nuclear weapon trials from Christmas Island. (Author's collection)

CHAPTER 11

V-Bombers Supreme 1957-1968

THE SECOND OF THE V-Bombers, the Vulcan, entered service in 1957 with No.1 Group, Bomber Command, but it was to be some time before the Canberra was completely replaced and *Musketeer* had demonstrated that the aircraft's effectiveness as a bomber had to be improved. In Europe the high-altitude *G-H* bombing role was still viable as a bludgeon, but pinpoint targeting was a problem and interception was becoming more of a danger. However, nuclear bombs small enough to be carried by the Canberra were about to be supplied by the Americans under Project E arrangements and the aircraft's low-level potential with such weapons was examined. Accepted as feasible, work started on devising safe escape manoeuvres and it was agreed that the Low Altitude Bombing System (LABS), originally developed in the USA, should be adopted. Nos.9 and 12 Squadrons were the first units to be involved, modification of their B.6 aircraft commencing in July 1957.

Meanwhile two crews from the Vulcan OCU underwent intensive training for the annual Bomber Command Competition and in June 1957, flying against experienced Valiant crews, they won four of the six trophies. Thus encouraged, AVM G.A. (Gus) Walker, AOC No.1 Group, asked Bomber Command to enter them in the prestigious USAF SAC Bombing, Navigation and Reconnaissance Competition of that year, and both Vulcan and Valiant teams were despatched to America on Operation *Longshot*. It proved only too apt a code-name for the competition was a tough one and the Vulcan crews were soundly beaten – a salutary lesson. The Valiants of No.3 Group did better, though not outstandingly so, being placed 27th out of the 45 teams competing.

Lincolns still remained in Bomber Command second-line service though in dwindling numbers, operating at Wyton with the Radar Reconnaissance Flight (RRF) and at Hemswell with No.199 Squadron and the remnants of 'Antler' and 'Arrow' Squadrons. In August 1957 No.543 Squadron temporarily took over the RRF, and the Hemswell units combined on 1 October as No.1321 Flight, reformed to continue ECM operations using Lincolns until Valiants of the reborn No.199 Squadron became operational in March 1958.

Meanwhile a plan calling for 144 front-line 'V-Bombers' by 1961 was approved in August 1957, 104 of them to be 'second-generation' Mk.2 aircraft replacing the older aircraft as they came off the production line. It did not prove quite such a simple and straightforward operation as might be imagined!

NATO Exercise *Strikeback* took place in September and the following month detachments of Valiants started going to Changi on Operation *Profiteer*, the V-Force back-up for *Firedog*. There was some disappointment when it was decided not to use them for active bombing operations unless the situation markedly deteriorated, and the crews spent their time 'showing the flag' and training on the Song Song bombing range.

Early in the autumn Canberras of No.76 Squadron returned to Edinburgh Field for Operation *Antler*, this series of atomic tests on the Maralinga Range culminating in a 25-kiloton explosion on 9 October 1957. The unit then moved to Christmas Island, where it was joined by a No.100 Squadron detachment of Canberra PR.7s in preparation for *Grapple X*, the first completely successful drop of a British hydrogen (thermo-nuclear) weapon from an aircraft, on 8 November from a No.49 Squadron Valiant.

With No.83 Squadron fully equipped with Vulcans, No.101 Squadron was reformed at Finningley in October 1957, and plans went ahead for the entry into service of the Victor, last of the

V-Bombers and technically the most advanced.

In February 1958 it was announced that British nuclear weapons in the megaton range were in production, and that a stand-off bomb was being developed for the second-generation V-Bombers. Also announced was the acceptance of an American offer of *Thor* intermediate-range ballistic missiles (IRBMs) to fill the gap until *Blue Streak* was ready. The *Thors* would go into service as soon as possible under an agreement lasting for five years unless terminated earlier by either Government on six months' notice.

No.83 Squadron embarked on a series of goodwill tours, three Vulcans going to Africa for visits to Uganda, Kenya and Southern Rhodesia in March, followed by two aircraft, one carrying AVM 'Gus' Walker, to Argentina and Brazil. Later in the year he was aboard a Vulcan which went eastwards to Turkey and the Phillipines, and was also demonstrated to the RAAF at Butterworth. No.101 Squadron were soon similarly employed, two Vulcans going to Vietnam in November 1958.

Three early Victor B.1s were delivered to Wyton in the spring of 1958 for the reborn RRF. They were fitted with *Yellow Aster* sidescan radar but the equipment was very troublesome, and after plans to fit the similar *Red Neck* in 40-foot-long underwing pods were abandoned the unit was disbanded in 1961.

The first Victors in front-line service joined No.10 Squadron at Cottesmore in April, just as No.214 Squadron commenced operational development of air-to-air refuelling using Valiant B(K).1 aircraft. It was a busy period for Valiants, the 'special' aircraft of No.49 Squadron being back on Christmas Island for *Grapple Y* alongside Canberras from Nos.76 and 58 Squadrons, while others went to Malta for NATO exercises *Medflex Fort* and *Medflex Bastion* during May. They were also entered for the annual SAC competition, but this time it was decided to play the

Flying from Waddington, the mighty Vulcan was a common sight around Lincolnshire from 1957 onwards. These white-painted B.1s were on No. 83 Squadron strength, the silver ones on No 230 OCU. (Air Ministry PRB 13950)

Americans at their own game and in July eight specially-prepared Valiants formed the 'SAC Bombing Squadron', both crews and aircraft receiving an intensive work-up before leaving for the USA.

No.49 Squadron returned to the Pacific in July 1958 for the *Grapple Z* work-up which culminated in two operational weapon drops in September. These were so successful that *Grapple M* was cancelled – the trials programme was complete. Back at Wittering No.49 Squadron aircraft were returned to standard and the unit joined No.3 Group's Order of Battle. Nos.76 and 58 Squadrons also returned to Britain, but 'C' Flight, No.542 Squadron remained in Australia and was renumbered No.21 Squadron on 1 October 1958, the unit continuing to fly its Canberra B.6s from Laverton until disbandment on 1 January 1959.

Meanwhile the first *Thor* IRBM had been handed over to the RAF on 19 August 1958, destined for No.77 Squadron, Feltwell. The RAF had built the sites, all on disused airfields, and was responsible for support facilities and manpower – the Americans provided the missiles.

No.15 Squadron reformed with Victor B.1s at Cottesmore on 1 September forming a Wing with

The Upwood Canberra Wing was still going strong. Illustrated is B.2 WJ641 of No.50 Squadron, September 1958. (MAP)

Victor B.1 XA936 of No.10 Squadron soon after entering service, September 1958. (B.I.P.P.A)

No.10 Squadron, but more interest was shown in the departure of the Valiants of the 'SAC Bombing Squadron' to March AFB on Operation *Lucky Strike*. Divided in two teams the 'Squadron' fought hard, the 'B' Team emerging 7th out of the 41 Wings participating, while the 'A' Team achieved a creditable 20th placing. The contest also provided the excuse for the first truly 'foreign' flight of an RAF Victor, when AVM K. 'Bing' Cross, AOC No. 3 Group, traversed the Atlantic on 13 October to witness events. He returned a week later, his aircraft covering the 2,480 miles from Gander to Marham in 4 hours 1 minute.

No.18 Squadron reformed on 16 December from 'C' Flight, No.199 Squadron, moving its Valiants to Finningley to provide room at Honington for No.57 Squadron to reactivate with Victors on 1 January 1959. From Binbrook Nos.9 and 12 Squadrons continued their regular *Sunspot* detachments to Luqa, and the future of the light bomber force seemed assured when the development of a strike/reconnaissance replacement for the Canberra, the TSR-2, was announced on 1 January

Canberra B.2 WJ616, which had already served with No.1321 Flight and No.199 Squadron in the countermeasures role, was taken over by No.18 Squadron in December 1958. (Author's Collection)

1959. In February No.9 Squadron started LABS training with their modified Canberras, followed by No.12 Squadron in March. Both used the Tarhuna range in Libya for working-up this complicated means of delivery, often operating from Idris rather than Luqa to reduce the transit time.

On 18 April 1959 a team from No.98 Squadron of No.1 Group, Bomber Command, carried out the first RAF live firing of a *Thor* missile from the test site at Vandenburg AFB, and a few days later a number of Vulcans of No.83 Squadron arrived at Goose Bay for Exercise *Eyewasher*, a test of the North American Air Defence System. Both Victors and Vulcans were now spreading their wings in all directions as the first *Lone Ranger*, *Polar Bear* and *Mayflight* detachments were made. The latter were the result of a dispersal plan put forward by Air Chief Marshal Sir Harry Broadhurst to reduce the risk of the V-Force receiving a knock-out blow from an aggressor. A *Mayflight* started with an operational stand-by followed by a scramble and a landing at a pre-briefed dispersal base. At first there were some terrible mix-ups, but with the building of Operational Readiness Platforms (ORPs) on the 36 selected airfields, proper 'domestic' facilities close by and good communications, the plan worked extremely well.

Nos.9 and 12 Squadrons transferred to Coningsby on 2 July and were assigned to NATO, joining Bomber Command's other Canberra bomber squadrons (Nos.35, 50, 100 and 139) under the operational control of the Supreme Allied Commander Europe (SACEUR) – though they remained special in being LABS-qualified with nuclear weapons. At much the same time Vulcans started supplementing Valiant detachments to Malaya, small numbers going at three-monthly intervals to Changi or Butterworth for Operation *Profiteer* during 1959-60.

No.214 Squadron had been steadily working up its flight refuelling role following the delivery of aircraft capable of 'wet' fuel transfers, and the Valiant/Valiant air-to-air refuelling operation quickly became routine, resulting in a series of distance records culminating on 9 July 1959 when Wg Cdr M.J. Beetham flew non-stop from Marham to Capetown (6,060 miles) in 11 hours 28 minutes at an average speed of 530 mph, air-refuelling twice.

Top right: *A* Blue Steel *missile nestling up against the specially shaped bomb bay doors of this version of the Vulcan B.2. (Author's collection)*

Right: *Fully fuelled and ready to launch, this* Thor *missile was one of three equipping No.97 Squadron at Hemswell. (No.97 Squadron records)*

For more than two years the Valiant had reigned supreme but by the middle of 1959, when air defence exercise *Mandate* took place, the Vulcan had overtaken the earlier aircraft in quality if not quantity, No.1 Group having No.83 Squadron at Waddington, No.101 Squadron at Finningley and No.617 at Scampton. No.617 Squadron got the 'plum' overseas trips, sending aircraft to the World Congress of Flight at Las Vegas in April, while in October three of the unit's aircraft went to New Zealand and by returning via the USA circumnavigated the world. The

squadron also found time to win the Laurence Minot, Sassoon and Armament Officer's Trophies in September, while No.83 Squadron won the individual crew awards for the best bombing and navigation performance. The Victor was also showing its potential and plans were made to transfer the Valiants to the tactical role, No.207 Squadron being placed at the disposal of SACEUR on 1 January 1960, replacing three Canberra squadrons disbanded during 1959 (Nos.50, 100 and 139).

That same month No.58 Squadron received some Canberra PR.9s and although the performance was somewhat disappointing, it did enable operations to be extended, particularly within the Arctic Circle, by operating from Bodo or Andoya in northern Norway.

On 31 March 1960, Harold Watkinson, the Minister of Defence, stated that new Mk.2 V-Bombers, fitted with the *Blue Steel* stand-off bomb, would 'hold the ring' until the mid-1960s when it was intended to replace this weapon by the Douglas AGM-87A *Skybolt* air-launched ballistic missile (ALBM), using the V-Force as the carrier. The deployment of the 60 RAF *Thor* IRBMs was completed with the delivery of three to No.150 Squadron at Carnaby during the month, the Force being split into four widely dispersed complexes centred on Feltwell, North Luffenham, Hemswell and Driffield. Each complex had a main and three satellite sites, and each site had three launching pads. By their nature the sites were isolated and the duty shifts tedious, the only variety provided by regular exercises and random 'no notice' practice alerts, some of which went as far as erecting and fuelling the missiles. Each site operated as an independent RAF squadron with its own technical and operations staff. The American input was small, though they remained responsible for initial training until May 1961, and they retained control over arming and firing clearance by means of

the 'dual key' system, a USAF officer being on duty on every site throughout the 24 hours of every day. Test firings showed the *Thor* to be extremely reliable and accurate – its only failing being the 15 minutes it took to prepare it for launch.

During 2/3 March 1960 a Valiant flown by Sqn Ldr Garstin and crew was air-refuelled twice as it flew 8,500 miles around the UK – a final test before successfully attempting the 8,110 miles to Singapore, completed in 15 hours 30 minutes (523mph) during May. The initial trial phase was then declared complete and the following month Javelin crews of No.23 Squadron started 'receiver' training and were air-refuelled non-stop to Akrotiri in August.

In July Victors of No.10 Squadron had taken over *Profiteer*, and though the 'Emergency' in Malaya was officially over at the end of August the detachments continued. There were cutbacks, however, including the cancellation of some Victor B.2s, ostensibly because the introduction of *Blue Steel* and *Skybolt* would enable Bomber Command to remain effective with fewer aircraft, it being planned to modify 72 Vulcans to each carry two *Skybolts*.

No.7 Squadron moved to Wittering in July 1960, enabling No.55 Squadron to reform at Honington in September and complete the second Victor B.1 Wing, while No.83 Squadron was officially reduced to cadre in preparation for Vulcan B.2s. In practice it became No.44 Squadron at Waddington, and a new No.83 Squadron was established at Scampton in October, receiving its first 'second-generation' Vulcan in December as the crews completed the OCU course.

Back in October 1958, Bomber Command had advocated that Victors and Vulcans should be fitted with an ECM package, the Mk.2s on the production line, the Mk.1s retrofitted. It proved easier to modify Victors and the first of the B.1A variants of the aircraft reached No.15 Squadron in August 1960, the first

No.83 Squadron was the first to receive Vulcan B.2s, among them XH563 in nuclear flash 'tone-down' finish. (Author's collection)

An impressive weapon - Valiant B.1 WP223 dropping a dummy Blue Danube *nuclear bomb, May 1959. (No.90 Squadron records)*

Vulcan B.1A, identifiable by a bulged tail cone, being delivered to No.617 Squadron three months later.

No.57 Squadron's Malayan detachment during the autumn of 1958 continued the usual routine, but the squadron also took part in the Phillipines' Aviation Week, and during the return home one of the Victors performed at the Khormaksar Air Display on 25 November, acclaimed as the 'star turn'. Victors and Vulcans were now frequent visitors at Luqa for *Sunspot* detachments while Canberras continued to go to Idris for LABS training. *Mayflight* and *Kinsman* exercises, the latter involving operations from dispersed bases, also increased in frequency, and *Micky Finn*, similar to *Mayflight* but without any notice, was also introduced.

In February 1961 the Defence Minister felt able to declare 'as it stands at this moment, Bomber Command is capable, by itself, of crippling the industrial power of any aggressor nation'. Strong words but probably accurate given the current abilities of surface-to-air missiles (SAMs) and high-altitude interceptors. It was also announced that it was planned to start deployment of *Skybolt* by the mid-1960s and that the weapon was to be fitted with British warheads. For 'free-fall' operations the *Blue Danube* and *Violet Club* were being replaced by *Yellow Sun Mk.1* and lighter-weight American nuclear weapons, two of which would fit in the bomb bay of a V-Bomber. The introduction of *Blue Steel* was also well advanced, and it was not surprising that the overall annual expenditure on the V-Force and *Thor* was running at some 10% of the entire defence budget.

The build-up and rationalization of the Vulcan force continued with the reformation of No.27 Squadron with B.2s at Scampton in April, the move of No.101 Squadron to Waddington in June, and to complete the Waddington Wing, the re-establishment of No.50 Squadron in August using a nucleus from No.617 Squadron. The latter unit was re-equipped with Mk.2 aircraft in September when the Scampton Wing commenced work-up as the Vulcan *Blue Steel* unit, while the *Yellow Sun Mk. 2* thermo-nuclear weapon was introduced to 'free-fall' V-Force squadrons. As the V-Force strength increased, the number of Bomber Command Canberras dwindled. No.76 Squadron disbanded in December 1960, Nos.9 and 12 Squadrons in July 1961, and the last bomber squadron, No.35, in September. The G-H ground stations, first used in 1943, finally closed down at the same time.

Meanwhile Vulcans and Victors had been fitted with flight refuelling probes and development work on the bombers culminated on 20/21 June 1961 with a non-stop flight from Britain to Australia by Sqn Ldr M.G. Beavis and his No.617 Squadron crew. Air-refuelled three times by Valiants operating from Cyprus, Pakistan and Singapore, they flew the 11,500 miles in 20 hours 3 minutes (573 mph). This flight, and others which followed at intervals were spectacular, but air-to-air refuelling of bombers actually had a low priority – until much later! The value of the tanker force was in extending the time on task of interception fighters and their ferry range – and it still is!

No.49 Squadron moved its Valiants over to Marham on 26 June to join Nos.148 and 207 Squadrons as a SACEUR-assigned unit. SACEUR insisted on rapid reaction to a threat and the squadrons each maintained a crew on immediate stand-by, initially in trailers near the Operations block, but later from a special Quick Reaction Alert (QRA) compound close to the aircraft.

The crew of a Vulcan B.1 climb aboard at Scampton for a practice 'scramble', 29 August 1960. (Central Press)

The rest of the V-Force operated a system of Alert States in times of international tension, ranging from *Blue* (30 minutes' warning), through *Amber* (cockpit readiness), to *Red* ('scramble'). 'No notice' dispersal exercises continued at any time and became more sophisticated, often ending with a *Matador* exercise designed to test the UK's air defences.

With Vulcan B.2s usually retained in Britain for deterrent duties and Victors responsible for the Far East detachments, the job of dealing with 'conventional' trouble in the Middle East where the ability to carry 21 1,000-lb 'iron' bombs was extremely useful, fell to the Waddington-based Vulcan B.1s. Regular visits to Akrotiri and Luqa soon paid off, for the ink was hardly dry on a new defence agreement between Britain and the oil-rich Ruler of Kuwait when Abdul Qarim Qassem, Ruler of Iraq, declared Kuwait part of his country and on 25 June 1961 began moving troops south. The following day British forces were placed on stand-by and in a

Valiant B(K).1 XD813 of No.90 Squadron refuelling Javelin FAW.9 XH768 of No.64 Squadron. (RAFM P18853)

surprise move entered Kuwait on the 29th, Vulcans moving to Cyprus in support. The Iraqis soon backed down and RAF aircraft returned to base, but it was a first-class demonstration of the effectiveness of prompt and determined action.

No.90 Squadron joined No.214 in assuming a flight refuelling role in August 1961, but rather surprisingly stayed at Honington, basically a Victor station. Further afield, Bomber Command continued to participate in the annual SAC competitions and was invited to take part in America's national air defence exercise, *Skyshield*, in October 1961. Acting as part of the 'attacking' forces four Vulcan B.2s of No.83 Squadron went in from the north at 56,000 feet – well above American bombers – and penetrated the defences with ease while interceptors were dealing with the SAC aircraft. It was a similar story from No.27 Squadron which approached the country from the Caribbean area, and while the scenario was not strictly comparable with conditions over Europe it was an encouraging result from Bomber Command's viewpoint.

A couple of months later Valiants were also crossing the Atlantic, two aircraft of No.543 Squadron leaving hurriedly for Jamaica to start a 10-day survey of hurricane-torn British Honduras on 6 December to help with the damage assessment.

In January 1962 it was announced that a 200-strong British Joint Trials Force was at Eglin AFB for *Skybolt* testing, and that the Vulcan modification programme was progressing well. Signalling a further upgrade in the V-Force the Victor B.2 entered front-line service with No.139 Squadron at Wittering the following month, the deployment of the bomber version being completed in May with the formation of No.100 Squadron. Coningsby was brought up to Class 1 V-Force standard and a new Vulcan B.2 Wing established there following the reformation of No.9 Squadron in March, No.12 Squadron in July and No.35 Squadron in December. As the Vulcan/Victor bomber force expanded so Valiant strength was reduced. In April Nos.90 and 214 Squadrons lost their bomber role and No.138 Squadron was disbanded, followed by No.7 which went out in September with a bang by dropping live sticks of 18 1,000-lb bombs on Salisbury Plain during a firepower demonstration for senior NATO officers.

Meanwhile the Marham Wing had steadily improved its low-level capability and in August 1962 No.49 Squadron became operational in the tactical role, Nos.148 and 207 Squadrons following within the next eight months. On the other side of the world a No.543 Squadron detachment completed Operation *Bafford*, a six-week survey of the Solomon Islands, Santa Cruz and New Hebrides operating from

The heavy reconnaissance element: Valiant B(PR)K.1 WZ396 of No.543 Squadron, Wyton, August 1960. (Author's collection)

Townsville (Australia), Port Moresby (Papua New Guinea) and Nadi (Fiji), and in August three Victors of No.139 Squadron went to Jamaica to take part in the country's independence celebrations. In the same area three Canberra PR.9s of No.58 Squadron started Operation *Thicket/Sabadilla*, a three-month survey of British Guyana and Trinidad which proved to be the swansong of the PR.9 with Bomber Command for they were withdrawn in November and the unit soldiered on with PR.7s.

The Soviets were deploying ballistic missiles in increasing numbers and the vulnerability of the V-Force, though lessened by the dispersal plan, was still cause for concern. The American system of air-refuelled airborne alert could not be employed because V-Bombers could not carry a second crew and trials at Waddington aimed at maintaining a credible airborne deterrent by changing over aircraft every six hours, proved impracticable. The only solution was the QRA concept, and in February 1962 it was extended to the whole of Bomber Command, one aircraft from each squadron being maintained in a fully-armed state with the crew accommodated close by on 15-minute readiness. With the introduction of 'on-line tele talk' communications between the Bomber Command controller and crews, and modification of the aircraft to allow simultaneous four-engine starts, the time from a 'scramble' call to airborne was reduced to less than four minutes, the anticipated minimum warning time. In times of tension with the aircraft already dispersed the whole force could be airborne in this time.

The V-Force was now an extremely efficient organization with a strong core of 'Select Star' crews, the top rating in a classification system which started with 'non-combat', and progressed through 'combat' and 'select' as expertise increased, though whether centralized servicing, introduced after trials at Cottesmore, was helpful was a matter of opinion. It resulted in the abandonment of the 'crew chief' concept which was widely considered a mistake, and in the event it was not long before the V-Force returned to 'squadron' first-line servicing.

By the beginning of October 1962 No.617 Squadron had achieved emergency operational capability with *Blue Steel* and would have used it had the 'Cuban Crisis' of that autumn resulted in war. The crisis erupted following the discovery of Soviet ballistic missile sites on Cuba, and in company with SAC the V-Force was brought up to a high readiness state with aircraft armed and bases sealed by patrols of armed guards. It was three tense days before the Russian leadership acceded to the American ultimatum, during which time, much to his chagrin, the Prime Minister, Harold Macmillan, would not let the C-in-C disperse the V-Force.

Blue Steel was turning out well. It allowed V-Bomber crews to turn away some 100 miles short of the target and thus avoid the more concentrated enemy defences, and could have been developed further but for the decision to supersede it with *Skybolt*, a missile abandoned as a failure by the Americans in December 1962. This was a terrible blow, for none of the alternatives hurriedly proposed by President John F. Kennedy were deemed feasible except the submarine-launched *Polaris*, and that meant an expensive building programme. Reluctantly it was accepted and ironically the last *Skybolt* test round performed perfectly three days later – impacting in the target area 1,000 miles down range. Efforts were made to resurrect *Blue Steel Mk.2* development, but as the V-Bombers were due to be withdrawn in 1968-69 the plan was rejected. In the meantime No.617 Squadron was declared fully operational with *Blue Steel* in February 1963 followed by Nos.27 and 83 Squadrons later in the year, and work-up with the missile by the Victor Wing at Wittering was begun.

On transfer to Bomber Command No.51 Squadron moved its Canberras and Comets into Wyton at the end of March, though remaining under operational control of the Air Ministry and retaining its special intelligence-gathering role. It was a gain balanced by the disbandment of No.18 Squadron, its role obsolescent now that virtually all operational Vulcans and Victors had ECM installed.

Concern over the survivability of the V-Force continued, but now focused on the vulnerability of the aircraft to SAMs. Despite the effect on the V-Bombers' range characteristics, interest in low-level operations increased at about the time that American bombs and *Yellow Sun Mk.1* were withdrawn from the V-Force and replaced by *Red Beard*, the British tactical weapon. Victor and Vulcan crews commenced training in this unfamiliar environment at an accelerated rate following agreement in May 1963 for the whole V-Force to come under SACEUR command for operations in support of NATO. The aircraft remained available for promoting British interests in 'out of NATO' areas, however, this somewhat convoluted arrangement being practised by *Sunspot* detachments of four or six aircraft, Central Treaty Organization (CENTO) exercises from Iranian bases, and *Lone Ranger* flights. The latter, involving a single V-Bomber, were a popular part of squadron life providing light relief from seemingly endless QRAs and alert exercises which did little for morale, especially following the apparent downgrading of Bomber Command after the *Skybolt* débâcle. More 'operational' were *Chamfron* detachments to the FEAF, commenced on 21 January 1963 when Victors of No.10 Squadron flew out to Butterworth as stand-by reinforcements as the Borneo Campaign and 'confrontation' with Indonesia hotted up.

Bomber Command's *Thor* force had been in service for less than three years when it was decided that the missiles were too vulnerable, withdrawal starting in January when No.240 Squadron 'stood down' at Breighton. Deactivation was rapid, the *Thor* ceasing to be part of Britain's deterrent on 15 August 1963 when the last of them was deactivated despite the lack of an immediate replacement, *Polaris* being still years away from operational service.

Conversely the V-Force was steadily gaining operational strength and at the end of the year three Valiant, six Victor and nine Vulcan bomber squadrons were available. In December the size of the *Chamfron* detachment was doubled, eight Victors of Nos.10 and 15 Squadrons going to Tengah following Indonesian threats to the sovereignty of newly independent Malaya. In January 1964 the detachment moved to

Loading checks being completed on Vulcan B.2 XL318 of No 617 Squadron and a Blue Steel *missile before crutching up, Scampton 1962. (via B. Robertson)*

Valiant B.1 WP213 of No.18 Squadron crammed full of jamming gear - at Finningley Battle of Britain Day, September 1962. (J.A. Todd)

Butterworth for low-level 'pop-up' bombing training and while there a crew dropped a stick of 35 live 1,000-lb bombs on the Song Song range as a demonstration of available firepower.

With Fylingdales Ballistic Missile Early Warning Radar operational from January the four-minute warning became much more realistic, and exercises concentrated on getting four V-Bombers off the ORP, onto the runway and accelerating for take-off within the required time, a quarter of the practice alerts being taken to this stage. In February 1964 it was disclosed that the V-Force was at its operational peak with 159 aircraft (50 Valiants, 39 Victors and 70 Vulcans) in 16 squadrons, but it was planned to increase the size of the tanker force, which would result in a reduction in bomber strength. Of the available aircraft 60% had to be serviceable within six hours of an alert and 80% within 12 hours; a tall order but practice alerts proved it possible!

The whole of the V-Force was now trained for both high- and low-level operations, including the *Blue Steel* units, this weapon having been modified for flight at heights down to 1,000 feet. Low-level penetration became the primary mode of operation in Europe, the Soviet air defences being faced with ground-hugging aircraft approaching anywhere along Russia's western border from North Cape to the Black Sea. This change of tactics and the availability of a variety of bombs designed for low-level release swung the odds in favour of the V-Force – at least in

Victor B.1A XH648 of No.15 Squadron releasing 35 1,000-lb bombs on the Song Song range, Malaya, 22 January 1964. (Handley Page A36 256)

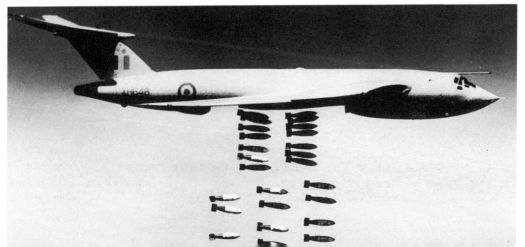

Valiants were given a coat of camouflage paint when assigned to NATO for low-level operations, as illustrated by B(K).1 XD822 of No.49 Squadron at Luqa, August 1964. (Author)

the short-term. To practice over terrain very similar to that covering large parts of the Soviet Union, much of the low-level training was in Canada under the control of the Bomber Command Detachment at Goose Bay, Labrador, a crew flying three of four approved routes during each visit. There were misgivings about low-level operations in aircraft designed for high-altitude flying, but they were allayed by fatigue life trials indicating only minor problems which could be dealt with easily – an unfortunate assumption as it turned out!.

Immediately after *Golf Club*, a Malaya air defence exercise held in February 1964, No.10 Squadron returned home and was disbanded, leaving Nos.15, 55 and 57 Squadrons to soldier on with the FEAF detachments. 'Confrontation' with Indonesia continued to escalate, resulting in a state of emergency being declared in Malaya in September, just as Victors were withdrawn and replaced by Vulcan B.2s of the Coningsby Wing (Nos.9, 12 and 35 Squadrons),

which became the Cottesmore Wing in November 1964.

Earlier, in June 1964, three Valiants of No.543 Squadron left Wyton on Operation *Pontiflex*, a very ambitious survey mapping the Rhodesias and Bechuanaland (now Zambia, Zimbabwe and Botswana) – an area of over 500,000 square miles. It took them 11 weeks to complete and revealed considerable errors in current maps. The same month No. 58 Squadron sent two Canberra PR.7s out to Singapore to assist No.81 Squadron with a photo survey of North Borneo, and in August the unit detached aircraft to Piarco, Trinidad, to complete the British Guyana survey begun as Operation *Thicket* in 1962.

In August a Valiant suffered a fracture of a wing main spar boom and inspection of other aircraft revealed widespread fatigue cracks. It was thought that the problem would be confined to the bomber variants but in fact all Valiants were affected, and

XM649 in the low-level role adopted by the standard Vulcan B.2 aircraft of the Waddington and Cottesmore Wings during 1964. (Hawker Siddeley/BAe A2/1/213)

Canberra PR.7 WT512 of No 58 Squadron on detachment at Labuan during the 'Confrontation', July 1964. (Author's collection)

though a modification programme was devised it was judged prohibitively expensive even if confined to the tanker and photo-reconnaissance aircraft. Despite the obvious problems arising from the sudden withdrawal of the tanker fleet, all Valiants were therefore grounded on 9 December 1964, and disbandments followed, starting with No.214 Squadron on 28 February and finishing with the last of the bomber squadrons, Nos.49 and 207, on 1 May 1965.

No.543 Squadron was not disbanded, receiving Victor B(SR).2 aircraft, a variant first considered for development in 1960. It had a photographic pack in the bomb bay – eight F.96 and four F.49 cameras for day use, and the F.89 for night work when photoflashes were also carried. The remainder of the bomb bay was taken up with two large fuel tanks which increased the range to over 4,000 miles, and in the maritime radar reconnaissance role one aircraft could cover vast areas, it being claimed that every ship in the Mediterranean could be plotted in a single seven-hour sortie.

The loss of the Valiants was undoubtedly a blow,

but potentially much worse was the cancellation of the TSR-2, announced with ill-concealed glee during the new Chancellor's budget speech on 6 April 1965, right at the height of Bomber Command's forced reorganization. Current plans had to be tested, however, and C-in-C Bomber Command arranged for C-in-C FEAF to request a Vulcan reinforcement detachment – unbeknown to the unit concerned. After realistic delays to simulate political release and diplomatic clearances, a 'no notice' Exercise *Spherical* was ordered at midnight on 26 April 1965, tasking No.35 Squadron with the deployment of eight aircraft to Gan. Thirty-two hours later all were in position, and ready to move on to Butterworth and Tengah. They could have been operating within 60 hours of leaving Cottesmore – impressive by anyone's standards. The more routine Vulcan deployments, known as the *Matterhorn Rotation*, consisted of four aircraft on three-month detachments which continued until the end of 'confrontation' with Indonesia in August 1966. It was a heavy burden but good training in the 'conventional' role.

Victor SR.2 XM715, an example of the radar/photo reconnaissance variant in service with No.543 Squadron. (Author)

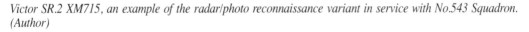

A Victor B.2R of the Wittering Wing (Nos.100 & 139 Squadrons) being flown energetically despite carriage of a Blue Steel *missile, 1964. (Author's collection)*

While the Victor SR.2s were non-operational the Canberras of No.58 Squadron did as much of No.543 Squadron's survey and general photographic work as possible, and fortunately it had been decided as early as 1962 that Victor B.1s would be converted into tankers when the 'second-generation' Mk.2s were all operational. Trials had already been completed by Handley Page enabling a 'crash' programme to be put in hand and Victor B(K).1As, equipped with wing-mounted refuelling pods, were rushed into service. They re-equipped No.55 Squadron which immediately commenced tanker training and in August 1965 the unit was able to 'top up' Lightnings of No.74 Squadron on their way to Akrotiri, coming back to the UK with No.19 Squadron aircraft 'in tow'.

After an agonised re-appraisal the Labour Government signed a contract for 50 General Dynamics F-111A aircraft in February 1966, Ministry of Defence (MoD) staff having decided that it would be capable of carrying out most of the tasks envisaged for the TSR-2. The same month the definitive Victor K.1 tanker entered service with No.57 Squadron, followed by a reformed No.214 Squadron in July, the last of the bomber Mk.1s having been disposed of a month earlier. No. 55 Squadron also received K.1 aircraft in February 1967 by which time Bomber Command was again stabilized as a compact but viable force. At Scampton were three *Blue Steel*-equipped Vulcan B.2 squadrons (Nos.27, 83 and 617), while Wittering housed two similarly equipped Victor B.2R units (Nos.100 and 139 Squadrons). Vulcans armed with 'free-fall' nuclear or conventional weapons were at Waddington (Nos.44, 50 and 101 Squadrons) and Cottesmore (Nos.9, 12 and 35), while the reconnaissance force at Wyton consisted of No.543 Squadron with Victor SR.2s, No.58 with Canberra PR.7s and the enigmatic No.51 Squadron, still with Comets and Canberras. Marham housed the Tanker Wing equipped with six two-point and 24 three-point Victor K.1s for Nos.55, 57 and 214 Squadrons and the Tanker Training Flight. The ferrying of fighters using flight refuelling was now routine, but taking them as far as Singapore was not, and some precise planning was required before Operation *Hydraulic*, the transfer of 13 Lightning F.6s of No.74 Squadron from Leuchars to Tengah in June 1967. The flight was made safely and nearly on schedule, in just four stages, the Lightnings making intermediate landings at Akrotiri, Masirah and Gan.

Comet 2SR XK695 of No.51 Squadron in September 1965. Note the numerous 'bulges' covering reconnaissance equipment. (Author)

Victors were modified for the air-to-air refuelling role in 1965, among them XH620 of No.55 Squadron, here replenishing Lightning F.6 XR768 of No.74 Squadron. (MoD PRB36240)

Despite the end of 'confrontation' with Indonesia in August 1966, Vulcans still continued to go to the Far East on month-long four-aircraft *Sunflower* detachments, during which they often went to Darwin for exercises with RAAF Mirages. Victor tankers also made the long trip to Tengah for *Malayan Litex* which enabled the Lightning pilots of No.74 Squadron to remain current in air-to-air refuelling (AAR).

On 16 June it was announced that No.3 Group would close down by the end of the year and in 1968 Fighter and Bomber Commands would merge as Strike Command. Though not a universally popular decision it was recognized as inevitable, and on 1 November No.1 Group took over operational control of all UK-based bomber and tanker forces, the reconnaissance element continuing to be administered and tasked by HQ Central Reconnaissance Establishment under direct MoD control.

No.12 Squadron was disbanded at the end of 1967 and its aircraft used to re-equip No.101 Squadron, the last Vulcan unit flying Mk.1As. It was the start of a planned decline in the strength of the V-Force, but in January 1968 the F-111 was cancelled on the dubious grounds that it was not needed following the decision

to withdraw from most Far East and Middle East commitments, and paradoxically this gave a new lease of life to the V-Force. SACEUR's plans required strong tactical bomber forces to counteract Warsaw Pact strength on the ground and he pleaded for the Vulcan's retention, the British Government finally agreeing to keep some 60 V-Bombers in service as part of the 'Flexible Response', even after *Polaris* took over the 'Deterrent'.

On 29 April 1968 the Secretary of State for Defence and RAF Chiefs were joined at Scampton by Marshals of the Royal Air Force Viscount Portal and Sir Arthur Harris and many other distinguished guests, including three VC holders, Gp Capt Cheshire, Wg Cdr Learoyd and WO Jackson, for Bomber Command's disbandment parade. As the ensign was lowered three V-bombers, a Vulcan, Victor and a Valiant (XD816 was still flying on trials work) flew overhead in salute.

The following day RAF High Wycombe became HQ Strike Command and Bomber Command's task was over. For 33 years it had been the country's premier offensive force, striving hard to uphold its motto: 'Strike Hard, Strike Sure'.

CHAPTER 12

Training

AT THE END OF THE First World War the RAF had a training organization second to none, able to send the Independent Force in France well-trained pilots, observers and gunners; but soon after the Armistice all aircrew training units except *ab initio* schools for pilots and specialist schools for maritime aviators were closed down. Pilots then completed their training on their first front-line squadron, while observers and gunners were chosen from volunteer ground tradesmen and given *ad hoc* instruction as bomb aimers and gunners on their unit.

This 'on the job' system continued throughout the notorious 'Ten Year Rule'* period, and for several years after its abrogation in 1932. Because the performance of front-line aircraft in the 1920s and early 1930s was only slightly more advanced than that of pilot training machines, the system worked reasonably well; but as early as April 1934 the AOC-in-C Air Defence Great Britain, Air Marshal Sir Robert Brooke-Popham, was pointing out that the amount of basic instructional flying required by newly-arrived pilots on the five night bomber squadrons under his command absorbed a quarter of the annual flying hours allocation and that this situation would be clearly untenable following the outbreak of war. In his opinion the burden was already affecting efficiency and would get worse as the new breed of monoplane bombers currently under development entered service. He recommended the formation of a special school for twin-engined and night flying training, suggestions taken up by Air Commodore Tedder, Director of Training, but without effect. The official answer was that no 'special' training could be undertaken during the expansion period.

*See Chapter 1

Thus life on a front-line bomber squadron continued much as it had done in the 1920s, consisting largely of triangular cross-country navigation exercises of about three hours' duration, local day and night flying, a certain amount of camera obscura 'bombing', and an annual visit to the armament camp for live bombing and gunnery. Searchlight 'co-operation' was introduced and gradually the annual defence exercise became more intensive and somewhat more realistic, while the installation of a Direction Finding (D/F) system in 1937 emphasized the importance of instrument flying for pilots and Wireless Telephony (W/T) operating skills for the gunners. But old habits die hard and progress in 'cloud' flying was very slow.

The successful training of volunteer observers and gunners depended entirely on an enlightened attitude from COs and by the mid-1930s it was generally accepted that this was an unsatisfactory situation. An Air Observers School (AOS) was opened at North Coates in January 1936 to give airmen volunteers a two-month course in bombing and gunnery. Navigation remained solely the province of pilots until mid-1937 when the course at North Coates was extended by a month to provide basic map-reading and 'dead reckoning' (DR) training for observers destined for medium bombers, enabling them to assist the pilot in these matters. 'Heavy' bombers carried two pilots, one of them responsible for the navigation following a 10-week course at the School of Air Navigation, Manston, or at civilian schools at Hamble and Shoreham. This arrangement continued into 1939 despite the declaration in May 1938 that the observer would have responsibility for navigation in wartime – an extraordinary situation!

Meanwhile Air Marshal Sir Arthur Tedder, still Director of Training at the Air Ministry, had laid down that 'the expansion of service squadrons was to be based on a reasoned training expansion programme' and that 'the object of training must be to produce pilots capable of going straight from the training organization to operational work in squadrons'. Sensible words which again fell on deaf ears because it was politically important to make a display of strength, and the six light and medium bomber types (Battle, Blenheim, Hampden, Wellesley, Wellington and Whitley) which entered service between March 1937 and October 1938 all went into the 'shop window', re-equipping operational squadrons. The size of Bomber Command did indeed increase by leaps and bounds under the impetus of the Expansion Schemes, new squadrons forming at a rapid rate, each requiring a nucleus of aircrew from operational units. Naturally the result was a serious dilution of experience on all units, and as forecast it was not long before none had a full complement of fully-trained trained crews.

Flying Training Schools (FTSs) were also in trouble, struggling desperately to produce sufficient pilots to man the aircraft flowing from the factories. In January 1935 it had been agreed to increase the pilot through-put by one-fifth to satisfy Expansion Scheme A, but Scheme C, approved in May, required a doubling of the number of pilot trainees. Expedients such as the reduction in the FTS course from nine to six months produced impressive increases in numbers, but a survey by a committee headed by Air Marshal Slessor concluded in April 1938 that the readiness of Bomber Command in March 1939 (the current 'declaration of war' date) would still be severely affected because the numbers of first-line aircrew would be inadequate for the 34 squadrons projected. Just as serious was the Committee's view that operations would only be sustainable for between seven and 12 weeks before wasting away because

there was still no aircrew replacement training policy or any plans for the advanced training of Volunteer Reserve (VR) pilots. It was a 'Catch 22' situation, for any attempt to provide such training would only exacerbate the situation in the short term, for the squadrons were the only source of the additional instructors required.

The Tedder Committee also considered the position regarding other aircrew categories. In October 1937 the observer flying badge had been re-introduced and in December the part-time concept was abandoned in principle, direct entry personnel being accepted and trained alongside serving airmen at North Coates. It quickly became obvious that the AOSs could not cope with the rapidly increasing requirement for observers, and that even when the planned civilian-manned Air Navigation Schools (ANS) were opened (the first in August 1938) there would be a shortfall. The team therefore recommended that bomber squadrons still equipped with obsolescent aircraft be immediately withdrawn from the front-line and employ training observers until adequate alternative methods were available. This recommendation was accepted, the Heyfords of Nos.97 and 166 Squadrons at Leconfield operating as an ANS for six months from 7 June 1938, providing 12-week courses similar in scope to the civilian schools.

Apart from the two-pilot concept the crew complement for the forthcoming 'heavy' bombers was still fluid. It was generally agreed that a five-man crew was required, but quite what the observer/-gunners 'mix' would be was uncertain, as was the position of volunteer tradesman. However, the Munich Crisis concentrated minds wonderfully and late in 1938 it was accepted that mobilization would make the position of tradesman/air gunners untenable. From 19 January 1939 all aircrew were regarded as in full-time employment and it was accepted that

No.108 Squadron became a Group Pool unit at the beginning of the war, using Blenheim IVs to provide budding bomber crews with advanced training. (Author's collection)

additional airmen would have to be provided to bring technical strengths of units up to establishment. It was also decided to amalgamate the wireless operator and air gunner categories in Bomber Command (and Coastal Command, except for flying boats), but recognised that this would be a slow process.

Meanwhile operational training problems had mounted. The difficulties which Sir Robert Brooke-Popham and Sir Arthur Tedder had prophesied materialized, and on 18 May 1938 the Chief of Air Staff, Air Chief Marshal Sir Cyril Newall stated in a memorandum: 'Training has not kept pace with the increased demands made on the fully-trained pilot due to increase in complexity of modern bomber aircraft. There is an "accident-prone zone" immediately following the arrival of a pilot at his squadron after leaving the FTS. There should be an interim stage of training between the two.' This time action was taken, a memo dated 12 December 1938 written by the Air Member for Supply & Organisation (AMSO), Air Marshal W.L. Welsh, recommending Advanced Training Centres, and on 3 January 1939 it was decided to call them Group Pools (GPs) and form six in Bomber Command. The scheme was dogged by a shortage of skilled personnel and in March it had to be amended, the GPs being held in abeyance, and nine of the 15 squadrons which had been deemed 'non-mobilizing' (Nos.7, 44 (later replaced by No.76), 52, 63, 75, 97, 104, 108 and 148 Squadrons) were required to carry out the function instead. Each was equipped with a number of Ansons for elementary navigation and map-reading, and the usual complement of operational-type aircraft to provide conversion flying, operational training and

In April 1940 No.185 Squadron was absorbed by No.14 OTU which continued as the Hampden advanced training unit – and used a few Dagger-powered Herefords. (MAP)

consolidation for VR personnel. Despite these welcome and sensible changes, too much flying by operational squadrons was still in the local area, navigation standards being such that a report dated 17 May 1939 stated that DR navigation above cloud could only be expected to bring an aircraft within some 50 miles of a 'long-range target'. Doubtless it was coincidence that three days later observers were made responsible for the navigation of all multi-seat bomber aircraft, in war or peace!

Night flying was another facet still being neglected, so much so that during 1938 out of some 162,500 hours of training only 14,000 hours were at night, and very little of that was on navigation exercises over the sea or countryside providing the conditions to be expected over 'blacked-out' enemy territory. Even the dedicated night flyers, the Whitley crews of No.4 Group, were denied proper bombing training because suitable ranges were not available until just prior to the outbreak of war. To complete the tale of woe gunnery training remained a problem, Ludlow-Hewitt feeling constrained to write to the Air Ministry in July 1939: 'As things are at present the gunners have no real confidence in their ability to use the equipment efficiently in war, and captains and crews have, I fear, little confidence in the ability of the gunners to defend them against destruction by enemy aircraft. Under these conditions it is unreasonable to expect these crews to press forward to their objectives in the face of heavy attack by enemy fighters.'

In August 1939 the non-mobilizable squadrons were 'pooled' and operated as Station units, being taken over on 5 September by No.6 Group, which had been working up to operational status since January, but was now redesignated No.6 (Training) Group. Three of No.6 Group's four Blenheim squadrons were handed over to No.2 Group, the one remaining being joined by an augmented number of GP squadrons; a total of 13*. Grouped by aircraft type in pairs on airfields in Oxfordshire and the East Midlands, the squadrons soon completely lost their identity as they wrestled with a flood of six-week courses, 'heavy' trainees flying 55 hours (including 22 at night) and 'light/medium' trainees 60 hours (18 at night). The task was two-fold: firstly to convert individuals onto operational type aircraft; and secondly, to weld them into a crew fit to be posted to a reserve squadron (Nos.78, 98, 101, 106, 185, 214 and 215 of which Nos.185 and 215 became GP units and the rest 'operational' in June 1940). These kept trainees in flying practice and provided more advanced training.

In December 1939 a conference at Bomber Command was told that 'conversion to type'

*See Appendix III, Order of Battle 25 September 1939

training was going well, but that night flying and 'cloud' (ie. instrument) flying practice was insufficient, especially on 'heavy' courses. These aspects were increasingly important, and it was decided to extend the length of courses and rename the GPs as Operational Training Units (OTUs). The change took effect on 8 April 1940 when eight OTUs (Nos.10-17 inclusive) were formed from the 14 current GP squadrons. The capacity of the OTUs remained insufficient to cope with the demand for new crews, however, and it was recognized that drastic action would have to be taken. The formation of new bomber squadrons was delayed until two more OTUs were in operation and even more dramatic, six new squadrons were dissolved in order to bring the current OTUs up to strength. Additionally the course flying hours for pilots who had completed FTS training on twin-engined aircraft was cut to 30. Not all had been so trained, for although the SFTSs had been divided into Group I (single-engined) and Group II (twin-engined) units in February 1940, some of the latter were forced to continue using Harts and Battles because of shortages – in June there were still 130 Hart variants in use. From July 1940 OTU trainees flew *Nickelling* sorties towards the end of their course to provide a degree of 'operational' experience, and later even mine-laying was carried out on occasion.

These changes were so successful that by the summer of 1940 the bottleneck in the supply of pilots had shifted to the SFTSs. In September the throughput was increased by 25%, formation and night flying being greatly reduced, and all specialized training such as bombing, gunnery and photography transferred to OTUs. In a further attempt to alleviate the shortfall an experimental training scheme was introduced. Specially selected trainee pilots with a total of 50 hours flying were posted direct to No.10 OTU (Whitleys) at Abingdon and No.13 OTU (Blenheims) at Bicester from their Elementary FTS. The X Course, as the experiment was called, lasted for 10 weeks and included 120 hours flying, and replaced training normally taking 20 weeks. The experiment was extended to Nos.11, 15, 19 and 20 OTUs in October but was found to be too dependant on good weather and a supply of hand-picked pupils, and so the scheme had to be abandoned. Instead the length of SFTS courses was cut to 10 weeks and 70 hours flying, resulting in trainee pilots arriving at OTUs with as little as 120 hours flying. The 30 hours on the OTU were plainly insufficient to bring these trainees up to first pilot standard on bombers, so in April 1941 Bomber Command reluctantly accepted that they would have to join squadrons as second pilots. In practice this resulted in an accumulation of partly-trained aircrew on operational squadrons and Bomber Command started pushing for a minimum 45 hours on the OTU. Provisional approval was given in January 1942, but the problem had already been solved by Air Marshal A.G.R. Garrod, the Air Member for Training, when he stipulated that pre-bomber OTU flying hours for pilots was to be 260.

By the end of 1941 only two SFTSs remained in Britain, the majority of training to 'wings' standard being performed in Commonwealth countries. This meant that pilots needed an 'acclimatization' course on return and this was provided by the formation of Advanced Flying Units.

Navigation, armament and wireless training passed through a similarly complicated series of changes. In April 1938 the Armament Training Camps were renamed Armament Training Schools, AOSs on the outbreak of war and Bombing & Gunnery Schools in

Whitley V N1412 served with No.19 OTU from August 1941 as ZV-J, its ex-78 Squadron codes roughly overpainted. (RAFM P570)

November 1939, reverting to AOSs when Air Gunnery Schools were formed in June 1941. Meanwhile wireless operator training, first carried out by Electrical & Wireless Schools, was undertaken by Signal Schools from September 1940, renamed Radio Schools in December 1942.

Four-engined aircraft, in the shape of the Stirling, had appeared in front-line service as early as August 1940 and by the end of the year Halifaxes were also re-equipping operational units. Crews had to convert to the new aircraft on squadrons because of a reluctance to dilute the front-line by diverting aircraft to training units – a partial return to pre-war practice. It proved acceptable during the build-up in strength which was very slow and involved experienced aircrew, but by the autumn of 1941 the conversion task was increasing rapidly and freshmen crews were being posted in. An extra layer of training had to be introduced, the aim being to reduce losses through accidents – some 9% of total output – by providing proper multi-engined type conversion and allowing pilots to achieve a minimum of 350 hours before joining a 'heavy' bomber squadron. In November 1941 two Conversion Flights (CFs) were formed, No.26 CF with Stirlings at Waterbeach, using 'C' Flight, No.7 Squadron as a nucleus, and No.28 CF with Halifaxes at Leconfield. Two more CFs were scheduled for December but were overtaken by events, Nos.1651 and 1652 Conversion Units (CUs) replacing the CFs on 3 January 1942, following a decision to establish one CU in each Group. The CUs could not cope with the whole of the immediate conversion task so CFs, equipped with four of the oldest aircraft, were formed on each 'heavy' squadron; a sensible way of preserving new aircraft from the rigours of 'circuits and bumps'. As Manchester-equipped squadrons received replacement Lancasters, similar CFs were formed, each with two Manchesters and two Lancasters.

The introduction of four-engined bombers also spawned a new crew member, the flight engineer. The requirement had been identified in January 1940 but nothing was done until February 1941 when the trade was formally established. Up to this time squadron fitters had performed the engineer's duty; now selected volunteer groundcrew were sent on gunner's courses followed by a manufacturer's course on the particular aircraft. The standard varied widely and the Air Ministry decided that the RAF would provide the technical training at No.4 School of Technical Training, St Athan, on courses which stabilized at six weeks' duration from the end of May 1942.

Meanwhile practical experience of Stirlings and Halifaxes convinced Air Vice Marshal MacNeece Foster, AOC No.6 Group, that the second pilot was little more than a passenger who far from gaining experience, actually regressed. He pointed out that Hampdens, which could only accommodate one pilot, flew long sorties without any difficulty, and he saw no reason why Wellingtons, Whitleys and, for that matter, four-engined aircraft should have more than one pilot. His report coincided with the growing realization that the steadily increasing complexity of the equipment and type of operation demanded either a higher standard of trainee or a reduction in the scope of their duties, and a complete overhaul of the crew composition of heavy bombers was put in hand. With the support of Air Marshal Garrod, Air Member for Training at the Air Ministry, the second pilot was officially dropped from both medium and heavy bombers on 29 March 1942, and the Pilot, Navigator, Bomb Aimer (PNB) scheme was introduced. Pilots had to be up to captaincy standard on arrival on the squadron, it being the practice for the pilot to be the aircraft captain regardless of rank; and to achieve higher standards without excessive wastage it was

When sufficient aircraft were available four-engined Conversion units were formed, the first being No.1651 CU in January 1942 equipped with Stirlings, including W7459/O. (MAP)

Within the operational Groups armament training was provided by target towing and gunnery Flights. Ex-78 Squadron Whitley V Z6640 was used by No.1484 Flight of No.4 Group in 1941. (MAP)

decided that the 90% of aircrew volunteers opting for pilot would be put through a 12-hour grading course on Tiger Moths. Aptitude would be assessed and those below the required standard would be reclassified as navigator or bomb-aimer, the duties of observer having already been so divided. The number of wireless operator/air gunners per crew was reduced to one, the two gunners no longer being subjected to a signals course, and to assist the pilot, the flight engineer took on additional duties.

In general the scheme was a great success, allowing each crew member to specialize and thus receive more thorough training than previously possible. In addition Bomber Command's insatiable demand for pilots was stemmed, and it was not long before surpluses began to be a problem! It did mean, however, that new pilots were thrown in at the deep end with little or no experience of operations before taking their own crew to war. When it was discovered, late in the year, that pilots who had done less than three trips as a second pilot only completed on average two operations as captain before being lost, while those with six 'experience' flights averaged eight 'ops' on their own, a series of cross-country exercises and a minimum of three operational flights as second pilot were introduced.

On 11 May 1942 No.6 Group was renumbered No.91, and No.7, which had been formed on 15 July 1940, became No.92 Group. Both were soon involved in Harris's 'Thousand Bomber' raids, for even a maximum effort by operational units could not produce the magic number. For the attack on Cologne on 30 May, No.91 Group provided 259 aircraft and No.92 Group another 108, the loss rate being an 'acceptable' 3.3%; but on the third mass attack, against Bremen on 25 June, the figures rose to 12.5% of Whitley and 11% of Wellington sorties. These were unsustainable losses, but nearly as bad was the training disruption involved in the preparation of aircraft to operational standard and their detachment

to other airfields, and it was significant that no more attacks of this magnitude were attempted until the front-line was strong enough to do so by itself.

Another 'diversion', but one much less disruptive, commenced in August. With the U-Boat menace at a peak Coastal Command asked for assistance with Bay of Biscay patrols, and it was decided that student crews at No.10 OTU would spend the last fortnight of the course at St Eval, flying anti-submarine sorties under the control of No.19 Group. Inexperience naturally limited their effectiveness, but the mere presence of their Whitleys was a deterrent and before the detachment ended in July 1943 it had made 1,848 sorties during which crews made 91 U-Boat sightings, 54 attacks and one 'kill'. The latter was on 14 June 1943 when a crew captained by Sgt A.J. Benson attacked and sank U-564. The aircraft was damaged and Benson had to 'ditch' after the starboard engine stopped, the aircraft and crew becoming one of the 33 from No.10 OTU which failed to return from Bay operations. The 'ditching' had been good, however, and after three days in their dinghies the crew were picked up by a French fishing boat and became PoWs, Benson receiving a well-deserved DFM and promotion to Warrant Officer.

To try and cope with the escalating training task caused by increasing numbers of squadrons and continuing heavy losses, an enlargement of CFs to eight aircraft was authorized. The change was not a success, however, and it was decided to replace them by more training units, officially formed as Heavy Conversion Units (HCUs) on 7 October, each with an establishment of 32 aircraft, though most were initially at half-strength. Nos.1651 and 1652 CUs were upgraded to HCUs and seven more were formed immediately, more following in 1943. A shortage of Lancasters forced increasing use of Stirlings and Halifaxes in December 1942, Nos.1654, 1656, 1660 and 1661 HCUs, which supplied Lancaster-equipped squadrons, having to make do with an establishment of 20 Halifaxes/Stirlings and 12 Lancasters.

Nos.13 and 17 OTUs supported the light bomber force concentrated in No.2 Group, both operating large numbers of Blenheims and a smaller number of Bostons. When the Mosquito element of the Group started to expand type conversion was handled by No.1655 CU, formed on 30 August 1942 at Horsham St Faith. Renamed No.1655 Mosquito Training Unit (MTU) on 18 October, training continued until 30 April 1943 when the imminent departure of No.2 Group to the Tactical Air Force resulted in disbandment, the aircraft being transferred to No.13 OTU which retained responsibility for No.2 Group replacements. However, a Mosquito element, gradually increasing in size, remained in Bomber

There was a surge in the number of HCUs in late 1942, among them No. 1661 HCU flying Manchesters and old Lancasters such as W4113/GP-J. (IWM CH11923)

Command and No.1655 MTU was reformed on 1 June in No.92 Group, transferring to No.8 (Pathfinder Force) Group a month later. Only experienced pilots and navigators were posted to Pathfinder Mosquito units so the task remained small until the build-up of the Light Night Striking Force, but by the end of 1944 it had outgrown the MTU and No.16 OTU was reformed in No.92 Group on 1 January 1945. Crews for all Mosquito bomber squadrons, eventually 12 in number, were provided by the unit.

Lancasters continued to be in short supply throughout 1943 and in November it was decided that HCUs should be completely equipped with Stirlings and Halifaxes, and an additional 'Finishing School' introduced for trainees earmarked for Lancaster-equipped Groups. These Lancaster Finishing Schools (LFSs), Nos.1, 3, 5, and 6, provided 12 hours' flying on Lancasters, and after joining their squadron crews normally received a further 12 hours before commencing operations.

Thus by mid-1944 a bomber crew would form at the OTU where they flew 80 hours on Wellingtons during a 10-week course. These started at fortnightly

intervals and varied in strength from 11 to 16 (occasionally 18) crews. The 'crewing up' procedure generally allowed individuals to choose each other, which sounds casual but was a system which worked well and continued throughout the war and for long afterwards. On completion of the OTU course the trainee crew went to a Stirling/Halifax HCU for five weeks, a week in ground school being followed by 40 hours' flying. The syllabus included bombing, air firing, fighter affiliation, navigation and radar training. Additional flight engineers were maintained at each HCU to give them 30 hours' flying experience prior to crewing up for the conversion course. A Lancaster crew then completed 12 hours with the Group LFS, which included a *Bullseye*, a navigational exercise which involved flying to a 'hostile' area of the UK where searchlight batteries attempted to illuminate the aircraft – valuable experience in avoiding detection as well as providing realistic training for the defence forces. This Bomber Command training was, of course, on top of that given overseas and by Flying Training Command (FTC), resulting in pilots of heavy bombers receiving an average of 440 hours prior to joining an operational squadron – over twice the flying provided in 1941. Navigators also had considerably more experience, some 200 flying hours.

The number of Bomber OTUs peaked at 22½ (an OTU with no satellite base counted as ¾ and one with two satellites as 1½) in December 1943. They normally operated four large Flights, and trainees moved from a basic conversion Flight to an 'applied' Flight, the latter often at a satellite base.

In addition to basic, advanced and conversion flying training, a number of other courses were operated by Bomber Command during the war. As the

Most numerous on OTUs were various variants of Wellington, among them Mk.X MF560/KJ-O of No.11 OTU at Westcott, late 1944. (RAFM P5013)

EB151/R, a Halifax V srs 1 (Special) of No.1663 HCU, which supplied crews for No.4 Group seen taking off from Rufforth in 1944. (IWM CH11529)

number of aircraft operating increased so did accidents caused by pilots trying to land at airfields affected by cloud, mist or fog. Radio beam 'blind' landing systems were widely introduced during 1940 and Blind Approach Training Flights formed on most major bases, the first at Wyton on 17 December 1940. They escalated in numbers rapidly during 1941, being known as Beam Approach Training Flights, a more accurate name, by the end of the year, but the main responsibility for such training was taken over by FTC in 1943 and BAT Flights started disappearing from bomber bases. They were replaced by Bomber (Defence) Training Flights providing fighter affiliation. The first six (Nos.1681-1686 inclusive)

formed on 5 June 1943 on Bomber Command training bases, equipped with Tomahawks, and were joined in 1944 by larger B(D)T Flights, one to each operational Group, these using Hurricane/Spitfire and Martinet aircraft.

Providing training for specialists were the *Gee* Training Flight at Hurn, the Radar Navigation Flight (H2S), the *G-H* Training Flight at Feltwell, the Pathfinder Navigation Training Unit, No.1323 Flight (No.8 Group), the Airborne Gunlaying for Turret Training Flight (No.8 Group) and No.1699 Fortress Training Flight (No.100 Group). More mundane were instructors' courses which became formalized as the war years rolled by, resulting in the Bomber Command Instructors' School being set up at Finningley on 5 December 1944. Pilots completed 35 hours of flying and 90 hours of lectures during the six-week course while navigators, signallers, engineers and gunners received 102 hours of instructional technique training in four weeks.

The overall training task was enormous. In a typical month, May 1944, the percentage of Bomber Command flying hours absorbed by the OTUs was 38.5%, by HCUs 17.3%, while operational squadrons accounted for 44.2%.

At the end of 1944 sufficient Lancasters were available to replace Stirlings in HCUs affiliated to Nos.1, 3, 5 and 6 (RCAF) Groups, and by March 1945 Halifaxes had also been supplanted on these units. The LFSs were then disbanded and aircrew reserves were

Armament training was taken over by the HCUs and included fighter affiliation, for which fighter aircraft were employed. This Hurricane I!C was at Lindholme with No.1662 HCU in 1945. (RAFM P16751)

Having served with No.625 Squadron, Lancaster III PB736 transferred to No.1654 HCU at the end of the war as JF-Z before moving to No. 1660 HCU. (MAP)

such that some Halifax HCUs were closed before the end of the war in Europe. Immediately after the German capitulation many more were disbanded, together with most of the bomber OTUs. By the end of August 1945 just five OTUs (Nos.10, 16, 17, 21 & 26) and three HCUs (Nos.1653, 1660 and 1668) remained in Bomber Command, these spending the immediate post-war period providing flights over the Ruhr for groundcrew and disposing of bombs in the North Sea.

By the autumn of 1946 the inevitable turmoil caused by the sudden cessation of hostilities had subsided and Bomber Command's once mighty training machine had been reduced to just three OTUs (Nos.16, 17 and 21) and a single HCU (No.1653), all in No.91 (Training) Group. Further rationalization resulted in the disbandment of the Group in March 1947 when the OTUs were transferred to FTC as Advanced Flying Schools (Nos.204, 201 and 202 respectively) and Operational Conversion Units (OCUs) were formed in Bomber Command, No.230 OCU from No.1653 HCU at Lindholme still with Lancasters, and No.231 OCU at Coningsby with Mosquitoes.

In July 1947 the Bomber Command Instructors' School was disbanded and part of it used to form the Instrument Rating & Examining Flight which operated until March 1953 to establish the new rating scheme using Lincolns. No.230 OCU converted to Lincolns in July 1948, to provide training on the aircraft that was now Bomber Command's mainstay though antiquated in comparison with American and even Soviet equipment. Boeing B-29s were 'borrowed' from the USAF, the first arriving in March

1950, and the Washington Conversion Unit (WCU) was established at Marham to provide eight-week courses for experienced 'four-engined bomber' crews. The first squadron, No.115, reformed in May 1950 after conversion and after a further seven squadrons had been converted the WCU disbanded on 1 September 1951 to form the nucleus of No.35 Squadron, which retained the training role in addition to being an operational unit.

With the run-down in the Mosquito force No.231 OCU disbanded in December 1949, only to reform two years later as the Canberra conversion unit established with 24 B.2 and 10 PR.3 aircraft. Canberras were already in service, the units at Binbrook converted in-situ with the help of an attached Jet Conversion Unit operating Meteors and a single Canberra and in practice none of the latter were available for the OCU until February 1952. Initially the OCU's strength was eight Mosquitoes, 10 Meteor PR.10s and an Anson, having absorbed the tasking of No.237 OCU, the photo-reconnaissance training unit, which had transferred to Bomber Command from Coastal Command in 1950. It was not until May 1953 that the first students assembled for the three-month Canberra course, and December before the Mosquitoes could be withdrawn.

Meanwhile the Bomber Command Bombing School (BCBS) had formed at Lindholme in October 1952 with Lincolns and Varsities, initially to provide visual bombing instruction but increasingly concentrating on the use of the NBS radar as the V-Force built up. No.230 OCU underwent considerable upheaval, the unit being renamed the Reserve Training Squadron early in 1953, No.1 Group

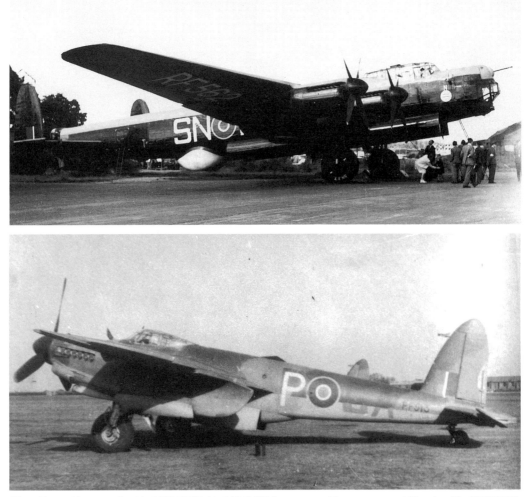

Top: *Formed by renaming No.1653 HCU, No.230 OCU first operated Lancasters and Lincolns, like RF562/SN-N. (Author's collection)*

Above: *After reorganisation No.231 OCU carried on Mosquito training, using Mk.XVIs including PF513 (an ex-16 OTU aircraft) for 'operational' exercises. (V. Hawley)*

operating a Lincoln Conversion Flight (LCF) at Waddington and No.3 Group a similar unit at Upwood from May onwards. This situation only lasted a few weeks, No.230 OCU reforming from the Conversion Flights at Upwood by August – only to be re-designated the LCF on 1 February 1955. No.232 OCU formed at Gaydon in readiness for the Vickers Valiant, first of the V-Bombers, for which the aircrew were hand-picked. Aircraft captains had to be rated 'above average' with at least 1,750 hours as first pilot and have completed a tour on Canberras, while co-pilots were required to have 700 hours 'in command' including a Canberra tour.

Navigator/plotters were to have completed 2½ years on the twin-jet, navigator/radar crewmen to have done the BCBS course using the 'Airborne Radar' training system, and signallers a full tour on Bomber, Coastal or Transport squadrons. Such personnel were

soon hard to find but the requirements were not relaxed until the V-Bombers had been in squadron service for some time, the first crews completing OCU training in May 1955.

In October 1955 the PR element of No.231 OCU moved to Merryfield with Canberras and Meteors, space being at a premium at Bassingbourn for the unit at its peak was churning out crews for some 38 RAF Canberra squadrons and running courses for Commonwealth and foreign personnel. The Merryfield detachment moved to Wyton in October 1956 and became No.237 OCU again, but in January 1958, as Canberra training markedly decreased, No.231 OCU was able to re-absorb the PR task and No.237 OCU was disbanded.

Meanwhile No.230 OCU had again reformed, at Waddington on 31 May 1956, in preparation for the arrival of the Avro Vulcan. The first was delivered in

No.231 OCU operated Canberras for many years, at one time working up a four-aircraft formation team using T.4s. (Air Ministry PRB12021)

July, service trials completed in December and training courses started in February 1957. Training on the third of the V-Bombers, the Handley Page Victor, commenced in November 1957 at Gaydon alongside the Valiant, by which time flight simulators were in use at both Nos.230 and 232 OCUs.

The Lincoln had proved a difficult aircraft for radar instructional purposes, being very cramped internally, but it was not until March 1960 that the first of five Hastings T.5s was delivered to the BCBS. Specially fitted out as 'NBS airborne classrooms' the improvement was immediately apparent and the Hastings of '1066 Squadron', as the BCBS was soon nicknamed, settled down to many years of steady service alongside the Varsities still in use for visual bombing training.

In 1952-53 No.231 OCU operated a few ex-237 OCU Mosquito PR.34s, among them RG229. (Author's collection)

Above: *No.232 OCU was formed at Gaydon on 1 March 1954 for Valiant training, WZ405 being one of the unit's aircraft. (Author)*

Below: *No.230 OCU reformed at Waddington in 1956 to train Vulcan crews. XA900 was one of the first deliveries and carried the Lincoln coat of arms on the fin and the unit badge on the forward fuselage. (Hawker Siddeley/BAe A2/56)*

Bottom: *Victor B.1 XA931 joined No.232 OCU in 1957, forming part of 'A' Flight at Gaydon. (MAP)*

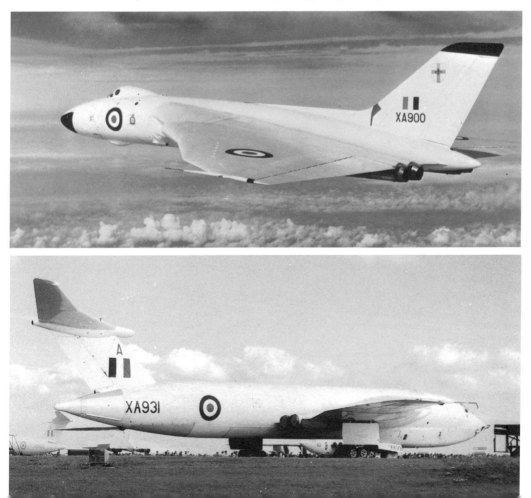

Top: *The Bomber Command Bombing School soldiered on with the Lincoln for many years, among them RA719, an immaculate ex-7 Squadron aircraft. (MAP)*

Above: *The replacement for the Lincolns with the BCBS was the Hastings T.5, which provided a much-improved training environment for NBS students. TG553 was photographed in October 1963. (Author)*

The first Vulcan B.2 was received on No.230 OCU on 1 July 1960 and joined 'B' Flight, Mk.1s continuing to operate with 'A' Flight until this variant was phased out of service in 1965. The Victor B.2 Trials Flight formed at Cottesmore in September 1961 as 'C' Flight, No.232 OCU, becoming the Victor Training Flight on 1 April 1962. It moved to Wittering in February 1964, operating its own aircraft until September, then borrowing squadron aircraft as required.

Valiant training suddenly ceased on 2 February 1965 following the discovery of extensive wing spar fatigue, and in June No.232 OCU was disbanded, the Victor ground school being integrated with No.230 OCU at Finningley (the latter unit having moved to the Yorkshire base in June 1961), while the Air Training Flight moved to Marham and was later renamed the Victor Tanker Training Flight. These proved to be the last changes in Bomber Command's training organization which remained stabilized long after No.3 Group was disbanded in 1967 and No.1 Group was taken over by Strike Command on 30 April 1968.

CHAPTER 13

Research and Development

THE RESEARCH AND DEVELOPMENT work carried out on radio/radar countermeasures of various types has been covered in Chapter 9. This chapter is concerned with the work on aircraft, navigation, bombing aids and armament.

Aircraft

Work on Specification B.9/32, which called for a replacement for the Sidestrand day bomber, and could be said to envisage the first of a new generation of 'modern' bomber aircraft, had already started when the 'Ten Year Rule'* was abandoned in March 1932, but submissions were seriously affected by pronouncements on aircraft weight limitations at the Geneva Disarmament Conference of 1933. The 6,300-lb limit being strongly advocated would have negated any chance of the requirements of B.9/32 being met and so the Air Staff gambled on it being abandoned and allowed Vickers and Handley Page to proceed with their proposals despite steadily escalating weight. They hedged their bets, however, by issuing P.27/32 which called for a single-engined aircraft with reduced armament but still capable of carrying a 1,000-lb load over a similar range while staying within the weight limit. From a number of tenders the Fairey design was chosen, but it was realized that aircraft designed to both specifications would take a long time to reach squadrons, so the Fairey B.19/27 Hendon monoplane, competitor of the Heyford and already tested in prototype form, was put into production and additional orders placed for the Hart and its derivative, the Hind.

Just as pressing was the development of a new night bomber and the Air Ministry's Supply and Research Department issued Specification B.3/34 for

*See Chapter 1

such an aircraft in July 1934, and then turned its attention to a replacement for the Hart/Hind by issuing Specification P.4/34 which called for a small manoeuvrable aircraft specifically tailored for 'battlefield operations'.

Belatedly it was realized that neither Heyfords or Hendons were a match for Hitler's new Luftwaffe, even at night, so an updated bomber version of the Handley Page 51 troop carrier was ordered 'off the drawing board' in August 1935 to B.29/35, to fill the gap while Armstrong-Whitworth's more advanced submission to B.3/34 was being developed into the Whitley.

All this activity gave the aircraft industry plenty to think about, but the Operational Requirements (OR) Branch of the Air Ministry had to look well into the future and issued in rapid succession Specification B.1/35, which was intended to take advantage of the more powerful engines in prospect; B.12/36, calling for a long-range, heavily-armed four-engined strategic bomber capable of carrying up to 2,000-lb sized bombs; and P.13/36 for a medium-range, twin-engined tactical bomber able to accommodate amongst other weapons, two 21-in torpedoes. It was the latter two that engendered most interest and proved more important, but they were also more contentious, causing considerable discussion and heated argument at both Government and Air Ministry level. Despite this they went ahead, Shorts and Supermarine being chosen to produce prototypes to B.12/36, while Handley Page and Avro tackled the equally difficult P.13/36. Prototypes of the Armstrong-Whitworth, Handley Page and Vickers submissions to B.1/35 were also ordered, but only the latter went ahead. It was built as the Warwick but did not enter service as a bomber, and strangely the tactical P.4/34 light bomber was quietly abandoned, the Hawker

A model of the Supermarine submission to Spec B.12/36. The contract was cancelled after destruction of the prototype during the bombing of the factory on 26 September 1940. (P.H.T. Green)

Henleys ordered to meet the requirement being transferred to a training role.

Meanwhile Shorts and Supermarine pressed on with work on the B.12/36, though hampered by the ruling that wing spans were not to exceed 100 feet so that existing hangars could be used. The aircraft which became the Short Stirling first flew on 13 May 1939, but unfortunately it was damaged on landing, which delayed things, and it was 7 May 1940 before the first production aircraft took to the air. The Supermarine Type 316 was dogged by the illness of the chief designer, R.J. Mitchell; the need to concentrate on Spitfire production; and the destruction of the prototypes when the factory was bombed on 26 September 1940. Although estimated performance was better than that of the Stirling some design features caused concern and it was clear that it would be seriously delayed, so it was cancelled.

Despite early setbacks due to inexperience with the manufacturing techniques required, Avro had their Rolls-Royce Vulture-powered P.13/36 prototype ready for a first flight on 25 July 1939. Early flight trials did not go smoothly but production deliveries of the Manchester commenced in August 1940 and, stressed for catapult take-off and dive-bombing, the aircraft proved immensely strong and capable of absorbing considerable punishment.

Doubts about the Vulture engine, concern over its availability, and the lack of alternative 2,000hp engines, had already caused the Air Ministry to ask Handley Page to redesign their P.13/36 submission, the HP.56, to take four Merlins instead. The change naturally resulted in delay but the HP.57, later known as the Halifax, flew on 25 October 1939. Flight trials were comparatively smooth but initial production deliveries were erratic.

The Vulture engine continued to give trouble and in December 1939 it was decided to re-engine the Manchester. Versions powered by the Napier Sabre or Bristol Centaurus engines then in development were rejected, and in the summer of 1940 the Avro design team completed drawings of the Manchester III, an extended-span variant powered by four Merlins. It was enthusiastically endorsed by the Air Ministry and conversion of an airframe commenced. The changes proved substantial and in November the Manchester III was renamed the Lancaster, the prototype flying on 9 January 1941. Despite fuel flow problems it was an instant success, proving to have a better performance than the Halifax. It was a war-winner!

On 25 November 1940 another war-winner, the de Havilland Mosquito, had made its first flight. The company first proposed an unarmed high-speed bomber in 1938 but Air Marshal Sir Wilfred Freeman, Air Member for Research and Development, was almost alone in supporting the project, his technical staff suspecting the performance estimates and general opinion believing that the Germans would have produced a faster fighter by the time the aircraft could be in service. A number of variations on the theme were projected during September and October 1939

The Warwick, an enlarged Wellington designed to meet Spec B.1/35, went into production, but despite much development effort, not into service with Bomber Command. (MAP)

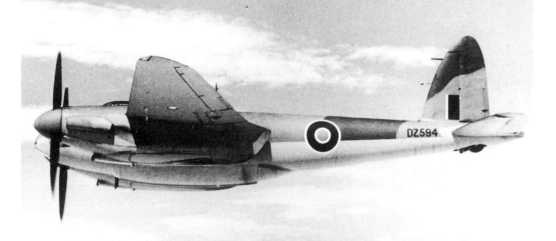

The very successful 'bulged' bomb bay which enabled the 4,000-lb Cookie to be carried by the Mosquito, is displayed by this development Mk.IV, DZ594. (British Official)

Much design work was put into the development of heavy-calibre defensive armament – in this instance a 40mm gun turret in a dorsal position on the much-modified Wellington II prototype, L4250. (MAP)

Steady development of the Halifax produced the very successful Hercules-powered Mk.III, here in prototype form still with square-cut wing tips. (MAP)

and Freeman finally got grudging agreement for a bomber reconnaissance version to be ordered, the go-ahead being given on 29 December 1939. More talks followed, with Freeman, now Vice Chief of Air Staff, continuing to champion the aircraft, and an order for 50 to B.1/40 was placed on 1 March 1940. It was nearly scuppered in May by Beaverbrook's 'super priority' scheme, and only saved by de Havillands promising 50 aircraft by the end of 1941 – which everyone knew was impossible! During the autumn of 1940 unease over the bomber version hardened, and by January 1941 none of the first 50 were scheduled as bombers, though it was suggested that such a variant might figure in the proposed follow-up order. In the event the final 10 airframes of the initial batch and 50 from the second were changed to bombers in July 1941, and the first bomber delivery was made on 15 November – not on schedule, but an outstanding effort nonetheless.

New variants of the Wellington, Stirling, Halifax and Lancaster were produced as the war proceeded, while the American industry provided the Boston,

Mitchell, Ventura and Fortress, of which only the Boston was a real Bomber Command success. There were also unsatisfactory aircraft from British industry, the Buckingham (an intended Blenheim replacement), and the 'rapid production' Albemarle joining the Warwick as bomber failures though built in considerable numbers. Additionally many specifications were issued which did not result in production, one of the most important, B.1/39, calling for a 9,000-lb bomb load to be carried over a range of at least 2,500 miles at a minimum cruising speed of 280 mph as a standard replacement for all current 'medium' and 'heavy' bombers. Nine design teams tendered proposals, those from Handley Page and Bristol being selected for development and prototype orders placed, though both were subsequently cancelled on the grounds that the loss of production during changeover to the new aircraft would not be worth the improved performance obtainable. Other aircraft projects abandoned for the same reason included the B.8/41 'Super Stirling' and the B.11/41 Mosquito replacement, and though Wellingtons fitted with pressure cabins went into small-scale production

Development of a high-altitude bomber version of the Wellington consumed much time and effort, both the Mk.V and VI being fitted with a pressurized crew compartment. W5798 was one of the Merlin-powered Mk.VI trials aircraft. (MAP)

they were scrapped, and the specially developed Vickers B.5/41 cancelled, when the Mosquito proved a capable high-altitude bomber.

Instead Vickers were allowed to convert the 'Wellington replacement' into a four-engined aircraft around which Specification B.3/42 was drafted. This called for a heavily-armed aircraft capable of carrying an 8,000-lb load over 1,400 miles, or 4,000-lb over 2,150 miles at cruising speeds well in excess of 300mph. Named the Windsor, development became tortuous and in the event even the Clyde-powered prop-jet version was cancelled in November 1945, only Merlin-powered prototypes having been flown. A stretched version of the Lancaster built to Specification B.14/43, which in many ways was the Windsor's competitor, did go into large-scale production as the Lincoln, but it did not enter service until late 1945 following teething troubles and reluctance to interfere with Lancaster production.

Proposals by Avro, Bristol, Miles, Shorts and Vickers for giant bombers all remained merely brochures, for Britain's aircraft industry was already stretched to the limit and such aircraft would have been years in development.

Apart from its greater range and more powerful armament the Lincoln represented little advance over the Lancaster, and in the era of the gas turbine it was already outdated. By 1944 designers had been making preliminary studies of jet-propelled bombers for some

The Vickers Windsor on display post-war. DW512 was the second prototype of this unsuccessful bomber aircraft. (MAP)

time, but it was the in-service appearance of the German Ar234 which provided a spur for the Operational Requirements Branch of the Air Ministry. During 1944-45 they evolved Specification B.3/45, which called for a Mosquito replacement with a cruising speed of 440 knots at 40,000 feet and a ceiling of not less than 50,000 feet – a quantum leap in bomber performance! It was written broadly around proposals by W.E.W. Petter who had recently joined the English Electric Company, and a contract for four prototypes of his A.1 project was placed with them in January 1946. Work on the aircraft proceeded rapidly, but the intended radar bombing system was soon way behind schedule and B.5/47 was issued for a tactical version employing visual bomb-aiming, an initial production order being placed before the prototype Canberra first flew. A target marker version to OR 302 was ordered but only a prototype produced, and both the Mk.2 and 6 bomber variants used by Bomber Command remained dependant on visual bombing aided by the elderly *G-H* system where available. Photographic reconnaissance versions of the basic bombers, culminating in the much-modified PR.9, were also produced and used by the Command.

Meanwhile the impact of nuclear weapons was being urgently considered and OR 229 was written around a four-jet replacement for the Lincoln capable of delivering a 10,000-lb 'shape' from 45,000 feet at 500 knots at a radius of 1,750 miles (i.e. a range of 3,500 miles). Specification B.35/46 was issued on 1 January 1947 to cover an amended OR, the required ceiling being increased to 50,000 feet with the range reduced to 3,350 miles as a trade-off. Six formal tenders were received by the closing date of May 1947, of which four could be considered aerodynamically advanced. The HP 80 and Avro 698 were selected, and because the aerodynamics involved were quite literally at the frontier of knowledge, prototypes of a simpler design were also ordered to an earlier Specification, B.14/46 – the Short Sperrin. In practice the Sperrin's position as a 'fall-back' was undermined by the acceptance of arguments put forward by Vickers for their Type 660, the firm guaranteeing to produce an aircraft which would fulfil most of the B.35/46 requirements using fully understood aerodynamics – and to do so quickly. Orders were placed for the Vickers aircraft to Specification B.9/48, and the designer, George Edwards, was as good as his word, the prototype making its first flight on 18 May 1951, and most of the production Valiants rolled off the lines ahead of schedule.

An attempt at a medium-range target marker was made with the Valiant B.2 to OR 285/Spec B.104P, but this impressive aircraft was not put into production,

and it was the turn of the Avro project, which had evolved as a tailless delta, and Handley Page's HP 80 'crescent' wing design, to take the stage.

After several quite radical design changes the prototype Avro Type 698, subsequently named the Vulcan, first flew on 30 August 1952, a few days after the first production contract was received. The HP 80, which became the Victor, also suffered alarms and excursions and further delay by having to be transferred to Boscombe Down for flight trials. It was not until 24 December 1952 that the prototype flew, and November 1957 before RAF deliveries began.

Meanwhile unmanned bombers were under consideration. Specification UB.109T of April 1951 called for a ramp-launched vehicle which could carry a 5,000-lb load 400 miles at 45,000 feet and 450 knots. The Bristol Aeroplane Company produced the Type 182 *Blue Rapier* and Vickers the *Red Rapier*, but both were cancelled in 1954 when at an advanced stage, manned bombers with stand-off weapons being preferred. The OR Branch also considered the development of a low-level strategic bomber as another way of reducing vulnerability, B.126T being issued for an aircraft capable of delivering a 10,000-lb nuclear weapon over a radius of 1,500 miles while flying at 500 feet and Mach 0.85. Shorts, Bristol and Avro submitted designs of which the latter's Type 721 was probably the most viable, but the concept was shelved.

By October 1955 the strategic plan for 10 years hence envisaged an IRBM (*Blue Streak*) and the Avro 730 reconnaissance bomber capable of a Mach 2.5 cruise at 60,000 feet carrying a large powered stand-off bomb. In the meantime the prospective enemy's fighters were improving and both Avro and Handley Page produced proposals for new and more powerful Mk.2 variants of their V-Bombers refined to improve their high-altitude abilities – and both went into service with updated electrics. Two years later the supersonic Avro 730 was suddenly cancelled and nuclear 'response' lay in the *Blue Steel* stand-off missile which was to be fitted to some V-Bombers, the *Thor* IRBM*, and ultimately its replacement, *Blue Streak**. The English Electric P.10D cruise missile was also projected for fitment on V-Bombers, and proposals were made for an enlarged Vulcan carrying six *Skybolt* airborne ballistic missiles, or 28 1,000-lb bombs in wing-mounted weapon pods (and another 10 in the bomb bay) over a 5,000-mile range. All these projects, including *Skybolt*, were subsequently cancelled and replaced by *Polaris*, a submarine-launched missile.

A Canberra tactical bomber/reconnaissance

*See Chapter 11

replacement was the subject of OR 339, to which the Buccaneer Mk.2 was proposed and rejected and the TSR-2 ordered and subsequently cancelled – as was the General Dynamics F-111 which replaced it. For a time the bomber/reconnaissance 'desk' of the OR Branch at the Ministry of Defence was virtually moribund; but designers continued to explore the field of tactical strike aircraft, and just as Bomber Command was disbanded Britain joined with other European countries in developing the Multi-Role Combat Aircraft (MRCA), which subsequently became the Tornado.

Navigation

Bomber Command started the war dependent on 'dead reckoning' navigation which required a good compass and an accurate wind at operating height for any hope of success. Such winds were not available over Germany, and even before the RAF's night offensive started in May 1940 it was becoming obvious that crews were having problems because of the inaccuracy of landfalls on return from leaflet 'raids'. Astro could be used but it was very dependent on the weather. Something more reliable had to be devised.

A fixing aid (a 'fix' being a position on a chart over which the aircraft had been at a specific time) using pulsed range signals from ground transmitters had been invented in 1938 but had remained undeveloped due to lack of funds. In June 1940 work restarted at the TRE and a simple cathode-ray tube display giving readings which could be plotted on a special navigational grid chart to give an accurate fix was produced. The equipment was enthusiastically reported on at a radio aids meeting on 16 October 1940 and a month later Bomber Command requested that *Gee* ('G' for Grid) be provided for all bomber aircraft. Early in 1941 the Air Staff got 'cold feet', believing that *Gee* would be immediately jammed and made useless, but the appointment of AVM R.H.M.S. Saundby as SASO Bomber Command changed such attitudes rapidly, and in April the TRE was tasked with constructing 24 hand-built sets. These were fitted in Wellingtons of No.115 Squadron for trials which started in August 1941 and success was immediate, the equipment proving both accurate and easy to use. Part of the trials involved sorties over Germany and unfortunately a *Gee*-equipped aircraft was lost on a sortie to Hanover. Tests were immediately suspended to maintain secrecy while 'productionised' equipment was manufactured, the formation of the TR1335 Development Unit on 14 December heralding resumption of trials. The unit was re-designated No.1418 Flight on 5 January 1942 and operated from

Marham, carrying out tests on the *Gee* chains and investigating its possible use for blind approaches, before amalgamating with the Bomber Development Unit on 20 July.

The equipment was also tested for target marking, a trial named *Crackers* being completed off the Isle of Man. No 3 Group crews dropping flares on *Gee* positioning – an early attempt at pathfinding which was not really conclusive! In August 1944 *Loran*, an American long-range navigation aid working on the same principle as *Gee* was tested and later used by No.8 Group Mosquitoes and some of the 'heavies'. It gave moderately accurate fixing at ranges out as far as Berlin.

Reliance on ground transmitters was inherently risky because not only could they be jammed but, perhaps worse, they could be distorted by 'meaconing' (the introduction of false beams). An airborne aid was the answer but its development proved difficult and the breakthrough came by accident during trials on the magnetron valve under development at the TRE for AI radar. During ground trials, Dr P.I. Dee noted that 'echoes' from built-up areas were much stronger than those from the countryside or the sea, and recognizing the potential he arranged for the rotating aerial in the flight trials Blenheim to be angled down so that the beam swept the ground. Initial tests confirmed that discrimination between the different 'echoes' was possible and development continued aimed at producing a map-like display using a cathode-ray tube with a rotating time base, known later as a Plan Position Indicator (PPI). A 'lash-up' was flown in April 1942 and proved

that outlines of towns could be distinguished, though there were many problems to be overcome before the production of H2S, as the equipment was called, could commence. Credit for the name 'H2S' is usually given to Lord Cherwell who nicknamed it 'Home Sweet Home' (soon reduced to H2S) because it had the potential to home straight to the target, but it is also suggested that it was so-called because its development was so difficult that it 'stank'!

The first serious obstacle was the secrecy surrounding the magnetron valve, aircraft carrying it being banned from flying over enemy-held territory, resulting in trials using the lower-powered Klystron valve, which proved unsatisfactory. It was the magnetron or nothing and on 15 July 1942 it was decided to go ahead and use it in H2S equipment. Tragically the TRE Halifax fitted with the first properly engineered H2S equipment had crashed on 7 June 1942, killing six leading experts, and Dr Lovell had to work desperately to regain lost ground. TRE flight trials resumed mid-July and were very successful, resulting in the development aircraft and three other H2S-fitted Halifaxes being delivered to No.1418 Flight for service tests, the first two arriving in October 1942.

With production 10-cm H2S Mk.II entering service Bomber Command called for a clearer picture, and Lovell started work on a 3-cm set. In January 1943 a set was converted to 'X' Band (as the 3-cm wavelength was called) and made its first flight in a Stirling on 11 March with encouraging results, the narrower beam improving definition considerably. Production problems were to be overcome by the

The 'mapping' ability of developed H2S can be seen in this 1945 photograph of the PPI display alongside a map of the Flensburg area of Germany. (British Official)

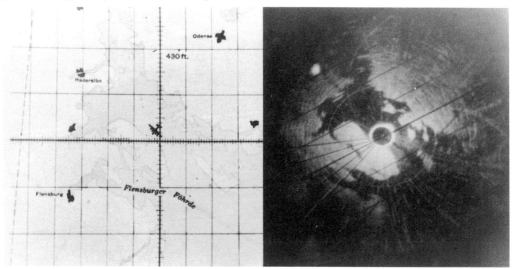

Much of the early development work on H2S radar involved Stirlings, including R9254. (MAP)

conversion of 200 British 10-cm sets to 3-cm format, but two months later the whole project was back in the melting pot following the failure of a series of attacks on Berlin being blamed on H2S. It was decided to equip six Lancasters of the Pathfinder Force with experimental TRE-built 3-cm H2S and run a properly organized trial, work starting in September. All six aircraft were ready for operations by mid-November and after a disappointing first sortie when faults developed, the equipment worked perfectly with results way above expectations – H2S Mk.III was a success.

The TRE now embarked on a 1¼-cm H2S, the *Lion Tamer* (later designated H2S Mk.VI), and early in 1944 also started refining H2S Mk.III by fitting an enlarged scanner, the revised equipment known as *Whirligig* H2S. After several changes of plan both were accorded equal priority with H2S Mk.IV, a straightforward development of the Mk.III, which most expert opinion considered would give the best results. Comparative trials started in July 1944 and the experts were proved right, the Mk.VI being unsatisfactory under operational conditions and the Mk.IIIF with six-foot scanner retained only for interim use by the Pathfinder Force, though in practice it was more widely used post-war.

Post-war development centred ·around the Navigation & Bombing System (NBS) in preparation for the V-Bombers. This used H2S Mk.9 high-definition mapping radar for basic information which was fed, with drift and ground speed inputs from *Green Satin* doppler, to the Navigation and Bombing Computer (NBC) Mk.2A.

For the Canberra *Blue Shadow* sideways-looking mapping radar was developed, and trials were carried out on *Red Neck*, a similar equipment intended for V-Bombers. Both suffered operationally from the need for specially prepared comparative maps to be carried in the aircraft.

Marking/Bombing aids

The discovery of the German *Knickebein*, *X Gerat* and *Y Gerat* bombing systems in 1940 led to unsuccessful attempts to attack the source using the beam itself. The TRE was asked to investigate blind bombing techniques in general, and A.H. Reeves and Dr F.E. Jones devised a system which they named *Oboe*, apparently because of the sound made by early transmissions. Equipment in the aircraft re-transmitted signals from two ground stations, enabling the distance to be measured electronically and the aircraft's position to be plotted very accurately. It could be used for fixing but its real value was as a marking/bombing aid, one station transmitting signals which, when followed by the pilot, kept the aircraft on a gently curving track, while the other, the Master station, calculated the bomb release point and transmitted it to the aircraft. The system was tested in a Wireless Investigation & Development Unit (WIDU) Wellington during the summer of 1941 and had one big disadvantage: one pair of ground stations could only control one aircraft at a time. Bomber Command staff were not universally enthusiastic, but did sanction trials by No.109 Squadron, suggesting that *Oboe* should be tried out on the German battlecruisers *Scharnhorst* and *Gneisenau* in Brest harbour. Several attacks were made in November and December 1941 using the equipment, but in fact the sorties were not true *Oboe* trials because a special radio beam was set up for tracking with an *Oboe* station sending the release signal, a system code-named *Trinity*.

The first full *Oboe* trial was made on 24 April 1942 and was very successful, bombing through cloud proving as accurate as visual daylight attacks. But the equipment's forte was target marking for which at least 28,000 feet altitude was required over Germany. It was planned to use pressurized Wellington VI aircraft which could operate at 35,000 feet while carrying a 4,000-lb load but the introduction of lighter target markers meant that the 2,000-lb load of the more versatile and reliable Mosquito was sufficient. Studies during the first six months of 1943 showed that *Oboe* was at least three times more accurate than H2S as a target marker – a staggering improvement. Further development, mainly to keep ahead of jamming, produced K *Oboe* in mid-1943, followed by the 'S' Band Mk.II in four variants: *Penwiper, Pepperbox, Fountain Pen* and *Album Leaf. Fountain Pen* (*Mk.IIF*) was the first of these to work properly, and went into service in February 1944, followed by *Album Leaf* (*Mk.IIM*) soon afterwards and *Oboe Mk.III* in July. The latter used modified ground stations which enabled four aircraft to be served at a time.

The answer to *Oboe*'s main shortcoming had been invented as early as 1940 but pigeon-holed until revived in November 1942 and made to work by Dr E. Franklin as *G-H*. It could be used simultaneously by large numbers of aircraft, for it was essentially *Oboe* in reverse, the main transmitter/receiver being aboard the aircraft. Transmitted pulses were returned by the ground station, the time taken measured and displayed as a range on a cathode-ray tube. The 'blip' was then compared with the desired range marker and adjustments made to the aircraft's track accordingly. Similarly a bomb release marker could be displayed on the tube and compared with the actual aircraft position on the track using the 'blip' from the second ground station. For a variety of reasons the effective maximum range was less than that of *Oboe*, and it was little used until mobile ground stations could be set up on the Continent after D-Day. It also required a highly-trained navigator capable of coping with the heavy workload involved in the system.

Bombs and Pyros

For 20 years after the Armistice of 1918, progress with properly developed British bombs was virtually nil. This was not due to a lack of foresight on the part of the Air Staff, a requirement for a range of new general purpose bombs up to a nominal 500-lb weight having been issued in 1921. The problem was the 'Ten Year Rule' which ensured that funds for research and development (R&D) remained desperately short, and although the whole point of having bombers was to deliver a bomb which worked, the weapons themselves had a very low priority! Redesigned 250-lb and 500-lb bombs, albeit inert ones, were available for trials in 1925 and demonstrated superior stability, giving a much more accurate trajectory than in-service weapons. Unfortunately tests on their explosive characteristics were made by firing them from a mortar – like a shell – and the whole range of General Purpose (GP) Mk.1 bombs were virtually useless when dropped from aircraft. The 1,000-lb bombs produced in small numbers in 1928 were not tested at all, it being assumed that they would behave in the same way as smaller ones!

In 1935 an Aircraft Bomb Sub Committee was formed and recommended a new 20-lb anti-personnel bomb to replace the Cooper, and a 40-lb bomb for use against vehicles and buildings. Both were approved and entered service late in 1938. Earlier that year the need for a 1,000-lb GP bomb was rediscovered and development of 2,000-lb versions was ordered. Changes were also made to both standard bombs, 250- and 500-lb GPs, but the production Mk.IV version still had Amatol (TNT/Ammonium Nitrate mix) fillings developed in the First World War; and the bombs were heavy-cased, having a charge-to-weight ratio (CWR) of only 30%. Totally unsuitable for anything but the softest-skinned targets, it was ironic that these standard GP bombs were first used in World War II against the armoured decks of German warships. They just bounced off, the result of neglect between the wars plainly visible.

When the Second World War started development of specialist bombs was rushed forward. Proper trials on existing types were also carried out and quickly confirmed that even when directed against 'ideal' targets the failure rate was disastrously high, nearly 50%, due largely to fuzes parting company on impact! Another shock was the discovery in 1941 that German bombs of similar size were approximately twice as effective against buildings as British GP variants. A better filling, RDX/TNT, was immediately introduced and the CWR increased in new bombs, classified as High Capacity (HC) for blast effect on buildings, and Medium Capacity (MC) for general targets. The MC bomb was better shaped than the GP and had a thinner casing, the CWR being increased to around 50%, while the HC had an extremely thin case and a CWR of some 85%. In addition, armour piercing and semi-armour-piercing (SAP) bombs were developed, these having forged-steel noses.

Bigger and better – Lancaster I (Special) PB995 during A&AEE trials of the 22,000-lb Grand Slam *bomb in early 1945. (RAFM P14426)*

The first 4,000-lb HC bombs, often called *Cookies*, looked like large oil drums, and were stabilized by a blunt conical nose and a cylindrical tail assembly. Calls for a 2,000-pounder followed, this appearing as a much slimmer and slightly longer weapon which went into production late in 1941.

Later versions of the 4,000-lb HC bomb were Amatex-filled like the 8,000- and 12,000-lb bombs which became available in September 1942 and September 1943 respectively. The 8,000-pounder was similar in design to the developed 4,000-lb HC Mk.IV, giving the appearance of being two of the smaller weapons bolted together. In fact its diameter was 38in, some 8in more than the standard *Cookie* and it was only produced in two sections for ease of transport. The 12,000-lb HC consisted of three 38-in diameter sections but had a conventional ballistic nose cone and a finned tail to overcome stability problems, and only modified Lancasters could carry it. Use against the Dortmund-Ems Canal in September 1943 was experimental and unsuccessful, but later trial attacks in February/March 1944 resulted in it being cleared for general service.

The 12,000-lb HC was nothing more than a very large blast bomb, and for hardened targets the 12,000-lb *Tallboy* Deep Penetration (DP) bomb was developed and first used in June 1944. The similar but much larger 22,000-lb *Grand Slam*, 25½ feet long and with a diameter of 46 inches, followed in March 1945, both these specialist weapons the work of the genius Barnes Wallis. Such bombs had been mooted in 1941 but rejected, then revived in June 1943 when the AoC No.5 Group suggested their use against canals. Aerodynamically shaped, the *Tallboy* had good ballistic qualities and could be aimed accurately. Its size was determined by the ability of current bomber aircraft to carry it, being a scaled-down version of

Wallis's original 10-ton proposal. Twenty-one feet long, it was Torpex-filled with a CWR of approximately 44%. Inspection of the massive concrete U-Boat pens on the French coast following *Overlord* convinced experts that the *Tallboy* could not penetrate them, and in July 1944 the C-in-C Bomber Command started pushing for production of the original version, cancelled in September 1943. Such a bomb, originally *Tallboy* (L) but renamed *Grand Slam* was intended to produce an 'earthquake' effect and be dropped from specially strengthened Lancasters, and while arguments raged over the need for such a weapon development work went ahead using the nine cases completed before the earlier cancellation. The first test drop was made on 18 October 1944 and the few problems soon sorted out, enabling a live trial of the weapon to be made on 13 March 1945.

There were a number of even more specialist bombs, of which the so-called 'bouncing bomb' used by the 'Dambusters' is the most well-known. Invented by the versatile Barnes Wallis and first proposed in April 1942 it was basically a 50-inch-diameter, 5-foot-wide cylinder slung across the bomb bay between two V-shaped arms which enabled it to be back-spun before low-level release so that it would 'skip' across water, but on contact with the wall of a dam would run down the face until detonated about 30 feet below the surface by a hydrostatic fuze. Trials with models demonstrated its practicality and approval for full-scale tests was given in June 1942. Work went ahead in conditions of great secrecy with the aim of producing an operational *Upkeep*, as it was code-named, by May 1943. Initial air drops of scaled-down versions from a Wellington were not encouraging but development went ahead and success came in January 1943, followed by instructions on 26 February to proceed with the conversion of Lancasters and

Upkeep: *Lancaster III ED817 carrying out dropping trials of the 'bouncing bomb' on Reculver Sands. (via J.D. Oughton)*

manufacture of the 9,150-lb weapon. Time was desperately short, but the May deadline was met and the results are well-known*.

Development of incendiary devices made even less progress during the 1920s than explosive ones, but in 1931 work started on a 20-lb weapon designed to eject a number of fire-raising bombs upon hitting the ground. It became the 25-lb Mk.I incendiary which went into production in 1937, but was not tested properly until April 1939 when it was found to be useless because the case broke up on impact. Attempts to remedy its faults all failed, and it was fortunate that the 4-lb incendiary, developed from a German weapon tested in September 1936, had also been put into production. It entered service in September 1937 and two years later some five million were available.

During the early days of the Second World War a variety of other incendiary devices were developed with very varied success. Incendiary 'leaves' intended to burn crops and forests were a failure, so were petrol bombs (literally five-gallon tins) weighing 45 lb. The 30-lb incendiary filled with a liquid phosphorus and rubber-benzol mixture was more effective and went into full-scale production in June 1941, but another 30-lb weapon filled with methane and petrol under pressure and designed to produce a jet of flame up to 15 feet in length was less successful. Much larger incendiary bombs were also produced, but the 4-lb and 30-lb versions were the only really successful ones, most of the heavier ones being converted into target markers. The most successful of these was *Red Blob* which used a 250-lb case, but most spectacular was *Pink Pansy* which weighed 2,700 lb and used a 4,000-lb HC carcass.

Specially developed target indicators (TIs) appeared during 1943 in two sizes, 250-lb and

*See Chapter 5

1,000-lb in weight. They contained coloured candles which were ejected by a small charge ignited by a barometric fuze. As the war developed the TIs became more complex, some phased so that they would burn for up to 20 minutes, these including the 250-lb *Spot Fire*. Others were sky markers, usually 4.5-in flares, which descended slowly on a parachute and burned for about three minutes, but candle TIs coloured red, green and yellow were also developed for the same purpose. A 30-lb *White Drip* magnesium sky marker was used mainly by the LNSF, and in January 1944 came cluster flares, some of which were hooded to prevent bomb aimers being dazzled. When large-scale day operations were started in the autumn of 1944, smoke puffs using 250-lb or 1,000-lb bomb cases were developed. For photography the impressive 4.5-in photoflash enabled night photos to be obtained from well over 30,000 feet.

Not all Bomber Command operations were against land targets, mine-laying being one of the tasks. After the usual desperately late start an air-drop version of the Admiralty M Mk.I magnetic mine was ordered in small numbers during July 1939 for use by the Fleet Air Arm and Coastal Command, and when Bomber Command became involved in sea mining the weapon was modified to cope with greater speeds and height of release. It was fitted with a nose fairing and drogue parachute and designated the 1,500-lb A Mk.1 mine, trials being completed in March 1940 and production versions becoming available in April. Further development eased manufacture and strengthened the weapon, while later versions included 'triggering' options – magnetic, acoustic or a combination. The A Mk.V, a 1,000-lb version, usually magnetically triggered, was introduced during 1941 and both continued in use throughout the remainder of the war, supplemented in 1944 by the 2,000-lb A Mk.VI which was more powerful and sophisticated. The main charges were Amatol or Minol and both 1,000-lb and 1,500-lb sea mines were used as parachute land mines code-named *Magnum* and *Tim* respectively. The latter weapons had increased explosive content and a domed nose and were very destructive as blast bombs.

For direct attacks on ships the standard GP and SAP bombs were used, but for 'high-value' warships sheltering in steep-sided fjords the 1,000-lb spherical bomb was hastily developed from the naval Mk.XIX contact mine. The body was filled with some 770 lb of Amatol and fitted with a Mk.XIV hydrostatic pistol set to detonate the weapon at a depth of 14-18 feet. The project was completed in under three months and used, unsuccessfully, at the end of March 1942 on just two *Tirpitz* attacks. The 5,600-lb Capital Ship bomb, a 38-inch-diameter turnip-shaped device was also developed. It had a unique 'ring charge' filling and was thought capable of sinking the most powerful warships – but failed to get the chance.

Although it had been agreed informally that full collaboration on weapons would continue between the USA and Britain until terminated jointly, nuclear co-operation came to an abrupt end unilaterally in August 1946 following the passing of the American Atomic Energy Act. The British Government felt very let down and decided it would have to independently develop nuclear weapons. The first British device was exploded on 3 October 1952 and a practical bomb, the 10,000-lb *Blue Danube*, was successfully dropped over Maralinga, Australia, on 11 October 1956. A thermo-nuclear (hydrogen) bomb warhead was under development but *Grapple* air drops in May 1957 were not completely successful so as a 'fall-back' *Orange Herald*, a high-yield fission bomb, was tested and production versions named *Violet Club* and *Yellow Sun Mk.1* entered service in 1958 and 1960 respectively. A successful H-Bomb warhead test was made under *Grapple 'X'* on 8 November, confirmed by *Grapple 'Y'* and *'Z'* in 1958, resulting in *Yellow Sun Mk.2*, the first British production thermo-nuclear weapon, entering service in 1961.

It had already become obvious that getting a free-fall bomb of any sort to a Russian target would become an increasingly doubtful proposition as defences improved, and it was estimated that high-altitude bombing would be suicidal by 1965. As early as 1949 work had started on *Blue Boar*, a bomb with TV guidance, but it was cancelled in 1954 in favour of stand-off weapons. IRBMs were also developed, the Hawker Siddeley *Blue Streak* being initiated in 1955, and Avro won the contract for the stand-off bomb in March 1956, producing the 35-foot-long *Blue Steel* which was inertially-guided and carried a *Red Snow* thermo-nuclear warhead. Its liquid fuel rocket motor gave it a range of about 100 miles. Though difficult to handle it worked well once the usual teething troubles had been eliminated, and went into service in 1963. Work was started on a much longer-range Mk.2 version but development was slow and it was cancelled in December 1959, the Air Staff pressing for the Douglas *Skybolt* air-launched ballistic missile to replace *Blue Steel* and the fixed-site *Thor* missile system. The Americans agreed to provide *Skybolt* from 1965, prompting the cancellation of *Blue Streak* in April 1960. It was therefore a severe shock when *Skybolt* was axed in December 1962 and replaced by the submarine-launched *Polaris*.

A comparatively small nuclear weapon, *Red Beard*, was also produced. Intended for low-level

tactical use it was also used for strategic bombing as an alternative to conventional bombs. The latter, mainly 500- and 1,000-lb MC, remained in production postwar and underwent little change until the 1960s when low-level operations resulted in the introduction of retarding devices to give aircraft time to escape the blast. Further development centred around 'smart' bombs and weapons specially designed for attacking airfields – but they were for the future.

Bomb-sights

A semi-automatic bomb-sight which made allowances for most of the variables involved in an accurate release point, including height, speed and wind strength/direction, had been developed in 1918, but the Air Staff held the view that equipment should be kept simple for inter-war years part-time bomb aimers; and in any case, lack of funds stifled its development. As a result Bomber Command entered the Second World War with the Mk.IX course-setting bomb-sight (CSBS) which was excellent – providing accurate information was fed into it and a long straight-and-level approach was made to the target. The first proviso was unlikely, the second undesirable!

The CSBS remained standard equipment until mid-1943 when the Mk.XIV gyro-stabilized vector sight started to supersede it. The Mk.XIV was not inherently as accurate as the CSBS, but results were better under operational conditions because it allowed evasive action during the run-up, only requiring the

The Valiant was employed for initial tests of Blue Steel, *WP204 being one of the aircraft involved. (BAe G1/64)*

aircraft to be held steady for the last 10 seconds before bomb release. It was also limited to 20,000 feet, aircraft operating above this height, mainly Mosquitoes, being fitted with the modified MK.XIVA.

Further work resulted in the MK.IIA stabilized automatic bomb-sight (SABS) being developed, and it first went into service with No.617 Squadron during 1944. Under ideal conditions it was incredibly accurate, errors of less than 100 yards from 20,000 feet being the norm. The 'T' series of tachometric sights were under development and post-war the T.2 was in service, followed by the T.3/T.4 variants used for visual bombing by Lincolns (T.2/.3), Canberras (T.2/.3/.4) and the V-Force (T.4). For blind bombing *G-H* was employed and the NBS system developed, the associated NBC providing signals for autopilot steering, and for automatic release of weapons if required, the prototype being ready for service trials early in 1956, operational use having to await ballistic information from the Pacific weapon tests.

Bomber Defence

As aircraft speeds increased the traditional single Lewis gun on a ring mounting used throughout the 1920s was replaced by more streamlined and manageable equipment, such as the Fairey 'High-Speed' mounting still in use on the Fairey Battle during 1939-40. The Hampden had a gun position faired into the underside of the fuselage using a special Handley Page mounting (useless in its original form) but the ventral defence of most medium/heavy bombers in the 1930s was a retractable 'dustbin' arrangement which gradually increased in complexity, but was virtually impossible to use.

The success of the power-operated nose turret developed for the Overstrand by Boulton Paul from a French design, sparked off a range of such turrets, the Bristol Aeroplane Company producing them for its own designs, while Fraser Nash manufactured a series suitable for other firms' aircraft. These included nose, tail and ventral turrets for the Whitley and Wellington replacing the manufacturer's own manually-operated 'birdcage'-type turrets. The latter mounted single .303-inch Vickers 'K' guns which had replaced the Lewis, but the power-operated variants usually sported pairs of guns though four were often squeezed into tail turrets. The calibre of guns in production aircraft remained the standard .303-inch, but belt-fed Brownings steadily replaced the Vickers in all turrets.

In 1936 the Air Ministry assumed responsibility for its guns, forming a small drawing office in the Royal Small Arms factory at Enfield and arranging for the establishment of an Armament Department at RAE Farnborough. Study contracts were placed for turrets mounting larger-calibre guns, it being realized that bombers were in danger of being outgunned by the new fighters already in production. The .5-inch Browning had already been tested and surprisingly rejected as no real improvement over the .303-inch. One-and-a-half pounders (40mm) and even 2-lb (70mm) guns were considered together with 'automatic' gun-laying, but despite much design and development work they all came to naught. Instead efforts were made to increase the firepower by simpler means. These included the design and manufacture of a new mounting for the Hampden by the small engineering company, Rose Brothers of Gainsborough, which enabled the number of guns at each position to be doubled, and the fitting of some Halifaxes, in particular the later Hercules-powered variants, with four-gun dorsal turrets. These went some way to replacing the nose turret removed from the aircraft to improve performance.

Ventral turrets, though attractive because they covered a blind spot and had a good field of fire, also had disadvantages. Their drag when lowered reduced speed by some 25mph, and their weight and complexity also mitigated against them. Despite this, work on the Fraser Nash FN 64 ventral turret, which was periscopically sighted, continued until 1942 when the general installation of H2S scanner cupolas under the fuselage of both Halifax and Lancaster bombers took precedence.

Later in the war the 13.5-mm (.5-inch) Browning and later the 20-mm calibre cannon were resurrected, and it was planned that Austin-built Lancasters would be fitted with the Bristol B.17 turret, mounting two 20-mm Hispano guns by the end of 1944. In the event the turret was not ready and FN 150 units had to be used instead – with two .303s! Many Canadian-built aircraft were completed with American Martin 0.5-inch gun turrets but there was little evidence that they made any difference, or indeed that the 20-mm cannon turrets would have done so either, for the real difficulty was training the guns on a highly manoeuvrable target like a fighter. The introduction of gyro-stabilized sights in place of reflector sights only went part way to solving the problem.

Tail turrets, especially the Frazer Nash FN 20, were the subject of constant complaint for they were cramped and difficult to see out of because the perspex was invariably badly scratched in service. Rose Brothers were again approached and in 1944 produced a new tail turret which was not only more spacious but mounted two .5-inch Browning guns. Aeroplane and Armament Experimental Establishment (A&AEE) trials reports were enthusiastic and service tests by No.101 Squadron confirmed that the turret was easier to operate, and that the removal of the rear facing perspex panels much increased visibility without causing discomfort.

Periscopic sights having proved largely ineffective, and remote-control systems such as that developed for the Windsor very troublesome, attention was directed to gun-directing radars under development by the TRE. The most advanced of the awkwardly-named Airborne Gunlaying for Turrets (AGLT), code-named *Village Inn*, was fitted to a few operational Lancasters towards the end of the war but had no chance to prove itself against the Luftwaffe. The similar Emerson APG-8 Blind Tracking Radar device was also tested but found to have no advantage over the generally more advanced AGLT.

Bomber aircraft developed post-1945 had no defensive armament, relying on speed and altitude for protection.

General Development

The first attempt to conduct bomber equipment trials on an organized basis was made when the Bomber Development unit formed at Boscombe Down on 17 November 1940 as part of the A & AEE, but it was not a success and it was disbanded six months later. The work was transferred to specialized units, in particular No. 109 Squadron and No. 1418 Flight – until 21 July 1942 when Bomber Command reformed the BDU at Gransden Lodge as an independent organisation, using No. 1418 Flight as a nucleus.

Initially the BDU was equipped with Wellingtons

Below: *Remote-controlled armament trials continued post-war using Lancaster LL780/G (for 'Guard'). The aircraft had 20mm turrets in the dorsal and ventral positions, sighted from a tail position. (via P.H.T. Green)*

Top right: *Remote-controlled gun barbettes intended for the Vickers Windsor being tested in a Warwick. (MAP)*

Bottom right: *A Rose rear turret fitted with AGLT equipment. (R.H. Hardy)*

and Mosquitoes for service trials of equipment at the development stage. Operational trials were carried out on *Gee* and during the autumn of 1942 extensive testing was done on H2S using the initial Halifax trials aircraft and Stirlings, the latter bearing the brunt of the testing. The BDU moved to Feltwell in April and Newmarket in September 1943, by which time five Stirlings were on strength, and trials on such diverse items as the Mk.VIII autopilot, Mk.IX sextant and Mk.IIG H2S had been completed. Later engine surging, flame damping, ultra-violet cockpit lighting, the photo-electric sun compass, FN 64 turret, SABS, *Oboe Mk.II* and the full range of the ECM equipment fitted to Main Force bombers were subjects of reports. Training on *G-H* was given to squadron navigation leaders and in February 1945 the unit returned to Feltwell and became involved in flight refuelling trials, 36 'line-and-grapple' refuelling flights using Lancaster 'tankers' and 'receivers' being made between May and August.

The BDU was disbanded on 27 November 1945 when it became the Central Bomber Establishment (CBE) Development Wing at Feltwell before joining the unit HQ at Marham in January 1946. Early CBE trials were largely concerned with improving the defensive armament of the Lincoln using test Lancasters. One was fitted with an FN 121 rear turret and on 27 March 1946 another arrived at Marham

Flight refuelling trials were pressed forward in 1945, intended for the Tiger Force. *(Flight Refuelling Ltd)*

fitted with remotely-controlled dorsal and ventral barbettes sighted from a position in the tail. Firing trials started in July but met immediate problems and the aircraft returned to Boulton Paul Ltd for modifications which took eight months, firing not being resumed for a year – and then promptly cancelled in August 1947 when the system was abandoned.

Lincolns gradually took over trials tasks from Lancasters and in May 1947 two aircraft, named *Excalibur* and *Crusader*, were fitted with the latest bombing and radar equipment and became regular globe-trotters on demonstration flights. Other Lincolns carried out tropical and arctic trials on H2S equipment, these continuing until the unit was disbanded at Lindholme in November 1949. There

followed a period when Command-instigated trials were carried out at squadron level or by outside agencies until the Bomber Command Development Unit (BCDU) was formed at Wittering in May 1954 using Canberras of No.100 Squadron for flight tests, joined later by Valiants of Nos. 138 and 214 Squadrons. The unit was responsible for the modification and evaluation of a wide variety of equipment, and for recommending tactics and operational procedures, including the initial service trials of the Valiant ECM installation and, during 1957-58, of the tanker/receiver 'probe-and-drogue' air refuelling system. The assisted take-off scheme for the Valiant using DH Super Sprite rockets was also evaluated and rejected.

In 1959 sufficient aircraft became available for a BCDU Trials Flight to be formed, with three Valiants and a couple of Canberras, the whole unit moving to Finningley on 1 March 1960. In June 1961 a Vulcan B.1 was received and by May 1964 the big delta had replaced both Canberras and Valiants. Low-level trials were a priority, but the development of a low-level bomb sight for the co-pilot and tests on a new jammer were also high on the list. Vulcans remained until October 1966 when, with no updated aircraft to spare, the unit reverted to 'borrowing' aircraft as required. It was absorbed by the Central Tactics and Trials Organization in 1968.

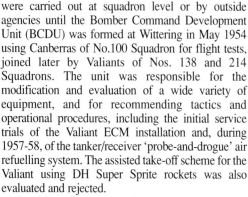

Left: *The Central Bomber Establishment's Lincoln 'Crusader' was well-known world-wide, but other Lincolns were on strength including SX975/ DF-C, equipped with H2S Mk.IVA. (Author's collection)*

Below: *The CBE also employed a fleet of Mosquitoes including Mk.XVI PF498 fitted with H2S, equipment which had been used in the latter stages of the war by No.8 Group. (Bristol Aeroplane Co 51839 via J.D. Oughton)*

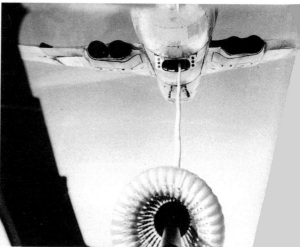

Top: *Valiants were used for intensive trials of 'probe-and-drogue' flight refuelling, most of the work involving WZ376 and WZ390. (Flight Refuelling Ltd 4590)*

Above: *One of the Bomber Command Development Unit's Valiants, WZ400, at Finningley 15 September 1962. (J.A. Todd)*

Right: *More 'probe-and-drogue' trials, this time testing the Victor tanker, 17 February 1967. (Author's collection)*

APPENDIX I

Command Formations

Bomber Command

Formed at Hillingdon House, RAF Uxbridge, on 14 July 1936 from HQ Air Defence Great Britain, reorganized on a functional basis. On formation it controlled Nos.1, 2 and 3 (Bomber) Groups, the Command being joined by Nos.4 and 5 Groups in 1937, and No.6 Group in 1939.

On 28 August 1939 HQ Bomber Command moved to Richings Park, Iver, and in March 1940 to a purpose-built site at Walter's Ash, Naphill, near High Wycombe, where it remained until the Command was merged on 30 April 1968 with Fighter Command to form Strike Command.

Air Officers Commanding-in-Chief

Name	Date of Appointment
Air Chief Marshal Sir John M. Steel KCB, KBE, CMG, GCB 1937	14 July 1936

HM King George VI with, from left, Air Marshal Sir Richard Peirse, AoC-in-C Bomber Command and Air Vice Marshal J. Baldwin, AoC No.3 Group, 1941. (via Chaz Bowyer Collection)

Name	*Date of Appointment*
Air Chief Marshal Sir Edgar R. Ludlow-Hewitt	12 September 1937
KCB, CMG, DSO, MC	
Air Vice Marshal (acting AM) C.F.A. Portal	2 April 1940
CB, DSO, MC, (ACM 25.5.40) KCB 1940	
Air Marshal (temp) Sir Richard E.C. Peirse	5 October 1940
KCB, DSO, AFC	
Air Vice Marshal J.E.A. Baldwin	8 January 1942
CB, CBE, DSO (acting AoC)	
Air Vice Marshal (acting AM) A.T. Harris	22 February 1942
CB, OBE, AFC (ACM (temp)) 16.8.44,	
KCB 1942, GCB 1945	
Air Marshal (temp) Sir Norman H. Bottomley	15 September 1945
KCB, CB, DSO, AFC (AM 1.1.46)	
Air Vice Marshal (acting AM) Sir Hugh W.L.	
Saunders	
KBE, CB, MC, DFC, MM (AM 1.7.47)	16 January 1947
Air Vice Marshal (acting AM) A.B. Ellwood	8 October 1947
CB, DSC (AM 1.7.49), KCB 1949	
Air Marshal Sir Hugh P. Lloyd	2 February 1950
KBE, CB, MC, DFC (ACM 1.4.51), KCB 1951	
Air Vice Marshal (acting AM) G.H. Mills	9 April 1953
CB, DFC (AM 1.1.54), KCB 1954	
Air Marshal Sir Harry Broadhurst	22 January 1956
KCB, KBE, DSO, DFC, AFC (ACM 14.2.57)	
Air Vice Marshal (acting AM) K.B.B. Cross	20 May 1959
CB, CBE, DSO, DFC (AM 1.7.61), KCB 1959	
Air Marshal Sir John Grandy	1 September 1963
KBE, CB, DSO, KCB 1964	
Air Chief Marshal Sir Wallace H. Kyle	19 February 1965
KCB, CBE, DSO, DFC	

Groups*

No.1
Reformed at Abingdon on 1 May 1936 from the Central Area of Air Defence Great Britain and designated No.1 (Bomber) Group. Mobilized on 24 August 1939 and ordered to France on 2 September 1939, becoming HQ Advanced Air Striking Force. A new No.1 Group began to form at Benson on 12 September in preparation for the move of more units to France, but this was postponed and the Group was disbanded on 22 December 1939.

Reformed 18 June 1940 at Hucknall to control the remnants of the Battle-equipped squadrons returning from France. HQ to Bawtry Hall, Bawtry, near Doncaster, Yorks, July 1941. On 1 November 1967 merged with No.3 Group, the combined unit being designated No.1 (Bomber) Group. Transferred to Strike Command on 30 April 1968.

No.2
Reformed at Abingdon on 20 March 1936 as No.2 (Bomber) Group, moving to Andover on 13 January 1937 and to Wyton in April 1938. In October 1939 the HQ took up residence in Castle Hill House, Huntingdon, where it remained until moving to the impressive Bylaugh Hall, East Dereham, Norfolk in May 1943 prior to transfer to the Tactical Air Force on 1 June 1943.

Air Chief Marshal Sir Harry Broadhurst, AoC-in-C Bomber Command, January 1956 to May 1959. (MoD PRB13565)

Heslington Hall, York, the wartime HQ of No.4 Group. Now part of York University. (Yorkshire Evening Press via J.D. Oughton)

No.3
On 1 May 1936 the HQ of Western Area was reformed as HQ No.3 (Bomber) Group at Andover and became part of Bomber Command on 14 July. Moved to Mildenhall on 13 January 1937, remaining there until March 1940 when the HQ was transferred to Exning, Suffolk. Returned to Mildenhall in January 1947 and on 1 November 1967 merged with No. 1 Group.

No.4
Reformed on 1 April 1937 from elements of No.3 Group with HQ temporarily at Mildenhall. Moved to Linton-on-Ouse on 29 June 1937 and to Heslington Hall, York in April 1940. On 7 May 1945 the Group transferred to Transport Command.

No.5
Reformed at Mildenhall on 1 July 1937 as an offshoot of No.3 (Bomber) Group. On 2 October 1937 the HQ moved to St Vincents, Grantham, a nineteenth century mansion. To Morton Hall, Swinderby in November 1943; disbanded on 15 December 1945.

No.6
Reformed during April 1936 as No.6 (Auxiliary) Group to administer Auxiliary Air Force units, the organization becoming No.6 (Bomber) Group on 1 January 1939. Commenced build-up as an operational unit but on 5 September 1939 became No.6 (Training) Group at Abingdon until redesignated No.91 Group on 11 May 1942. Reformed as No 6 (Bomber) Group, RCAF on 25 October 1942 with HQ temporarily at Linton-on-Ouse. Moved to Allerton Park near Knaresborough, Yorks on 6 December 1942 and became officially operational on 1 January 1943 with eight Canadian bomber squadrons transferred from No.4 Group under its command. The Group was transferred to Eastern Air Command, RCAF on 14 July 1945, the Rear HQ at Allerton Park being disbanded on 1 September 1945.

No.7
Reformed as a Training Group in Bomber Command on 15 July 1940 at Brampton Lodge, Huntingdon to administer OTUs. HQ moved to Winslow Hall, Winslow, Bucks on 1 September 1941 where it was renumbered No. 92 Group on 11 May 1942. Reformed on 20 September 1944 to control Bomber Command HCUs with HQ

at St Vincents, Grantham. Disbanded on 21 December 1945 when its units transferred to No.91 Group.

No.8
Reformed on 1 September 1941 as No.8 (Bomber) Group to control light bomber units with HQ at Brampton Grange, Hunts, but did not become operational and was disbanded on 28 January 1942. Reformed as No.8 (PFF) Group on 8 January 1943 from the Pathfinder Force which had been established on 15 August 1942, with HQ at Wyton, Hunts. On 5 May 1943 the HQ moved to Castle Hill House, Huntingdon until it was disbanded on 15 December 1945.

No.26
Reformed on 12 February 1940 as No.26 (Signals) Group with HQ at Cranwell, moving to Bridge House, Iver, Bucks on 27 March 1940 and joining Technical Training Command on 27 May to administer the Electrical & Wireless Schools (renamed Signals Schools on 1 September 1940). The Group was reorganised on 17 April 1941, the training element being transferred, leaving only operational signals units under Group command. No.26 Group was transferred to Bomber Command on 10 February 1942 to run the extensive signals communications network being built up, with HQ at Langley Hall, Slough. Absorbed No.60 Group on 9 November 1945 but disbanded on 25 April 1946 when it was itself absorbed by No.90 (Signals) Group.

No.91
Formed on 11 May 1942 with HQ at Abingdon, Oxon, by renumbering No.6 Group. Administered bomber training units until it was disbanded in March 1947.

No.92
Formed on 11 May 1942 at Winslow Hall, Bucks, by renumbering No.7 Group. Continued administering Bomber Command OTUs until disbanded on 15 July 1945.

No.93
Formed on 15 June 1942 with HQ at Lichfield, moving to Egginton Hall, Derby on 7 July 1942. Administered Bomber Command training units until disbanded on 14 February 1945.

No.100
Formed on 8 November 1943 at Radlett from No.80 Wing personnel and equipment. HQ moved to West Raynham on 3 December 1943 and Bylaugh Hall, near Swanton Morley, Norfolk on 1 January 1944. Disbanded on 17 December 1945.

*Details refer to Bomber Command service only.

Allerton Park near Knaresborough, Yorks. HQ of No.6 Group, RCAF. (RCAF)

APPENDIX II

Order of Battle 30 June 1937

No.1 (Bomber) Group   **Air Commodore S.W. Smith** OBE
  No.15 Squadron   Hind   Abingdon
  No.18 Squadron   Hind   Upper Heyford
  No.21 Squadron   Hind   Lympne
  No.34 Squadron   Hind   Lympne
  No.40 Squadron   Hind   Abingdon
  No.57 Squadron   Hind   Upper Heyford
  No.62 Squadron   Hind   Abingdon
  No.90 Squadron   Hind   Bicester
  No.101 Squadron   Overstrand   Bicester
  No.103 Squadron   Hind   Usworth
  No.105 Squadron   Audax   Harwell
  No.107 Squadron   Hind   Harwell
  No.113 Squadron   Hind   Upper Heyford
  No.218 Squadron   Hart   Upper Heyford
  No.226 Squadron   Audax   Harwell
  No.233 Squadron   Hind   Upper Heyford

No.2 (Bomber) Group   **Air Commodore S.J. Goble** CBE, DSO, DSC
  No.12 Squadron   Hind   Andover
  No.35 Squadron   Gordon   Worthy Down
  No.44 Squadron   Hind   Andover
  No.49 Squadron   Hind   Worthy Down
  No.52 Squadron   Hind/Audax   Upwood
  No.63 Squadron   Hind/Battle   Upwood
  No.83 Squadron   Hind   Turnhouse
  No.98 Squadron   Hind   Hucknall
  No.104 Squadron   Hind   Hucknall
  No.108 Squadron   Hind   Farnborough
  No.114 Squadron   Audax/Blenheim   Wyton
  No.139 Squadron   Hind/Audax   Wyton
  No.142 Squadron   Hind   Andover
  No.207 Squadron   Gordon   Worthy Down
  No.602 Squadron   Hind   Abbotsinch
  No.605 Squadron   Hind   Castle Bromwich

No.3 (Bomber) Group   **Air Vice Marshal P.H.L. Playfair** CB, CVO, MC

No.9 Squadron	Heyford	Scampton
No.37 Squadron	Harrow	Feltwell
No.38 Squadron	Heyford/Hendon	Marham
No.50 Squadron	Hind	Waddington
No.61 Squadron	Audax/Anson	Hemswell
No.77 Squadron	Audax	Finningley
No.88 Squadron	Hind	Waddington
No.99 Squadron	Heyford	Mildenhall
No.102 Squadron	Heyford	Finningley
No.110 Squadron	Hind	Waddington
No.115 Squadron	Hendon	Marham
No.144 Squadron	Audax/Anson	Hemswell
No.149 Squadron	Heyford	Mildenhall
No.211 Squadron	Audax	Mildenhall
No.214 Squadron	Harrow	Feltwell

Note: Finningley transferred to No.4 Group on 29 June 1937. Nos.77 and 102 Squadrons moved to Honington on 7 July 1937.

No.4 (Bomber) Group   **Air Commodore A.T. Harris** OBE, AFC

No.7 Squadron	Wellesley/Heyford	Finningley
No.10 Squadron	Whitley/Heyford	Dishforth
No.51 Squadron	Virginia/Anson	Boscombe Down
No.58 Squadron	Virginia/Anson	Boscombe Down
No.75 Squadron	Virginia/Anson	Driffield
No.76 Squadron	Wellesley	Finningley
No.78 Squadron	Heyford	Dishforth
No.97 Squadron	Heyford	Leconfield
No.166 Squadron	Heyford	Leconfield
No.215 Squadron	Virginia/Anson	Driffield

No.6 (Auxiliary) Group   **Air Commodore J.C. Quinnell** DFC

No.500 Squadron	Hind	Manston
No.501 Squadron	Hart	Filton
No.502 Squadron	Hind	Aldergrove
No.503 Squadron	Hart	Waddington
No.504 Squadron	Hind	Hucknall
No.603 Squadron	Hart	Turnhouse
No.609 Squadron	Hart	Yeadon
No.610 Squadron	Hart	Hooton Park
No.611 Squadron	Hart	Speke

Order of Battle
25 September 1939

Advanced Air Striking Force, France		**Air Vice Marshal P.H.L. Playfair** CB, CVO MC
No.12 Squadron	Battle	Berry-au-Bac
No.15 Squadron	Battle	Conde/Vraux
No.40 Squadron	Battle	Betheniville
No.88 Squadron	Battle	Mourmelon-le-Grande
		(Det. at Perpignan/La Salanque)
No.103 Squadron	Battle	Challerange
No.105 Squadron	Battle	Villeneuve
		(Dets. at Perpignan/La Salanque
		& Echemines)
No.142 Squadron	Battle	Berry-au-Bac
		(Det. at Perpignan/La Salanque)
No.150 Squadron	Battle	Ecury-sur-Coole
		(Det. at Perpignan/La Salanque)
No.218 Squadron	Battle	Auberines-sur-Suippes
		(Det. at Perpignan/La Salanque)
No.226 Squadron	Battle	Reims
		(Det. at Perpignan/La Salanque)
Air Component, France		
No.18 Squadron	Blenheim	Roye
No.57 Squadron	Blenheim	Roye
No.1 (Bomber) Group		**Air Vice Marshal A.C. Wright** AFC
Reforming - no units		
No.2 (Bomber) Group		**Air Vice Marshal C.T. Maclean** CB, DSO, MC
No.21 Squadron	Blenheim	Watton
No.82 Squadron	Blenheim	Watton
No.101 Squadron*	Blenheim	West Raynham
No.107 Squadron	Blenheim	Wattisham
No.110 Squadron	Blenheim	Wattisham
No.114 Squadron	Blenheim	Wyton
No.139 Squadron	Blenheim	Wyton

No.3 (Bomber) Group   **Air Vice Marshal J.E.A. Baldwin** CB, OBE, DSO
   No.9 Squadron   Wellington   Honington
   No.37 Squadron   Wellington   Feltwell
   No.38 Squadron   Wellington   Marham
   No.99 Squadron   Wellington   Newmarket
   No.115 Squadron   Wellington   Marham
   No.149 Squadron   Wellington   Mildenhall
   No.214 Squadron*   Wellington   Methwold
   No.215 Squadron*   Wellington   Bassingbourn

No.4 (Bomber) Group Air Vice Marshal A. Coningham DSO, MC, DFC, AFC
   No.10 Squadron   Whitley   Dishforth
   No.51 Squadron   Whitley   Linton-on-Ouse
   No.58 Squadron   Whitley   Linton-on-Ouse
   No.77 Squadron   Whitley   Driffield
   No.78 Squadron*   Whitley   Dishforth
   No.102 Squadron   Whitley   Driffield

No.5 (Bomber) Group   **Air Vice Marshal A.T. Harris** OBE, AFC
   No.44 Squadron   Hampden   Waddington
   No.49 Squadron   Hampden   Scampton
   No.50 Squadron   Hampden   Waddington
   No.61 Squadron   Hampden   Hemswell
   No.83 Squadron   Hampden   Scampton
   No.106 Squadron*   Hampden   Cottesmore
   No.144 Squadron   Hampden   Hemswell
   No.185 Squadron*   Hampden   Cottesmore

No.6 (Training) Group   **Air Vice Marshal W.F. MacNeece Foster** CB, CBE, DSO, DFC
   No.7 Squadron   Hampden   Upper Heyford
   No.35 Squadron   Battle   Cranfield
   No.52 Squadron   Battle   Benson
   No.63 Squadron   Battle   Benson
   No.75 Squadron   Wellington   Harwell
   No.76 Squadron   Hampden   Upper Heyford
   No.90 Squadron   Blenheim   Upwood
   No.97 Squadron   Whitley   Abingdon
   No.98 Squadron*   Battle   Hucknall (lodger)
   No.104 Squadron   Blenheim   Bicester
   No.108 Squadron   Blenheim   Bicester
   No.148 Squadron   Wellington   Harwell
   No.166 Squadron   Whitley   Abingdon
   No.207 Squadron   Battle   Cranfield

*Reserve squadrons

APPENDIX IV

Order of Battle
1 January 1941

No.1 (Bomber) Group   **Air Vice Marshal R.D. Oxland** OBE

No.12 Squadron	Wellington	Binbrook
No.103 Squadron	Wellington	Newton
No.142 Squadron	Wellington	Binbrook
No.150 Squadron	Wellington	Newton
No.300 (Polish) Squadron	Wellington	Swinderby
No.301 (Polish) Squadron	Wellington	Swinderby
No.304 (Polish) Squadron	Wellington	Syerston
No.305 (Polish) Squadron	Wellington	Syerston

No.2 (Bomber) Group   **Air Vice Marshal J.M. Robb** DSO, DFC

No.18 Squadron	Blenheim	Great Massingham
No.21 Squadron	Blenheim	Watton
No.82 Squadron	Blenheim	Watton
No.101 Squadron	Blenheim	West Raynham
No.105 Squadron	Blenheim	Swanton Morley
No.107 Squadron	Blenheim	Wattisham
No.114 Squadron	Blenheim	Horsham St Faith
No.139 Squadron	Blenheim	Horsham St Faith

No.3 (Bomber) Group   **Air Vice Marshal J.E.A. Baldwin** CB, CBE, DSO

No.7 Squadron	Stirling	Oakington
No.9 Squadron	Wellington	Honington
No.15 Squadron	Wellington	Wyton
No.40 Squadron	Wellington	Wyton
No.57 Squadron	Wellington	Feltwell
No.75 Squadron	Wellington	Feltwell
No.99 Squadron	Wellington	Newmarket
No.115 Squadron	Wellington	Marham
No.149 Squadron	Wellington	Mildenhall
No.214 Squadron	Wellington	Stradishall
No.218 Squadron	Wellington	Marham
No.271 Squadron*	Harrow/Bombay/Albatross	Doncaster
No.311 (Czech) Squadron	Wellington	East Wretham
No.419 (SD) Flight	Whitley/Lysander	Stradishall
No. 3 Photo Recce Unit	Spitfire/Wellington	Oakington

*Heavy transport unit

No.4 (Bomber) Group   **Air Vice Marshal A. Coningham** DSO, MC, DFC, AFC

No.10 Squadron	Whitley	Leeming
No.35 Squadron	Halifax	Linton-on-Ouse
No.51 Squadron	Whitley	Dishforth
No.58 Squadron	Whitley	Linton-on-Ouse
No.77 Squadron	Whitley	Topcliffe
No.78 Squadron	Whitley	Dishforth
No.102 Squadron	Whitley	Topcliffe

No.5 (Bomber) Group   **Air Vice Marshal N.R. Bottomley** CBE, DSO, AFC

No.44 Squadron	Hampden	Waddington
No.49 Squadron	Hampden	Scampton
No.50 Squadron	Hampden	Lindholme
No.61 Squadron	Hampden	Hemswell
No.83 Squadron	Hampden	Scampton
No.106 Squadron	Hampden	Finningley
No.144 Squadron	Hampden	Hemswell
No.207 Squadron	Manchester	Waddington

No.6 (Training) Group   **Air Vice Marshal W.F. MacNeece Foster** CB, CBE, DSO, DFC

No.10 OTU	Whitley/Anson	Abingdon
No.11 OTU	Wellington/Anson	Bassingbourn
No.12 OTU	Wellington/Anson	Benson
No.15 OTU	Wellington/Anson	Harwell
No.18 OTU	Wellington/Anson	Bramcote
No.19 OTU	Whitley/Anson	Kinloss
No.20 OTU	Wellington/Anson	Lossiemouth

No.7 (Training) Group   **Acting Air Commodore L.H. Cockey**

No.13 OTU	Blenheim/Anson	Bicester
No.14 OTU	Hampden/Hereford/ Anson	Cottesmore
No.16 OTU	Hampden/Hereford/ Anson	Upper Heyford
No.17 OTU	Blenheim/Anson	Upwood

APPENDIX V

Order of Battle
9 January 1942

No.1 (Bomber) Group	Air Vice Marshal R.D. Oxland OBE	
No.12 Squadron	Wellington	Binbrook
No.103 Squadron	Wellington	Elsham Wolds
No.142 Squadron	Wellington	Waltham
No.150 Squadron	Wellington	Snaith
No.300 (Polish) Squadron	Wellington	Hemswell
No.301 (Polish) Squadron	Wellington	Hemswell
No.304 (Polish) Squadron	Wellington	Lindholme
No.305 (Polish) Squadron	Wellington	Lindholme
No.458 Squadron, RAAF	Wellington	Holme-on-Spalding Moor
No.460 Squadron, RAAF	Wellington	Breighton
No.1481 Flight	Lysander/Wellington	Binbrook

No.2 (Bomber) Group	Air Vice Marshal A. Lees DSO, AFC	
No.18 Squadron	Blenheim	Wattisham (Det. in Northern Ireland)
No.21 Squadron*	Blenheim	Luqa
No.82 Squadron	Blenheim	Watton
No.88 Squadron	Boston	Attlebridge
No.105 Squadron	Blenheim/Mosquito	Horsham St Faith
No.107 Squadron	Blenheim/Boston	Great Massingham
No.110 Squadron	Blenheim	Wattisham
No.114 Squadron	Blenheim	West Raynham
No.226 Squadron	Blenheim/Boston	Swanton Morley
No.1482 Flight	Lysander/Blenheim	West Raynham

*No.21 Squadron in Malta but still part of No.2 Group

No.3 (Bomber) Group	Air Vice Marshal J.E.A. Baldwin CB, CBE, DSO	
No.7 Squadron	Stirling	Oakington
No.9 Squadron	Wellington	Honington
No.15 Squadron	Stirling	Wyton
No.40 Squadron*	Wellington	Alconbury (Det.)
No.57 Squadron	Wellington	Feltwell
No.75 (NZ) Squadron	Wellington	Feltwell
No.99 Squadron	Wellington	Waterbeach
No.101 Squadron	Wellington	Oakington
No.115 Squadron	Wellington	Marham

No.138 (SD) Squadron	Whitley/Halifax/ Lysander	Stradishall
No.149 Squadron	Stirling	Mildenhall
No.214 Squadron	Wellington	Honington
No.218 Squadron	Wellington/Stirling	Marham
No.271 Squadron**	Harrow/Albatross/ Hudson	Doncaster
No.311 (Czech) Squadron	Wellington	East Wretham
No.419 Squadron, RCAF	Wellington	Mildenhall
No.1483 Flight	Lysander/Wellington	Newmarket
No.1651 Conversion Unit	Stirling	Newmarket

*Main echelon of No.40 Squadron at Luqa, Malta
**Heavy transport unit

No.4 (Bomber) Group — Air Vice Marshal C.R. Carr CBE, DFC, AFC

No.10 Squadron	Halifax	Dishforth
No.35 Squadron	Halifax	Linton-on-Ouse
No.51 Squadron	Whitley	Dishforth
No.58 Squadron	Whitley	Linton-on-Ouse
No.76 Squadron	Halifax	Middleton-St George
No.77 Squadron	Whitley	Leeming
No.78 Squadron	Whitley	Croft
No.102 Squadron	Whitley/Halifax	Dalton
No.104 Squadron*	Wellington	Driffield
No.405 Squadron, RCAF	Wellington	Pocklington
No.1484 Flight	Lysander/Battle	Driffield
No.1652 Con Unit	Halifax	Marston Moor

*Main echelon of No.104 Squadron at Luqa, Malta

No.5 (Bomber) Group — Air Vice Marshal J.C. Slessor DSO, MC

No.44 Squadron*	Lancaster	Waddington
No.49 Squadron	Hampden	Scampton
No.50 Squadron	Hampden	Skellingthorpe
No.61 Squadron	Manchester	Woolfox Lodge
No.83 Squadron	Hampden/Manchester	Scampton
No.97 Squadron	Manchester	Coningsby
No.106 Squadron	Hampden	Coningsby
No.144 Squadron	Hampden	North Luffenham
No.207 Squadron	Manchester	Bottesford
No.408 Squadron, RCAF	Hampden	Balderton
No.420 Squadron, RCAF	Hampden	Waddington
No.455 Squadron, RAAF**	–	Swinderby

*No.44 Squadron non-operational
**No.455 Squadron echelon without aircraft

No.6 (Training) Group — Air Vice Marshal W.F. MacNeece Foster CB, CBE, DSO, DFC

No.10 OTU	Whitley	Abingdon
No.11 OTU	Wellington	Bassingbourn
No.12 OTU	Wellington	Chipping Warden
No.15 OTU	Wellington	Harwell
No.18 OTU	Wellington	Bramcote
No.19 OTU	Whitley	Kinloss
No.20 OTU	Wellington	Lossiemouth
No.21 OTU	Wellington	Moreton-in-the-Marsh

| No.23 OTU | Wellington | Pershore |
| No.27 OTU | Wellington | Lichfield |

Note: OTUs also used Anson and other trainers, but only Whitley and Wellington used operationally. Sundry Flights attached for gunnery and beam training.

No.7 (Training) Group   **Air Commodore L.H. Cockey**
No.13 OTU	Blenheim/Boston	Bicester
No.14 OTU	Hampden	Cottesmore
No.16 OTU	Hampden	Upper Heyford
No.17 OTU	Blenheim	Upwood
No.25 OTU	Wellington/	Finningley
	Manchester	

See No.6 Group note

No.8 (Bomber) Group   **Acting Air Commodore D.F. Stevenson** CBE, MC, DSO
| No.90 Squadron | Fortress | Polebrook |

Order of Battle
4 March 1943

No.1 (Bomber) Group	Air Vice Marshal E.A.B. Rice CB, CBE, MC	
No.12 Squadron	Lancaster	Wickenby
No.100 Squadron	Lancaster	Waltham/Grimsby
No.101 Squadron	Lancaster	Holme-on-Spalding Moor
No.103 Squadron	Lancaster	Elsham Wolds
No.166 Squadron	Wellington	Kirmington
N0.199 Squadron	Wellington	Ingham
No.300 (Polish) Squadron	Wellington	Hemswell
No.301 (Polish) Squadron	Wellington	Hemswell
No.305 (Polish) Squadron	Wellington	Hemswell
No.460 Squadron, RAAF	Lancaster	Breighton
No.1481 BG Flight	Whitley/Lysander	Lindholme
No.1656 HCU	Lancaster/Halifax	Lindholme
No.1662 HCU	Lancaster/Halifax	Blyton

No.2 (Bomber) Group	Air Vice Marshal J.H. D'Albiac CB, DSO	
No.21 Squadron	Ventura	Methwold
No.88 Squadron	Boston	Oulton
No.98 Squadron	Mitchell	Foulsham
No.105 Squadron	Mosquito	Marham
No.107 Squadron	Boston	Great Massingham
No.139 Squadron	Mosquito	Marham
No.180 Squadron	Mitchell	Foulsham
No.226 Squadron	Boston	Swanton Morley
No.464 Squadron, RAAF	Ventura	Feltwell
No.487 Squadron, RNZAF	Ventura	Feltwell
No.1482 BG Flight	Martinet/Ventura	West Raynham
No.1655 Trg Unit	Mosquito/Blenheim	Marham

No.3 (Bomber) Group	Air Vice Marshal R. Harrison CB, CBE, DFC, AFC	
No.15 Squadron	Stirling	Bourn
No.75 (NZ) Squadron	Stirling	Newmarket
No.90 Squadron	Stirling	Ridgewell
No.115 Squadron	Wellington/Lancaster	East Wretham
No.138 (SD) Squadron	Halifax	Tempsford
No.149 Squadron	Stirling	Lakenheath

No.161 (SD) Squadron	Lysander/Halifax/ Hudson/Havoc/ Albemarle	Tempsford
No.192 (SD) Squadron	Halifax/Wellington/ Mosquito	Gransden Lodge
No.214 Squadron	Stirling	Chedburgh
No.218 Squadron	Stirling	Downham Market
No.271 Squadron*	Harrow	Doncaster
No.1483 BG Flight	Lysander/Wellington	Marham
No.1651 HCU	Stirling	Waterbeach
No.1657 HCU	Stirling	Stradishall
Bomber Development Unit	Wellington/Halifax/ Stirling/Lancaster	Gransden Lodge

*Heavy transport unit

No.4 (Bomber) Group   **Air Vice Marshal C.R. Carr** CBE, DFC, AFC

No.10 Squadron	Halifax	Melbourne
No.51 Squadron	Halifax	Snaith
No.76 Squadron	Halifax	Linton-on-Ouse
No.77 Squadron	Halifax	Elvington
No.78 Squadron	Halifax	Linton-on-Ouse
No.102 Squadron	Halifax	Pocklington
No.158 Squadron	Halifax	Lisset
No.196 Squadron	Wellington	Leconfield
No.429 Squadron, RCAF	Wellington	East Moor
No.431 Squadron, RCAF	Wellington	Burn
No.466 Squadron, RAAF	Wellington	Leconfield
No.1484 BG Flight	Lysander/Whitley	Driffield
No.1652 HCU	Halifax	Marston Moor
No.1658 HCU	Halifax	Ricall
No.1663 HCU	Halifax	Rufforth

No.5 (Bomber) Group   **Air Vice Marshal the Hon R.A. Cochrane** KBE, CB, AFC

No.9 Squadron	Lancaster	Waddington
No.44 Squadron	Lancaster	Waddington
No.49 Squadron	Lancaster	Fiskerton
No.50 Squadron	Lancaster	Skellingthorpe
No.57 Squadron	Lancaster	Scampton
No.61 Squadron	Lancaster	Syerston
No.97 Squadron	Lancaster	Woodhall Spa
No.106 Squadron	Lancaster	Syerston
No.207 Squadron	Lancaster	Langar
No.467 Squadron, RAAF	Lancaster	Bottesford
No.1485 BG Flight	Manchester/Martinet	Fulbeck
No 1654 HCU	Manchester/Halifax/ Lancaster	Wigsley
No 1660 HCU	Stirling	Swinderby
No 1661 HCU	Manchester/Halifax/ Lancaster	Winthorpe

No.6 (Bomber) Group   **Air Vice Marshal G.E. Brookes** OBE

No.405 Squadron, RCAF	Halifax	Topcliffe
No.408 Squadron, RCAF	Halifax	Leeming
No.419 Squadron, RCAF	Halifax	Middleton St George

No.420 Squadron, RCAF	Wellington	Middleton St George
No.424 Squadron, RCAF	Wellington	Topcliffe
No.425 Squadron, RCAF	Wellington	Dishforth
No.426 Squadron, RCAF	Wellington	Dishforth
No.427 Squadron, RCAF	Wellington	Croft
No.428 Squadron, RCAF	Wellington	Dalton
No.1659 HCU	Halifax	Leeming

No.8 (PFF) Group　　　　**Acting Air Commodore D.C.T. Bennett** DSO

No.7 (PFF) Squadron	Stirling	Oakington
No.35 (PFF) Squadron	Halifax	Graveley
No.83 (PFF) Squadron	Lancaster	Wyton
No.109 (PFF) Squadron	Mosquito	Wyton
No.156 (PFF) Squadron	Lancaster	Warboys
No.1655 (M) Trg Unit	Mosquito	Marham

No.26 (Signals) Group　　　　**Air Vice Marshal O.G.W. Lywood** CB, CBE
Numerous Ground Signals units

No.91 (Training) Group　　　　**Acting Air Commodore H.S.P. Walmsley** CBE, MC, DFC

No.10 OTU	Whitley	Abingdon
No.15 OTU	Wellington	Harwell
No.19 OTU	Whitley	Kinloss
No.20 OTU	Wellington	Lossiemouth
No.21 OTU	Wellington	Moreton-in-the-Marsh
No.22 OTU	Wellington	Wellesbourne Mountford
No.23 OTU	Wellington	Pershore
No.24 OTU	Whitley	Honeybourne

Note: OTUs also operated Anson/Defiant/Lysander aircraft but only Wellingtons and Whitleys operationally. Numerous Flights attached for gunnery and beam training.

No.92 (Training) Group　　　　**Group Captain S. Graham MC**

No.11 OTU	Wellington	Westcott
No.12 OTU	Wellington	Chipping Warden
No.13 OTU	Blenheim	Bicester
No.14 OTU	Wellington	Cottesmore
No 16 OTU	Wellington	Upper Heyford
No.17 OTU	Blenheim	Upwood
No.26 OTU	Wellington	Wing
No.29 OTU	Wellington	North Luffenham
No.1473 Flight	Wellington/Anson	Finmere

See No.91 Group note

No.93 (Training) Group　　　　**Air Commodore A.P. Richie AFC**

No.18 OTU	Wellington	Bramcote
No.25 OTU	Wellington	Finningley
No.27 OTU	Wellington	Lichfield
No.28 OTU	Wellington	Wymeswold
No.30 OTU	Wellington	Hixon
No.81 OTU	Whitley	Whitchurch Heath

See No.91 Group note

Order of Battle
6 June 1944

No.1 (Bomber) Group **Air Vice Marshal** E.A.B. RICE CB, CBE, MC

No.12 Squadron	Lancaster	Wickenby
No.100 Squadron	Lancaster	Grimsby
No.101 Squadron	Lancaster	Ludford Magna
No.103 Squadron	Lancaster	Elsham Wolds
No.166 Squadron	Lancaster	Kirmington
No.300 (Polish) Squadron	Lancaster	Faldingworth
No.460 Squadron, RAAF	Lancaster	Binbrook
No.550 Squadron	Lancaster	North Killingholme
No.576 Squadron	Lancaster	Elsham Wolds
No.625 Squadron	Lancaster	Kelstern
No.626 Squadron	Lancaster	Wickenby
No.1656 HCU	Lancaster/Halifax	Lindholme
No.1662 HCU	Halifax	Blyton
No.1667 HCU	Halifax	Sandtoft
No.1 Lancaster Finishing School	Hemswell	

No.3 (Bomber) Group **Air Vice Marshal R. Harrison** CB, CBE, DFC, AFC

No.15 Squadron	Lancaster	Mildenhall
No.75 (NZ) Squadron	Lancaster	Mepal
No.90 Squadron	Stirling/Lancaster	Tuddenham
No.115 Squadron	Lancaster	Witchford
No.138 (SD) Squadron	Halifax/Stirling	Tempsford
No.149 Squadron	Stirling	Methwold
No.161 (SD) Squadron	Hudson/Lysander/ Halifax	Tempsford
No.218 Squadron	Stirling	Woolfox Lodge
No.514 Squadron	Lancaster	Waterbeach
No.622 Squadron	Lancaster	Mildenhall
No.1651 HCU	Stirling	Wrattling Common
No.1653 HCU	Stirling	Chedburgh
No.1657 HCU	Stirling	Shepherds Grove
No.1678 HCU	Lancaster	Waterbeach
Bomber Development Unit	Lancaster/Halifax/ Stirling/Mosquito	Newmarket
No.3 Lancaster Finishing School		

No.4 (Bomber) Group	**Air Vice Marshal C.R. Carr** CB, CBE, DFC, AFC	
No.10 Squadron	Halifax	Melbourne
No.51 Squadron	Halifax	Snaith
No.76 Squadron	Halifax	Holme-on-Spalding Moor
No.77 Squadron	Halifax	Full Sutton
No.78 Squadron	Halifax	Breighton
No.102 Squadron	Halifax	Pocklington
No.158 Squadron	Halifax	Lissett
No.346 Squadron, FAF	Halifax	Elvington
No.466 Squadron, RAAF	Halifax	Driffield
No.578 Squadron	Halifax	Burn
No.640 Squadron	Halifax	Leconfield
No.1652 HCU	Halifax	Marston Moor
No.1658 HCU	Halifax	Ricall
No.1663 HCU	Halifax	Rufforth

No.5 (Bomber) Group	**Air Vice Marshal the Hon R.A. Cochrane** CBE, AFC	
No.9 Squadron	Lancaster	Bardney
No.44 Squadron	Lancaster	Dunholme Lodge
No.49 Squadron	Lancaster	Fiskerton
No.50 Squadron	Lancaster	Skellingthorpe
No.57 Squadron	Lancaster	East Kirkby
No.61 Squadron	Lancaster	Skellingthorpe
No.83 Squadron	Lancaster	Coningsby
No.97 Squadron	Lancaster	Coningsby
No.106 Squadron	Lancaster	Metheringham
No.207 Squadron	Lancaster	Spilsby
No.463 Squadron, RAAF	Lancaster	Waddington
No.467 Squadron, RAAF	Lancaster	Waddington
No.617 Squadron	Lancaster/Mosquito	Woodhall Spa
No.619 Squadron	Lancaster	Dunholme Lodge
No.627 Squadron	Mosquito	Woodhall Spa
No.630 Squadron	Lancaster	East Kirkby
No.1654 HCU	Stirling	Wigsley
No.1660 HCU	Stirling	Swinderby
No.1661 HCU	Stirling	Winthorpe
No.5 Lancaster Finishing School		

No.6 (Bomber) Group, RCAF	**Air Vice Marshal C.M. McEwen** CB, MC, DFC	
No.408 Squadron, RCAF	Lancaster	Linton-on-Ouse
No.419 Squadron, RCAF	Lancaster	Middleton St George
No.420 Squadron, RCAF	Halifax	Tholthorpe
No.424 Squadron, RCAF	Halifax	Skipton-on-Swale
No.425 Squadron, RCAF	Halifax	Tholthorpe
No.426 Squadron, RCAF	Halifax	Linton-on-Ouse
No.427 Squadron, RCAF	Halifax	Leeming
No.428 Squadron, RCAF	Halifax/Lancaster	Middleton St George
No.429 Squadron, RCAF	Halifax	Leeming
No.431 Squadron, RCAF	Halifax	Croft
No.432 Squadron, RCAF	Halifax	East Moor
No.433 Squadron, RCAF	Halifax	Skipton-on-Swale
No.434 Squadron, RCAF	Halifax	Croft
No.1659 HCU	Halifax	Topcliffe
No.1664 HCU	Halifax	Dishforth
No.1666 HCU	Lancaster	Wombleton

No.8 (PFF) Group	**Air Vice Marshal D.C.T. Bennett** CBE, DSO	
No.7 Squadron	Lancaster	Oakington
No.35 Squadron	Lancaster	Graveley
No.105 Squadron	Mosquito	Bourn
No.109 Squadron	Mosquito	Little Straughton
No.139 Squadron	Mosquito	Upwood
No.156 Squadron	Lancaster	Upwood
No.405 Squadron, RCAF	Lancaster	Gransden Lodge
No.571 Squadron	Mosquito	Oakington
No.582 Squadron	Lancaster	Little Straughton
No.635 Squadron	Lancaster	Downham Market
No.692 Squadron	Mosquito	Graveley
No.1409 (Met) Flight	Mosquito	Wyton
No.1655(M) Trg Unit	Mosquito	Warboys

No.26 (Signals) Group	**Air Vice Marshal O.G.W. Lywood** CB, CBE	
Numerous Ground Signals units		

No.91 (Training) Group	**Air Vice Marshal J.A. Gray** DFC, GM	
No.10 OTU	Whitley	Stanton Harcourt
No.19 OTU	Whitley	Kinloss
No.20 OTU	Wellington	Lossiemouth
No.21 OTU	Wellington	Moreton-in-the-Marsh
No.22 OTU	Wellington	Wellesbourne Mountford
No.24 OTU	Wellington	Honeybourne

Note: Also used Anson, Hurricane, Martinet, Oxford aircraft but only Whitley and Wellington operationally. Flights for gunnery training, etc attached.

No.92 (Training) Group	**Air Vice Marshal H.K. Thorold** CBE, DSO, DFC, AFC	
No.11 OTU	Wellington	Westcott
No.12 OTU	Wellington	Chipping Warden
No.14 OTU	Wellington	Market Harborough
No.16 OTU	Wellington	Barford St John
No.17 OTU	Wellington	Silverstone
No.26 OTU	Wellington	Wing
No.29 OTU	Wellington	Bruntingthorpe
No.84 OTU	Wellington	Desborough

See No.91 Group note

No.93 (Training) Group	**Air Vice Marshal O.T. Boyd** CB, OBE, MC, AFC	
No.18 OTU	Wellington	Finningley
No.27 OTU	Wellington	Lichfield
No.28 OTU	Wellington	Wymeswold
No.30 OTU	Wellington	Hixon
No.82 OTU	Wellington	Ossington

See No.91 Group note

No.100 (SD) Group	**Air Commodore E.B. Addison** CBE	
No.23 Squadron	Mosquito	Little Snoring
No.85 Squadron	Mosquito	Swannington
No.141 Squadron	Mosquito	West Raynham
No.157 Squadron	Mosquito	Swannington

No.169 Squadron	Mosquito	Great Massingham
No.192 Squadron	Wellington/Halifax/ Mosquito	Foulsham
No.199 Squadron	Stirling	North Creake
No.214 Squadron	Fortress	Oulton
No.223 Squadron	Liberator	Oulton
No.239 Squadron	Mosquito	West Raynham
No.515 Squadron	Mosquito	Little Snoring
No.1699 Flight	Fortress	Sculthorpe
Bomber Support Development Unit	Mosquito	Foulsham

Note: All operational Groups also established with Bomber Defence and Beam Approach Training Flights.

Order of Battle
6 May 1945

No.1 (Bomber) Group   **Air Vice Marshal R.S. Blucke** CBE, DSO, AFC
  No.12 Squadron   Lancaster   Wickenby
  No.100 Squadron   Lancaster   Elsham Wolds
  No.101 Squadron   Lancaster   Ludford Magna
  No.103 Squadron   Lancaster   Elsham Wolds
  No.150 Squadron   Lancaster   Hemswell
  No.153 Squadron   Lancaster   Scampton
  No.166 Squadron   Lancaster   Kirmington
  No.170 Squadron   Lancaster   Hemswell
  No.300 (Polish) Squadron   Lancaster   Faldingworth
  No.460 Squadron, RAAF   Lancaster   Binbrook
  No.550 Squadron   Lancaster   North Killingholme
  No.576 Squadron   Lancaster   Fiskerton
  No.625 Squadron   Lancaster   Scampton
  No.626 Squadron   Lancaster   Wickenby

No.3 (Bomber) Group   **Air Vice Marshal R. Harrison** CB, CBE, DFC, AFC
  No.15 Squadron   Lancaster   Mildenhall
  No.75 (NZ) Squadron   Lancaster   Mepal
  No.90 Squadron   Lancaster   Tuddenham
  No.115 Squadron   Lancaster   Witchford
  No.138 Squadron   Lancaster   Tuddenham
  No.149 Squadron   Lancaster   Methwold
  No.186 Squadron   Lancaster   Stradishall
  No.195 Squadron   Lancaster   Wratting Common
  No.218 Squadron   Lancaster   Chedburgh
  No.514 Squadron   Lancaster   Waterbeach
  No.622 Squadron   Lancaster   Mildenhall
  Bomber Development Unit   Halifax/Lancaster   Feltwell
      Mosquito/Spitfire
      Beaufighter/Anson

No.4 (Bomber) Group   **Air Vice Marshal J.R. Whitley** CBE, DSO, AFC
  No.10 Squadron   Halifax   Melbourne
  No.51 Squadron   Halifax   Leconfield
  No.76 Squadron   Halifax   Holme-on-Spalding Moor
  No.77 Squadron   Halifax   Full Sutton

No.78 Squadron	Halifax	Breighton
No.102 Squadron	Halifax	Pocklington
No.158 Squadron	Halifax	Lisset
No.346 Squadron, FAF	Halifax	Elvington
No.347 Squadron, FAF	Halifax	Elvington
No.466 Squadron, RAAF	Halifax	Driffield
No.640 Squadron	Halifax	Leconfield

No.5 (Bomber) Group — **Air Vice Marshal H.A. Constantine** CBE, DSO

No.9 Squadron	Lancaster	Bardney
No.44 Squadron	Lancaster	Spilsby
No.49 Squadron	Lancaster	Syerston
No.50 Squadron	Lancaster	Skellingthorpe
No.57 Squadron	Lancaster	East Kirkby
No.61 Squadron	Lancaster	Skellingthorpe
No.106 Squadron	Lancaster	Metheringham
No.189 Squadron	Lancaster	Bardney
No.207 Squadron	Lancaster	Spilsby
No.227 Squadron	Lancaster	Strubby
No.463 Squadron, RAAF	Lancaster	Waddington
No.467 Squadron, RAAF	Lancaster	Waddington
No.617 Squadron	Lancaster/Mosquito	Woodhall Spa
No.619 Squadron	Lancaster	Strubby
No.630 Squadron	Lancaster	East Kirkby

No.6 (Bomber) Group — **Air Vice Marshal C.M. McEwen** CB, MC, DFC

No.408 Squadron, RCAF	Halifax/Lancaster	Linton-on-Ouse
No.415 Squadron, RCAF	Halifax	East Moor
No.419 Squadron, RCAF	Lancaster	Middleton St George
No.420 Squadron, RCAF	Halifax/Lancaster	Tholthorpe
No.424 Squadron, RCAF	Lancaster	Skipton-on-Swale
No.425 Squadron, RCAF	Halifax/Lancaster	Tholthorpe
No.426 Squadron, RCAF	Halifax	Linton-on-Ouse
No.427 Squadron, RCAF	Lancaster	Leeming
No.428 Squadron, RCAF	Lancaster	Middleton St George
No.429 Squadron, RCAF	Lancaster	Leeming
No.431 Squadron, RCAF	Lancaster	Croft
No.432 Squadron, RCAF	Halifax	East Moor
No.433 Squadron, RCAF	Lancaster	Skipton-on-Swale
No.434 Squadron, RCAF	Lancaster	Croft

No.7 (Training) Group — **Air Vice Marshal E.A.B. Rice** CB, CBE, MC

No.1651 HCU	Lancaster	Woolfox Lodge
No.1652 HCU	Halifax	Marston Moor
No.1653 HCU	Lancaster	North Luffenham
No.1654 HCU	Lancaster	Wigsley
No.1656 HCU	Lancaster	Lindholme
No.1659 HCU	Halifax	Topcliffe
No.1660 HCU	Lancaster	Swinderby
No.1661 HCU	Lancaster	Winthorpe
No.1663 HCU	Halifax	Rufforth
No.1666 HCU	Lancaster	Wombleton
No.1667 HCU	Lancaster	Sandtoft
No.1668 HCU	Lancaster	Bottesford

Bomber Command	Wellington/Halifax/	Finningley
Instructors' School*	Lancaster/Oxford/	
	Master/Spitfire	

Note: Bomber Command Instructors' School aircraft were non-operational.

No.8 (PFF) Group   Air Vice Marshal D.C.T. Bennett CB, CBE, DSO

No.7 (PFF) Squadron	Lancaster	Oakington
No.35 (PFF) Squadron	Lancaster	Graveley
No.83 (PFF) Squadron*	Lancaster	Coningsby
No.97 (PFF) Squadron*	Lancaster	Coningsby
No.105 (PFF) Squadron	Mosquito	Bourn
No.109 (PFF) Squadron	Mosquito	Little Staughton
No.128 Squadron	Mosquito	Wyton
No.139 (PFF) Squadron	Mosquito	Upwood
No.142 Squadron	Mosquito	Gransden Lodge
No.156 (PFF) Squadron	Lancaster	Upwood
No.162 Squadron	Mosquito	Bourn
No.163 Squadron	Mosquito	Wyton
No.405 (PFF) Squadron, RCAF	Lancaster	Linton-on-Ouse
No.571 Squadron	Mosquito	Oakington
No.582 (PFF) Squadron	Lancaster	Little Staughton
No.608 Squadron	Mosquito	Downham Market
No.627 (PFF) Squadron*	Mosquito	Woodhall Spa
No.692 Squadron	Mosquito	Graveley
No.1323 Flight	Lancaster	Warboys
No.1409 (Met) Flight	Mosquito	Wyton
Pathfinder Navigation Training Unit	Lancaster/Mosquito/ Oxford	Warboys

*Nos.83, 97 and 627 Squadrons detached to No.5 Group

No.26 (Signals) Group   Air Vice Marshal O.G.W. Lywood CB, CBE
Numerous Ground Signals units

No.91 (Training) Group   Air Vice Marshal J.A. Gray CBE, DFC, GM

No.10 OTU	Wellington	Abingdon
No.19 OTU	Wellington	Kinloss
No.20 OTU	Wellington	Lossiemouth
No.21 OTU	Wellington	Moreton-in-the-Marsh
No.22 OTU	Wellington	Wellesbourne Mountford
No.24 OTU	Wellington	Honeybourne
No.27 OTU	Wellington	Lichfield
No.30 OTU	Wellington	Gamston

No.92 (Training) Group   Air Vice Marshal G.S. Hodson CBE, AFC

No.11 OTU	Wellington	Westcott
No.12 OTU	Wellington	Chipping Warden
No.14 OTU	Wellington	Market Harborough
No.16 OTU	Mosquito	Upper Heyford
No.17 OTU	Wellington	Silverstone
No.29 OTU	Wellington	Bruntingthorpe
No.84 OTU	Wellington	Desborough
No.85 OTU	Wellington	Husbands Bosworth

No.100 (BS) Group   **Air Vice Marshal E.B. Addison** CB, CBE

No.23 (BS) Squadron	Mosquito	Little Snoring
No.85 (BS) Squadron	Mosquito	Swannington
No.141 (BS) Squadron	Mosquito	West Raynham
No.157 (BS) Squadron	Mosquito	Swannington
No.169 (BS) Squadron	Mosquito	Great Massingham
No.171 (BS) Squadron	Halifax	North Creake
No.192 (BS) Squadron	Halifax/Mosquito	Foulsham
No.199 (BS) Squadron	Halifax	North Creake
No.214 (BS) Squadron	Fortress	Oulton
No.223 (BS) Squadron	Liberator/Fortress	Oulton
No.239 (BS) Squadron	Mosquito	West Raynham
No.462 (BS) Squadron	Halifax	Foulsham
No.515 (BS) Squadron	Mosquito	Little Snoring
No.1692 (BS) Flight	Mosquito/Wellington	Great Massingham
No.1699 Trg Flight	Fortress	Oulton
Bomber Support Development Unit	Mosquito/Halifax/ Lancaster	Swanton Morley

Note: All Groups also established with Bomber Defence Flights.

Order of Battle
1 December 1960

No.1 (Bomber) Group	Air Vice Marshal J.G. Davis CB, OBE, MA	
No.9 Squadron	Canberra	Coningsby
No.12 Squadron	Canberra	Coningsby
No.18 Squadron	Valiant	Finningley
No.44 Squadron	Vulcan	Waddington
No.83 Squadron	Vulcan	Waddington
No.97 Squadron	Thor	Hemswell
No.98 Squadron	Thor	Driffield
No.101 Squadron	Vulcan	Finningley
No.102 Squadron	Thor	Full Sutton
No.104 Squadron	Thor	Ludford Magna
No.106 Squadron	Thor	Bardney
No.142 Squadron	Thor	Coleby Grange
No.150 Squadron	Thor	Carnaby
No.226 Squadron	Thor	Catfoss
No.240 Squadron	Thor	Breighton
No.269 Squadron	Thor	Caistor
No.617 Squadron	Vulcan	Scampton
No.230 OCU	Vulcan	Waddington
Bomber Command Bombing School	Hastings/ Varsity	Lindholme

No.3 (Bomber) Group	Air Vice Marshal M.H. Dwyer CB, CBE	
No.7 Squadron	Valiant	Wittering
No.10 Squadron	Victor	Cottesmore
No.15 Squadron	Victor	Cottesmore
No.35 Squadron	Canberra	Upwood
No.49 Squadron	Valiant	Wittering
No.55 Squadron	Victor	Honington
No.57 Squadron	Victor	Honington
No.58 Squadron	Canberra	Wyton
No.76 Squadron	Canberra	Upwood
No.77 Squadron	Thor	Feltwell
No.82 Squadron	Thor	Shepherds Grove
No.90 Squadron	Valiant	Honington
No.107 Squadron	Thor	Tuddenham
No.113 Squadron	Thor	Mepal**

No.130 Squadron	Thor	Polebrook
No.138 Squadron	Valiant	Wittering
No.144 Squadron	Thor	North Luffenham
No.148 Squadron	Valiant	Marham
No.207 Squadron	Valiant	Marham
No.214 Squadron	Valiant	Marham
No.218 Squadron	Thor	Harrington
No.220 Squadron	Thor	North Pickenham
No.223 Squadron	Thor	Folkingham
No.254 Squadron	Thor	Melton Mowbray
No.543 Squadron	Valiant	Wyton
Radar Reconnaissance Flight	Victor	Wyton
No.231 OCU	Canberra	Bassingbourn
No.232 OCU	Victor/Valiant	Gaydon
Bomber Command Development Unit	Valiant	Wyton

Bomber Command Squadrons 1936-1968

No	From*	To*	Aircraft Type	From	To
7	14/7/36	8/4/40	Heyford II/III	7/36	4/38
			Wellesley	4/37	4/38
			Whitley II	3/38	12/38
			Whitley III	11/38	5/39
			Anson	3/39	4/40
			Hampden	4/39	4/40
	30/4/40	20/5/40	Hampden (ntu)		
	1/8/40	1/1/56	Stirling I	8/40	8/43
			Stirling III	3/43	8/43
			Lancaster I/III	5/43	1/50
			Lincoln 2	9/49	1/56
	1/11/56	30/9/62	Valiant 1	11/56	9/62
9	14/7/36	13/7/61	Heyford III	7/36	3/39
			Wellington I	1/39	10/41
			Wellington II	3/41	8/41
			Wellington III	7/41	8/42
			Wellington I	5/42	6/42
			Lancaster I/III	9/42	12/45
			Lancaster VII	11/45	4/46
			Lancaster I/III	5/46	7/46
			Lincoln 2	7/46	5/52
			Canberra 2	5/52	6/56
			Canberra 6	9/55	7/61
	1/3/62	30/4/68	Vulcan 2	4/62	4/68
10	14/7/36	7/5/45	Heyford III	7/36	7/37
			Whitley I	3/37	6/39
			Whitley IV	5/39	5/40
			Whitley V	5/40	12/41
			Halifax I	12/41	8/42
			Halifax II	12/41	3/44
			Halifax III	3/44	5/45
	15/1/53	15/1/57	Canberra 2	1/53	12/56
	15/4/58	1/3/64	Victor 1	4/58	3/64
12	14/7/36	13/7/61	Hart	8/36	10/36**

No	From*	To*	Aircraft Type	From	To
			Hind	10/36	2/38
			Battle	2/38	11/40+
			Wellington II	11/40	11/42
			Wellington III	8/42	11/42
			Lancaster I/III	11/42	7/46
			Lincoln 2	8/46	4/52
			Canberra 2	5/52	6/55
			Canberra 6	5/55	7/61
			Canberra 2	8/57	3/59
	1/7/62	31/12/67	Vulcan 2	7/62	12/67
15	14/7/36	15/4/57	Hind	7/36	7/38
			Battle	6/38	12/39+
			Blenheim IV	12/39	10/40+
			Wellington I	11/40	5/41
			Stirling I	4/41	4/43
			Stirling III	1/43	12/43
			Lancaster I/III	12/43	3/47
			Lincoln 2	2/47	11/50
			Washington 1	2/51	4/53
			Canberra 2	5/53	4/57
	1/9/58	1/10/64	Victor 1	9/58	10/64
18	14/7/36	11/11/42	Hind	7/36	5/39
			Blenheim I	5/39	5/40+
			Blenheim IV	2/40	9/42++
			Blenheim V	9/42	11/42
	1/8/53	1/2/57	Canberra 2	8/53	1/57
	17/12/58	31/3/63	Valiant 1	12/58	3/63
21	14/7/36	1/6/43	Hind	7/36	8/38
			Blenheim I	8/38	9/39
			Blenheim IV	9/39	7/42++
			Ventura I/II	5/42	6/43
	21/9/53	30/6/57	Canberra 2	9/53	6/57
	1/10/58	15/1/59	Canberra 2/6	10/58	1/59
23	2/6/44	25/9/45	Mosquito VI	6/44	9/45
			Mosquito XXX	8/45	9/45
27	1/6/53	31/12/57	Canberra 2	6/53	12/57
	1/4/61	30/4/68	Vulcan 2	4/61	4/68
34	14/7/36	12/8/39	Hind	7/36	7/38
			Blenheim I	7/38	8/39
35	14/7/36	8/4/40	Gordon	7/36	9/37**
			Wellesley	7/37	5/38
			Battle	4/38	2/40
			Anson	7/39	4/40
			Blenheim IV	11/39	4/40
	7/11/40	23/2/50	Halifax I	11/40	2/42
			Halifax II	10/41	1/44

No	From*	To*	Aircraft Type	From	To
			Halifax III	10/43	3/44
			Lancaster I/III	3/44	9/49
			Lincoln 2	8/49	2/50
	1/9/51	11/9/61	Washington 1	9/51	2/54
			Canberra 2	4/54	9/61
	1/12/62	30/4/68	Vulcan 2	12/62	4/68
37	26/4/37	12/11/40	Harrow	4/37	6/39
			Wellington I	5/39	11/40
38	14/7/36	12/11/40	Heyford III	7/36	7/37
			Hendon II	11/36	1/39
			Wellington I	11/38	11/40
40	14/7/36	14/2/42	Hind	7/36	8/38
			Battle	7/38	12/39+
			Blenheim IV	12/39	11/40
			Wellington I	11/40	2/42
	28/10/53	1/2/57	Canberra 2	10/53	2/57
44	8/3/37	15/7/57	Hind	3/37	12/37
			Blenheim I	12/37	2/39
			Anson	2/39	6/39
			Hampden	2/39	12/41
			Lancaster I/III	12/41	9/47
			Lincoln 2	10/45	5/46
				12/46	3/47
				5/47	1/51
			Washington 1	2/51	1/53
			Canberra 2	4/53	7/57
	10/8/60	30/4/68	Vulcan 1	8/60	9/67
			Vulcan 2	9/66	4/68
49	14/7/36	1/8/55	Hind	7/36	12/38
			Hampden	9/38	4/42
			Manchester	4/42	6/42
			Lancaster I/III	6/42	5/50
			Lincoln 2	10/49	7/55
	1/5/56	1/5/65	Valiant 1	5/56	12/64
50	3/5/37	31/1/51	Hind	5/37	1/39
			Hampden	12/38	4/42
			Manchester	4/42	6/42
			Lancaster I/III	5/42	10/46
			Lincoln 2	7/46	1/51
	15/8/52	1/10/59	Canberra 2	8/52	10/59
	1/8/61	30/4/68	Vulcan 1	8/61	10/66
			Vulcan 2	1/66	4/68
51	15/3/37	7/5/45	Virginia X	3/37	2/38
			Anson	3/37	2/38
			Whitley II	2/38	12/39
			Whitley III	8/38	3/40
			Whitley IV	11/39	5/40
			Whitley V	1/40	10/42

No	From*	To*	Aircraft Type	From	To
			Halifax II	11/42	1/44
			Halifax III	1/44	5/45
	31/3/63	30/4/68	Canberra 6	3/63	4/68
			Comet 2R	3/63	4/68
			Hastings 1	3/63	3/67
52	18/1/37	6/4/40	Hind	1/37	12/37
			Battle	11/37	4/40
			Anson	2/39	4/40
55	1/9/60	30/4/68	Victor 1	9/60	4/68
57	14/7/36	9/12/57	Hind	7/36	3/38
			Blenheim I	3/38	5/40
			Blenheim IV	3/40	11/40
			Wellington I	11/40	6/42
			Wellington II	7/41	11/41
			Wellington III	1/42	9/42
			Lancaster I/III	9/42	5/46
			Lincoln 2	8/45	5/51
			Washington 1	4/51	3/53
			Canberra 2	5/53	12/57
	1/1/59	30/4/68	Victor 1	1/59	
58	14/7/36	7/4/42	Virginia X	7/36	1/38
			Anson	2/37	11/37
			Whitley I	10/37	4/38
			Whitley II	10/37	7/39
			Heyford III	4/39	5/39
			Whitley III	5/39	4/40
			Whitley V	3/40	4/42
	1/50	30/4/68	Mosquito 34	1/50	12/53
			Anson 19	1/50	12/51
			Lincoln 2	11/50	9/51
			Mosquito 35	11/51	3/54
			Canberra 3	12/53	10/55
			Canberra 7	1/55	4/68
			Canberra 9	1/60	3/63
61	8/3/37	31/3/58	Audax	3/37	4/37
			Anson	3/37	2/38
			Blenheim I	1/38	3/39
			Hampden	2/39	10/41
			Manchester	6/41	6/42
			Lancaster I/III	4/42	6/46
			Lancaster II	1/43	3/43
			Lincoln 2	5/46	8/54
			Canberra 2	8/54	3/58
62	3/5/37	11/8/39	Hind	5/37	3/38
			Blenheim I	2/38	8/39
63	15/2/37	6/4/40	Hind	2/37	4/37
			Audax	3/37	8/37

No	From*	To*	Aircraft Type	From	To
			Battle	5/37	4/40
			Anson	3/39	4/40
75	15/3/37	15/10/45	Virginia X	3/37	9/37
			Anson	3/37	10/37
				3/39	10/39
			Harrow	9/37	7/39
			Wellington I	7/39	1/42
			Wellington III	1/42	11/42
			Stirling I	10/42	7/43
			Stirling III	3/43	4/44
			Lancaster I/III	3/44	10/45
			Lincoln II	9/45	10/45
76	12/4/37	8/4/40	Wellesley	4/37	4/39
			Hampden	3/39	4/40
			Anson	5/39	4/40
	30/4/40	20/5/40	Hampden (ntu)		
	1/5/41	7/5/45	Halifax I	5/41	3/42
			Halifax II	10/41	4/43
			Halifax V	2/43	2/44
			Halifax III	1/44	4/45
			Halifax VI	3/45	5/45
	9/12/53	30/12/60	Canberra 2	12/53	12/55
			Canberra 6	12/55	12/60
77	14/6/37	7/5/45	Audax	6/37	11/37
			Wellesley	11/37	11/38
			Whitley III	11/38	10/39
			Whitley V	9/39	10/42
			Halifax II	10/42	6/44
			Halifax V	4/44	5/44
			Halifax III	5/44	3/45
			Halifax VI	3/45	8/45
	1/9/58	10/7/63	Thor (missile)	9/58	7/63
78	1/11/36	7/5/45	Heyford III	11/36	10/37
			Whitley I	7/37	12/39
			Whitley IV	6/39	6/40
			Whitley V	8/39	3/42
			Halifax II	3/42	1/44
			Halifax III	1/44	4/45
			Halifax VI	4/45	5/45
82	14/6/37	20/3/42	Hind	6/37	3/38
			Blenheim I	3/38	9/39
			Blenheim IV	8/39	3/42**
	1/50	1/9/56	Lancaster 1	1/50	12/53
			Canberra 3	11/53	2/55
			Canberra 7	10/54	9/56
	22/7/59	10/7/63	Thor (missile)	7/59	7/63
83	4/8/36	1/1/56	Hind	8/36	12/38
			Hampden	11/38	1/42
			Manchester	12/41	6/42

No	From*	To*	Aircraft Type	From	To
			Lancaster I/III	5/42	7/46
			Lincoln 2	7/46	12/55
	21/5/57	10/8/60	Vulcan 1	7/57	8/60
	10/10/60	30/4/68	Vulcan 2	10/60	4/68
85	30/4/44	26/6/45	Mosquito XIII	4/44	5/44
			Mosquito XVII	4/44	11/44
			Mosquito XXX	11/44	6/45
88	7/6/37	1/6/43	Hind	6/37	12/37
			Battle	12/37	8/41+
			Boston I/II	2/41	8/41
			Blenheim I	2/41	7/41
			Blenheim IV	7/41	2/42
			Boston III	7/41	6/43
90	15/3/37	6/4/40	Hind	3/37	6/37
			Blenheim I	5/37	4/39
				9/39	4/40
			Blenheim IV	3/39	4/40
	3/5/41	10/2/42	Fortress I	5/41	2/42
			Blenheim IV	10/41	2/42
	7/11/42	1/9/50	Stirling I	11/42	5/43
			Stirling III	3/43	6/44
			Lancaster I/III	5/44	9/47
			Lincoln 2	4/47	8/50
	4/10/50	1/5/56	Washington I	1/51	3/54
			Canberra 2	11/53	5/56
	1/1/57	1/3/65	Valiant 1	3/57	12/64
97	14/7/36	8/4/40	Heyford III	7/36	2/39
			Anson	2/39	4/40
			Whitley II/III	2/39	4/40
	30/4/40	20/5/40	Whitley (ntu)		
	25/2/41	1/1/56	Manchester	2/41	2/42
			Hampden	7/41	8/41
			Lancaster I/III	1/42	7/46
			Lincoln 2	7/46	12/55
	1/12/59	24/5/63	Thor (missile)	12/59	5/63
98	14/7/36	31/7/40	Hind	7/36	6/38
			Battle	6/38	6/40
	12/9/42	1/6/43	Mitchell II/III	9/42	6/43
	1/8/59	18/4/63	Thor (missile)	8/59	4/63
99	14/7/36	12/2/42	Heyford III	7/36	11/38
			Wellington I	10/38	2/42
			Wellington II	7/41	10/41
100	14/12/42	1/9/59	Lancaster I/III	12/42	5/46
			Lincoln 2	5/46	4/54
			Canberra 2	4/54	9/59
			Canberra 6/8	8/56	9/59
			Canberra 7	8/56	6/57

No	From*	To*	Aircraft Type	From	To
	1/5/62	30/4/68	Victor 2	5/62	4/68
101	14/7/36	1/2/57	Overstrand	7/36	8/38
			Blenheim I	6/38	4/39
			Blenheim IV	4/39	7/41
			Wellington I	4/41	2/42
			Wellington III	2/42	10/42
			Lancaster I/III	10/42	8/46
			Lincoln 2	8/46	6/51
			Canberra 2	6/51	8/54
			Canberra 6	6/54	1/57
	15/10/57	30/4/68	Vulcan 1	1/58	1/68
			Vulcan 2	1/68	4/68
102	7/36	8/5/45	Heyford II/III	7/36	11/38
			Whitley III	10/38	1/40
			Whitley V	11/39	2/42
			Halifax II	12/41	5/44
			Halifax III	5/44	2/45
			Halifax VI	2/45	5/45
	1/8/59	27/4/63	Thor (missiles)	8/59	4/63
103	10/8/36	25/11/45	Hind	8/36	8/38
			Battle	7/38	10/40+
			Wellington I	10/40	7/42
			Halifax II	7/42	10/42
			Lancaster I/III	10/42	11/45
104	14/7/36	6/4/40	Hind	7/36	5/38
			Blenheim I	5/38	4/40
			Anson	5/39	4/40
			Blenheim IV	11/39	4/40
	7/3/41	14/2/42	Wellington II	4/41	2/42
	22/7/59	24/5/63	Thor (missiles)	7/59	5/63
105	12/4/37	1/2/46	Audax	4/37	10/37
			Battle	8/37	5/40+
			Blenheim IV	6/40	12/41++
			Mosquito IV	11/41	3/44
			Mosquito IX	6/43	8/45
			Mosquito XVI	3/44	2/46
106	1/6/38	18/2/46	Hind	6/38	7/38
			Battle	7/38	5/39
			Anson	5/39	9/39
			Hampden	5/39	3/42
			Manchester	2/42	6/42
			Lancaster I/III	5/42	2/46
	22/7/59	24/5/63	Thor (missiles)	7/59	5/63
107	10/8/36	1/6/43	Hind	9/36	9/38
			Blenheim I	8/38	6/39
			Blenheim IV	5/39	2/42++
			Boston III	1/42	6/43
	22/7/59	10/7/63	Thor (missile)	7/59	7/63

No	From*	To*	Aircraft Type	From	To
108	4/1/37	6/4/40	Hind	1/37	6/38
			Blenheim I	6/38	4/40
			Anson	5/39	4/40
			Blenheim IV	10/39	4/40
109	10/12/40	1/2/57	Whitley V	12/40	1/41
			Anson	12/40	6/42
			Wellington I	12/40	12/42
			Wellington VI	3/42	7/42
			Lancaster I	7/42	10/42
			Mosquito IV	12/42	5/44
			Mosquito IX	6/43	9/45
			Mosquito XVI	3/44	12/48
			Mosquito 35	4/48	7/52
			Canberra 2	8/52	12/54
			Canberra 6	12/54	1/57
110	18/5/37	6/3/42	Hind	5/37	1/38
			Blenheim I	1/38	9/39
			Blenheim IV	6/39	3/42++
113	18/5/37	29/4/38	Hind	5/37	4/38
	22/7/59	10/7/63	Thor (missile)	7/59	7/63
114	1/12/36	12/11/42	Hind	12/36	3/37
			Audax	3/37	4/37
			Blenheim I	3/37	5/39
			Blenheim IV	5/39	9/42
			Blenheim V	9/42	11/42
115	15/6/37	1/3/50	Hendon II	6/37	8/37
			Harrow	6/37	6/39
			Wellington I	3/39	2/42
			Wellington III	2/42	3/43
			Lancaster II	3/43	5/44
			Lancaster I/III	3/44	1/50
			Lincoln 2	9/49	2/50
	13/6/50	1/6/57	Washington 1	6/50	3/54
			Canberra 2	2/54	5/57
128	15/9/44	31/3/46	Mosquito XX	9/44	11/44
			Mosquito XXV	10/44	11/44
			Mosquito XVI	10/44	3/46
130	1/12/59	23/8/63	Thor (missile)	12/59	8/63
138	25/8/41	1/9/50	Lysander III	8/41	3/42
			Whitley V	8/41	11/42
			Halifax II	8/41	8/44
			Stirling IV	6/44	3/45
			Lancaster I/III	3/45	9/47
			Lincoln 2	9/47	8/50
	1/1/55	1/4/62	Valiant 1	2/55	4/62

No	From*	To*	Aircraft Type		From	To
139	3/9/36	9/12/41	Hind		9/36	7/37
			Blenheim I		7/37	9/39
			Blenheim IV		7/39	12/41++
	8/6/42	31/12/59	Blenheim V		6/42	11/42
			Mosquito IV		6/42	7/44
			Mosquito IX		9/43	8/44
			Mosquito XX		12/43	8/45
			Mosquito XVI		2/44	7/48
			Mosquito XXV		10/44	5/45
			Mosquito 35		2/48	1/53
			Canberra 2		11/52	7/55
			Canberra 6		2/55	12/59
	1/2/62	30/4/68	Victor B.2		2/62	4/68
141	3/12/43	7/9/45	Beaufighter VI		12/43	1/44
			Mosquito II		12/43	8/44
			Mosquito VI		8/44	4/45
			Mosquito XXX		4/45	9/45
142	3/12/36	19/12/42	Hind		1/37	4/38
			Battle ·		3/38	11/40+
			Wellington II		11/40	10/41
			Wellington IV		10/41	9/42
			Wellington III		9/42	12/42
	25/10/44	28/9/45	Mosquito XXV		10/44	9/45
	22/7/59	24/5/63	Thor (missile)		7/59	5/63
144	11/1/37	22/4/42	Overstrand		1/37	2/37
			Anson		1/37	9/37
			Audax		3/37	9/37
			Blenheim I		8/37	4/39
			Hampden		3/39	4/42
	1/12/59	23/8/63	Thor (missile)		12/59	8/63
148	7/6/38	20/5/40	Audax		6/37	7/37
			Wellesley		6/37	11/38
			Heyford III		11/38	3/39
			Wellington I		3/39	5/40
			Anson		4/39	4/40
	4/11/46	1/7/55	Lancaster I		11/46	2/50
			Lincoln 2		1/50	6/55
	1/7/56	1/5/65	Valiant 1		7/56	12/64
149	12/4/37	1/3/50	Heyford III		4/37	3/39
			Wellington I		3/39	12/41
			Stirling I		11/41	7/43
			Stirling III		2/43	9/44
			Lancaster I/III		8/44	11/49
			Lincoln 2		10/49	3/50
	9/8/50	31/8/56	Washington 1		11/50	2/53
			Canberra 2		3/53	8/56
150	8/8/38	27/1/43	Battle		8/38	9/40+
			Wellington I		10/40	12/42

No	From*	To*	Aircraft Type	From	To
			Wellington III	9/42	1/43
	1/11/44	7/11/45	Lancaster I/III	11/44	11/45
	1/8/59	9/4/63	Thor (missile)	8/59	4/63
153	7/10/44	28/9/45	Lancaster I/III	10/44	9/45
156	14/2/42	25/9/45	Wellington I	2/42	6/42
			Wellington III	2/42	1/43
			Lancaster I/III	1/43	9/45
157	7/5/44	16/8/45	Mosquito XIX	5/44	5/45
			Mosquito XXX	2/45	8/45
158	14/2/42	7/5/45	Wellington II	2/42	6/42
			Halifax II	6/42	12/43
			Halifax III	12/43	5/45
			Halifax VI	4/45	5/45
161	15/2/42	9/3/45	Lysander III	2/42	6/45
			Hudson I	2/42	8/44
			Whitley V	2/42	12/42
			Halifax II	9/42	12/42
			Halifax V	10/42	10/44
			Albemarle II	10/42	4/43
			Havoc I	10/42	12/43
			Hudson III/V	9/43	6/45
			Stirling III/IV	9/44	3/45
162	16/12/44	14/7/46	Mosquito XXV	12/44	7/46
			Mosquito XX	2/45	7/46
163	25/1/45	10/8/45	Mosquito XXV	1/45	5/45
			Mosquito XVI	5/45	8/45
166	1/11/36	6/4/40	Heyford III	11/36	9/39
			Whitley I	6/39	2/40
			Whitley III	12/39	4/40
	27/1/43	18/11/45	Wellington III	1/43	4/43
			Wellington X	2/43	9/43
			Lancaster I/III	9/43	11/45
169	7/12/43	10/8/45	Mosquito II	1/44	7/44
			Mosquito VI	6/44	8/45
			Mosquito XIX	1/45	8/45
170	15/10/44	15/11/45	Lancaster I/III	10/44	11/45
171	7/9/44	27/7/45	Stirling III	9/44	1/45
			Halifax III	10/44	7/45
180	11/9/42	1/6/43	Mitchell II	9/42	6/43
185	1/3/38	8/4/40	Hind	3/38	7/38
			Battle	6/38	6/39
			Hampden	6/39	5/40

No	From*	To*	Aircraft Type	From	To
			Hereford	8/39	4/40
			Anson	8/39	4/40
189	15/10/44	20/11/45	Lancaster I/III	10/44	11/45
192	4/1/43	22/8/45	Wellington I/III	1/43	3/43
			Wellington X	1/43	1/45
			Mosquito IV	1/43	3/45
			Halifax II	3/43	7/43
			Halifax V	7/43	3/44
			Halifax III	3/44	8/45
			Mosquito XVI	2/45	8/45
195	1/10/44	14/8/45	Lancaster I/III	10/44	8/45
196	7/11/42	1/12/43	Wellington X	12/42	7/43
			Stirling III	7/43	12/43
199	7/11/42	29/7/45	Wellington III	11/42	4/43
			Wellington X	3/43	6/43
			Stirling III	7/43	3/45
			Halifax III	2/45	7/45
	17/4/52	15/12/58	Lincoln 2	4/52	9/57
			Mosquito 36	4/52	3/54
			Canberra 2	7/54	12/58
			Valiant 1	5/57	12/58
207	4/7/36	19/4/40	Gordon	8/36	11/37
			Wellesley	9/37	4/38
			Battle	4/38	4/40
			Anson	7/39	4/40
	1/11/40	1/3/50	Manchester	11/40	3/42
			Hampden	7/41	8/41
			Lancaster I/III	3/42	8/49
			Lincoln 2	7/49	2/50
	29/5/51	27/3/56	Washington 1	7/51	3/54
			Canberra 2	3/54	3/56
	1/4/56	1/5/65	Valiant 1	6/56	2/65
211	24/6/37	12/5/38	Audax	7/37	10/37
			Hind	8/37	5/38
214	14/7/36	27/7/45	Virginia X	7/36	4/37
			Harrow II	1/37	6/39
			Wellington I	5/39	4/42
			Wellington II	11/41	12/41
			Stirling I	4/42	2/44
			Stirling III	2/43	1/44
			Fortress II	1/44	7/45
			Fortress III	11/44	7/45
	5/11/46	30/12/54	Lancaster I	11/46	3/50
			Lincoln 2	2/50	12/54
	21/1/56	1/3/65	Valiant 1	1/56	12/64
	1/7/66	30/4/68	Victor 1	7/66	4/68

No	From*	To*	Aircraft Type	From	To
215	14/7/36	22/5/40	Virginia X	7/36	9/37
			Anson	2/37	11/37
			Harrow	8/37	12/39
			Wellington I	7/39	5/40
			Anson	1/40	4/40
218	14/7/36	10/8/45	Hart	7/36	3/38
			Battle	1/38	5/40+
			Blenheim IV	7/40	11/40
			Wellington I	11/40	2/42
			Wellington II	5/41	12/41
			Stirling I	1/42	6/43
			Stirling III	2/43	8/44
			Lancaster I/III	8/44	8/45
	1/12/59	23/8/63	Thor (missile)	12/59	8/63
220	22/7/59	10/7/63	Thor (missile)	7/59	7/63
223	23/8/44	29/7/45	Liberator IV	8/44	6/45
			Fortress II/III	4/45	7/45
	1/12/59	23/8/63	Thor (missile)	12/59	8/63
226	15/3/37	1/6/43	Audax	3/37	11/37
			Battle	10/37	5/41+
			Blenheim IV	5/41	12/41
			Boston III	11/41	6/43
			Mitchell II	5/43	6/43
	1/8/59	9/3/63	Thor (missile)	8/59	3/63
227	7/10/44	5/9/45	Lancaster I/III	10/44	9/45
239	9/12/43	1/7/45	Mosquito II	1/44	8/44
			Mosquito VI	8/44	1/45
			Mosquito XXX	1/45	7/45
240	1/8/59	8/1/63	Thor (missile)	8/59	1/63
254	1/12/59	23/8/63	Thor (missile)	12/59	8/63
269	22/7/59	24/5/63	Thor (missile)	7/59	5/63
300	1/7/40	2/1/47	Battle	7/40	11/40
			Wellington I	12/40	9/41
			Wellington IV	8/41	1/43
			Wellington III	1/43	4/43
			Wellington X	3/43	3/44
			Lancaster I/III	4/44	10/46
301	22/7/40	7/4/43	Battle	7/40	11/40
			Wellington I	10/40	8/41
			Wellington IV	8/41	4/43
304	22/8/40	7/5/42	Battle	8/40	11/40
			Wellington I	11/40	5/42

No	From*	To*	Aircraft Type	From	To
305	29/8/40	5/9/43	Battle	8/40	11/40
			Wellington I	11/40	7/41
			Wellington II	7/41	8/42
			Wellington IV	8/42	5/43
			Wellington X	5/43	8/43
311	29/7/40	28/4/42	Wellington I	8/40	4/42
346	15/5/44	20/10/45	Halifax V	5/44	6/44
			Halifax III	6/44	4/45
			Halifax VI	3/45	10/45
347	20/6/44	20/10/45	Halifax V	6/44	7/44
			Halifax III	7/44	4/45
			Halifax VI	3/45	10/45
405	23/4/41	5/9/45	Wellington II	5/41	4/42
			Halifax II	4/42	9/43
			Lancaster I/III	8/43	5/45
			Lancaster X	5/45	9/45
408	15/6/41	5/9/45	Hampden	6/41	9/42
			Halifax V	9/42	12/42
			Halifax II	12/42	10/43
			Lancaster II	10/43	9/44
			Halifax III	9/44	2/45
			Halifax VII	9/44	5/45
			Lancaster X	5/45	9/45
415	26/7/44	15/5/45	Halifax III	7/44	5/45
			Halifax VII	3/45	5/45
419	15/12/41	5/9/45	Wellington I	1/42	11/42
			Wellington III	2/42	11/42
			Halifax II	11/42	4/44
			Lancaster X	3/44	9/45
420	19/12/41	16/5/43	Hampden	1/42	8/42
			Wellington III	8/42	4/43
			Wellington X	2/43	5/43
	6/11/43	12/6/45	Halifax III	12/43	5/45
			Lancaster X	4/45	6/45
424	15/10/42	15/5/43	Wellington III	10/42	5/43
	6/11/43	15/10/45	Halifax III	12/43	1/45
			Lancaster I/III	1/45	10/45
425	25/6/42	15/5/43	Wellington III	8/42	5/43
	10/12/43	12/6/45	Halifax III	12/43	5/45
			Lancaster X	5/45	6/45
426	15/10/42	25/5/45	Wellington III	10/42	4/43
			Wellington X	4/43	6/43
			Lancaster II	7/43	5/44

No	From*	To*	Aircraft Type	From	To
			Halifax III	4/44	6/44
				12/44	3/45
			Halifax VII	6/44	5/45
427	7/11/42	31/5/46	Wellington III	11/42	3/43
			Wellington X	2/43	5/43
			Halifax V	5/43	3/44
			Halifax III	1/44	5/45
			Lancaster I/III	3/45	5/46
428	7/11/42	31/5/45	Wellington III	11/42	4/43
			Wellington X	4/43	6/43
			Halifax V	6/43	1/44
			Halifax II	11/43	6/44
			Lancaster X	6/44	5/45
429	7/11/42	31/5/46	Wellington III	11/42	8/43
			Wellington X	1/43	8/43
			Halifax II	8/43	1/44
			Halifax V	11/43	3/44
			Halifax III	3/44	3/45
			Lancaster I/III	3/45	5/46
431	13/11/42	6/6/45	Wellington X	12/42	7/43
			Halifax V	7/43	4/44
			Halifax III	3/44	10/44
			Lancaster X	10/44	6/45
432	1/5/43	15/5/45	Wellington X	5/43	11/43
			Lancaster II	10/43	2/44
			Halifax III	2/44	7/44
			Halifax VII	7/44	5/45
433	25/9/43	15/10/45	Halifax III	11/43	1/45
			Lancaster I/III	1/45	10/45
434	15/6/43	9/6/45	Halifax V	6/43	5/44
			Halifax III	5/44	12/44
			Lancaster X	12/44	6/45
			Lancaster I/III	2/45	3/45
455	6/6/41	26/4/42	Hampden	7/41	4/42
458	25/8/41	20/3/42	Wellington IV	8/41	1/42
460	15/11/41	10/10/45	Wellington IV	11/41	9/42
			Halifax II	8/42	10/42
			Lancaster I/III	10/42	10/45
462	12/8/44	24/9/45	Halifax III	8/44	9/45
463	25/11/43	25/9/45	Lancaster I/III	11/43	9/45
464	15/8/42	1/6/43	Ventura I/II	9/42	6/43

No	From*	To*	Aircraft Type	From	To
466	15/10/42	7/5/45	Wellington II	10/42	11/42
			Wellington X	11/42	9/43
			Halifax II	9/43	11/43
			Halifax III	11/43	5/45
			Halifax VI	5/45	5/45
467	7/11/42	30/9/45	Lancaster I/III	11/42	9/45
487	15/8/42	1/6/43	Ventura II	9/42	6/43
500	14/7/36	7/11/38	Hart	7/36	3/37
			Hind	2/37	11/38
501	14/7/36	1/12/38	Hart	7/36	3/38
			Hind	3/38	12/38
502	14/7/36	27/11/38	Wallace	7/36	4/37
			Hind	4/37	11/38
503	14/7/36	1/11/38	Hart	7/36	11/38
			Hind	6/38	11/38
504	14/7/36	31/10/38	Wallace	7/36	5/37
			Hind	5/37	10/38
513	15/9/43	21/11/43	Stirling III	10/43	11/43
514	1/9/43	22/8/45	Lancaster II	9/43	7/44
			Lancaster I/III	6/44	8/45
515	15/12/43	10/6/45	Beaufighter II	12/43	4/44
			Mosquito II	2/44	4/44
			Mosquito VI	3/44	6/45
540	1/50	31/3/56	Mosquito 34	1/50	9/53
			Canberra 3	12/52	10/54
			Canberra 2	6/53	9/54
			Canberra 7	6/54	3/56
541	1/50	7/6/51	Spitfire 19	1/50	5/51
			Meteor 10	12/50	6/51
542	17/5/54	1/10/55	Canberra 3	5/54	10/55
	1/11/55	1/10/58	Canberra 2/6/7	11/55	10/58
543	1/7/55	30/4/68	Valiant 1	7/55	2/65
			Victor 1	5/65	12/65
			Victor 2	12/65	4/68
550	25/11/43	1/11/45	Lancaster I/III	11/43	10/45
571	5/4/44	20/9/45	Mosquito XVI	4/44	9/45
576	25/11/43	19/9/45	Lancaster I/III	11/43	9/45

No	From*	To*	Aircraft Type		From	To
578	14/1/44	15/4/45	Halifax III		1/44	3/45
582	1/4/44	11/9/45	Lancaster I/III		4/44	9/45
602	14/7/36	1/11/38	Hind		7/36	11/38
603	14/7/36	24/10/38	Hart		7/36	2/38
			Hind		2/38	10/38
605	14/7/36	1/1/39	Hart		7/36	9/36
			Hind		8/36	1/39
607	14/7/36	23/9/36	Wapiti		7/36	9/36
608	14/7/36	16/1/37	Wapiti		7/36	1/37
	1/8/44	24/8/45	Mosquito XX		8/44	4/45
			Mosquito XXV		10/44	4/45
			Mosquito XVI		3/45	8/45
609	14/7/36	8/12/38	Hart		7/36	1/38
			Hind		1/38	12/38
610	14/7/36	1/1/39	Hart		7/36	5/38
			Hind		5/38	1/39
611	14/7/36	1/1/39	Hart		7/36	4/38
			Hind		4/38	1/39
617	23/3/43	15/12/55	Lancaster I/III		3/43	6/45
			Mosquito VI		4/44	3/45
			Lancaster VII		6/45	9/46
			Lincoln 2		9/46	1/52
			Canberra 2		1/52	4/55
			Canberra 6		2/55	12/55
	1/5/58	30/4/68	Vulcan 1		5/58	7/61
			Vulcan 2		9/61	4/68
619	18/4/43	18/7/45	Lancaster I/III		4/43	7/45
622	10/8/43	15/8/45	Stirling III		8/43	1/44
			Lancaster I/III		12/43	8/45
623	10/8/43	6/12/43	Stirling III		8/43	12/43
625	1/10/43	7/10/45	Lancaster I/III		10/43	10/45
626	7/11/43	14/10/45	Lancaster I/III		11/43	10/45
627	12/11/43	30/9/45	Mosquito IV		11/43	9/45
			Mosquito XX		7/44	9/45
			Mosquito XXV		10/44	9/45
			Mosquito XVI		3/45	9/45
630	15/11/43	18/7/45	Lancaster I/III		11/43	7/45

No	From*	To*	Aircraft Type	From	To
635	20/3/44	1/9/45	Lancaster III	3/44	8/45
			Lancaster VI	7/44	11/44
640	7/1/44	7/5/45	Halifax III	1/44	3/45
			Halifax VI	3/45	5/45
692	1/1/44	20/9/45	Mosquito IV	1/44	6/44
			Mosquito XVI	3/44	9/45

*   Bomber Command Service dates
**   To Middle East on detachment 1936
\+   To AASF 1939/40
\+\+   To Malta on detachment 1941/42

Data – Operational Bombers used by the Command

Name	Cruising Speed (mph)	Radius of Action (miles)	Weapon Load (lbs)	Armament
Audax	138	220	224	2 x .303"
Battle	200	525	1000	2 x .303"
Blenheim I	200	460	1000	3 x .303"
		560	Nil	
Blenheim IV	180	730	1000	5 x .303"
		975	Nil	
Boston III	200	510	2000	7 x .303"
		1065	Nil	
Canberra 2	0.72M	1155	6000	Nil
Canberra 6	0.72M	1700	6000	Nil
Fortress I	230	925	4000	14 x .303"
		1430	Nil	5 x .5"
Gordon	110	300	500	2 x .303"
Halifax I	195	500	13000	8 x .303"
		870	8500	
		1360	1500	
Halifax II srs 1A	190	325	13000	9 x .303"
		830	5250	
		1050	1500	
Halifax III	215	465	13000	9 x .303"
		885	7250	
		1200	500	
Halifax V	190	415	13000	9 x .303"
		1160	1000	
Halifax VI	225	485	13000	9 x .303"
		985	6500	
		1245	2500	
Halifax VII	225	535	12000	9 x .303"
		1100	4500	or 5 x .303" & 2 x .5"
Hampden I	155	490	4500	6 x .303"
		840	2000	
Harrow	163	625	3000	4 x .303"
		920	Nil	

Name	Cruising Speed (mph)	Radius of Action (miles)	Weapon Load (lbs)	Armament
Hart	140	235	520	2 x .303"
Hendon	125	680	1660	3 x .303"
Heyford III	115	200	3000	3 x .303"
		460	1600	
Hind	132	215	510	2 x .303"
Lancaster I/III/X	216	520	22000*	6 x .303"
		830	14000	or 8 x .303"
		1125	5500	
		1575	Nil	
Lancaster II	210	500	14000	10 x .303"
		1160	4000	
Lincoln II	215	1125	14000	6 x .5"
		1465	4150	or 5 x .5" & 2 x 20mm
Manchester	185	600	10350	8 x .303"
		885	8100	
Mitchell II	210	475	6000	6 x .5"
		820	4000	
Mosquito IV/XX/XXV	265	935	2000**	Nil
		810	3000	
		1020	Nil	
Mosquito IX	245	685	5000	Nil
		935	1000	
Mosquito XVI	245	685	4000	Nil
		890	2000	
Overstrand	140	270	1600	3 x .303"
Stirling I	160	370	14000	8 x .303"
		1025	3500	
		1165	1500	
Stirling III	200	295	14000	8 x .303"
		1005	3500	
		1220	Nil	
Valiant 1	0.82M	1750	21000	Nil
Ventura	175	475	2500	4 x .303"
		1220	Nil	
Virginia X	70	490	3000	3 x .303"
Victor 1	0.92M	1250	35000	Nil
Victor 2	0.94M	2000	35000	Nil
Vulcan 1	0.92M	1500	21000	Nil
Vulcan 2	0.95M	2000	21000	Nil
Wallace II	135	235	580	2 x .303"
Washington 1	220	500	17500	10 x .5"
		1500	6000	
		2050	Nil	
Wellesley	188	1295	2000	2 x .303"
Wellington I	165	600	4500	6 x .303"
		1275	1000	

*Mk.I only
**Some Mk.IVs capable of carrying a single 4000-lb bomb with radius of action reduced to 715 miles

Name	Cruising Speed (mph)	Radius of Action (miles)	Weapon Load (lbs)	Armament
Wellington IC	170	625	4500	6 x .303"
		1100	1500	
Wellington II	175	700	4500	6 x .303"
		870	3500	
		1225	1250	
Wellington III	180	770	4500	8 x .303"
		1100	1500	
Wellington IV	175	490	4500	6 x .303"
		750	2700	
		1090	500	
Wellington X	180	665	4500	6 x .303"
		945	1500	
Whitley I	150	625	4220	2 x .303"
Whitley II	150	650	3500	2 x .303"
Whitley III	150	650	5500	4 x .303"
Whitley IV	165	625	7000	5 x .303"
		900	Nil	
Whitley V	165	235	7000	5 x .303"
		825	3000	

Note: Cruising speeds rather than the more usual maximum speeds are quoted because the former are more applicable to bomber operations. Similarly, radius of action is given instead of range which tends to give a false impression of performance. Most of the data has been obtained from official sources and relates to normal operation by average crews – it will tend to indicate a lower performance than manufacturer's figures obtained under ideal conditions. For special operations using specially modified aircraft, the radius of action/load figures could be improved considerably.

APPENDIX XII

Wartime Statistics

ACCURATE ASSESSMENT OF tonnage is impossible to calculate because some aircraft were lost *en route* the target, the figures in the tables being reasonable assumptions based on quantities despatched. Sortie and loss figures have been obtained from official returns issued by the Air Ministry News Service Ref A.M.B. No 19312 & 19042 dated July 1945.

Annual Comparison: Bombing/Mining Sept 1939-May 1945

Year	Bombing		Mining		Losses
	Sorties	Tons	Sorties	Tons	
1939	591	30			40
1940	22473	13000	762	510	509
1941	32012	31500	1055	700	985
1942	35338	45500	9574	6300	1543
1943	65068	157000	13834	9000	2457
1944	166844	525500	17500	13000	2904
1945	67483	181500	4582	3300	708

Sorties/Tonnage by Aircraft Type 1939-45

Type	Sorties		Tons	Type	Sorties		Tons
	Bombing	Other			Bombing	Other	
Battle	237	-	85	Lightning	-	9	½
Beaufighter	-	12	-	Lysander	-	72	-
Blenheim	11332	882	3000	Manchester	983	286	1800
Boston	1597	12	950	Mitchell	96	-	80
Fortress	51	1289	45	Mosquito	28639	11157	26500
Halifax	73312	9461	22500	Mustang	6	-	½
Hampden	12893	3648	9100	Stirling	11074	7366	27800
Hudson	-	278	-	Ventura	997	-	726
Lancaster	148403	7789	608000	Wellington	37412	9997	41800
Liberator	-	662	-	Whitley	8996	862	9800

Note: Total number of Bomber Command Sorties 389,809

Bomb Tonnage by Targets/Year

Year	1939	1940	1941	1942	1943	1944	1945
Towns	-	135	12300	35600	131000	184000	66000
Defences	-	1860	-	60	3200	155000	26000
Transport	-	2100	6100	135	2800	98300	28000
Oil	-	1700	500	10	50	48000	47000
Naval	30	2800	8800	5300	8700	9500	11100
Aircraft (Factories/ Airfields)	-	2100	1000	1500	1600	18500	600
Special Industries	-	1000	1300	1300	7000	7600	1200
Misc	-	1000	1300	1400	2300	2300	500

Casualties

Aircrew killed on Operations (including POWs):   47,268

of which RAF: 32,980
RAAF: 3,417
RCAF: 8,240
RNZAF: 1,439
SAAF: 20
Other Dominions/Colonials: 29
Poles: 753
Other Allies: 390

Aircrew killed on non-ops duty: 8,090
Aircrew wounded on operations: 4,200
Aircrew wounded on non-ops: 4,203

Aircraft lost on operations   8,655
lost on non-ops: 2,127

Aircraft damaged on operations   5,572

Enemy aircraft claimed in combat

Destroyed: 1,191
Probably destroyed: 310
Damaged: 897

Tallboy & Grand Slam Usage

No. of 12,000-lb *Tallboys* dropped: 854
No. of 22,000-lb *Grand Slams* dropped: 41

Glossary and Abbreviations

AASF — Advanced Air Striking Force
ACM — Air Chief Marshal
AEAF — Allied Expeditionary Air Force
AFB — Air Force Base
AFC — Air Force Cross
AFV — Armoured Fighting Vehicle
AGLT — Airborne Gun Laying for Turret
AI — Airborne Interception
Airborne Cigar — R/T jamming equipment
AOC — Air Officer Commanding
AVM — Air Vice Marshal

BAFF — British Air Forces in France
BEF — British Expeditionary Force (to France)
Bgdr Gen — Brigadier General
Big Ben — Sorties aimed at jamming supposed V-2 rocket radio-control system
Boozer — Warning Receiver
BS — Bomb Squadron
BS(H) — Bomb Squadron (Heavy)
BS(P) — Bomb Squadron (Photographic)
Bullseye — Bomber Command exercise involving searchlight batteries of AA Command

CAS — Chief of Air Staff
CB — Companion of the Order of the Bath
CBE — Companion of the Order of the British Empire
CENTO — Central Treaty Organization
Chamfron — Bomber Command operation supporting FEAF
Chowhound — USAAF operation dropping supplies to Dutch
C-in-C — Commander-in-Chief
Circus — Combined Fighter & Bomber Command operation intended to provoke response from Luftwaffe

CO — Commanding Officer
Cookies — Slang name for British 4,000-lb MC bombs
CTs — Communist Terrorists (Malaya)
CU — Conversion Unit
CWR — Charge to Weight Ratio (bombs)

Dartboard — Equipment for disrupting enemy night fighter R/T & W/T control channels
D/F — Direction Finding
DFC — Distinguished Flying Cross
Ditch — Slang name for emergency descent into the sea
DR — Dead Reckoning
Droop Snoot — P-38 Lightning with elongated nose
Drumstick — Equipment for disrupting enemy W/T channels
DSO — Distinguished Service Order
ECM — Electronic Counter Measures
EW — Early Warning

FAA — Fleet Air Arm
F/E — Flight Engineer
Fishpond — Warning device using H2S equipment
'Flak' — Anti-aircraft gunfire (specifically German)
Flg Off — Flying Officer
Flower — Fighter Command intruder operation
F/Sgt — Flight Sergeant
FTC — Flying Training Command
FuG — Funkgerät (German Radio/radar set)

Gardening — Mining
GCI — Ground-Controlled Interception
Gen — General
G-H — Target location and marking aid
GP — Group Pool

Grand Slam	British 22,000-lb bomb	PRU	Photographic Reconnaissance Unit
Ground Cigar	Equipment for disrupting enemy night fighter control channels	*Quisling*	Norwegian collaborators (with Germans)
Ground Grocer	Equipment for jamming enemy AI radar	RAAF	Royal Australian Air Force
Gp Capt	Group Captain	RAF	Royal Air Force
		Razzle	Incendiary device
HCU	Heavy Conversion Unit	RCAF	Royal Canadian Air Force
HQ	Headquarters	RCM	Radio Counter Measures
		RFC	Royal Flying Corps
IFF	Identification Friend or Foe	*Roadstead*	Anti-shipping operation
IRBM	Intermediate-Range Ballistic Missile	RNAS	Royal Naval Air Service
		RNZAF	Royal New Zealand Air Force
Jostle	High-powered jammer of enemy R/T transmissions	R/T	Radio Telephony
		SABS	Stabilized Automatic Bomb-Sight
KBE	Knight Commander of the Order of the British Empire	SAC	Strategic Air Command
		SAP	Semi-armour piercing (bombs)
KCB	Knight Commander of the Order of the Bath	SASO	Senior Air Staff Officer
		SD	Special Duties
		Seelöwe	Proposed German invasion of Britain
LFS	Lancaster Finishing School	*Serrate*	Homing device (onto German AI)
LNER	London & North Eastern Railway	Sgt	Sergeant
LNSF	Light Night Striking Force	SHAEF	Supreme Headquarters Allied Expeditionary Force
Lt Gen	Lieutenant General		
		Shaker	Target marking technique
Mahmoud	British night fighter sortie to specific point over enemy territory to engage German night fighters	*Shiver*	Jammer for enemy GCI radars
		Sqn	Squadron
		Sqn Ldr	Squadron Leader
Maj Gen	Major General	SWF	Special *Window* Force
Mandrel	Equipment for jamming enemy EW radars	*Tallboy*	British 12,000-lb AP bomb
Manna	Bomber Command operation to drop supplies to Dutch	TI	Target Indicator
		Tinsel	Device to disrupt enemy R/T control channels
MC	Military Cross		
MoD	Ministry of Defence	TRE	Telecommunications Research Establishment
Monica	Radar emission detector (British)		
Moonshine	Equipment producing spurious returns on *Freya* EW radar	UE	Unit Establishment
MPU	Message Pick-up	USAAF	United States Army Air Force
		VC	Victoria Cross
Naxos	Radar emission detector (German)		
NBC	Navigation & Bombing Computer	WA	Western Air (Plans)
NBS	Navigation & Bombing System	WAAF	Women's Auxiliary Air Force
Nickelling	Leaflet-dropping operation	WCU	Washington Conversion Unit
		Wg Cdr	Wing Commander
OBE	Order of the British Empire	WIDU	Wireless Investigation & Development Unit
OCU	Operational Conversion Unit		
OR	Operational Requirement	*Wilde Sau*	German single-seat fighter night operation
ORP	Operational Readiness Platform		
OTU	Operational Training Unit	W/T	Wireless Telephony
		WO	Warrant Officer
Pampa	Planned meteorological sortie		
Pointblank	Combined Bomber Command/ USAAF 8th AF directive	*Zahme Sau*	German twin-engined night fighters operating independently

Index